Information Security and Privacy in Smart Devices:

Tools, Methods, and Applications

Carlos Rabadão
Computer Science and Communication Research Centre, Polytechnic of Leiria, Portugal

Leonel Santos
Computer Science and Communication Research Centre, Polytechnic of Leiria, Portugal

Rogério Luís de Carvalho Costa
Computer Science and Communication Research Centre, Polytechnic of Leiria, Portugal

A volume in the Advances in Information Security, Privacy, and Ethics (AISPE) Book Series

Published in the United States of America by
  IGI Global
  Information Science Reference (an imprint of IGI Global)
  701 E. Chocolate Avenue
  Hershey PA, USA 17033
  Tel: 717-533-8845
  Fax: 717-533-8661
  E-mail: cust@igi-global.com
  Web site: http://www.igi-global.com

Library of Congress Cataloging-in-Publication Data

Names: Rabadao, Carlos, 1965- editor.
Title: Information security and privacy in smart devices : tools, methods,
  and applications / Carlos Rabadao, Leonel Santos, Rogerio Luis de
  Carvalho Costa, editors.
Description: Hershey, PA : Engineering Science Reference, [2023] | Includes
  bibliographical references and index. | Summary: "This research book of
  contributed chapters brings together research challenges, innovative
  insights, and trends related to solutions, methods, processes, and
  applications for maintaining information security and privacy in
  intelligent environments by covering a wide range of topics, including
  cybersecurity, privacy, IoT, networks, data protection regulations
  compliance, and information systems"-- Provided by publisher.
Identifiers: LCCN 2022033919 (print) | LCCN 2022033920 (ebook) | ISBN
  9781668459911 (h/c) | ISBN 9781668459928 (s/c) | ISBN 9781668459935
  (eISBN)
Subjects: LCSH: Mobile communication systems--Security measures. |
  Smartphones--Security measures. | Data privacy.
Classification: LCC TK5105.59 .I5265 2023 (print) | LCC TK5105.59 (ebook)
  | DDC 621.3845--dc23/eng/20220909
LC record available at https://lccn.loc.gov/2022033919
LC ebook record available at https://lccn.loc.gov/2022033920

This book is published in the IGI Global book series Advances in Information Security, Privacy, and Ethics (AISPE) (ISSN: 1948-9730; eISSN: 1948-9749)

British Cataloguing in Publication Data
A Cataloguing in Publication record for this book is available from the British Library.

For electronic access to this publication, please contact: eresources@igi-global.com.

Advances in Information Security, Privacy, and Ethics (AISPE) Book Series

ISSN:1948-9730
EISSN:1948-9749

Editor-in-Chief: Manish Gupta State University of New York, USA

MISSION

As digital technologies become more pervasive in everyday life and the Internet is utilized in ever increasing ways by both private and public entities, concern over digital threats becomes more prevalent.

The **Advances in Information Security, Privacy, & Ethics (AISPE) Book Series** provides cutting-edge research on the protection and misuse of information and technology across various industries and settings. Comprised of scholarly research on topics such as identity management, cryptography, system security, authentication, and data protection, this book series is ideal for reference by IT professionals, academicians, and upper-level students.

COVERAGE

- Cookies
- IT Risk
- Internet Governance
- Computer ethics
- Telecommunications Regulations
- Information Security Standards
- Security Information Management
- Security Classifications
- Electronic Mail Security
- Access Control

IGI Global is currently accepting manuscripts for publication within this series. To submit a proposal for a volume in this series, please contact our Acquisition Editors at Acquisitions@igi-global.com or visit: http://www.igi-global.com/publish/.

Titles in this Series

701 East Chocolate Avenue, Hershey, PA 17033, USA
Tel: 717-533-8845 x100 • Fax: 717-533-8661
E-Mail: cust@igi-global.com • www.igi-global.com

Table of Contents

Detailed Table of Contents

Chapter 1
Responsible and Safe Home Metering: How to Design a Privacy-Friendly
Metering System 1
    Libor Polčák, Brno University of Technology, Czech Republic

The European directive on energy efficiency requires that all meters in multi-apartment buildings installed after 25 October 2020 shall be remotely readable devices when technically feasible and cost-effective in terms of being proportionate to the potential energy savings. The European Commission Recommendation of 9 March 2012 on preparations for the roll-out of smart metering systems (2012/148/ EU) explicitly mentions that smart metering predominantly processes personal data. This chapter recommends how to design a metering system that fully conforms to legal regulations. The main contribution is the recommendation of eight steps for data controllers that make metering systems legally compliant. Additionally, the chapter lists recommendations for smart meter manufacturers that remove the burden of being a controller of the processing. The recommendations apply to the distribution of electricity, water, gas, heat, cooling, and other energies. The chapter shows that the recommendations can be generalized for smart home deployments.

Chapter 2
Security and Performance of Knowledge-Based User Authentication for
Smart Devices 41
    Alec Wells, York St. John University, UK
    Aminu Bello Usman, York St. John University, UK

A secure authentication system ensures that the claimant is the genuine user attempting to access the system and that it is not susceptible to misidentification, forgetfulness, or reproduction. While technological advancements in the authentication process continue to advance, most authentication systems still have room for improvement, particularly in terms of accuracy, tolerance to various security attacks, noise, and scalability as the number of smart devices grows. In this chapter, the authors look at the security, effectiveness, and drawbacks of knowledge-based, ownership-based, location-based, and social-based authentication systems, as well as some unresolved issues and potential future research directions.

The pervasiveness of smart devices, i.e., components equipped with feedback loops, sensing, and telecommunications for remote management, bring interesting research opportunities for incorporating contextual cybersecurity information through cyber threat intelligence (CTI). This approach enriches analysis by aggregating contextual information gathered from a myriad of unstructured data sources such as application logs, sensing data, blog posts, selected Internet-based commentary on security, vulnerability reports, and a host of other sources. The main difficulty regarding CTI is how to best integrate data into the design of protective measures. This chapter will discuss ways of leveraging CTI using a myriad of smart devices present in cyber-physical systems and internet-of-things with applications to the smart grid and smart buildings. The author will showcase the use of CTI in smart environments and how to incorporate and integrate data from multiple sources directly into the analysis efforts. The chapter will end with research perspectives and future work.

The technological development observed in recent years has led to the expansion of automotive systems communication capabilities. Consequently, several security vulnerabilities and additional attack surfaces that a threat agent can potentially exploit are increased. The most employed communication protocol in a vehicle is the controller area network (CAN) serial bus protocol, designed with robust fault tolerance in mind, but little to no concern for security. This chapter offers a primer on the controller area network typical architecture, what messages are used in communication, its error management system, and its vulnerabilities. Possible CAN attack surfaces and attack methods are also presented, followed by an exposition on intrusion detection systems (IDS) as a potential solution to the security concerns raised by CAN bus vulnerabilities. Several case studies on IDS implementations for secure CAN bus systems are also presented, including a recently proposed framework to facilitate further development in this field of study.

Guilherme Santo, ESTG, Polytechnic of Leiria, Portugal
Leonel Santos, CIIC, ESTG, Polytechnic of Leiria, Portugal
Rogério L. C. Costa, CIIC, Polytechnic of Leiria, Portugal
Carlos Rabadão, CIIC, ESTG, Polytechnic of Leiria, Portugal

Intelligent transportation systems are an area that have been in discussion for a lot of time, more precisely since in the 90's. With the advances in technology, it has been possible to start implementing this type of system, which brings a lot of benefits to people's lives; like, for example, making their road trips more secure and efficient. It also helps the environment, due to people spending less time in transit, and is a system that complements the emerging industry of smart cities. It all sounds good, except when it comes to security and privacy. This chapter will present these systems and their security and privacy concerns, including vulnerabilities that can be exploited if the due measures are not considered and implemented, which are even harder to obey because of privacy regulations like the general data protection regulation (GDPR).

Veena Gadad, RV College of Engineering, India
Sowmyarani C. N., RV College of Engineering, India

Privacy preserving data publishing (PPDP) provides a suite of anonymization algorithms and tools that aim to balance the privacy of sensitive attributes and utility of the published data. In this domain, extensive work has been carried out to preserve the privacy of single sensitive attributes. Since most of the data obtained from any domain includes multiple sensitive attributes (MSAs), there is a greater need to preserve it. The data sets with multiple sensitive attributes allow one to perform effective data analysis, research, and predictions. Hence, it is important to investigate privacy preserving algorithms for multiple sensitive attributes, which leads to higher utilization of the data. This chapter presents the effectiveness and comparative analysis of PPDP algorithms for MSAs. Specifically, the chapter focuses on privacy and utility goals and illustrates implications of the overall study, which promotes the development of effective privacy preservation techniques for MSAs.

The recent trends in the healthcare sector have catalyzed the emergence of several healthcare ecosystems. The inevitable and innate health data exchange amongst ecosystem components for provisioning of healthcare services as well as secondary use has raised several trust issues. The consent is a predominant mechanism to ensure privacy preserving, secure and ethical exchange, as well as sharing of health records of a patient by establishments. The proposed consent management system supports the life cycle of consent given by the patient or their authorized entity as well as validation and delegation of consent by a provider for health records requested by a user in an ecosystem. It reinforces different types as well as flavors of consent to strike a balance between privacy protection, ease of use, and patient safety. It supports the simple, flexible, and efficient management of consent at different granularity of health resource, user, and purpose. This is enabled by embedding consent structure in tree representation of EHR and a tree traversal algorithm for conflict resolution.

Misinformation is always a serious problem for the general public, especially during a pandemic. People constantly receive text messages of related coronavirus news and its cures from their smartphones, which have become major devices for communication these days. These health text messages help people update their coronavirus knowledge repeatedly and better manage their health, but some of the messages may mislead people and may even cause a fatal result. This research tries to identify mobile health text misinformation by using various effective information retrieval methods including lexical analysis, stopword removal, stemming, synonym discovery, various message similarity measurements, and data fusion. Readers will learn various information retrieval methods applied to contemporary research: mobile misinformation detection. Experiment results show the accuracy of the proposed method meets the expectation but still has room for improvement because misinformation detection is intrinsically difficult, and no satisfactory methods have been found yet.

Chapter 9

    Desmond Onyemechi Okocha, Bingham University, Nigeria
    Judith Oyiza Isah, Bingham University, Nigeria
    Samuel Akpe, Bingham University, Nigeria

Advances in technology have provided people with unparalleled opportunities to communicate efficiently and in real time. Adults with an inappropriate sexual interest in children have also benefited from developments in information and communications technology, using it to establish contact with them, to develop relationships, and to groom potential victims for sexual abuse and exploitation. Based on this, this study examined how social media has become a gateway for online child grooming. The study was anchored on the luring communication theory. The study adopted in-depth interview as its research design. The study used purposive sampling technique to draw a sample size of 15 experts. Findings from the study revealed that since the introduction of social media platforms, the amount of child sexual abuse content has been increasing yearly as these platforms have become a channel that offenders use in soliciting and sharing of explicit images and videos of minors.

Preface

As technology continues to advance, smart devices have become commonplace in our daily lives. From smartphones to the internet of things (IoT), these devices offer exceptional convenience, ease of use, and powered new intelligent services. Their application enabled the rise of smart homes, intelligent cities, smart agriculture, and Industry 4.0. However, smart devices collect and share large amounts of data, including private data, such as the habits and preferences of their users, making information security and privacy become increasingly critical because cybersecurity incidents in intelligent environments may impact services used by millions across the world and make private information public.

Because smart devices are so important in today´s world and also are ubiquitous and used in almost every aspect of our lives, the security and privacy of these devices and all the data present on them have become an essential concern. The topic of this book is of utmost importance in the current scenario where privacy breaches and data thefts are rampant. *Information Security and Privacy in Smart Devices: Tools, Methods, and Applications* is a comprehensive book to help readers understand the complex landscape of smart device security and privacy. The book covers research challenges, innovative insights, and trends related to solutions, methods, processes, and applications for maintaining information security and privacy in intelligent environments.

Covering topics such as information retrieval methods, electronic health records, and misinformation detection, this premier reference source is an excellent resource for security professionals, government officials, business leaders and executives, IT managers, hospital administrators, students of higher education, librarians, researchers, and academicians.

Current intelligent metering systems commonly process personal data. Chapter 1 discusses the design of remotely readable metering systems that fully conform to legal regulations. The chapter presents eight steps for data controllers that make metering systems legally compliant and lists recommendations for intelligent meter manufacturers that remove the burden of being a data processing controller. The recommendations apply to the distribution of several types of energy and can be generalized for intelligent home deployments.

Strong authentication systems help reduce malicious users' access to sensitive information, but creating a secure authentication process is still a considerable concern in cyberspace. Chapter 2 discusses the security, effectiveness, and drawbacks of authentication systems based on distinct authentication factors, like knowledge, ownership, location, and social data, as well as some unresolved issues and future research directions.

Recent technological innovations turned a myriad of devices, from smartphones to IoT devices, into daily life. On the other hand, it also highly increased the number of unstructured data sources available. Contextual cybersecurity information gathered from data sources such as sensing data, application logs, and vulnerability reports may be aggregated and used with Cyber Threat Intelligence (CTI) to assist cybersecurity officers in making timely decisions. Chapter 3 showcases the use of CTI in intelligent environments and how to incorporate and integrate data from multiple sources directly into the analysis efforts.

The technological innovations observed in recent years also boosted the change of automotive vehicles from purely mechanical system platforms into complex multisystem platforms that integrate mechanical and computerized systems and communication capabilities. The controller area network (CAN) serial bus is the most employed communication protocol in vehicles. Such a protocol was designed with robust fault tolerance but little concern for security. Chapter 4 describes the CAN's typical architecture and its vulnerabilities. The chapter discusses using intrusion detection systems (IDS) as a potential solution to the security concerns raised by CAN bus vulnerabilities and also presents several case studies on IDS implementations for secure CAN bus systems.

Chapter 5 deals with security and privacy concerns in the context of the Intelligent Transportation System. Although these systems have been studied for a long time, their implementation started in more recent years. Intelligent Transportation systems are very relevant in the context of smart cities, as they reduce the time spent in transit and make road trips more secure and efficient. Still, these systems are subject to several vulnerabilities that can be exploited if the due measures are not considered and implemented. On the other hand, regulations like the General Data Protection Regulation (GDPR) may difficult the implementation of countermeasures.

Indeed, preserving privacy became a major concern in recent years. Privacy-Preserving Data Publishing (PPDP) algorithms and tools aim to balance the privacy protection of sensitive data and the utility of anonymized data. Chapter 6 reviews the use of PPDP in the presence of Multiple Sensitive Attributes. The chapter presents a comparative analysis of the effectiveness of PPDP algorithms, focusing on privacy and utility goals.

Balancing privacy preservation and the utility of data is also one of the goals of the Consent Management System that Chapter 7 proposes. The consent is a mechanism to ensure privacy preserving, secure and ethical exchange of health records and the system is applied in the context of health data exchange amongst components in healthcare ecosystems. The system Chapter 7 describes supports the management of consent at distinct granularities of health resource, user, and purpose.

While rapid advances in technology have provided unparalleled opportunities for efficient, real-time communication, they have also led to new behaviors and unwanted effects. One of these is the rapid dissemination of misinformation. Chapter 8 deals with mobile health text misinformation detection. Chapter proposals use various information retrievals methods, like lexical analysis and synonym discovery, together with message similarity measurements and data fusion in the context of mobile text misinformation detection.

Another undesired use of the communication capabilities of current intelligent systems is their employment by adults with an inappropriate sexual interest in children to establish contact, develop relationships, and groom potential victims for sexual abuse and exploitation. Chapter 9 presents a study anchored on the Luring Communication theory on how social media has become a gateway for online child grooming. The chapter also discusses the effects that the introduction of social media platforms has on child sexual abuse content and how such platforms have become a channel that offenders use.

In conclusion, *Information Security and Privacy in Smart Devices: Tools, Methods, and Applications* is an important source for anyone interested in the security and privacy of smart devices. The book provides valuable insights and practical applications that can help readers navigate the dense landscape of smart device security and privacy. We hope that readers will find this book informative and useful in their work and research.

Carlos Rabadão
Computer Science and Communication Research Centre, Polytechnic of Leiria, Portugal

Leonel Santos
Computer Science and Communication Research Centre, Polytechnic of Leiria, Portugal

Rogério Luís de Carvalho Costa
Computer Science and Communication Research Centre, Polytechnic of Leiria, Portugal

Acknowledgment

The editors appreciate the work and commitment of the authors and reviewers. They also thank FCT - Fundação para a Ciência e a Tecnologia, as this work is partially funded by FCT - Fundação para a Ciência e a Tecnologia, I.P., through project UIDB/04524/2020, and under the Scientific Employment Stimulus - Institutional Call - CEECINST/00051/2018.

Chapter 1
Responsible and Safe Home Metering: How to Design a Privacy-Friendly Metering System

Libor Polčák
Brno University of Technology, Czech Republic

ABSTRACT

The European directive on energy efficiency requires that all meters in multi-apartment buildings installed after 25 October 2020 shall be remotely readable devices when technically feasible and cost-effective in terms of being proportionate to the potential energy savings. The European Commission Recommendation of 9 March 2012 on preparations for the roll-out of smart metering systems (2012/148/EU) explicitly mentions that smart metering predominantly processes personal data. This chapter recommends how to design a metering system that fully conforms to legal regulations. The main contribution is the recommendation of eight steps for data controllers that make metering systems legally compliant. Additionally, the chapter lists recommendations for smart meter manufacturers that remove the burden of being a controller of the processing. The recommendations apply to the distribution of electricity, water, gas, heat, cooling, and other energies. The chapter shows that the recommendations can be generalized for smart home deployments.

INTRODUCTION

The European Union (EU) takes the impact of people on the environment seriously. Previous research has shown that transparent energy metering can reduce consumption (March et al., 2017; Kaatz, 2017; Beal & Flynn, 2015; Liu et al., 2015). Moreover, meters can detect tampering (Monedero et al., 2015) and water leakage (Britton et

DOI: 10.4018/978-1-6684-5991-1.ch001

al., 2013, Lima & Navas, 2012). Consequently, the current text of the EU directive on energy efficiency mandates the deployment of remotely readable and cost-effective provisioning of billing and consumption information for heating and cooling and domestic hot water for each building unit, where technically feasible and cost-effective in terms of being proportionate in relation to the potential energy savings (Directive Articles 9b (1) and 9c; European Parliament and Council, 2018).

The EU Directive on common rules for the internal electricity market provides requirements for smart metering systems (Directive 2019/944/EU, Article 20; European Parliament and Council, 2019). Specifically, the consumption data need to be available securely: "the security of the smart metering systems and data communication shall comply with relevant Union security rules, having due regard of the best available techniques for ensuring the highest level of cybersecurity protection while bearing in mind the costs and the principle of proportionality" (Directive 2019/944/EU, Article 20(b); European Parliament and Council, 2019). "The privacy of final customers and the protection of their data shall comply with relevant Union data protection and privacy rules" (Directive 2019/944/EU, Article 20(b); European Parliament and Council, 2019). Nevertheless, the deployment of smart metering for electricity metering is not mandatory and should be decided by each EU member state through an assessment (Directive 2019/944/EU, Article 19(2); European Parliament and Council, 2019).

A well-designed metering system can help to reduce energy consumption. However, current literature also highlights that the success of metering systems depends on their security (Kumar et al., 2019). As energy distribution is considered critical to our societies, smart metering network operators and manufacturers should consider robust security and privacy features from the beginning (Kumar et al., 2019). Poorly designed metering systems risk incompatibilities with data protection laws (Polčák & Matoušek, 2022). Cuijpers & Koops (2012) describe the failure of smart metering deployment in the Netherlands due to detailed readouts; the proposed Dutch law supposed processing data that were not minimized and not necessary. The main goal of this chapter is to assist in designing metering systems conforming to the data protection law. Data protection authorities can ban a metering system that unlawfully processes personal data or issue an order to redesign the system. Such a ban or a redesign would increase the cost of the deployment. Recall that the EU law mandates balancing the metering system deployment based on the costs and its potential for energy savings. Hence, this chapter aims to provide advice on the requirements stemming from data protection laws to assist in designing a metering system correctly from the beginning.

This chapter focuses on legal requirements for remotely readable metering systems. The research methodology is as follows. The author of this chapter researched the cases of the Court of Justice of the European Union (CJEU) concerning data protection issues together with the guidance of the European Data Protection Board (EDPB) and its predecessor Article 29 Data Protection Working Party concerning EU General Data Protection Regulation 2016/679/EU (GDPR, European Parliament and Council, 2016) requirements, smart metering, and other related topics like the Internet of things. Additionally, the chapter's research methodology involved studying research papers on privacy and security issues in smart metering. The research also considered smart metering data protection development in the United States and Canada. In summary, this chapter does not propose any new metering system. Rather, this chapter brings together data protection law requirements and applies them to metering systems in general. The requirements are applicable from small deployments to deployments spanning countries; considered metering systems involve electricity, water, gas, heat, cooling, and other energy distribution systems.

The text of the chapter argues that data processed by the metering systems are often personal data. Hence, European Parliament and Council (2016) (General Data Protection Regulation, GDPR, Regulation 2016/679/EU) typically applies. Consequently, the requirements of European Parliament and Council (2016) (GDPR, Regulation 2016/679/EU) on controllership, data minimization, transparency, and fairness must be fulfilled. Moreover, the chapter provides suggestions on architecting and deploying metering systems that fully conform to law requirements. To facilitate the understanding, the chapter introduces multiple scenarios of possible smart metering systems, ranging from a small deployment without a permanent reading infrastructure to a full electricity smart grid. Finally, the chapter generalizes the requirements for smart homes.

BACKGROUND

This section introduces key terms related to advanced energy consumption metering. Later, this section focuses on the data protection issues connected with remotely readable metering systems from the law position and reviews related work.

Terminology Related to Metering Systems and Smart Grids

There is not a single type of a metering system. Some are deployed in a single building, whereas others span a whole country. A smart electricity grid typically consists of many heterogeneous systems (Kumar et al., 2019, Knap & Samani, 2013). In contrast, remote readout also covers meters periodically transmitting metering data without any permanent reading infrastructure (Polčák & Matoušek, 2022).

- **Automatic Metering Readout (AMR)** allows only communication initiated by the meters and often without the possibility of sending data to the meter. The meters are typically not directly connected to a wired network and are powered by batteries. The goal is to minimize the power requirements of the meter. To do so, the meter does not listen for any incoming transmissions. Instead, the meter sends readouts during predefined intervals (e.g., periodically). These messages might be processed either by an occasionally available device or a permanent infrastructure.
  - **Readings by an occasionally available device:** These readings need a reading service that periodically reads the meters by visiting the building or reading the readouts from a car parked in the vicinity of the building. Hence, there are no additional costs for permanent reading devices (e.g., gateways between the metering protocols and the internet protocol suite TCP/IP), and it is not necessary to provide a durable connection to the internet. Such deployment is suitable if the only goal is to provide billing information, but it is impossible to provide real-time information on events like water leakage. However, a meter can detect events such as attempted fraud. Nevertheless, the reading service would learn about the incident with delay.
  - **Readings by a permanent infrastructure:** As the battery-powered meter's signal typically spans only tens or hundreds of meters and the data need to be processed across a city or a country, a permanent architecture composed of gateways can relay the readings to a different medium. For example, data can be aggregated from all local meters and relayed to the metering facility over the internet. As the metering facility can process the data in real time, it can timely react to detected events, such as suspected fraud or water leakage. All data from a meter can be analyzed and evaluated by the reading facility if the customer wishes to benefit from the detailed information on energy consumption, for example, to learn about activities that result in very high consumption.
- **Advanced Metering Infrastructure (AMI)**, also called **smart grid**, for example, by Kumar et al. (2019). Mohassel et al. (2014) and Knapp & Samani (2013) describe AMI thoroughly. The infrastructure is heterogeneous and hierarchical; it includes smart meters, communication networks, data management systems, and means to integrate collected data into software platforms and interfaces. AMI allows bidirectional communication, typically initiated by the infrastructure. AMI does not need meters that send data periodically. Instead, the infrastructure begins each readout. Typical AMI meters allow advanced features to improve the reliability, efficiency, and sustainability of the grid. For example, connected devices can negotiate with

the network the optimal time to consume resources (for example, to charge an electric vehicle during the night). AMI allows for negotiation of providing energy back to the network, for example, from solar panels mounted on residential buildings.

Remote readouts may be employed for different purposes (Kumar et al., 2019; Knapp & Samani, 2013):

- **Metering for billing** performs the same functionality as legacy analog metering. The goal is to meter consumption and issue a bill.
- **Metering for operations** is used to optimize the efficiency and reliability of the network. For example, the utility company may analyze patterns in energy consumption and predict future workload.
  - ○ Cuijpers & Koops (2012) mention remote energy quality detection, the ability to turn the power supply off to deal with fraudulent or nonpaying customers and to deal with disasters.
  - ○ Accident detection is another operational example. Britton et al. (2013) claim that current estimations assume customer postmeter leakage accounts for up to 10% of total water consumption, particularly in the residential sector. They report significant water savings resulting from the early detection of household leaks. Smart metering provides water utilities with a powerful tool to identify rapidly and take action in case of a postmeter leakage.
- **Value-added services** let the user benefit from smart metering. For example, the user can receive suggestions on how to improve energy consumption (Chen et al., 2011), or the smart grid may instruct cooperative appliances in the household to use electricity at low prices during off-peak times (Knapp & Samani, 2013).

Smart metering systems typically employ protocols like ZigBee (IEEE 802.15.4), Z-wave, Wi-Fi (IEEE 802.11), MobileFi (IEEE 802.20), WiMAX (IEEE 802.16), powerline communication (PLC), mesh networks on unlicensed radio, and Wireless M-Bus (Kumar et al. 2019; Brunschwiler, 2013). Concentrated data are sometimes carried over the internet using TCP/IP (Kumar et al., 2019).

RELATED LITERATURE

Orlando & Vandevelde (2021) focused on the EU law and found the EU approach correct but not optimal. They think that personal data should be collected for the public interest (as the GDPR legal basis); they highlight several requirements of the law, such as identifying the entities, such as data subjects, controllers, and processors. Knyrim & Trieb (2011) also highlight the need to base the deployment on legal bases other than consent. Lee & Hess (2021) compared privacy regulations of smart residential meters in Canada, France, the Netherlands, Norway, the United Kingdom, and the United States. They identified strategies that help gain public confidence: (1) opt-out policies for mounting a smart meter, (2) opt-in policies for provisioning of highly granular data that allow identification of activities, (3) rules for data storage and data sharing, and (4) independent monitoring and supervision on privacy-related practices.

As discussed above, metering systems differ in complexity. Hence, each deployment may result in a different set of threats. Kumar et al. (2019) offers an overview of the threats appearing in the metering systems, including advanced persistent threats, targeted attacks, privacy issues, denial of service radio subversion, credential compromise, illegal access, message modification, man-in-the-middle attacks, data analysis, misuse of private data, routing attacks, meter compromise or intrusion, location migration, and cloning. The threats endanger individuals (customers), the metering systems, and the ability of utilities to distribute energy. According to Kumar et al. (2019), privacy threats are not fully understood in the metering systems. An attacker can be an insider or an outsider, the attackers can connect directly to the network, or they can use logical access through insecure components and other means (Kumar et al., 2019).

Chen et al. (2011) showed that readouts with 15-minute periods reveal household activities, such as taking a shower or using a washing machine or dishwasher. Some devices have a distinct pattern of energy consumption that can be used to fingerprint a device (Lisovich et al., 2010; Kelly & Knottenbelt, 2015). Consequently, a remote adversary can reveal the manufacturer or even the model of household appliances without ever entering the household. Such information is convenient for burglars, profiling, and marketing (Kumar et al., 2019; Polčák & Matoušek, 2022).

A related issue is zero-consumption detection. Energies like water or gas are typically not used in an unoccupied property. Even though some electrical appliances can run in standby mode, the electricity consumption in an unoccupied property generally is much lower compared to the periods when the property is occupied. Erol-Kantarci & Mouftah (2013) and Lisovich et al. (2010) point out the risks.

Several privacy-enhancing techniques deployable by residents appeared in the literature. Backes & Melser (2012), Kalogridis et al. (2010), McLaughlin et al. (2011), Yang et al. (2012), Armel et al. (2013), Zeifman & Roth (2011) mention a battery mounted after a smart electricity meter at the edge of the household grid. Such a battery hides peaks in energy consumption with an almost constant charging current. However, the battery approach is expensive when applied to hide occupancy patterns, so Chen et al. (2014) proposed preventing occupancy detection using the thermal energy storage of large elastic heating loads already present in many homes, such as electric water and space heaters. Orlando & Vandevelde (2021) question if such approaches are an obstacle to the potential of smart meters in terms of benefits. Specifically, both batteries and heaters in unoccupied flats waste (some) energy.

Rial et al. (2018) propose a sophisticated approach that encrypts metered data with a key shared with the residents. Later, residents need to: (1) decrypt the metered values on their devices and (2) compute costs. The approach ensures that the utility can verify the cost computation. Moreover, Rial et al. (2018) also propose extensions for future demand predictions, fraud detection, and profiling. However, Kumar et al. (2019) argue that it is widely accepted that public and private key-based mechanisms are considerably expensive concerning computational complexities.

Homomorphic encryption allows to encrypt and share information between multiple parties in a way in which arithmetic operations can be done on encrypted data without the need to decrypt the data first. Abreu & Pereira (2022) note that two main disadvantages of homomorphic encryption for smart grids are its complexity and that meters are not independent. Using homomorphic encryption, it is possible to aggregate data from multiple meters without revealing the specific consumption of the meters to the metering facility.

Kumar et al. (2019) show that encryption-related issues are an open topic in current literature. Symmetric encryption is fast but needs a complex key management solution. Asymmetric keys simplify key management but suffer from bad performance on resource-hungry devices. Homomorphic systems and public key infrastructure are often too expensive, especially considering battery-powered devices (Esposito & Ciampi, 2015; Kumar et al., 2019). Homomorphic encryption generates larger messages (Esposito & Ciampi, 2015; Kumar et al., 2019).

Smart meters are often wireless (Kumar et al., 2019). Consequently, they suffer from jamming and spoofing attacks (Kumar et al., 2019; Polčák & Matoušek, 2022; Brunschwiler, 2013). The mitigation of this threat is through detection techniques that create alerts, and the misbehaving devices can be identified (Kumar et al., 2019). A metering system can mitigate a replay attack with enforced integrity detection. For example, Polčák & Matoušek (2022) describe an attacker that can store metering messages and replay them later to lower the bill. Although the studied system tracked time in the metering messages, it did not use the time stamp to detect integrity violations.

Comparison to this chapter: The related work identified many relevant problems and solutions. However, none of the work provides a clear set of instructions that can be followed by the parties participating in the smart metering and manufacturers of the smart meters. Rial et al. (2018) proposed a privacy-preserving approach that was tested by real utilities. However, this chapter provides more general guidance.

Following the guidance, one can be determined that the proposal of Rial et al. (2018) fulfills data protection requirements. However, other architecture and deployments that are not based on Rial et al. (2018) are also compliant. Orlando & Vandevelde (2021) focused on the law and what is missing, but they do not give detailed technical guidance. This chapter generalizes the advice given by Polčák & Matoušek (2022). Their advice considers a specific deployment. In contrast, this chapter focuses on metering systems in general.

EU Data Protection Law and Rules

The fact that metering systems process personal data is a well-established concept in the literature (Lee & Hess, 2021; Orlando & Vandevelde; 2021; Knyrim & Trieb, 2011). This section focuses on the interpretation of the regulatory bodies. Orlando & Vandevelde (2021) cover the history of soft law that has clarified crucial aspects. The European Commission set up a task force related to smart grid operations; one group consisted of European data protection authorities (DPAs) established in all member states. These authorities were grouped in the Article 29 Data Protection Working Party (GDPR transformed the working party into EDPB). The Article 29 Data Protection Working Party (2011) produced its Opinion 12/2011, expressing its view that metered data are often personal data.

The European Commission applied the Article 29 Working Party Opinion (2011) (Opinion 12/2011) on smart metering to the Commission Recommendation of March 9, 2012 (European Commission, 2012) on preparations for the roll-out of smart metering systems (2012/148/EU, European Commission, 2012). Through Programming Mandate M/487 EN, the European Commission (2011) also asked the European Standard Bodies to revise and secure standards for smart metering. Even though the standards were revised, some literature provides evidence that the revised standards were not always implemented in practice (Polčák & Matoušek, 2022). Nevertheless, Commission Recommendation is not legally binding. However, data protection regulations like European Parliament and Council (2016) (GDPR, Regulation 2016/679/EU) are legally binding.

The Recommendation 2012/148/EU (European Commission, 2012) states in recital 6 that "Smart metering systems allow processing of data, including predominantly personal data." The author of this chapter adds that smart metering is also deployed in factories and other industrial deployments. Additionally, smart metering is deployed in public buildings, hotels, and other facilities where the measured data are aggregated for the whole building or even a campus. Hence, not all data are personal. Recital 30 of European Parliament and Council (2016) (GDPR, Regulation 2016/679/EU) recognizes that identifiers provided by devices may be used to identify them. Moreover, the CJEU (2016) (in Case C-582/14) considered a dynamic IP address personal data, provided that there are reasonable means that can be used to identify the person.

Recitals 10 and 11 of the Recommendation 2012/148/EU (European Commission, 2012) clarifies European Parliament and Council (2016) (GDPR, Regulation 2016/679/EU, Article 25) on data protection by design and by default: "security features should be built into smart metering systems before they are rolled out and used extensively. Such features can effectively improve consumers' control over the processing of personal data." National data protection authorities should stimulate the principle in the early phases of the roll-out.

European Parliament and Council (2016) (GDPR, Regulation 2016/679/EU) deals with data protection impact assessment in Article 35. Recital 15 of the Recommendation 2012/148/EU (European Commission, 2012) argues that an assessment of the data protection impact should be carried out prior to the roll-out of smart metering systems. European Commission (2014) (Recommendation 2014/724/EU) later clarified the requirements for data protection impact assessment.

European Parliament and Council (2016) (GDPR, Regulation 2016/679/EU) lists several obligations. Article 4 provides definitions for basic terms like personal data, processing, controller (the entity that decides the means and purposes of the processing), and processor (an entity that processes personal data on behalf of the controller). Article 5(1) declares the basic rules for processing: lawfulness, fairness, and transparency, and Article 5(2) puts restrictions on the processing like purpose limitation and data minimization; the controller is responsible for the demonstration of compliance (accountability principle). Article 6 provides legal bases for processing (note that all except consent allow processing only strictly necessary personal data).

CJEU (2010, 2013, 2014, 2017, 2019a) decided several cases that dealt with the condition of necessity (C-92/09 and C-93/09, point 86; C-473/12, point 39; C-212/13, point 28; C-13/16, point 30; C-708/18, points 40–45). In essence, CJEU is strict on considering what is necessary and what is not. CJEU is also strict on considerations of what is data minimization (see, C-708/18, points 48–51, CJEU, 2019a). Case C-708/18 (CJEU, 2019a) assessed a deployment of a video surveillance system. CJEU decided that as the controller applied less invasive measures before applying more intrusive measures, the controller fulfilled the minimization principle. The lesson to be taken is that it is necessary to try, or at least consider, less privacy-invasive measures before applying more intruding measures.

European Parliament (2021) (Resolution 2021/C 494/11) recently evaluated European Parliament and Council (2016) (GDPR, Regulation 2016/679/EU). In the resolution, the European Parliament "Expresses its concern about the uneven and sometimes non-existent enforcement of the GDPR by national DPAs more than two years after the start of its application, and therefore regrets that the enforcement situation has not substantially improved compared to the situation under Directive

95/46/EC." The author interprets the text as evidence that European Parliament and Council (2016) (GDPR, Regulation 2016/679/EU) enforcement is lacking and that many processing activities are not in line with the regulation. According to the resolution, EDPB should adopt guidelines to determine the conditions under which ICT manufacturers should be considered controllers. EDPB did not publish the guidelines yet. One of the contributions of this chapter is to anticipate and manifest what should be in the guidelines.

Cuijpers & Koops (2012) described the failed roll-out of smart metering in the Netherlands as due to the flawed regulations without respecting the law from the beginning. The proposal did not clearly define processing parties and purposes; there was no data protection impact assessment; and the proposal did not respect principles of data privacy by design. Two smart-metering bills expected mandatory roll-out for every household with 15 minutes readout periods for electricity and hourly readouts for gas. Energy suppliers were supposed to derive detailed information about energy consumption so that consumers could adapt their behavior for greater efficiency. The meters were supposed to cut out the household from the energy supply for fraudulent behavior and nonpayers. The Dutch Senate blocked the two bills in 2009 due to privacy concerns. Privacy concerns led to the Dutch Data Protection Authority being asked to give advice on the bill. The authority raised concerns about the lack of legitimate processing basis opaque access to the personal data of different parties. Consequently, the proposal was amended: (1) to require explicit consent to transfer the frequent readouts, (2) daily readouts would be mandatory, and (3) all data protection conditions like purpose limitation or data subjects' rights would apply. The authority deemed the legislation compliant with the Dutch Data Protection Act.

Nevertheless, the Dutch Consumer Union let Cuijpers & Koops (2008) evaluate the bills in the light of Article 8 of the European Convention on Human Rights (ECHR) Article 8. The report concluded that: (1) the processing of quarter-hourly and hourly readings to grid managers, (2) the daily readings to grid managers and suppliers, and (3) the compulsory roll-out of smart meters to all households were not (proven to be) necessary in a democratic society and the roll-out would violate ECHR (Cuijpers & Koops, 2012). Additionally, the report found that the government provided too little evidence to assess the necessity of the built-in switch that was supposed to cut out the household from the energy distribution remotely, as it introduces new opportunities for abuse, for example, by remote adversaries (Cuijpers & Koops, 2012).

The text of the law was updated by: (1) improving the coherence of the management of end-user data by the parties involved, (2) improving transparency and awareness by requiring the publishing of annual reports on the processing, (3) the smart meters were no longer obligatory, and (4) the law explicitly refined purposes of processing, such as billing and network management. The law passed in 2011 (Cuijpers & Koops, 2012). In summary, the roll-out was delayed by several years, and the final rules significantly changed. Zhou & Brown (2016) described the Netherlands as a laggard in smart meter deployment.

Zhou & Brown (2016) compared smart meters deployment in Finland, Sweden, Denmark, Germany, and the Netherlands. Finland and Sweden have a high smart meter deployment ratio, while Germany and the Netherlands have a low deployment. Interestingly, Zhou & Brown (2016) mention only Germany and the Netherlands as countries with opposition from the public due to privacy and security concerns. However, Germany was the only country with a negative cost-benefit analysis that resulted in the reported adoption slowdown. Nevertheless, Finland specified purposes for processing, obligations for data transmissions and storage, data security and protection, and rights for data subjects. The desire of accurate billing mainly drove deployment in Sweden. Although Sweden does not require smart metering, the requirement for monthly readings lets the market select smart metering as the optimal path.

Orlando & Vandevelde (2021) researched the Flemish (a part of Belgium) implementation of electricity distribution. The Flemish Regulator of the Electricity and Gas Market has to publish regular reports to the public and government. The law lists specific cases with mandatory digital meters and specifies the processing of metering data which provides a legal basis under Article 6(e) European Parliament and Council (2016) (GDPR, Regulation 2016/679/EU). The law limits the purposes of processing. The law specifies legal roles, including defining conditions under which a controller can employ a processor. Finally, the law creates specific rules for risk management and conducting data protection impact assessments, further clarifying Articles 32 and 35 of European Parliament and Council (2016) (GDPR, Regulation 2016/679/EU).

Table 1 summarizes the papers of Orlando & Vandevelde (2021), Cuijpers & Koops (2012), and Zhou & Brown (2016). The lesson learned is that public scrutiny or obliging the principle of privacy by design leads into detailed conditions and regulations provided by law. As European Parliament and Council (2016) (GDPR, Regulation 2016/679/EU) is generic, laying down specific criteria in sector law removes some burden from the controllers. Most countries decided on improved transparency and specifying data rights for customers.

Let us compare the European status to the United States. California established the 15/15 rule (Lee & Hess, 2021; Kaatz, 2017) that allows a utility to share data if it aggregates 15 or more customers and if each customer comprised less than 15% of the group's aggregated consumption (California Public Utilities Commission, 2014). New York State Public Service Commission (2018) adopted a 4/50 rule meaning a minimum of four households, each accounting for less than 50% of the total consumption. Orlando & Vandevelde (2021) think that providing such a threshold that is well reasoned would be beneficial for European utility companies. After specifying concrete numbers that make aggregated personal data anonymous and, hence, not protected by data protection rules, the controllers would not need to evaluate their anonymization techniques. A future research question is selecting the number of households and maximum household consumption so that it is guaranteed that a household cannot be reidentified.

Table 1. Comparison of privacy and security-related forces that enables the smooth deployment of smart metering

Country/region	Finland	Sweden	Denmark	Germany	Netherlands (after public scrutiny)	Flanders
Clear specification of roles	Yes	No	Unknown	Unknown	Yes	Yes
Clear list of operations	Yes	No	Unknown	Unknown	Yes	Yes
Mandatory deployment	Unknown	No	Yes	No, negative cost-benefit analysis	Opt-out	Under specific circumstances
Additional transparency requirements	Unknown	No	Unknown	Unknown	Annual reports of processing	Yes
Specific security obligations	Yes	No	Unknown	Yes	Yes	Yes
Specific data rights for customers	Yes, for example, data access	No	Yes, for example, data access	Yes, choose a third party to operate the metering point	Yes, for example, setting the period of readouts	Yes, for example, data access rights, identification of personal data
Assessed by data protection authority or other bodies	Unknown	Unknown	Unknown	Unknown	Yes	Unknown

Note. Data acquired by Orlando & Vandevelde (2021), Cuijpers & Koops (2012), and Zhou & Brown (2016).

In the US case of Naperville Smart Meter Association v. Naperville, the Seventh Circuit Decision (2018) overturned the lower court decision based on previous decisions on legacy analog meters. The Seventh Circuit court stated that:

Using traditional energy meters, utilities typically collect monthly energy consumption in a single lump figure once per month. By contrast, smart meters record consumption much more frequently, often collecting thousands of readings every month. Due to this frequency, smart meters show both the amount of electricity being used inside a home and when that energy is used (United States Court of Appeals for the Seventh Circuit Decision, 2018, Naperville Smart Meter Association v. Naperville).

The court decided that the city has an interest in collecting the data in this specific case. Additionally, the city benefited from the policy of not sharing the data without a search warrant or court order. The court has left open a question of readouts with a period lower than 15 minutes. The court also highlighted that the city could have avoided the controversy if they had given the residents the option to avoid a smart meter.

Designing A Smart Metering System

The previous section established that metering systems deployed in residential areas are intrinsically personal data. European Parliament and Council (2016) (GDPR, Regulation 2016/679/EU) requires each processing operation of personal data to be proportionate, necessary, and processed personal data to be minimized. As this claim is quite vague, the author will expand this law requirement into several steps that the entities running a metering system (including a smart grid) need to apply. Later, the section focuses on manufacturers of smart meters.

Entity Running a Metering System

Step 1: The controller, the entity planning to run a metering system, has to list all the operations carried out by the planned metering system. Alternatively, a controller can carry these steps during an audit of an existing metering system to determine legal compliance. This step yields a set of operations, such as the need to know the current meter value to provide billing, the need to monitor consumption during a period to detect water leakage, or the analysis of patterns and energy usage to provide suggestions to reduce consumption.

- Note that it is necessary to list all processing operations in advance. The Purpose Limitation Principle prevents controllers from gathering personal data for one purpose, like billing, and later, using the same data for a different purpose. The use for an incompatible purpose is only possible with the consent of the data subject. As the controller might find a different legal basis for additional processing purposes, it is preferable for the controller to list all purposes in advance.

Step 2: The controller must determine the data needed to achieve each selected goal. The controller needs to differentiate between personal data and other data, as personal data requires better protection (Regulation 2016/679/EU, Opinion 05/2014, Article 29 Data Protection Working Party, 2014). The controller should minimize required personal data to the most necessary extent.

- For example, when the law mandates that the controller performs a yearly billing, only one readout is necessary (Opinion 12/2011, Article 29 Data Protection Working Party, 2011). Hence, the frequency of the readouts is directly prescribed in the law in this case.
- The controller can determine that an approach of Rial et al. (2018) or homomorphic encryption can be applied. Consequently, only the customer can access unencrypted data. Orlando & Vandelvelde (2021) note that such an approach does not create anonymous data. However, the author of this chapter thinks that it demonstrates compliance with data minimization, the principle of data protection by design (GDPR, Regulation 2016/679/EU, Article 25, European Parliament and Council, 2016), and the application of technical and organizational security measures (GDPR, Regulation 2016/679/EU, Article 32, European Parliament and Council, 2016). Note that data protection by design refers to the current technological state. Hence, a controller finding that the market does not offer any product detecting necessary events could demonstrate the need to perform frequent readouts to collect data needed to evaluate the events.
- Activities such as fraud detection and water leakage detection need very frequent readouts. Polčák & Matoušek (2022) report meters that perform computations to detect events such as possible fraud or water leakage without requiring frequent readouts to leave the device. There was no court of justice decision directly applicable to this case. However, the author of this text believes that detecting events directly in the meters demonstrates compliance with the principle of data protection by design (GDPR, Regulation 2016/679/EU, Article 25, European Parliament and Council, 2016). Article 29 Data Protection Working Party (2013) (Opinion 05/2013) lists detection of fraudulent activities by mining fraudulent data as compatible with data protection laws, providing that the controller applies safeguards to minimize risks and undue impact on data subjects.
- The controller might need to decide how to reach the same goal from several possibilities. For example, suppose that the controller wants to differentiate between peak and off-peak hours. One option is to read the metered value each time the peak hours start or end. Another option is to deploy a meter that can separately meter consumption for peak and off-peak hours. Note that the latter option allows the controller to read the metered consumption less frequently, demonstrating adherence to the data minimization principle.

Again, the controller can find that there is no suitable meter offering the needed functionality; the wording of the European Parliament and Council (2016) (GDPR, Regulation 2016/679/EU, Article 25) enables the controller to demonstrate that the market does not offer any other meter collecting sufficient data.

- European Parliament and Council (2016) (GDPR, Regulation 2016/679/EU) applies only to personal data. The controller should consider the option not to process personal data, for example, for operational processing that does not require personal data but, for example, works with aggregated data. The utility can gather aggregated data in the part of the metering system that carries the energy aggregated during transport before the pipes or wires reach homes and residential buildings or in large substations (McKenna et al., 2012). Article 29 Data Protection Working Party (2014) (Opinion 05/2014) gives examples of anonymization techniques.

Step 3: The controller needs to decide the lawfulness of processing for each selected goal (GDPR, Regulation 2016/679/EU, Article 6, European Parliament and Council, 2016); for example, is the processing a legal obligation, or is it necessary to perform the contract (e.g., differentiate between peak and off-peak hours)?

- The controller can decide to pursue their legitimate interests in the processing—for example, to keep the grid functioning. In such a case, the controller needs to demonstrate that their interests are not overridden by the legitimate interests of data subjects in being private in their homes. In particular, the controller should weigh other possibilities to achieve the same goal.
  - ○ For example, the controller can realize that it does not need the metered value for each household separately to predict future demand. Instead, the controller can employ consumption data from a distribution network that aggregates many households (Knyrim & Trieb, 2011).
  - ○ Another example is to use data from a distribution network composing many households to determine that there is no possibility of fraud in a part of the network. Once a part of the distribution network looks like there might be a fraudulent customer, the controller can decide to collect data from each household in the network segment. The controller should stop processing further data on each household once it establishes that the particular household does not exhibit fraudulent behavior.
- If there is no other possible basis in Article 6 (GDPR, Regulation 2016/679/EU, Article 6, European Parliament and Council, 2016), the controller can decide to offer the service as an added value with the consent of the customer

(each data subject). Such a decision could be reached, for example, by providing detailed graphs about the consumption of the individual household. Such a decision would empower customers to watch their consumption and act accordingly. Not interested in the detailed consumption analysis, other customers could keep their data private. As Orlando & Vandevelde (2021) and Knyrim & Trieb (2011) warn, utilities should avoid the need for consent for operational and billing services of the metering system. The author of this text recommends relying only exceptionally on a consent.

- Suppose the market analysis performed in the second step revealed that the controller needs to deploy a metering device providing more frequent data than necessary. In that case, the controller should reevaluate if the legal basis allows such an interpretation. The more disparity between the absolutely necessary frequency of meter readouts and the actual reading frequency, the more questionable the processing is (Cuijpers & Koops, 2012; Knyrim & Trieb, 2011). Hence, the author of this text recommends depending on more frequent readouts than absolutely necessary, only exceptionally in well-grounded cases.

- The reliance on consent or different contracts (different tariffs, value-added services) may introduce the need for customizable readouts. AMI deployments typically offer the needed customization, but AMR deployments may not be suitable (Polčák & Matoušek, 2022).

- The Article 29 Data Protection Working Party (2013) (Opinion 05/2013) lists transparency, predictability, and user control as related concepts to purpose limitation. The processing must be predictable and sufficiently related to the original purpose of processing. In the case of the metering data, unrelated purposes might be incompatible with legal bases, such as legitimate interests, as the data subject does not predict such processing. In the context of smart metering, unrelated purposes are, for example, marketing activities based on the detected appliances. The data subject interested in getting energy supplies does not suspect automatic profiling of their activities. The Article 29 Data Protection Working Party (2013) (Opinion 05/2013) lists two examples related to smart monitoring:

  ○ The first example relates to cooperation between tax authorities (for example, to detect occupied flats that are declared unoccupied) or law enforcement (for example, to detect cannabis factories) on one side and the utilities on the other. The Article 29 Data Protection Working Party concluded that such cooperation is possible only under strict conditions of (nowadays) Article 23 of the European Parliament and Council (2016) (GDPR, Regulation 2016/679/EU), that is, there needs to be a legislative measure that respects the essence of the fundamental rights and freedoms and is a necessary and proportionate measure in a democratic society to safeguard national security, defense, public security, or other exceptions listed by the Article 23, European Parliament and Council (2016) (GDPR, Regulation 2016/679/EU).

○ The second example is about an analytics tool that detects anomalies in usage patterns. As the controller identifies high risks for data subjects, they consult their plan with regulatory authorities responsible for the electricity grid and data protection (see Articles 35 and 36, European Parliament and Council, 2016) (GDPR, Regulation 2016/679/EU). The controller gets approval for the plan, provided that additional safeguards are in place to minimize the risks of any undue impact on the data subjects like technical and organizational measures, fair and effective procedures to correct any inaccurate results, and transparency towards the data subjects.

Step 4: The controller should decide the envisaged time limits for the collected personal data erasure. For example, the controller is legally obliged to keep (or forward) some data from the smart meters, for example, monthly or yearly readouts. For data collected only for further computation, for example, to detect events, such as water leakage or fraud, the controller can decide that data are needed only for a limited time, sometimes only a fraction of a second. The controller complies with the data minimization principle by processing the data for a minimal period.

Step 5: The controller should reflect other parties taking part during the processing:

• The controller can realize that they want to outsource a part of the processing to another party, for example, because it is cheaper. Such processing is allowed if the controller conforms to Article 28 of the European Parliament and Council (2016) (GDPR, Regulation 2016/679/EU).

• Multiple parties determine the purposes and means of the processing (GDPR, Regulation 2016/679/EU, Article 26, European Parliament and Council, 2016).

○ The electricity market comprises several entities like energy suppliers, distributors, and retail sellers. Multiple parties need some data. For example, both the distributor and the retail seller need the billing value. Consequently, one of the entities typically performs the readout and shares the metered value with the other party.

○ Recall that the European Commission Recommendation of March 9, 2012 (European Commission, 2012) on preparations for the roll-out of smart metering systems (2012/148/EU) calls for a clear determination of the responsibilities of data controllers and data processors. CJEU recently decided on several cases concerning issues in controllership (see C-210/16, CJEU, 2018a; C-25/17, CJEU, 2018b; and C-40/17, CJEU, 2019b). For example, Advocate General Mengozzi (2018, paragraph 68) considers it necessary to rely upon a factual rather than a formal analysis. The European Parliament (2021) Resolution of March 25, 2021 on the Commission evaluation report on the implementation of the General Data Protection Regulation 2 years after its application (GDPR, 2020/2717(RSP), European Parliament, 2021) explicitly mentions ICT manufacturers being considered controllers of personal data.

- Polčák & Matoušek (2022) reported a case in which an association of coowners (condominium) deployed an AMR metering system with frequent readouts offered by a supplier. The association was interested in providing billing. However, the supplier installed a metering system that performs frequent readouts (with a period of tens of seconds). Who is the controller of the data in the frequent readouts, and who decides the purposes of the processing? Polčák & Matoušek (2022) only speculate about the accurate answer to this question. The supplier could have prevented the uncertainty by revealing the readout period. Consequently, the controller could have established that there is no legal basis for such transfers unless the inhabitants of each household give their free consent. Additionally, the parties should have signed a contract in conformance with European Parliament and Council (2016) (GDPR, Regulation 2016/679/EU, Article 26). Such a contract arrangement would demonstrate adherence to the accountability principle.

Step 6: The controller should determine technical and organizational security measures (GDPR, Regulation 2016/679/EU, Article 32, European Parliament and Council, 2016). The controller should focus on the availability, integrity, confidentiality, authentication, identification of authorized personnel, nonrepudiation, access control, accountability, and auditing (GDPR, Regulation 2016/679/EU, European Parliament and Council, 2016; Kumar et al., 2019). A typical smart metering system is heterogeneous. The controller needs to identify the assets, responsibilities of the employees, threats, risks, and possible mitigations. Kumar et al. (2019) provide a thorough list of risks associated with metering networks of all sizes. Moreover, they identified solutions to some of the threats. Nevertheless, some of the identified threats are still open research problems. Known threats evolve, and the complexity of the deployed smart network often increases as new functionality is added and parts of the networks are replaced by new equipment. Hence, this step needs to be repeated, and the threats and risks revised. The controller should have a policy specifying the events that trigger the security reevaluation. The author of this chapter advises the controller to follow security standards like ISO/IEC 27000 that give holistic guidance on how to achieve secure deployment.

- Not only are the security measures essential for the data protection of the consumers, but they are also crucial for maintaining the stability of the metering systems. For example, Komninos et al. (2014) give an example of smart homes using parked electric cars' batteries to offer network energy during a high load. A man-in-the-middle attacker can massively drop the acknowledgment messages by the smart grid, resulting in unstable electricity network conditions.
- The system should be resilient against impersonation attacks (Komninos et al., 2014). An impersonating adversary can order the system to turn all devices on-premise on (with a financial burden on the customer) or off (with possibly life-threatening consequences if electrical life support systems are deployed).
- Asghar et al. (2017) mention tempered electric and gas meters in the United Kingdom, even though the tampering may result in explosions and even deaths. To overcome the issue, they recommend employing a scalable access control mechanism and application of low-level code of the smart meters.

Step 7: Once the controller completes the six steps above, they determine all crucial information to create records of processing activities (GDPR, Regulation 2016/679/EU, Article 30, European Parliament and Council, 2016). The records of processing activities enable the controller to prepare transparent information (GDPR, Regulation 2016/679/EU, Articles 12 and 13, European Parliament and Council, 2016). Cuijpers & Koops (2012) and Asghar et al. (2017) show that consumers need to be adequately informed about the risks and privacy implications of smart meters. Additionally, the controller should determine that there are means to allow data subjects to exercise the rights for data access (GDPR, Regulation 2016/679/EU, Article 15, European Parliament and Council, 2016), rectification (GDPR, Regulation 2016/679/EU, Article 16, European Parliament and Council, 2016), erasure (GDPR, Regulation 2016/679/EU, Article 17, European Parliament and Council, 2016), restriction of processing (GDPR, Regulation 2016/679/EU, Article 18, European Parliament and Council, 2016), and data portability (GDPR, Regulation 2016/679/EU, Article 20, European Parliament and Council, 2016).

- This step poses a risk for the controller. While data subjects should have means to exercise their rights, this process should not infringe on the rights of other data subjects. McKenna et al. (2012) raise the issue of multiple persons living in a single household. How can the controller distinguish between personal data belonging to a parent and an adolescent child, or distinguish between a landlord and a tenant? The author of this chapter suggests that the controller needs to evaluate each request on a case-by-case basis. The controller should prepare in advance for such requests and determine the process that determines if the request does not interfere with the rights of other individuals.

Step 8: As an additional step, the controller should increase the transparency of the processing. That is not strictly required by European Parliament and Council (2016) (GDPR, Regulation 2016/679/EU) but can be required by some national data protection laws. Additionally, as covered in Table 1, transparency can facilitate the deployment of smart metering. For example, the controller can allow the residents (data subjects) to read wireless data sent by the meters, offer access to the algorithms that analyze the metering data, or publish the data protection impact assessment or regular reports on the processing.

- The offer to read data demonstrates compliance with the rights for the data access (GDPR, Regulation 2016/679/EU, Article 15, European Parliament and Council, 2016) and data portability (GDPR, Regulation 2016/679/EU, Article 20, European Parliament and Council, 2016). For example, some residents do not want the controller to collect frequent readouts that are not necessary (Knyrim & Trieb, 2011). However, a resident wants to process the readouts themselves or forward them to an IoT vendor of the resident's choice. Such an option enables the customers to detect events such as water leakage as early as possible. Moreover, the customers could detect events tailored to a specific household (for example, the IoT controller can report any gas consumption when all household members are away as a gas leakage).
- The additional steps improve transparency (GDPR, Regulation 2016/679/EU, Articles 12 and 13, European Parliament and Council, 2016). The author of this chapter thinks that the more transparent the metering is, the less likely it encounters opposition. Moreover, transparency can improve the system's resiliency, and independent audits can improve the metering system. Data subjects that can validate the metering systems fear less compared to residents left in the dark about the data collected on their household.

Table 2 summarizes the steps and the European Parliament and Council (2016) (GDPR, Regulation 2016/679/EU) principles affected during each step.

Table 2. Summary of the steps

Steps	Step summary
1. List processing operations	Transparency, purpose limitation, accountability
⇓	
2. Specify needed data	Fairness, transparency, purpose limitation, data minimization, accountability, data protection by design, risks for data subjects
⇕	
3. Legal basis for processing	Lawfulness, fairness, transparency, purpose limitation, necessity, accountability, legal bases, data protection by default, risks for data subjects, data protection impact assessment
⇕	
4. Storage duration	Lawfulness, fairness, transparency, data minimization, accountability, data protection by design and default, risks for data subjects, data protection impact assessment
⇓	
5. Identify other parties	Transparency, accountability
⇓	
6. Security measures	Accountability, risks for data subjects
⇓	
7. Records of processing and data subjects' rights	Lawfulness, fairness, transparency, purpose limitation, data minimization, accountability, legal bases, data protection by design and default, data subjects' rights
⇓	
8. Transparency and data access	Fairness, transparency, necessity, data subjects' rights

Note. The author of the chapter expects that the controller might iterate between steps 2–3 as they learn more details on the processing and risks for data subjects.

Manufacturers and Distributors of Components for Metering Systems

Recall that in the second and third steps, the entities running a metering system needed to perform a market analysis to identify meters with an adequate and preferably strictly necessary frequency of readouts and process only necessary information. A responsible manufacturer (or distributor) of remotely readable meters and other components for smart metering and smart grids should be transparent in documenting the capabilities and risks of the devices.

To facilitate the deployment of metering systems, the manufacturers and distributors should clearly explain the benefits of the meters. For example, they can educate on the risk of postmeter leakage, which accounts for up to 10% of total water consumption (Britton et al., 2013). Recall that the entity running the meter needs to justify the costs in proportion to the expected energy savings (Directive 2018/2002/ EU, European Parliament and Council, 2018). A controller determining the purposes of processing (steps 1 and 2 above) can precisely justify the processing only if the manufacturers and distributors provide transparent and precise information.

The manufacturers should make the devices configurable. Some protocols like Wireless M-Bus (EN 13757) need frequent data transmissions. Polčák & Matoušek (2022) reported meters sending data with a period of tens of seconds or minutes. As some deployments (like billing) do not need such frequent readouts, the manufacturer should allow a household member to configure the frequency of the readouts. For example, it is technically possible to keep sending the same metered value for each transmission for a whole month. As faulty or tampered gas or electricity meters can cause explosions (Asghar, 2017), the manufacturers should consider allowing verification of the meters' firmware, for example, by an independent certification body.

A metering system can consist of a web interface, application, or a similar user interface facing the resident of a metered household. Such an interface can provide historical data on billing and consumption. Recall that the controller needs to decide on envisaged time limits for the erasure of the collected personal data (step 4 above, GDPR, Regulation 2016/679/EU, Article 5(1)(e), European Parliament and Council, 2016). Hence, the web interface and the underlying database need to erase data after the period during which the controller needs the data. The vendor should allow the user to consent to keep data longer than necessary.

The manufacturer and the distributor should clearly describe the security model and support. For example, is the security strong enough to protect confidentiality, integrity, availability, authenticity, and other security functions? What are the privacy goals (Kumar et al., 2019)? Will there be software updates for the device? Are there any known attacks against the devices? Is it possible to pay for security support, or is it included in the price of the meter? What is the envisioned threat model?

The manufacturer should incorporate the possibility of using encrypted personal data and cryptographic proofs (Rial et al., 2018) or homomorphic encryption. As mentioned above, such an approach demonstrates legal conformance, does not leak private data to energy distributors, and does not need excessive additional resources. If such approaches are not applicable, the manufacturer should enable the meter to compute some operations like fraud detection directly in the meter so that the consumption data do not need to be processed and collected by other elements of the metering architecture.

Some of the above recommendations are motivated by business incentives. The author of this paper believes that a meter detecting events like meter tampering or water leakage should sell better than a meter without such configurability. However, the manufacturers and distributors must also be motivated by the data protection law.

The European Parliament (2021) Resolution of March 25, 2021 on the Commission evaluation report on the implementation of the General Data Protection Regulation 2 years after its application (GDPR, 2020/2717(RSP); European Parliament, 2021), explicitly considers ICT manufacturers as controllers according to Article 4(7) (GDPR, Regulation 2016/679/EU, European Parliament and Council, 2016), as they determine the means of processing. Although such a statement is not lawfully binding, the manufacturers (and distributors) should be aware of the possibility of them being a controller. The author of this text believes that manufacturers and distributors should avoid any possibility of them being identified as actual controllers (if they do not have a business model depending on them being a controller). Controllers have many legal requirements that can be avoided by the manufacturers by offering sufficient transparency to the actual controllers.

Considered Scenarios

This section applies the data protection recommendation to metering systems (scenarios) and clarifies the views of the author of this chapter.

Scenario A: Manual Water Remote Readout

This scenario deals with a building, that is, owned by an association of co-owners or a condominium. The building is composed of many units. Each building unit has a water meter that can be read remotely. However, there is no additional permanent infrastructure. Such a metering system is cost effective, as it does not require permanent reading, and the electricity consumption is minimal. However, a person needs to enter the building or read the data in front of the building, as the signal strength is sufficient for readouts from the vicinity only. The controller is the association of co-owners. However, as it is a small entity without any knowledge of security in information technologies, it will need help to manifest conformance with the law.

Step 1: The controller decides that it needs to process data to provide billing. Additionally, the controller is interested in detecting events (Polčák & Matoušek, 2022). Although the metering system cannot warn about accidents in real time, as there is no reading infrastructure, the meters can detect tampering, backflow, and similar events (Polčák & Matoušek, 2022).

Step 2: The controller determines that it needs monthly data readouts to comply with Directive 2018/2002/EU (European Parliament and Council, 2018). For each detectable event, the controller only needs information if the event was or was not detected during the previous month.

Step 3: The controller decides to process billing information as a legal obligation. The controller will process events as its legitimate interests, as it will process only strictly necessary information to prevent fraud and ensure proper billing.

Step 4: The controller will keep personal data for the period required by law. For personal data that are not required by law, like the detected events, the controller can store such personal data for the duration of the investigation that explains and settles the event.

Step 5: The controller does not plan to buy a reading set. It will buy a specialized service to perform the reading.

Step 6: The controller will ensure organizational and security measures as a service offered by the manufacturer of the meter.

Steps 7–8: These steps do not add any technical steps and are out of the scope of this chapter.

The manufacturer of the meters has to help the controller. The manufacturer does not want to be considered a controller, so it discloses all information regarding data transfers to the controller. This should include any quirks of the protocol, such as the necessity to transfer data much more often than needed, as explained in the case of a Wireless M-Bus described in a deployment by Polčák & Matoušek (2022). The manufacturer takes several steps to account for the compliance of deployed meters with the law. Although the meters send data every minute, all messages contain the same readout from the beginning of the month. The meters keep several recent readings in local memory to detect the events. To increase transparency and facilitate the expansion of the systems, the manufacturer gives the controller instructions on how to read the messages and switch the meters to more frequent readouts. Tenants in the building can buy their own reading sets to track their consumption. The manufacturer also offers a paid service (that gives it additional revenue) that tracks all changes in related standards, data protection laws, and published security threats. The service will warn the controller in case there is any problem. The meters can be updated to fix bugs or be updated according to new requirements.

Scenario B: Manual Gas Remote Readout

In this scenario, a gas distributor (controller) installs meters to building units. The meters send data wirelessly and are not connected to any permanent infrastructure. Similarly to scenario A, a car needs to park in front of the building to read out the metering data. The signal strength is sufficient for readouts from the vicinity only.

Steps 1–4: The motivations of the controller are the same as in Scenario A (see the concrete steps above).

Step 5: The controller will perform the reading by itself. However, the controller decides to store the readouts in the cloud. The controller needs to ensure that all provisions that are out of the scope of this paper are met (European Data Protection Board, 2021; C-311/18, CJEU, 2020).

Step 6: The controller is large enough to organize the security by itself. Nevertheless, it will cooperate with the manufacturer of the meters and react to any vulnerability found. Additionally, it will review related work biannually to consider new risks for the processing.

Steps 7–8: These steps do not add any technical steps and are out of the scope of this chapter.

Similarly, to Scenarios A and B, there are many variants that influence the outcome of the analysis only slightly.

Scenario C: Permanent Infrastructure—Frequent Readouts

In this scenario, a gas distributor (controller) installs meters to building units in a small city. The meters send data wirelessly to a radio station mounted on the building of the distributor in the city. The signal strength is sufficient for the readouts.

Step 1: The controller decides that it needs to process data to provide billing. Additionally, the controller is interested in detecting events like meter tampering or backflow. The metering system will warn about accidents in real time.

Step 2: The controller determines that it needs monthly data readouts to comply with Directive 2018/2002/EU (European Parliament and Council, 2018). The controller does not find any meter on the market that detects all required events, so it will need frequent readouts.

Step 3: The controller decides to process billing information as a legal obligation. The controller will process events as its legitimate interests. However, as the amount of data required is high, it will consult with its data protection authority (GDPR, Regulation 2016/679/EU, Articles 35 and 36, European Parliament and Council, 2016). The controller and the supervisory data protection authority decide to apply additional safeguards including public reports, incentives to review the algorithms, or the possibility of opt-out. The controller might be ordered to postpone the processing and run a pilot study with volunteers. If the controller is large enough, it might conduct a business contract with a manufacturer to deliver meters suitable for the task. The controller can deploy meters detecting fraud and leakage in suitable locations like where the flow is aggregated.

Step 4: The controller will keep personal data for the period required by law. For personal data that are not required by law, like the readouts to detected events, the controller will immediately delete the data unless it detects an event. The controller will store personal data that triggered the event for the duration of the investigation that explains and settles the event.

Steps 5–8: See the scenarios above.

Scenario D: Permanent Infrastructure— Optional Processing Based on Consent

This scenario is similar to Scenario A. However, the controller decides to deploy a permanent reading infrastructure. The infrastructure consists of gateways that forward the readouts through the internet to a server collecting and processing the data. The advantage for the association is that the billing is performed automatically. All tenants have access to the metered data in real time. Moreover, the deployment can detect water leaks. The association decides that preventing the risk of a water leak and giving the possibility to the tenants to track and optimize the consumption outweigh the cost of the reading infrastructure.

The steps needed to be taken by the controller are very similar to Scenario A. Table 3 introduces the new processing activities. Step 4 is similar to Scenario A.

Table 3. Additional processing of the controller

Step 1	Step 2	Step 3
Water leak detection	Event detected by meter	Legitimate interests, see the reasoning for similar processing in Scenario A
Detailed information on water consumption	Detailed data like the consumption at the time of each message from the meter	Consent of the tenants. The meter needs to be switched manually.

Note. Each line represents one processing activity.

The service provider will offer a paid service that enables the controller to allow the tenants to see the detailed consumption. As detailed consumption tracking is not strictly necessary, the controller cannot force all tenants to allow the processing. As a result, such data will be collected only with freely given consent. Some tenants will participate, and others will not.

Scenario E: Detection of Unlawful Water Consumption During Drought

In this scenario, a local water distributor installs meters to building units and households in a city. The meters send data wirelessly to radio stations mounted on communal buildings in the city. The signal strength is sufficient for the readouts. In essence, this scenario is similar to Scenario C. However, in this case, local authorities ask the distributor to give them data on unusual patterns in consumption that might reveal temporarily banned activities like filling pools.

In this case, there are two controllers. The water distributor deployed the metering system similar to the discussion in Scenario C. The local authorities are a different controller (C-175/20, 2022, CJEU,2022). Hence, the local authorities need to go through the identified steps by themselves:

Step 1: Personal data are needed to identify illegal water usage.

Step 2: The local authorities can ask for: (1) detailed readings, (2) identified events, and (3) running algorithms on the data in possession of the local water distributor. In all three cases, the local distributor is the processor that acts on behalf of the local authorities.

Step 3: The local authorities decide that the processing is necessary for the performance of a task carried out in the public interest (GDPR, Regulation 2016/679/EU, Article 6(e), European Parliament and Council, 2016). However, unless there is a law following Article 23, European Parliament and Council (2016) (GDPR, Regulation 2016/679/EU), the processing cannot be carried out.

Step 4: The law identified in step 3 will likely specify the period for how long the local authorities keep the data or how the period should be calculated. Otherwise, local authorities should immediately delete personal data for households without suspicion. The local authorities will keep suspicious data during the investigation of the incident or for the time required by the law governing the investigations.

Step 5: Both the water distributor and local authorities are controllers. The water distributor is a processor of local authorities. Depending on additional circumstances out of the scope of this chapter, there might be additional processors.

Step 6: Both parties need to negotiate the security measures to transfer personal data with regard to the sensitivity of the data.

Step 7: The local authorities need to prepare the records of processing activities and are responsible to obey user rights.

Scenario F: Undocumented Data Transmitted by the Meters

A controller deployed a metering system similar to the Scenarios A–D. The controller fulfilled all its responsibilities and deployed the system. The police investigate a burglary in one of the households and learn that the burglars used data transmitted wirelessly by the metering systems to reveal occupancy periods of the household. The police forward the case of the metering system to the data protection authority. The controller demonstrates that it deployed meters that were supposed to provide monthly readouts with Directive 2018/2002/EU (European Parliament and Council, 2018), and the documentation does not mention more frequent readouts. The supervisory authority fines the manufacturer of the meters and orders replacing the meters.

The manufacturer did not follow the advice given in this chapter and was not transparent. As a consequence, it was the manufacturer that decided that frequent data are collected on data subjects. However, such processing was not lawful, as it was not collected for legitimate purposes in a transparent manner.

Scenario G: Security Breach

An adversary managed to get access to the database collected in Scenario D. A data subject sues the controller for the data breach. As the controller followed the steps listed in this chapter, it can demonstrate that all personal data were processed lawfully, fairly, and in a transparent manner. As the controller can demonstrate a legal basis for storing all leaked data in the database, and it was able to demonstrate that all security measures were in place as required by Article 32 of European Parliament and Council (2016) (GDPR, Regulation 2016/679/EU), the lawsuit is dismissed.

For example, the Supreme Administrative Court of the Czech Republic recently stated that a controller could not be held responsible for any security breach, and the data protection authority needs to demonstrate that the level of security was not appropriate to the risk of a breach (Supreme Administrative Court of the Czech Republic, 2021).

Scenario H: Electrical Energy Grid

Knapp & Samani (2013) give an overview of an electrical grid. There are producers of energy like fossil, nuclear, solar, hydroelectric, and wind power plants. The electricity is carried by the transmission and distribution layer. At this stage, the electricity is carried by high-voltage transmission. Transformers can increase (step up) or decrease (step down) voltages. Households are connected to the distribution network, each having a meter. A household can generate electricity, for example, with a solar panel. A household can also utilize devices that communicate with the network, for example, to negotiate the best time to consume energy.

Several entities play a role in the architecture. Energy producers need to know and predict how much energy to produce. Transmission entities need to prevent the network from blackout. They need to balance the amount of energy accepted for the transmission with the consumed energy. They also need models for anticipating the imminent behavior of the network. They also need data to perform billing. Distribution network operators need data to perform billing. Households need means to communicate with other parties to negotiate energy consumption and price. Note that such deployments facilitate complex pricing schemes. Energy can be ordered in advance but also bought at the last moment. As a result, many personal data controllers appear—producers, transmission, and distributors need to process personal data. Table 4 contains processing activities, needed data, and possible legal basis for such operation. Note that it is out of the scope of this chapter to provide an exhaustive list of processing activities in the smart grid. The listed processing activities are examples of activities that can be performed.

Table 4. An example of processing activities in a smart electrical grid

Entity	Step 1	Step 2	Step 3	Step 5
Producer	Price negotiation	Negotiated price, consumption period, energy sold, and energy consumed	Performance of a contract	(Some) data shared with transmission and distribution
Transmission	Billing	Aggregated data for the billing period. Dynamical contracts accepted by producers.	Performance of a contract	
Distribution	Billing	Aggregated data for the billing period. Dynamical contracts accepted by producers.	Performance of a contract	
Distribution	Fraud prevention	Aggregated data, in case of suspicion, detailed data	Legitimate interests, steps taken so that the interests of the controller are not overridden by the interests of the data subject	(Some) data shared with distribution, law enforcement, etc.
Producer, transmission, distribution	Predict future load	Aggregated data collected by transformers	Personal data are not processed, so these steps do not apply.	

Note. Each line represents one processing activity.

Of course, this scenario can be expanded. The amount of personal data will depend on the specific parameters of each deployment. The purpose of this example is to illustrate that aggregated data greatly simplify the obligations of data controllers. The key question is how to get the aggregated data. As Recommendation 2012/148/EU (European Commission, 2012) and European Parliament (2021) Resolution 2021/ C494/11 suggest, the best time to answer the question is before the deployment. The earlier the processing activities are detected, the lower the time to design or redesign the grid.

GENERALIZATION OF THE RECOMMENDATIONS FOR SMART HOMES

The European Commission (2014) (Recommendation 2014/724/EU) on the data protection impact assessment highlights that data from smart grids can be combined with other sources, such as geolocation data, tracking and profiling on the internet, video surveillance systems, and radio frequency identification (RFID) systems. According to the Recommendation, Article 29 Working Party and Commission

(2014) see smart metering as a foreshadowing of the IoT. This section reiterates the steps suggested above in the context of IoT deployment.

Devices typically appearing in smart homes, like smart bulbs, smart thermostats, smart plant watering, or smart ovens, produce and process personal data. Such devices often propagate data to the servers of the manufacturer or service provider (e.g., running in the cloud). According to European Parliament and Council (2016) (GDPR, Regulation 2016/679/EU), these service providers are data controllers.

Consequently, the controllers need to:

- track the operations (step 1 above),
- determine data needed to achieve the goal, including data minimization and necessity (step 2),
- decide the lawfulness of the processing (step 3),
- decide the envisaged time limits (step 4),
- reflect other parties (step 5),
- determine technical and organizational security measures (step 6),
- create the records of processing, and check that there are means to exercise the rights (step 7).

The author of this text thinks that step 8 typically does not make sense for IoT deployments. The difference is that in smart metering, the consumers typically cannot decide that they do not want the metering. In IoT, the customer decides to engage in a business contract with the controller. Step 8 is optional and aims to facilitate smart metering deployment.

FUTURE RESEARCH DIRECTIONS

The author of this chapter agrees with Orlando & Vandelvelde (2021) that current guidelines for smart metering lack clear guidance on the aggregation of data. Recall California, New York, and the rule that specifies the minimal number of households and maximal share of consumption of each household. Such numbers are understandable and implementable. Nevertheless, such a rule does not exist in Europe. According to Article 29 Data Protection Working Party (2014) Opinion 05/2014 on anonymization techniques, every case needs to be considered independently. Nevertheless, a branch of future research can focus on testing the rules of California, New York, or similar rules. Can such a rule guarantee that the aggregated data cannot be reversed? If not, do we need to add additional households, lower the maximal consumption, or add other constraints like spreading the consumption into small time bins?

This chapter identified multiple scenarios. However, there are likely other scenarios. Are there other requirements for these scenarios? Moreover, the chapter generalized the findings to smart homes. However, IoT also covers deployments that do not process personal data. One future research direction can focus on various flavors of IoT and the need for personal data.

From the law's point of view, the roles of the parties can be blurred. Possible research can focus on identifying the roles of each party. Who needs to be a controller, and who may be considered only a processor?

Another open question is the minimal subset of functionality and configurability of a meter. Cuijpers & Koops (2012) describe the failed attempt at smart meter roll-out in the Netherlands. One of the obstacles to the roll-out was that the meters were planned to be controllable remotely. Hence, identifying a minimal set of functionalities can help with legal certainty as well as in courts.

Kumar et al. (2019) cover the open security issues well (GDPR, Regulation 2016/679/EU, Article 32, European Parliament and Council, 2016). According to their paper, most of the research is evaluated by simulation instead of real-world devices. Only a few researchers evaluate their security properties with real smart meters, probably due to the limited access to real-world devices. Another issue lies in applying homomorphic and advanced cryptography to meters that need to conserve power. Advanced key distribution schemes are an open issue, as current schemes are vulnerable or have high computational costs. The limited communication bandwidth in metering networks results in the need to design secure and efficient routing protocols. Wireless transfers are inherently vulnerable to jamming and spoofing attacks. Another open research question, according to the paper, is the need for detailed data. Finally, they identified the need for security and privacy assessment tools.

Additionally, open research questions concern the practical large-scale deployment of homomorphic encryption smart meters or smart meters using cryptographic proofs (Rial et al., 2018) in multiple EU member states. The research should focus on facilitating such deployments. What are the benefits for manufacturers and utilities? Can the benefits be made more significant?

CONCLUSION

Our lifestyles depend on functioning utilities. It is well understood that energy consumption can be reduced by eliminating waste. The improvements in leakage detection can save up to 10% of the water (Britton et al., 2013). Fraud and energy theft harm the utilities. Smart metering provides the possibility to improve energy consumption. However, the deployment of smart networks brings several challenges to the design and operation of critical infrastructure. The network or individuals can be targeted, and, for example, an attack can stop energy distribution and harm individuals or companies (Kumar et al., 2019). It is well understood that a secure system needs to be designed securely from the beginning (Kumar et al., 2019). This chapter provides an overview of the metering networks, known threats, and the literature. The main contribution lies in specifying detailed steps that achieve conformance with data protection laws. A metering system designed according to the steps outlined in this chapter is resilient to threats and processes only necessary personal data. The chapter illustrates the application of scenarios and the steps ranging from a small deployment to a full-scale grid. The requirements apply to any energy distribution system, provided that the system meters the consumption of individual persons and, in some countries, small groups of persons. Moreover, the author argues that the steps can help smart home device manufacturers in designing data protection-compliant devices and services.

REFERENCES

Abreu, Z., & Pereira, L. (2022). Privacy protection in smart meters using homomorphic encryption: An overview. *WIREs*, *12*(4), 1–16. doi:10.1002/widm.1469

Armel, K., Gupta, A., Shrimali, G., & Albert, A. (2013). Is disaggregation the holy grail of energy efficiency? The case of electricity. *Energy Policy*, *52*(1), 213–234. doi:10.1016/j.enpol.2012.08.062

Asghar, M. R., Dán, G., Miorandi, D., & Chlamtac, I. (2017). Smart meter data privacy: A survey. *IEEE Communications Surveys and Tutorials*, *19*(4), 2820–2835. doi:10.1109/COMST.2017.2720195

Backes, M., & Melser, S. (2012). Differentially private smart metering with battery recharging. *IACR Cryptology*, 183. https://eprint.iacr.org/2012/183

Beal, C. D., & Flynn, J. (2015). Toward the digital water age: Survey and case studies of Australian water utility smart-metering programs. *Utilities Policy*, *32*, 2–37. doi:10.1016/j.jup.2014.12.006

Britton, T. C., Stewart, R. A., & O'Halloran, K. R. (2013). Smart metering: Enabler for rapid and effective post meter leakage identification and water loss management. *Journal of Cleaner Production*, *54*, 166–176. doi:10.1016/j.jclepro.2013.05.018

Brunschwiler, C. (2013). *Wireless M-Bus security*. Black Hat.

California Public Utilities Commission. (2014). *Decision adopting rules to provide access to energy usage and usage-related data while protecting privacy of personal data*. CPUC. https://docs.cpuc.ca.gov/PublishedDocs/Published/G000/M090/K845/90845985.PDF

Chen, D., Irwin, D., Shenoy, P., & Albrecht, J. (2014). *Combined heat and privacy: Preventing occupancy detection from smart meters*. In *2014 IEEE International Conference on Pervasive Computing and Communications*, (pp. 208–215). IEEE.

Chen, F., Dai, J., Wang, B., Sahu, S., Naphade, M., & Lu, C.-T. (2011). *Activity analysis based on low sample rate smart meters*. In *Proceedings of the 17th ACM International Conference on Knowledge Discovery and Data Mining*, (pp. 240–248). ACM. 10.1145/2020408.2020450

Court of Justice of the European Union. (2010). *Joint Case C-92/09 and C-93/09 (2010). Volker und Markus Schecke GbR (C-92/09) and Hartmut Eifert (C-93/09) v. Land Hessen*. [*Volker und Markus Schecke GbR (C-92/09) and Hartmut Eifert (C-93/09) v. Land Hessen*.] Europea. https://curia.europa.eu/juris/liste.jsf?num=C-92/09

Court of Justice of the European Union. (2013). *Case C-473/12. Institut professionnel des agents immobiliers (IPI) v Geoffrey Englebert and Others*. [*Professional Institute of Realtors (IPI) v Geoffrey Englebert and Others*.]. Europa. https://curia.europa.eu/juris/liste.jsf?num=C-473/12

Court of Justice of the European Union. (2014). Case C-212/13. *František Ryneš v Úřad pro ochranu osobních údajů*. [*František Ryneš in the Office for Personal Data Protection*.] Europa. https://curia.europa.eu/juris/liste.jsf?num=C-212/13

Court of Justice of the European Union. (2016). Case C-582/14. *Patrick Breyer v. Bundesrepublik Deutschland*. Europea. https://curia.europa.eu/juris/liste.jsf?num=C-582/14

Court of Justice of the European Union. (2017). Case C-13/16. *Valsts policijas Rīgas reģiona pārvaldes Kārtības policijas pārvalde v. Rīgas pašvaldības SIA "Rīgas satiksme"*. [*Order Police Department of the Riga Region Administration of the State Police v. Riga Municipality Ltd. "Rīgas satiksme"*.]. Europea. https://curia.europa.eu/juris/liste.jsf?num=C-13/16

Court of Justice of the European Union. (2018a). Case C-210/16. *Unabhängiges Landeszentrum für Datenschutz Schleswig-Holstein v Wirtschaftsakademie Schleswig-Holstein GmbH*. [*Unabhängiger Landeszentrum für Datenschutz Schleswig-Holstein v Wirtschaftsakademie Schleswig-Holstein GmbH*.]. Europa. https://curia.europa.eu/juris/liste.jsf?num=C-210/16

Court of Justice of the European Union. (2018b). Case C-25/17. *Jehovah witness.* Europa. *https://curia.europa.eu/juris/liste.jsf?num=C-25/17*

Court of Justice of the European Union. (2019a). Case C-708/18. *TK v. Asociaţia de Proprietari bloc M5A-ScaraA. [TK v. Association of Owners block M5A-ScaraA.].* Europa. https://curia.europa.eu/juris/liste.jsf?num=C-708/18

Court of Justice of the European Union. (2019b). Case C-40/17. *Fashion ID GmbH & Co.KG v Verbraucherzentrale NRW eV.* https://curia.europa.eu/juris/liste. jsf?num=C- 40/17

Court of Justice of the European Union. (2020). Case C-311/18. *Data Protection Commissioner v. Facebook Ireland Limited a Maximillian Schrems.* Europa. https:// curia.europa.eu/juris/liste.jsf?num=C- 311/18

Court of Justice of the European Union. (2022). Case C-175/20. *„SS" SIA v. Valsts ieņēmumu dienests. ["SS" Ltd. v. State Revenue Service.]* https://curia.europa.eu/ juris/liste.jsf?num=C- 175/20

Cuijpers, C., & Koops, B.-J. (2008). The 'smart meters' bill: A privacy test based on article 8 of the ECHR. *Study commissioned by the Dutch Consumers' Association.* English version available from the authors, see Cuijpers, C., & Koops, B.-J. (2012), footnote 39.

Cuijpers, C., & Koops, B.-J. (2012). Smart metering and privacy in Europe: Lessons from the Dutch case. In *European data protection: Coming of age* (pp. 269–293). Springer.

Erol-Kantarci, M., & Mouftah, H. T. (2013). Smart grid forensic science: Applications, challenges, and open issues. *IEEE Communications Magazine, 51*(1), 68–74. doi:10.1109/MCOM.2013.6400441

Esposito, C., & Ciampi, M. (2015). On security in publish/subscribe services: A survey. *IEEE Communications Surveys and Tutorials, 17*(2), 966–997. doi:10.1109/ COMST.2014.2364616

European Commission. (2011). Programming Mandate M/487 EN. *Programming mandate addressed to CEN, CENELEC and ETSI to establish security standards.* European Commission. https://ec.europa.eu/growth/tools-databases/mandates/index. cfm?fuseaction=search.detail&id=472

European Commission. (2012). Recommendation 2012/148/EU. *Commission Recommendation of 9 March 2012 on preparations for the roll-outroll-out of smart metering systems. Official Journal of the European Union, L, 73*(9), 9–22.

European Commission. (2014). Recommendation 2014/724/EU. *Commission Recommendation of 10 October 2014 on the data protection impact assessment template for smart grid and smart metering systems. Official Journal of the European Union, L, 300*(63), 63–68.

European Commission. (2011). Article 29 Data Protection Working Party. *Opinion 12/2011 on smart metering.* Europea. https://ec.europa.eu/justice/article-29/documentation/opinion recommendation/files/2011/wp183_en.pdf

European Commission. (2013). Article 29 Data Protection Working Party. *Opinion 05/2013 on purpose limitation.* Europea. https://ec.europa.eu/justice/article-29/documentation/opinion-recommendation/files/2013/wp203_en.pdf

European Commission. (2014). Article 29 Data Protection Working Party. *Opinion 05/2014 on anonymization techniques.* Europea. https://ec.europa.eu/justice/article-29/documentation/opinion-recommendation/files/2014/wp216_en.pdf

European Data Protection Board. (2021). *Recommendations 01/2020 on measures that supplement transfer tools to ensure compliance with the EU level of protection of personal data Version 2.0.* Europa. https://edpb.europa.eu/system/files/2021-06/edpb_recommendations_202001vo.2.0_supplementarymeasurestransferstools_en.pdf

European Parliament. (2021) *European Parliament Resolution 2021/C 494/11. European Parliament Resolution of 25 March 2021 on the Commission evaluation report on the implementation of the General Data Protection Regulation two years after its application (2020/2717(RSP)). European Parliament. Official Journal of the European Union* C 494/129-138.

European Parliament and Council. (2016). *General Data Protection Regulation (GDPR). Regulation 2016/679/EU. Official Journal of the European Union* L 119, 4.5.2016, 1–88.

European Parliament and Council. (2018). Directive 2018/2002/EU. *Amending Directive 2012/27/EU on energy efficiency. European Parliament and Council. Official Journal of the European Union* L 328, 21.12.2018, p. 210–230.

European Parliament and Council. (2019). Directive 2019/944/EU. *On common rules for the internal market for electricity and amending Directive 2012/27/EU.* European Parliament and Council. Official Journal of the European Union L *158, 14.6.2019, 125–199.*

Kaatz, J. (2017). Resolving the conflict between new and old: A comparison of New York, California and other state DER proceedings. *The Electricity Journal, 30*(9), 6–13. doi:10.1016/j.tej.2017.10.005

Kalogridis, G., Efthymiou, C., Denic, S., Lewis, T., & Cepeda, R. (2010). Privacy for smart meters: towards undetectable appliance load signatures. In *2010 First IEEE International Conference on Smart Grid Communications*, 232–237. 10.1109/SMARTGRID.2010.5622047

Kelly, J., & Knottenbelt, W. (2015). The UK-DALE dataset, domestic appliance-level electricity demand and whole-house demand from five UK homes. *Scientific Data, 2*(1), 1–14. doi:10.1038data.2015.7 PMID:25984347

Knapp, E. D., & Samani, R. (2013). *Applied cyber security and the smart grid.* Elsevier Inc.

Knyrim, R., & Trieb, G. (2011). Smart metering under EU data protection law. *International Data Privacy Law, 1*(2), 121–128. doi:10.1093/idpl/ipr004

Komninos, N., Philippou, E., & Pitsillides, A. (2014). Survey in smart grid and smart home security: Issues, challenges and countermeasures. *IEEE Communications Surveys and Tutorials, 16*(4), 1933–1954. doi:10.1109/COMST.2014.2320093

Kumar, P., Lin, Y., Bai, G., Paverd, A., Dong, J. S., & Martin, A. (2019). Smart grid metering networks: A survey on security, privacy and open research issues. *IEEE Communications Surveys and Tutorials, 21*(3), 2886–2927. doi:10.1109/COMST.2019.2899354

Lee, D., & Hess, D. J. (2021). Data privacy and residential smart meters: Comparative analysis and harmonization potential. *Utilities Policy, 70*, 101188. doi:10.1016/j.jup.2021.101188

Lima, C. A. F., & Navas, J. R. F. (2012). Smart metering and systems to support a conscious use of water and electricity. *Energy, 45*(1), 528–540. doi:10.1016/j.energy.2012.02.033

Lisovich, M. A., Mulligan, D. K., & Wicker, S. B. (2010). Inferring personal information from demand-response systems. *IEEE Security and Privacy, 8*(1), 11–20. doi:10.1109/MSP.2010.40

Liu, A., Giurco, D., & Mukheibir, P. (2015). Motivating metrics for household water-use feedback. *Resources, Conservation and Recycling, 103*, 29–46. doi:10.1016/j.resconrec.2015.05.008

March, H., Morote, Á.-F., Rico, A.-M., & Saurí, D. (2017). Household smart water metering in Spain: Insights from the experience of remote meter reading in Alicante. *Sustainability*, *9*(4), 582. doi:10.3390u9040582

McKenna, E., Richardson, I., & Thomson, M. (2012). Smart meter data: Balancing consumer privacy concerns with legitimate applications. *Energy Policy*, *41*, 807–814. doi:10.1016/j.enpol.2011.11.049

McLaughlin, S., McDaniel, P., & Aiello, W. (2011). Protecting consumer privacy from electric load monitoring. In *Proceedings of the 18th ACM Conference on Computer and Communications Security*, (pp. 87–98). ACM. 10.1145/2046707.2046720

Mengozzi, P. (2018). Opinion of Advocate General Mengozzi. *CJEU Case C-25/17, ECLI:EU:C:2018:57*. https://curia.europa.eu/juris/liste.jsf?num=C-25/17

Mohassel, R. R., Fung, A., Mohammadi, F., & Raahemifar, K. (2014). A survey on advanced metering infrastructure. *Electrical Power and Energy Systems*, *63*, 473–484. doi:10.1016/j.ijepes.2014.06.025

Monedero, I., Biscarri, F., Guerrero, J. I., Roldán, M., & León, C. (2015). An approach to detection of tampering in water meters. *Procedia Computer Science*, *60*, 413–421. doi:10.1016/j.procs.2015.08.157

New York State Public Service Commission. (2018). *Order Adopting Whole Building Energy Data Aggregation Standard*. NYPSC.https://documents.dps.ny.gov/public/Common/ViewDoc.aspx?DocRefId=%7B4C4CE28E-54CC-4514-967D-B513678E3F37%7D

Orlando, D., & Vandelvelde, W. (2021). Smart meters' roll out, solutions in favour of a trust enhancing law in the EU. *Journal of Law. Technology & Trust*, *2*(1). Advance online publication. doi:10.19164/jltt.v2i1.1071

Polčák, L., & Matoušek, P. (2022). *Metering homes: do energy efficiency and privacy need to be in conflict*? In *Proceedings of the 19th International Conference on Security and Cryptography*, Lisboa, Portugal. 10.5220/0011139000003283

Rial, A., Danezis, G., & Kohlweiss, M. (2018). Privacy-preserving smart metering revisited. *International Journal of Information Security*, *17*(1), 1–31. doi:10.100710207-016-0355-8

Supreme Administrative Court of the Czech Republic. (2021). *Internet Mall, a.s. v. Úřad pro ochranu osobních údajů [Internet Mall, a.s. Office for Personal Data Protection]*. SACCR. https://www.nssoud.cz/files/SOUDNI_VYKON/2021/0238_1As__2100033S_20211111111159.pdf

United States Court of Appeals for the Seventh Circuit. (2018). *Naperville Smart Meter Association v. Naperville - Seventh Circuit Decision*. United States Court of Appeals for the Seventh Circuit.

Yang, W., Li, N., Qi, Y., Qardaji, W., McLaughlin, S., & McDaniel, P. (2012). *Minimizing private data disclosures in the smart grid*. In ACM Conference on Computer and Communications Security, Raleigh, North Carolina. 10.1145/2382196.2382242

Zeifman, M., & Roth, K. (2011). Nonintrusive appliance load monitoring: Review and outlook. *IEEE Transactions on Consumer Electronics*, *57*(1), 76–84. doi:10.1109/TCE.2011.5735484

Zhou, S., & Brown, M. A. (2016). Smart meter deployment in Europe: A comparative case study on the impact of national policy schemes. *Journal of Cleaner Production*, *144*, 22–32. doi:10.1016/j.jclepro.2016.12.031

ADDITIONAL READING

Article 29 Data Protection Working Party (2014*). Opinion 8/2014 on Recent Developments on the Internet of Things*. Europa. https://ec.europa.eu/justice/article-29/documentation/opinion-recommendation/files/2014/wp223_en.pdf

Edwards, L. (2016). Privacy, security and data protection in smart cities: A critical eu law perspective. *European Data Protection Law Review*, *2*(1), 28–58. doi:10.21552/EDPL/2016/1/6

European Court of Human Rights. (2022). *Guide on Article 8 of the European Convention on Human Rights*. ECHR. https://www.echr.coe.int/documents/guide_art_8_eng.pdf

European Data Protection Board. (2020). *Guidelines 4/2019 on Article 25 Data Protection by Design and by Default Version 2.0*. EDPB. https://edpb.europa.eu/sites/default/files/files/file1/edpb_guidelines_201904_dataprotection_by_design_and_by_default_v2.0_en.pdf

European Data Protection Board. (2021). *Guidelines 07/2020 on the concepts of controller and processor in the GDPR Version 2.1*. EDPB. https://edpb.europa.eu/system/files/2021-07/eppb_guidelines_202007_controllerprocessor_final_en.pdf

Finster, S., & Baumgart, I. (2015). Privacy-aware smart metering: A survey. *IEEE Communications Surveys and Tutorials*, *17*(2), 1088–1101. doi:10.1109/COMST.2015.2425958

Jakobi, T., Patil, S., Randall, D., Stevens, G., & Wulf, V. (2019). It is about what they could do with the data: A user perspective on privacy in smart metering. *ACM Transactions on Computer-Human Interaction*, *26*(1), 1–44. doi:10.1145/3281444

Langås, M., Løfqvist, S., Katt, B., Haugan, T., & Jaatun, M. G. (2021). *With a little help from your friends: Collaboration with vendors during smart grid incident response exercises. European Interdisciplinary Cybersecurity Conference (EICC)*. Association for Computing Machinery, New York, NY, USA, 46–53. 10.1145/3487405.3487654

Petrlic, R. (2019). The General Data Protection Regulation: From a data protection authority's (technical) perspective. *IEEE Security and Privacy*, *17*(6), 31–36. doi:10.1109/MSEC.2019.2935701

Singh, J., & Cobbe, J. (2019). The security implications of data subject rights. *IEEE Security and Privacy*, *17*(6), 21–30. doi:10.1109/MSEC.2019.2914614

KEY TERMS AND DEFINITIONS

Advanced metering infrastructure (AMI): This is heterogeneous and hierarchical; it includes smart meters, communication networks, data management systems, and means to integrate collected data into software platforms and interfaces. AMI allows bidirectional communication, typically initiated by the infrastructure. Typical AMI meters allow advanced features to improve the reliability, efficiency, and sustainability of the grid. For example, connected devices can negotiate with the network the optimal time to consume resources (for example, to charge an electric vehicle during the night).

Automatic metering readout (AMR): This allows only communication initiated by the meters and often without the possibility of sending data to the meter. The meters are typically not directly connected to a wired network and are powered by batteries. The goal is to minimize the power requirements of the meter. The meters are typically read by a person that enters the building or parks a car in the vicinity. There might be a permanent infrastructure to read the meters.

Court of Justice of the European Union (CJEU): This is the highest court in the European Union. Courts in the European Union should take into account its case law.

Controller: This is an entity defined by GDPR that specifies the means and purposes of the processing of personal data.

Personal data: These are any data that can be directly or indirectly connected to a natural person, for example, by using identifiers.

Privacy: This is a concept that allows a person to keep information hidden from the general public. It is connected to the right to respect for private and family life in the European Convention of Human Rights and respect for private and family life, protection of personal data of the European Charter of Fundamental Rights.

Processor: This is an entity cooperation with the controller processing personal data according to the instructions of the controller.

Smart meter: This is a device with capabilities like remote readout, remote control, price negotiation, etc. A typical smart meter does not offer all capabilities.

Chapter 2
Security and Performance of Knowledge–Based User Authentication for Smart Devices

Alec Wells
York St. John University, UK

Aminu Bello Usman
York St. John University, UK

ABSTRACT

A secure authentication system ensures that the claimant is the genuine user attempting to access the system and that it is not susceptible to misidentification, forgetfulness, or reproduction. While technological advancements in the authentication process continue to advance, most authentication systems still have room for improvement, particularly in terms of accuracy, tolerance to various security attacks, noise, and scalability as the number of smart devices grows. In this chapter, the authors look at the security, effectiveness, and drawbacks of knowledge-based, ownership-based, location-based, and social-based authentication systems, as well as some unresolved issues and potential future research directions.

INTRODUCTION

Authentication is the process of verifying an identity claim using the users' knowledge (e.g., secret questions, passwords, PINs), their possessions or ownership (e.g., ID cards, mobile phones, tokens), their location, other social accounts, or their biometrics

DOI: 10.4018/978-1-6684-5991-1.ch002

(e.g., biometrics, fingerprints, iris scans, signatures) of which can all be referred to as different authentication factors (Flu, 2015). The purpose of authentication is to establish confidence, that the user trying to access technology, is the user themselves and to only allow the user access to their account/sensitive information. Strong authentication systems help to reduce potential fraudsters and other hackers from gaining access to sensitive information they should not have access to. The need of a secure authentication process is still a sizable concern in cyberspace to establish the integrity and authenticity of a claimant while accessing anything from technologies, applications to network systems. With the growth of smart technologies in many different sectors such as hospitals, financial sectors, the military, aviation, etc. there is an even greater need to determine the authenticity of a genuine user.

A secure authentication process ensures that the claimant is the legitimate user trying to access the system and the authentication process is not susceptible to misplacement, forgetfulness, or reproduction. Whilst technological progress in the authentication process continues to evolve, most of the authentication systems still have more room for improvement, particularly in their accuracy, tolerance to various security attacks, noisy environments, and scalability as the number of individuals increases (Poh, Bengio, & Korczak, 2002). The classification of user authentication factors can be seen in Figure 1, which classifies authentication factors in to five main categories, Knowledge-based, Biometric (inherence)-based, Ownership-based, Location-based, and Social-based authentication factors.

The knowledge-based authentication (KBA) is a flexible tool in digital identity proofing protocols and solutions. As the name suggests, knowledge-based authentication factors seek to prove the identity of the claimant accessing the technology or service, using private and secret pieces of information to prove the claimant's identity. KBA can be offered in many formats, making it a valuable and flexible authentication mechanism in many cybersecurity architectures. Knowledge-based factors are based on information only the user should know such as a username and password or personal identification number (PIN).

Ownership-based authentication factors are based on something the user has, such as cards, smartphones, or other tokens. For instance, one of the most prevalent examples of ownership-based factors are payment cards, utilized by banks that each possess a unique combination of numbers and security information from one another. Another example of ownership-based factors is the usage of tokens that are issued to the user to use to sign in.

Figure 1. A Taxonomy of Authentication Factors - A breakdown of each authentication method and a list of examples for each type

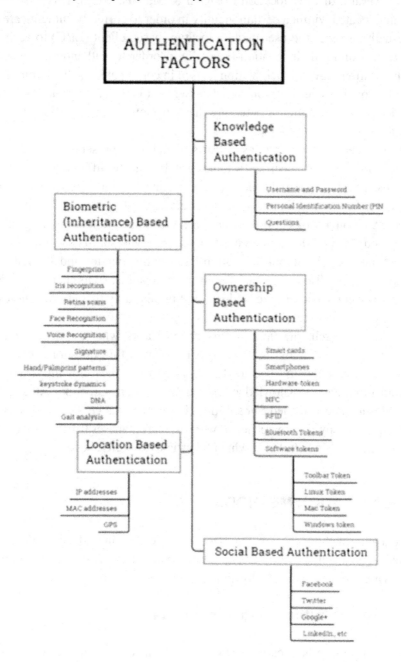

The location-based authentication factors use the claimant's identity to detect its presence at a distinct location (Trojahn & Marcus, 2012). It is based on the user being located within a certain vicinity in order to correctly authenticate them. This usually involves the user using a location-based client (LBC) to verify with a server containing their location-based ID in order to authenticate themselves. Usually location-based authentication is used in combination with another form of authentication, however location-based authentication can also be used on its own, to get access to a machine or detecting that a person is at a specified area – such as an entrance.

The chapter is structured as follows: Section 2 presents an overview of authentication systems; specifically looking at the various different factors and how they are used in single and multi-factor authentication. Section 3 discusses knowledge-based authentication, again providing an overview and looking at the attacks done on KBA. Section 4 looks at ownership-based authentication comparing the types of token and also looking at the security issues of ownership-based authentication. Section 5 provides a brief look at location-based authentication and the challenges it presents. Section 6 discusses social-based authentication and its challenges. Finally, Section 7 is a conclusion of the findings within this study that also discusses open issues and potential future research.

The key research question of this chapter asks what is the current state of authentication methods as a whole? To answer this question, papers were researched between the time period of 1994-2020, using the following search terms: Authentication, Factor, Knowledge, Ownership, Token, Location, Attack, Brute-Force, Masquerade, Blended Substitution, False Acceptance, Phishing, Guessing, Password & Entropy. The search terms were used in databases IEEE, Science Direct, Springer and Google Scholar of which 87 articles are referenced.

AUTHENTICATION METHODS

Authentication methods can be categorized in two groups, single-factor authentication, and multi-factor authentication. The descriptions of the two user authentication methods are provided in the following sections.

Single-Factor Authentication Methods

The single-factor authentication method simply involves using only one method or 'factor' to verify the user's identity and authenticate themselves. Single-factor authentication can involve any type of factor from knowledge-based factors like passwords or PIN numbers, to ownership-based factors such as bank cards or cell phones, other factors such as inherence factors like a user's fingerprints or iris, or social factors such as google accounts, or location factors such as their GPS location (Turner, 2016).

Many different literature, technology-based companies and agents consider single-factor authentication to be inadequate for preventing fraud, especially for that of high-risk transactions related to banking (Council, 2005) (Tiwari, Sanyal, Abraham, Knapskog, & Sanyal, 2011). This is simply because if you only have one factor protecting your account, if that was to ever leak, then access to the account can be immediately gained by an intruder. Studies such as (Veľ Asquez & Rodrıguez, 2018) also suggest that in regard to single-factor authentication using knowledge factors, users find it hard to remember passwords for a long time, or remember different passwords for multiple accounts, hence leakages are much more likely, without a second alternative factor also being used. This is especially a concern nowadays, considering the amount of data breaches that have occurred in recent years where multiple users accounts and passwords have been leaked. Even disregarding data breaches, many passwords can be cracked due to users using weak or even default passwords, allowing hackers easy access to accounts. When users are valuing authentication, the main considerations they have are with the usability and security of the authentication (Khan & Zahid, 2010). Although many users consider multi-factor authentication to be safer and more secure than single-factor, users also consider single-factor to be more user friendly, as shown in the study (Gunson, Marshall, Morton, & Jack, 2011) in which participants considered single factor to be easier, more straightforward and quicker than multi-factor authentication.

Multi-Factor Authentication Methods

Multi-factor authentication utilizes a similar process to that of single-factor authentication. However, the primary difference between the two is that multi-factor authentication will only authenticate the user after they have presented two or more factors to verify their identity (Turner, 2016). Similar to single-factor authentication, these can be based on the same factors seen their such as knowledge, ownership, behavioral, location or social. In multi-factor authentication, the authentication process can ask for pieces of evidence from the same type of factor i.e. two knowledge-based factors like a password and security question or two different types of factor, such as a fingerprint and PIN code.

Multi-factor authentication while considered much more secure than single-factor authentication, does however have a few drawbacks. For instance, just like single-factor authentication, two-factor authentication is not immune to being hacked and is just as vulnerable to many different types of attacks. Another concern with multi-factor's feasibility is when only one factor is available to authentication themselves, such as for example, if a user is using a mobile authenticator, in a rare circumstance that mobile phone might not be available due to battery loss, lack of signal or it being stolen. Two-factor authentication can also be equally susceptible to users having their credentials stolen from phishing-based attacks. For instance, one such example is Man-in-the-Middle attacks, where attackers will create spoofed versions of websites for users to type their credentials into for the attacker to steal and use on the real website. Alternatively, other attacks that two-factor authentication is not immune to is the likes of Trojan attacks where a hacker can piggyback on a user's login session to make their own fraudulent transactions (Schneier, 2005).

The main deployment of multi-factor authentication has been through phone authentication apps that users can tie to most online accounts. This authentication follows the method of first receiving credentials that have one identifier between a first and second principal (such as an email address). The user's knowledge of the first identifier is first verified (such as a password) and an authentication credential is then generated (Burch & Carter, 2010). This is often seen with smartphones via an app to generate codes for the user to receive and then enter when they sign in (Drokov, Punskaya, & Tahar, 2015). This has been one of the most common deployments of multi-factor authentication due to how integrated phones are in modern society – allowing them to be nearly always available, except in extenuating circumstance.

Other prominent examples of multi-factor authentication are seen in the world of banking that utilizes both knowledge and possession-based factors. In order to pay via a credit card in person, a user must have both the bank card itself to put in the card reader and know the PIN code in order to complete the transaction. Alternatively, multi-factor authentication is seen for a network service by monitoring a session at a firewall applying a profile based on the new session and performing an action based on the authentication profile (Murthy et al., 2020).

Overall, despite single-factor authentication being considered inadequate at preventing fraud, it is still commonly used as it considered both faster and more convenient for the user compared to the safer yet slightly more cumbersome multi-factor authentication. Several important services, such as banking, have multi-factor authentication as a requirement, whereas less important services simply provide it as an optional extra layer of security. Single-factor and multi-factor can be used with all different authentication factors in various combinations, such as with biometrics, when two different biometrics are combined together, is referred to as multimodal biometrics. This is elaborated in the following sections.

KNOWLEDGE-BASED AUTHENTICATION

The two most widely used methods of users' authentication using KBA are: static (shared secrets) and instant (also known as dynamic KBA). The Static KBA is based on a pre-defined or agreed set of questions or shared secret information between the authentication parties involved. Mostly, static KBA relies on factoid recall, which is information known specifically to the user, which include questions such as what your is mother's maiden name, what street did you grow up on, or what was your first pet etc, and is commonly used by email providers, banks, financial services or other companies to authenticate different users (Chokhani, 2004).

On the contrary, instant KBA uses methods and algorithms to dynamically develop a set of personal questions and answers to authenticate a user, and it does not require the user to have provided the questions and answers beforehand (Flu, 2015). These dynamic questions provide randomized right and wrong answer choices based on data found for the subject by the KBA system. Regardless, in practical usage, both versions of KBA usually require a form of initial registration against an existing database to create the credentials. KBA then usually requires access to the server to verify the factoids/credentials in the login mechanism (Chokhani, 2004).

One of the attributes of KBA is password entropy - a measure of how unpredictable a password is. Password entropy estimates how many trials an attacker (either by guessing or brute force) would need, on average, to guess the password correctly. In other words, the more difficult to predict or guess the password entropy, the more secure the KBA is. Given a password with a character size L, we can compute the password entropy using the following equation 1 below (MLB9252, 2011).

$$E = Log_2(R^L) \tag{1}$$

Where E is the password entropy, R is the pool of unique password char- acters, and L is the number of characters in each password. Subsequently, R to the power of L is the number of possible password combination and the equation is the number of bits of entropy.

Security Attacks on Knowledge-Based Authentication Factors

The KBA attacks Taxonomy in Figure 2 presents the classification of KBA attacks, of which there are a few main types we cover; social engineering, guessing attacks and brute force attack.

Social Engineering Attacks on Knowledge Based Authentication Factors

The social engineering (SE) attack is manipulating the target (a person) to obtain information by a social engineer – an attacker. So far, SE is the most superior form of KBA attacks as users themselves are the attacks' targets. Successful social engineering attacks can be incredibly damaging and highly lucrative. In a SE attack, the attacker takes on a legitimate personnel's disguise to convince the victim to give out their sensitive information. The attacker can execute the attack in person by interacting with the target to gather desired information about the target(s) or use specialized software. A distinctive feature of SE attacks to KBA compared with the other forms of attacks on KBA, is social engineering attacks exploits human weaknesses and that it may be challenging to address the problem of human weaknesses.

The attacks' operators of social engineering attacks against KBA can be classified into two approaches. Social engineering attacks include social-based attacks (using psychological skills to collect KBA information) (Granger, 2001) (Salahdine & Kaabouch, 2019), and computer-based attacks (the use of sophisticated technical tools to obtain KBA information) (Krombholz, Hobel, Huber, & Weippl, 2015). In turn, depending on how the attack is conducted, social engineering attacks can be classified into three categories, physical, technical and socio-technical (or social) based attacks. Physical-based attacks refer to physical actions the attack does, such as dumpster diving, to obtain information. Technical-based attacks refer to attacks using technical approaches – using technical tools and methods to harvest users' KBA information. Technical types of attacks to KBA are mainly carried out over the Internet using a specialized tool such as Maltego to gather and aggregate target's information from different Web resources or social networks. Finally, social-based attacks refer to exploiting relationships with the victim, utilizing psychology and emotion to trick the victim into giving information and is currently one of the most powerful forms of KBA attacks used by of social engineers. Examples of these forms of attacks include "road apples" attacks, an attack using a USB containing a Trojan horse or baiting attacks (Stasiukonis, 2006). Social-engineering attacks have often shown to be very effective, for example a study investigated the vulnerability of hospital employees sharing their passwords through social engineering attacks with 73% of respondents sharing their password (Medlin, Cazier, & Foulk, 2008).

Table 1 presents different forms of social engineering attacks in relation to two different approaches to social engineering attacks. Examples of attacks can include shoulder surfing attack, which is a form of social engineering attack used to obtain information from the target using direct observation techniques, such as looking over victim's shoulder to obtain victims' passwords, PINs, or secret information. Dumpster diving attack is another form of social-based attack to recover information about

Table 1. Social engineering attacks' operators on knowledge-based authentication factors

Attack Operator	Shoulder Surfing	Dumpster Diving attacks	Reverse Diving Attacks	Water holing attacks	Crawling or spidering attacks	Baiting Attacks	Advanced Persistent Threat	Spear Phishing attack	Voice Phishing Attacks	Man in the Middle Attacks	SMS Phishing	Catphishing	Clone Phishing	Whale Phishing
Social-Based Attack	☑	☑	☑		☑	☑		☑	☑			☑		
Computer-based Attack		☑	☑	☑	☑	☑	☑	☑	☑	☑	☑	☑	☑	☑

the habits, activities, and interactions of individuals or organization from discarded phone books, hard drives that have not properly been scrubbed or surfing through people's curbside garbage. "A dumpster can be a valuable source of information for attackers, who may find personal data about employees, manuals, memos and even print-outs of sensitive information" (Koyun & Janabi, 2017).

The Reverse Social Engineering (RSE) attack has three stages: sabotage, advertising and assisting. Initially, an attacker can sabotage the company's or individual access credentials. The attacker can then convince the target that he/she is ready to solve the problem.

When the victim asks for help, the social engineer will resolve the problem they created earlier while, for example, asking the victim for their password ("so I can fix the problem") or telling them to install certain software, etc. (Krombholz et al., 2015).

Other forms of SE attacks on KBA include water holing attacks - strategically targeting frequent users of a website by infecting one or a few frequent users (Edwards et al., 2017), spidering attacks - often a more automated and thorough form of phishing attack gather all small details (Dale, 2021), baiting attacks - similar to phishing attacks but as a Trojan horse, providing a good incentive or gift to the user in exchange (Fan, Lwakatare, & Rong, 2017), advanced persistent threat - which is repeated usage of the same technique to wear the victim down, often gaining and then maintain a foothold (Daly, 2009) and phishing attacks. We provide in the following section, a detailed description about phishing attack on KBA.

As presented in Figure 2 there are different forms of phishing attacks: whaling phishing, spear phishing attack, and vishing phishing, etc. Spear phishing attack is usually directed at specific individuals or companies to gather and use personal information about the target to increase chances of successful attacks (Ho et al., 2017). Whaling phishing (Whaling email) is a highly targeted phishing attack mostly against financial institutions and payment services. Through social engineering, the attacker can encourage the victim to perform a secondary action, such as initiating a wire transfer of funds. Whaling phishing are more sophisticated than generic phishing emails as they often target senior executives (Chiew, Yong, & Tan, 2018). Other forms of phishing attacks include the catfishing attack in which the attacker pretends to be someone else the target would be interested in, to lure the target into giving information they wouldn't usually give to the attacker (Simmons & Lee, 2020). There is also voice phishing and SMS phishing, which both involve the user spoofing phones either through landlines or SMS pretending to be someone else by changing their caller ID (Choi, Lee, & Chun, 2017; Mishra & Soni, 2019). Clone phishing meanwhile is where an attacker takes something legitimate, such as a website or email and makes a copy of it, however, they can replaces attachments or links with something malicious or steal the users data (Banu & Banu, 2013). In the Man-in-the-Middle (MITM) phishing attack, the phisher places himself or herself in the middle of two ways communication between the victim and a web-based application to eavesdrop and collect sensitive information that the victim is submitting to a web-based application (Chiew et al., 2018).

Figure 2. Knowledge-Based Authentication Attack's Taxonomy - An illustration of various types of knowledge-based authentication and the type of attacks they can be attacked by

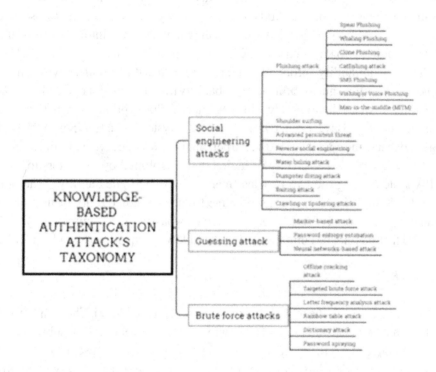

Guessing Attacks on Knowledge Based Authentication Factors

The popular methods of KBA guessing attacks can be classified into three types: Markov-based, neural networks-based (recognise relationships in data the same way a human brain operates), and Entropy estimation (guessing based on the expected entropy). The study (Narayanan & Shmatikov, 2005) argued that the distribution of letters in easy to remember KBA factors (e.g, passwords) is likely to be similar to the distribution of letters in the users' native language. The authors applied "Markov modelling techniques from natural language processing to reduce the size of the password space to be searched and increases the chances of guessing the password". Meanwhile the study ([Dürmuth] et al., 2015) proposed a "Markov model-based password cracker that generates password candidates according to their occurrence probabilities". The study (Weir et al., 2009) applied a" probabilistic context free grammar based upon a training set of previously disclosed passwords template to generate word-mangling rules for password cracking". Finally, the study (Hitaj et al., 2019) applied "machine learning algorithms to propose password guessing technique based on generative adversarial networks (GANs) to learn users' password distribution information from password leaks".

The use of Bayesian network (BN) models in probabilistic reasoning and information theory provides a valid metric for entropy estimation of human-selected passwords. The proposed BN-KBA model in (Chen, 2007) is intuitively appealing in that it captures two key metrics of KBA as the model parameters, particularly the likelihood memorability (probability that a claimant with true identity recalls the factoid correctly) and guessability (the probability that an impostor correctly guesses the factoid). In that vein, the study (Chen & Liginlal, 2007) proposed a methodology for implementing a Bayesian network based KBA system. The findings in the study suggested that in the context of KBA, the personal knowledge revealed from a variety of online sources can be directly or indirectly be exploited by imposters to attack a KBA system using the two metrics (memorability and guessability). The other reason for KBA being compromised is due to the of predictability of user choice on the guessability of KBA. For example, given a password, the guessability of the password factoids can be computed using the following equation (Chokhani, 2004).

$$P_{KBA,j} = \pi_i P_{i,j}$$

Where $P(KBA, j)$ is the probability of compromising KBA by j. The claimant type is j. The ith factoid is i and the probability to guess by factoid i is $P_{i,j}$, subsequently, the convenience of a KBA system is valued as important as the obscurity (difficulty of guessing) variable; thus, guessability of KBA can be a reason why alternative solutions are being explored, though the guessability of KBA is made worse by the fact that many users use common, easy to guess passwords, such as '123456' which was used by over 23.2 million breached accounts (NCSC, 2019). In addition, with the rich data repository available on resources such as online social networks and the cutting-edge machine learning techniques, the guessability an attacker would achieve can be substantially improved. Subsequently resources such as online social networks, may put imprudent KBA designs at risk.

Brute Force Attacks on Knowledge Based Authentication Factors

A brute force attack on KBA is the act of trial and error to gain access via trying multiple combinations of password. There are different forms of brute force attack to KBA including offline cracking attack (taking a password from a password storage file that has been recovered from the system) (Blocki, Harsha, & Zhou, 2018), letter frequency analysis attack (replace popular letters in ciphertext with common letters in the used language) (CRYPTO-IT, 2020), or targeted brute force attacks which primarily uses input dictionary creation programs and password guess generators (to target other accounts with previously compromised account details) (Tools, n.d.) (Salamatian et al., 2020). Another form of brute force attack on KBA is rainbow table attack which enables the recovery feasibility of long, human chosen passwords, which computes hashes of the large set of available strings, rather than specifically calculating a hash function for every string present and comparing them to the target (ParthDutt, n.d.) (Marforio et al., 2016; Zhang, Tan, & Yu, 2017).

A more refined version of the brute force attack is a dictionary attack, a type of attack that only utilizes the possibilities most likely to succeed rather than cycling through every option like a brute force attack (Jablon, 1997). Similarly, password spraying also utilizes the most common passwords, but instead targets multiple accounts at once, to try to gain entry into any account regardless of the user (Joseph et al., 2021). There also exists the danger of password cracking, where attackers try recover passwords from data that has already been transmitted, usually via a brute-force attack, however since the password has already been transmitted the attackers know the cryptographic hash of the password, allowing them to brute-force more effectively (Weir, 2010).

While there are many different attacks against knowledge-based factors, there are several countermeasures that users can do, to try make them as secure as possible. One of the simplest and yet best ways to deal with various attacks, is to have strong, uncommon passwords that utilize multiple different types of characters, numbers, and case (Shay et al., 2014). By using stronger passwords, simple attacks such as brute-force and dictionary attacks are far less likely to succeed. Likewise, having different passwords for every account or changing passwords often can help keep accounts secure in the event of a data breach, though many would argue that" changing password often can inflict needless pain, cost and risk to the user," (Lance, 2019) though could still be considered good practice. Beyond that, users should simply be careful to avoid any suspicious software/emails and always look for good identifiers, such as the padlock in the address bar to signify the website is encrypted. Depending on the types of attacks, other forms of attacks' countermeasures include multi-factor authentication, account lockouts after multiple failed attempts, user training, and antivirus software (Dejan, 2018). Alternatively, the study (Bhardwaj & Goundar

2021) proposes for preventing brute force attacks on Cloud services that a 3-tier structure is superiors to that of single tier infrastructure, applying various firewalls to different tiers such as networks and web applications.

Despite the perceived risk of KBA, it is still widely used and has many metrics." KBA is very easy to use and easy to understand. This is because it has been one of the standard means of authentication and KBA, such as passwords, are the most common form of authentication" (for Cybersecurity, n.d.). Likewise, from an admin and logistical point of view, KBA is very attractive. It requires no additional hardware beyond a standard keyboard, unlike for instance biometrics, which means it can be easily used by anyone for anything and anywhere. Due to this, it is cheaper to implement for business than more costly methods, such as biometrics (Raza, Iqbal, Sharif, & Haider, 2012), and is also fairly easy to administer for both home and business owners. Further, studies have suggested that the possible starting point for addressing the vulnerability of KBA credentials is to understand the status of uses' password reuse behavior since many studies suggested that the same login credentials are used for many more accounts and reused much more often than previously expected (Bang, Lee, Bae, & Ahn, 2012).

OWNERSHIP-BASED AUTHENTICATION

Ownership-based authentication factors are based on something the user has, such as cards, smartphones, tokens etc. For instance, one of the most prevalent examples of ownership-based factors are payment cards, utilized by banks that each possess a unique combination of numbers and security information from one another. Another example of ownership-based factors is the usage of tokens that are issued to the user to use to sign in. As we've moved into a more digital age, one of the most common forms of ownership-based factors is within mobile phones to deliver a single use code, either through receiving a code through text messages or via an authentication-based app that would provide a code when you attempt to login.

Payment cards are an extremely common form of ownership-based factors and are usually issued by banks. A bank card has a unique string of numbers as well as data such as an expiry date and security code that is tied to a user's band account. Bank cards can come in many different forms, with the most common being credit and debit cards. Similarly, many banks also use a form of tokens (electronic key) or one-time use passwords (a password that is generated for that specific sign-in request) to authenticate users and the server. Authentication apps and messages are being used for a variety of online accounts to be used in conjunction with passwords as a form of two-factor authentication, some examples include the google authenticator and windows authenticator apps. Alternatively, mobile phones can also be used as a token by using Bluetooth wireless communication, using the phone token as a challenge-response protocol (Kunyu, Jiande, & Jing, 2009). We also see tokens being applied to cloud computing, as seen when multi-layer tokens were used with honey passwords to authenticate users at different fog nodes to deter various attacks such as should surfing, password guessing and denial of service attacks (Rayani, Bhushan, & Thakare, 2018). Another form of ownership-based authentication is a smart card or integrated circuit card (ICC card) - an electronic authorization device, used to control access to a resource. The ICC card is typically a plastic credit card-sized card with an embedded integrated circuit (IC) chip (ISO/IEC, 2007). A smart card can be in either the form of card with metal contacts to electrically connect to the internal chip, connect contactless, or in both forms (Kuo & Lo, 1999). Smart cards contain a users' authentication, small data storage, and application processing components to perform input/output (I/O) functions. In terms of applications, most

organizations used smart cards for single sign-on (SSO) (using the same ID for multiple services) for pass-through authentication system. For example, studies such as Li et al. (2012, 2013) have proposed schemes that utilized smart cards for scenarios such as multi-server architecture and insecure network environments. Both approaches include a control server which chooses a master key and four phases: registration, login, authentication/session key and the password change phase. Alternatively, the study (Li & Hwang, 2010) also proposed a smart card scheme that uses a one-way hash function with verification and smart cards that is unique due to the usage of randomized numbers in place of timestamps for resisting replay attacks. Another example is in the study (Li, Niu, Ma, Wang, & Liu, 2011), which proposed a improved biometric scheme using smart cards that supports session key agreements, which allowed the scheme to be more resistant to man-in-the-middle attacks. Other forms of ownership-based factors include NFC (near-field communication)-tag authentication, which uses a unique key that is encoded onto the tag, which when scanned reveals the item (Chen et al., 2010). RFID (radio frequency identification) involves a similar process to NFC- tags but transmits the data using radio waves (Lim & Kwon, 2006). Cellphones can be used as ownership-based factors in many ways from providing one-time passwords through phone apps and SMS messages or as digital certifications using public key infrastructure (Contributor, 2014). Finally, hardware-tokens, which come in several forms, which we expand upon in the following section (Shablygin et al., 2013).

Categories of Hardware-Token

Hardware-token can be categorized into synchronous and asynchronous Tokens. For synchronous tokens, time synchronization between the token and authentication server is used as part of the authentication process, whereas asynchronous does not.

Synchronous Tokens

With synchronous token, a server keeps the records of a serial number for each authorized token, the user associated with the token, and the time. Using these three pieces of information, a server can predict the dynamic code generated by the token. As illustrated in Figure 3, synchronous tokens have two subcategories of which they can be, either clock-based or counter-based tokens. The clock-based, One Time Password (OTP) tokens are dependent on time-sensitive codes which have to be used within a certain timeframe, often expiring if not used within the correct amount of time. Many authentication apps are time based and will have to be used quickly before being replaced by another key. This means usually only the user will have enough time to access the correct code within the necessary time window (Jøsang, 2018).

The second type of synchronized token is counter-based OTP tokens. Counter-based OTP tokens (sometimes referred to as event-based OTP) generate a form of 'password' from two pieces of internal information. The two pieces of information are the secret key (or seed) which is only known by the token and the second piece of information is the moving factor, aka the counter. To give out a token, the OTP feeds the counter number into an algorithm with the token seed as the key; this produces a 160-bit value that is reduced down usually to 6-8 digits for the user to use as an OTP. When the token is pressed, the counter is incremented when a OTP is successfully validated. The key difference between counter and clock-based OTP is that counter-based uses purely internal data rather than external data (Smith, 2018).

Asynchronous Tokens

Alternative to synchronized tokens are asynchronous tokens, also known as challenge-response tokens. Challenge-response authentication defines one party proposes a challenge or question to the other. The second party can then perform the challenge or task by using information only available to it. The types of challenge questions can be static or dynamic. Static questions are predefined that the user has previously selected for instance "name of first pet" etc. Dynamic questions are created from extracting public data about the user such as a "previous street address" (Jøsang, 2018) (Rouse, 2018). Asynchronous tokens are not synchronized with a central server" and thus, the most common types are challenge-response tokens. Challenge-response authentication is often done using cryptographic techniques to prevent eavesdropping. Hence, many challenge-response tokens use encryption keys when generating the challenge, so that the responder must also use the key to create an encrypted response (Konigs, 1991).

Figure 3. Categories of Authentication Tokens - A breakdown of the two types of tokens and various examples of each

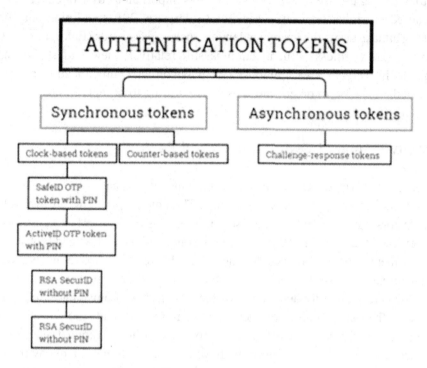

Client to Authenticator Protocol

Alternatively, other types of ownership authentication exist. For example, with smartphones, protocols such as FIDO2, which is a form of password less authentication that uses WebAuthn and the FIDO Client to Authenticator Protocol 2. FIDO2 is able to authenticate the user by contacting a device such as a mobile phone, this could be done via the use of biometric features, such as by using touch ID. FIDO2 then uses a challenge-response protocol by using a pair of keys, that are individually generated for each service, that when verified, will authenticate the user (Lyastani, Schilling, Neumayr, Backes, & Bugiel, 2020). This approach is different in that it doesn't use tokens and hence is not susceptible to the likes of phishing or credential stuffing attacks since no text message or token is inputted by the user. FIDO2 improves upon the base of the original FIDO which only covered using public key cryptography for mobile devices, whereas FIDO2 also supports browsers from Microsoft, Mozilla and Google and is being adopted by many areas such as banking, telecoms and other sectors (Dunkelberger, 2018).

Many believe that passwordless authentication can be the future of authentication, due to it lacking the use of passwords, which is important as 81% of data breaches are caused by stolen or weak passwords (Enterprise, 2017) and nine out of ten phishing attacks target the users' credentials such as passwords (Enterprise, 2016). However, passwordless authentication is still relatively new and studies have sought to investigate user opinions with passwordless authentication as single factor authentication to determine if users are willing to accept a replacement for passwords (Lyastani et al., 2020).

Security Issues of Ownership-Based Factors

Ownership-based factors, however, are not immune to being hacked and they too have disadvantages that can inconvenience the user. The simplest problem with ownership-based factors is in the event that the user loses possession of their factor, or worse it is stolen, then the user cannot access their account and the user would both require a replacement token and request for the old card/token to be made invalid. When the data of an ownership-based factor is fixed, like for banking cards such as debit and credit cards, the individual details on them are at risk of phishing-based attacks and due to the rise of online commerce and banking, has made these details more vulnerable to those types of attacks. In 2016, 1.09 million banking Trojan attacks were detected and 47.78 percent of them were from the usage of a phony banking website/page to steal credentials from users (Stephen, 2019). Most phishing attacks are due the naivety of many users in signs of phishing and hence being unable to distinguish real sites from fake sites. Studies have looked into protocols that leverage communication between the service to provide security alert indications when in the presence of malicious applications for mobile devices, though even these require the user to be careful and alert for potential phishing (Marforio et al., 2016).

There are studies in the literature that have found that utilizing text message-based authentication can also be insecure, when researchers were able to get into a Gmail account to hack Gmail, all they required was a name and a phone number. The hackers were able to exploit a SS7 weakness to intercept SMS text messages from only knowing the number itself, allowing them access into Gmail accounts through password resetting and then proceed to do another reset (Thomas, 2017). This shows the dangers of having multi-factor authentication can also add more vulnerabilities to security, as hackers could be intercepting the codes, despite the user having possession of the device. Tokens have many vulnerabilities, though given there are many different types of tokens, these are not mutually exclusive. Tokens share the most common issue with ownership-based factors being the user either losing it, or having it stolen. In the event of having a card/token stolen, a user could be compromised, which is why tokens and other ownership-based factors are usually used in conjunction with knowledge-based factors as multi-factor authentication. However, credit cards are also vulnerable to SQL injection attacks as well as unpatched systems, or storage of unnecessary data (Braintree, 2007). In addition, systems utilizing a network for authentication can be vulnerable to man-in-the-middle attacks, where the attacker spoofs the" go-between" to solicit the token output from the user. Alternatively, a compromised token may be used for an SQL injection attack (maliciously entering an SQL statement into an entry field to be executed by the system) to tamper with the database containing user's data by exploiting input validation flaws.

LOCATION-BASED AUTHENTICATION

Location-based authentication (LBA) factors are more uncommon compared to the likes of knowledge or ownership-based factors. LBA is based on the user (or an object) being located within a certain vicinity in order to correctly authenticate them. This usually involves the user using a location-based client (LBC) to verify with a server containing their location-based ID to authenticate themselves or alternatively perhaps a consumer might use a portable consumer device that is used to conduct a transaction at a merchant (Zhang, Kondoro, & Muftic, 2012). Mostly, LBA is used by financial industries to increase profitability of credit card companies by reducing the accumulated losses due to fraud.

Technology companies and network administrators are using building services that use geolocation security checks to verify the location of a user before granting access to an application, a network or entire system, like for instance GPS. For example, network administrators are using IP addresses to access the origin of network traffic and to know ascertain the users' location before granting service to the user. However, this can be bypassed by using IP tunneling (a channel between two networks to transport a network protocol) (Koutny & Sykora, 2010), a VPN or anonymous routing protocols (a specific way routers communicate with one another) (Kumari & Kannammal, 2009). In addition, MAC addresses, which are unique to individual computing devices, can be implemented as a location-based authentication factor to ensure that a system is only accessed from a limited number of authorized devices (Turnbull & Gedge, 2012). Location-based authentication can also be used to discern that a user has perhaps been compromised, as for instance it would seem odd a user that usually logs in within a certain postcode would be logging in from a different machine perhaps located on the other side of the world.

Location-based authentication systems with mobile devices transitions, is mostly used for electronic transactions on a financial institution's online website. The process of authentication may involve verifying whether a mobile device (such as a cellular telephone) is proximate to a computer from which the transaction is being performed (Ashfield, Shroyer, & Brown, 2012). If the mobile device is sufficiently proximate, then the transaction may be approved. Otherwise, it can be rejected. To enable location-based authentication, a special combination of objects is required. First, the claimant must present a sign of identity. Secondly, the individual who is to be authenticated has to carry at least one human authentication factor that may be recognized on the distinct location and thirdly, the distinct location must be equipped with a means capable to determine the coincidence of individual at this distinct location (Hammad & Faith, 2017). Some studies investigated different forms of location-based authentication in a product supply chain with machine-learning techniques, by which they show suspicious products can be automatically recognized from the incomplete location information (Lehtonen, Michahelles, & Fleisch, 2007). To detect fraudulent transactions, studies have proposed a Location-based Authentication (LBA) system by which a fraud-score can be generated to indicate whether an attempted transaction should be authorized or not. (Eden & Avigad, 2012).

Challenges of Location-Based Authentication

Location-based authentication is not without its issues however, for instance one large consideration about location-based authentication is that the location used by a user is more publicly available knowledge than that of a password. Attackers could learn of a user's location through various tracking means and then appear at that same location. The accuracy of GPS signals is also crucial to the success of location-based authentication (Sharma, 2005). Alternatively, more sophisticated hackers might be able to spoof their location through various means such as through a VPN meaning that the location-based authentication would have to be more sophisticated to prevent this (Harber, 2022). Location-based authentication also relies on generating cryptographic keys based on the user's location which in turn could be brute-forced by an attacker, especially if that attacker knew the rough location of a user which would reduce the amount of attempts for a brute-force attack dramatically.

Location-based authentication does however have many advantages. Primarily adding an extra layer to authentication as it will only allow successful sign in from specific locations. This could be useful for a company that would only want employees on site being able to login, or for regular users with their home desktops only allowing specific locations such as their house or on mobile the town/city they live in. Unlike ownership-based factors, location-based factors cannot be stolen. Also, if location-based factors were being used for a certain building or home, then unlike most other authentication factors there could be several physical layers of protection, primarily door locks etc. to keep unwanted hackers from getting in. It also isn't necessary to set up specialized infrastructure for location-based authentication as it can be built into existing devices and mobile networks (Zhang et al., 2012).

SOCIAL-BASED AUTHENTICATION

Throughout the last few years, many web-based logins have adopted the ability to use social login. Social login allows users to authenticate themselves for services by using a login from their preferred social network account such as Facebook, Twitter, Google, LinkedIn and many others, rather than setup an account with the service. There are many benefits to using a social login instead of having an account for each online service. For example, users don't need to remember multiple usernames and passwords for their accounts, the user establishes one connection to a reliable identity provider, which provides "reduced password fatigue" and lowers the need for the website to have significant infrastructure or security protocols" (Gafni & Nissim, 2014). Similarly, certain social media accounts are also being used for single sign on, such as Facebook, which allows users to use a single set of login credentials to access multiple services. In turn, by using single sign-on, it helps uses mitigates the need to manage and remember their different accounts and passwords (Fang et al., 2001).

Challenges of Social-Based Authentication

Social login however does have some concerns. For example, one issue is the privacy of the user. Many sites ask the user for lots of unnecessary personal information, not to mention any account would in turn be linked to the user's social media, which means users may lack anonymity on certain websites. This is also concerning as those websites with less infrastructure and security could be more easily compromised. A concern many users may have when using social login, is that if an attacker were to gain access to the user's social media, then they would potentially be able to access many accounts through their social login, hence strong passwords are a must (Gafni & Nissim, 2014). By using services for social-based or single-sign on, users are also creating a single point of failure so that if that service was ever down, they would be unable to access any of their other services, making them especially vulnerable to denial-of service attacks (Ellison, Hodges, & Landau, 2002).

CONCLUSION

In conclusion, many traditional means of authentication are considered to be outdated. Hence, many alternate methods of authentication are being sought out. Example of such outdated methods include; knowledge-based factors like passwords which while considered the norm and are widely used - have many potential security concerns as identified in section 4. This includes social-based attacks and computer-based attacks like social engineering, brute force and guessing-based attacks. As outlined in section 5, ownership-based authentication similarly has concerns being used as the sole means of authentication due to concerns such as misplacing or having the authentication factor being stolen, hence can only really be used in multi-factor-based authentication. Likewise, location-based authentication as presented in section 6 also displays many challenges, such as technologies like a VPN that can spoof sensors, as well as in section 7 in which presents the issues with social-based authentication mainly that it creates a single point of failure.

Open Issues

There are many open challenges that need to be solved in the field of authentication, such as the user's opinion and usage of knowledge-based factors. Given that they are the standard mode of authentication yet are often considered one of the weaker authentication factors. Hence there is a general need for better cyber hygiene amongst users, given the user themselves is often considered the factor most likely to cause a security breach, there needs to be a better way of keeping the user safe. For ownership-based authentication, although it can be attacked like other forms of authentication, one of the standout challenges currently is SQL injection attacks, being very popular for hacking common ownership factors such as credit cards, as hackers can gain the access to the details of the item, without owning the item. One topic of research interest would be developing better protection from SQL injection attacks for ownership-based factors. Specifically, regarding location-based authentication; one of the biggest open issues facing location-based authentication is the use of VPNs or Virtual Private Networks which are becoming increasingly popular. The reason is because with a VPN, a user could mask their position from where they are logging in from, disrupting the accuracy of the location-based authentication, hence, it could be important to solve this issue in the coming future. One issue that plagues all authentication types is the concern for privacy, which has come to the forefront after the introduction for GDPR regulations. As such many authentication methods should better consider how they will handle users' data in order to keep the users' data safe and private.

Future Research

Cloud computing and multi-server networks has had a large spike in activity over the last few years with many services offerings more ways to utilize cloud computing or virtual desktop devices, though with new technology there are also new vulnerabilities and it is important to develop sufficient countermeasures and understand the possible dangers of using technologies to be prepared against them. Alternatively, there are many promising developments with virtual reality, with many considering it as a possible means of authentication. Studies could investigate users' opinions on using virtual reality as a means to authentication themselves or how virtual reality is able to handle different attacks. To a lesser degree there is a similar interest in developing augmented reality technologies and similarly to virtual reality, may be considered as a possible means of authentication and how to best authenticate oneself while using augmented reality. Such research topics could be investigating users' opinions of authentication or investigating the attacks on augmented reality and defenses. Given all forms of authentication suffer from privacy concerns after the introduction of GDPR regulations it is of importance that privacy is considered in the design of authentication systems. Once such future research to address these could be the implantation of privacy principles such as privacy by design when designing privacy concerning authentication solutions, for example a framework of authentication.

REFERENCES

Ashfield, J., Shroyer, D., & Brown, D. (2012, October 23). *Location based authentication of mobile device transactions.* Google Patents. (US Patent 8,295,898)

Bang, Y., Lee, D.J., Bae, Y.S., & Ahn, J.H. (2012). Improving information security management: An analysis of id–password usage and a new login vulnerability measure. *International Journal of Information Management, 32* (5), 409–418.

Banu, M. N., & Banu, S. M. (2013). A comprehensive study of phishing attacks. *International Journal of Computer Science and Information Technologies*, 4(6), 783–786.

Bhardwaj, A., & Goundar, S. (2021). Comparing single tier and three tier infrastructure designs against DDoS attacks. In *Research Anthology on Combating Denial-of-Service Attacks* (pp. 541–558). IGI Global. doi:10.4018/978-1-7998-5348-0.ch028

Blocki, J., Harsha, B., & Zhou, S. (2018). *On the economics of offline password cracking. In 2018 ieee symposium on security and privacy (sp).* IEEE.

Braintree. (2007). *Top 5 vulnerabilities leading to credit card data breaches.* Braintree Payments. https://www.braintreepayments.com/blog/top-5-vulnerabilities-leading-to-credit-card-data-breaches/

Burch, L. L., & Carter, S. R. (2010, June 15). *Methods and systems for multi- factor authentication.* Google Patents. (US Patent 7,739,744)

Chen, W. D., Hancke, G. P., Mayes, K. E., Lien, Y., & Chiu, J. H. (2010). Using 3g network components to enable nfc mobile transactions and authentication. In 2010 ieee international conference on progress in informatics and computing (Vol. 1). IEEE.

Chen, Y. (2007). A bayesian network model of knowledge-based authentication. *AMCIS 2007 Proceedings, 423.* AMC.

Chen, Y., & Liginlal, D. (2007). Bayesian networks for knowledge-based authentication. *IEEE Transactions on Knowledge and Data Engineering*, *19*(5), 695–710. doi:10.1109/TKDE.2007.1024

Chiew, K. L., Yong, K. S. C., & Tan, C. L. (2018). A survey of phishing attacks: Their types, vectors and technical approaches. *Expert Systems with Applications*, *106*, 1–20. doi:10.1016/j.eswa.2018.03.050

Choi, K., Lee, J. L., & Chun, Y. T. (2017). Voice phishing fraud and its modus operandi. *Security Journal*, *30*(2), 454–466. doi:10.1057j.2014.49

Chokhani, S. (2004). Knowledge based authentication (kba) metrics. In Kba symposium-knowledge based authentication: Is it quantifiable. CSRC.

Contributor, T. T. (2014, December). What is mobile authentication? *Tech Target.* https://www.techtarget.com/searchsecurity/definition/mobile-authentication

Council, F. F. I. E. (2005). *Authentication in an internet banking environment. FFIEC agencies.* FFIE Council.

CRYPTO-IT. (2020, -03-09). Frequency analysis (Vol. 2020) (No. 29th June). *Crypto.* http://www.crypto-it.net/eng/attacks/frequency-analysis. html#:~:text=Frequency%20analysis%20is%20one%20of,are%20used%20with%20 different%20frequencies.&text=Based%20on%20that%2C%20one%20can,texts%20 written%20in%20other%20languages

Dale, W. (2021, 7 Sep). The top 12 password-cracking techniques used by hackers (Vol. 2022) (No. 02/02/). *IT Pro.* https://www.itpro.co.uk/security/34616/the-top-password-cracking-techniques-used-by-hackers

Daly, M. K. (2009). Advanced persistent threat. *Usenix, Nov, 4* (4), 2013–2016.

Dejan, T. (2018, December 3,). How to prevent brute force attacks with 8 easy tactics. *Phoenix Nap.* https://phoenixnap.com/kb/prevent-brute-force-attacks

Drokov, I., Punskaya, E., & Tahar, E. (2015, January 27). *System and method for dynamic multifactor authentication.* Google Patents. (US Patent 8,943,548)

Dunkelberger, P. (2018). Fido2 puts biometrics at heart of web security. *Biometric Technology Today, 2018*(8), 8–10. doi:10.1016/S0969-4765(18)30126-7

Dürmuth, M., Angelstorf, F., Castelluccia, C., Perito, D., & Chaabane, A. (2015). OMEN: Faster password guessing using an ordered markov enumerator. In Engineering Secure Software and Systems: 7th International Symposium, ESSoS 2015, Milan, Italy, March 4-6, 2015. [Springer International Publishing.]. *Proceedings, 7*, 119–132.

Eden, T., & Avigad, B. (2012). *Location based authentication system.* (US Patent US8321913B2)

Edwards, M., Larson, R., Green, B., Rashid, A., & Baron, A. (2017). Panning for gold: Automatically analysing online social engineering attack surfaces. *Computers & Security, 69*, 18–34. doi:10.1016/j.cose.2016.12.013

Ellison, G., Hodges, J., & Landau, S. (2002). Security and privacy concerns of internet single sign-on. *Liberty v1*(6).

Enterprise, V. (2016). *Data breach investigations report. Report.* Verizon Enterprise.

Enterprise, V. (2017). 2017 data breach investigations report. Verizon Enterprise.

Fan, W., Lwakatare, K., & Rong, R. (2017). Social engineering: Ie based model of human weakness for attack and defense investigations. *International Journal of Computer Network & Information Security, 9*(1), 1–11. doi:10.5815/ijcnis.2017.01.01

Fang, Y., Kao, I.-L., Milman, I. M., & Wilson, G. C. (2001, June 5). *Single sign-on (sso) mechanism personal key manager.* Google Patents. (US Patent 6,243,816)

Flu, K. (2015). *Knowledge-based authentication (kba). for Cybersecurity.* HSGAC. https://www.hsgac.senate.gov/imo/media/doc/Testimony-Fu-2015-06-02-REVISED%2021.pdf

Gafni, R., & Nissim, D. (2014). To social login or not login? exploring factors affecting the decision. *Issues in Informing Science and Information Technology, 11*(1), 57–72. doi:10.28945/1980

Granger, S. (2001). Social engineering fundamentals, part i: Hacker tactics. *Security Focus*, (December), 18.

Gunson, N., Marshall, D., Morton, H., & Jack, M. (2011). User perceptions of security and usability of single-factor and two-factor authentication in automated telephone banking. *Computers & Security*, *30*(4), 208–220. doi:10.1016/j.cose.2010.12.001

Hammad, A., & Faith, P. (2017). *Location based authentication.* (US Patent US10163100B2)

Harber, L. M. (2022, January 19th). Fake gps: top 5 vpns for spoofing your location. *Tom's Guide.* https://www.tomsguide.com/uk/best-picks/fake-gps-vpn

Hitaj, B., Gasti, P., Ateniese, G., & Perez-Cruz, F. (2019). Passgan: A deep learning approach for password guessing. In *International conference on applied cryptography and network security* (p. 217-237). Springer. 10.1007/978-3-030-21568-2_11

Ho, G., Sharma, A., Javed, M., Paxson, V., & Wagner, D. (2017). Detecting credential spearphishing in enterprise settings. In *26th USENIX security symposium (USENIX security 17)* (p. 469-485). Springer.

ISO/IEC. (2007, -10). Identification cards part 2: Cards with contacts. ISO.

Jablon, D. P. (1997). Extended password key exchange protocols immune to dictionary attack. In *Proceedings of ieee 6th workshop on enabling technologies: Infrastructure for collaborative enterprises* (p. 248-255). IEEE. 10.1109/ENABL.1997.630822

Joseph, T., Bruchim, G. Z., Gofman, I., & Ashkenazy, I. G. (2021, August 31). *Credential spray attack detection.* Google Patents. (US Patent 11,108,818)

Jøsang, A. (2018). *Lecture 9: User authentication.* UIO. https://www.uio.no/studier/emner/matnat/ifi/IN2120/h18/lectures/in2120-2018-l09-user-authentication.pdf

Khan, H. Z. U., & Zahid, H. (2010). Comparative study of authentication techniques. *International Journal of Video & Image Processing and Network Security IJVIPNS*, *10*(04), 9.

Konigs, H.-P. (1991). Cryptographic identification methods for smart cards in the process of standardization. *IEEE Communications Magazine*, *29*(6), 42–48. doi:10.1109/35.79401

Koutny, T., & Sykora, J. (2010). Lessons learned on enhancing performance of networking applications by ip tunneling through active networks. *International Journal on Advances in Internet Technology*, *3*(3 & 4), 2010.

Koyun, A., & Janabi, E. A. (2017). Social engineering attacks. [JMEST]. *Journal of Multidisciplinary Engineering Science and Technology*, *4*(6), 7533–7538.

Krombholz, K., Hobel, H., Huber, M., & Weippl, E. (2015). Advanced social engineering attacks. *Journal of Information Security and applications, 22*, 113-122.

Kumari, E. H. J., & Kannammal, A. (2009). Privacy and security on anonymous routing protocols in manet. In *2009 second international conference on computer and electrical engineering* (*Vol. 2*, pp. 431–435). IEEE. 10.1109/ICCEE.2009.147

Kunyu, P., Jiande, Z., & Jing, Y. (2009). *An identity authentication system based on mobile phone token. In 2009 ieee international conference on network infrastructure and digital content*. IEEE.

Kuo, C.-C., & Lo, M. (1999, December 14). *Secure open smart card architecture*. Google Patents. (US Patent 6,003,134)

Lance, S. (2019, June 27,). Time for password expiration to die. *SANS*. https://www.sans.org/security-awareness-training/blog/time-password-expiration-die

Lehtonen, M., Michahelles, F., & Fleisch, E. (2007). Probabilistic approach for location-based authentication. In *1st international workshop on security for spontaneous interaction iwssi* (Vol. 2007). IEEE.

Li, C.-T., & Hwang, M.-S. (2010). An efficient biometrics-based remote user authentication scheme using smart cards. *Journal of Network and Computer Applications, 33*(1), 1–5. doi:10.1016/j.jnca.2009.08.001

Li, X., Niu, J., Khan, M. K., & Liao, J. (2013). An enhanced smart card based remote user password authentication scheme. *Journal of Network and Computer Applications, 36*(5), 1365–1371. doi:10.1016/j.jnca.2013.02.034

Li, X., Niu, J.-W., Ma, J., Wang, W.-D., & Liu, C.-L. (2011). Cryptanalysis and improvement of a biometrics-based remote user authentication scheme using smart cards. *Journal of Network and Computer Applications, 34*(1), 73–79. doi:10.1016/j.jnca.2010.09.003

Li, X., Xiong, Y., Ma, J., & Wang, W. (2012). An efficient and security dynamic identity based authentication protocol for multi-server architecture using smart cards. *Journal of Network and Computer Applications, 35*(2), 763–769. doi:10.1016/j.jnca.2011.11.009

Lim, C. H., & Kwon, T. (2006). Strong and robust rfid authentication enabling perfect ownership transfer. In *International conference on information and communications security* (p. 1-20). Springer. 10.1007/11935308_1

Lyastani, S. G., Schilling, M., Neumayr, M., Backes, M., & Bugiel, S. (2020). Is fido2 the kingslayer of user authentication? a comparative usability study of fido2 passwordless authentication. In 2020 ieee symposium on security and privacy (sp) (pp. 268–285). IEEE.

Marforio, C., Masti, R. J., Soriente, C., Kostiainen, K., & Capkun, S. (2016). Hardened setup of personalized security indicators to counter phishing attacks in mobile banking. In *Proceedings of the 6th workshop on security and privacy in smartphones and mobile devices* (p. 83-92). ACM. 10.1145/2994459.2994462

Medlin, B. D., Cazier, J. A., & Foulk, D. P. (2008). Analyzing the vulnerability of US hospitals to social engineering attacks: How many of your employees would share their password? [IJISP]. *International Journal of Information Security and Privacy*, 2(3), 71–83. doi:10.4018/jisp.2008070106

Mishra, S., & Soni, D. (2019). Sms phishing and mitigation approaches. In *2019 twelfth international conference on contemporary computing (ic3)* (p. 1-5). IEEE. 10.1109/IC3.2019.8844920

MLB9252. (2011). How to calculate pass- word entropy. *RIT Cyber Self Defense*. https://ritcyberselfdefense.wordpress.com/2011/09/24/how-to-calculate-password-entropy/

Murthy, A. S., Ganesan, K., Mangam, P. M., Jandhyala, S. S., & Walter, M. (2020, January 28). *Multifactor authentication as a network service*. Google Patents. (US Patent 10,547,600)

Narayanan, A., & Shmatikov, V. (2005). Fast dictionary attacks on passwords using time-space tradeoff. *In Proceedings of the 12th acm conference on computer and communications security* (p. 364-372). ACM. 10.1145/1102120.1102168

NCSC. (2019) *Most hacked passwords revealed as uk cyber survey exposes gaps in online security*. NCSC. https://www.ncsc.gov.uk/news/most-hacked-passwords-revealed-as-uk-cyber-survey-exposes-gaps-in-online-security

ParthDutt. (n.d.). Understanding rainbow table attack (Vol. 2020) (No. 29th June). Retrieved from https://www.geeksforgeeks.org/understanding-rainbow-table-attack/

Poh, N., Bengio, S., & Korczak, J. (2002). A multi-sample multi-source model for biometric authentication. In *Proceedings of the 12th ieee workshop on neural networks for signal processing* (p. 375-384). IEEE. 10.1109/NNSP.2002.1030049

Rayani, P. K., Bhushan, B., & Thakare, V. R. (2018). Multi-Layer Token Based Authentication Through Honey Password in Fog Computing. [IJFC]. *International Journal of Fog Computing*, *1*(1), 50–62. doi:10.4018/IJFC.2018010104

Raza, M., Iqbal, M., Sharif, M., & Haider, W. (2012). A survey of password attacks and comparative analysis on methods for secure authentication. *World Applied Sciences Journal*, *19*(4), 439–444.

Rouse, M. (2018). challenge-response authentication. *Search Security*. https://searchsecurity.techtarget.com/definition/challenge-response-system

Salahdine, F., & Kaabouch, N. (2019). Social engineering attacks: A survey. *Future Internet*, *11*(4), 89. doi:10.3390/fi11040089

Salamatian, S., Huleihel, W., Beirami, A., Cohen, A., & Medard, M. (2020). Centralized vs decentralized targeted brute-force attacks: Guessing with side-information. *IEEE Transactions on Information Forensics and Security*, *15*, 3749–3759. doi:10.1109/TIFS.2020.2998949

Schneier, B. (2005). The failure of two-factor authentication. *Schneier*. https://www.schneier.com/blog/archives/2005/03/the_failure_of.html

Shablygin, E., Zakharov, V., Bolotov, O., & Scace, E. (2013). *Token management*. (US Patent US8555079B2)

Sharma, S. (2005). *Location based authentication*. Sharma.

Shay, R., Komanduri, S., Durity, A. L., Huh, P. S., Mazurek, M. L., Segreti, S. M, & Cranor, L. F. (2014). Can long passwords be secure and usable? In *Proceedings of the sigchi conference on human factors in computing systems* (p. 2927-2936). ACM. 10.1145/2556288.2557377

Simmons, M., & Lee, J. S. (2020). Catfishing: A look into online dating and impersonation. In *International conference on human-computer interaction* (p. 349-358). Springer. 10.1007/978-3-030-49570-1_24

Smith, N. (2018). Hotp vs totp: What's the difference? *Microcosm*. https://www.microcosm.com/blog/hotp-totp-what-is-the-difference

Stasiukonis, S. (2006). Social engineering, the usb way. *Dark Reading, 7*.

Stephen, M. (2019, Jan 2,). Phishing attacks in the banking industry. *Info Institute*. https://resources.infosecinstitute.com/category/enterprise/phishing/the-phishing-landscape/phishing-attacks-by-demographic/phishing-in-the-banking-industry/

Thomas, B. (2017). All that's needed to hack gmail and rob bitcoin: A name and a phone number. *Forbes.* https://www.forbes.com/sites/thomasbrewster/2017/09/18/ss7-google-coinbase-bitcoin-hack/#338f7a5f41a4

Tiwari, A., Sanyal, S., Abraham, A., Knapskog, S. J., & Sanyal, S. (2011). A multi-factor security protocol for wireless payment-secure web authentication using mobile devices. arXiv preprint arXiv:1111.3010

Tools, R. S. (n.d.). *Password cracking tools.* Google. https://sites.google.com/site/reusablesec/Home/password-cracking-tools

Trojahn, M., & Marcus, P. (2012). *Towards coupling user and device locations using biometrical authentication on smartphones. In 2012 international conference for internet technology and secured transactions.* IEEE.

Turnbull, R. S., & Gedge, R. (2012). *Location based authentication.* (US Patent US8321913B2)

Turner, D. M. (2016, 01 August). Digital authentication - the basics. *Cryptomathic.* https://www.cryptomathic.com/news-events/blog/digital-authentication-the-basics

Vel´asquez, I., Caro, A., & Rodr´ıguez, A. (2018). Authentication schemes and methods: A systematic literature review. *Information and Software Technology, 94*, 30-37.

Weir, C. M. (2010). *Using probabilistic techniques to aid in password cracking attacks.*

Weir, M., Aggarwal, S., Medeiros, B. D., & Glodek, B. (2009). Password cracking using probabilistic context-free grammars. In *2009 30th ieee symposium on security and privacy* (p. 391-405). IEEE. 10.1109/SP.2009.8

Zhang, F., Kondoro, A., & Muftic, S. (2012). Location-based authentication and authorization using smart phones. In *2012 ieee 11th international conference on trust, security and privacy in computing and communications* (p. 1285-1292). IEEE. 10.1109/TrustCom.2012.198

Zhang, L., Tan, C., & Yu, F. (2017). An improved rainbow table attack for long passwords. *Procedia Computer Science, 107*, 47–52. doi:10.1016/j.procs.2017.03.054

Chapter 3
Leveraging Cyber Threat Intelligence in Smart Devices

Ricardo M. Czekster

iD https://orcid.org/0000-0002-6636-4398

Aston University, UK

ABSTRACT

The pervasiveness of smart devices, i.e., components equipped with feedback loops, sensing, and telecommunications for remote management, bring interesting research opportunities for incorporating contextual cybersecurity information through cyber threat intelligence (CTI). This approach enriches analysis by aggregating contextual information gathered from a myriad of unstructured data sources such as application logs, sensing data, blog posts, selected Internet-based commentary on security, vulnerability reports, and a host of other sources. The main difficulty regarding CTI is how to best integrate data into the design of protective measures. This chapter will discuss ways of leveraging CTI using a myriad of smart devices present in cyber-physical systems and internet-of-things with applications to the smart grid and smart buildings. The author will showcase the use of CTI in smart environments and how to incorporate and integrate data from multiple sources directly into the analysis efforts. The chapter will end with research perspectives and future work.

INTRODUCTION

Modern critical infrastructure is highly interconnected and data intensive. Providing continuous operation to a range of stakeholders in such large attack surfaces mandates a strong cybersecurity posture. Analysts and officers sitting on the edge

DOI: 10.4018/978-1-6684-5991-1.ch003

of the infrastructure must trace and monitor failures to enhance protective measures and violations perpetrated by malicious actors. However, the staggering number of components, services, and devices that participate in this environment feeding data into information management systems is simply overwhelming. These difficulties demand system analysts and respond teams to quickly react and respond to events and alarms. The job of these domain experts with focus on cybersecurity involves tackling multiple data sources for identifying and thwarting cyber-attacks before they propagate any further. The problems are compounded by the sheer number of data sources namely application logs from intrusion detection system and firewalls, external and internal data feeds, and other information sources to consider when assessing risk or determining breaches.

This reflects today's societal objectives to provide seamless services to customers connecting to critical infrastructure. Coordination systems exchanges messages and instantaneously collect data to allow the remote-control of devices and to operate machinery unbounded by geographical barriers. It is worth mentioning that enterprise information systems are mandated nowadays to collect large longitudinal data originating from a plethora of systems, because it may be indicative of potential malicious incursions lurking on the infrastructure. Another issue concerns security threats that hide sophisticated malicious incursions aiming to destabilize systems and promote disruptions that cause damage and financial loss, among other substantial shortcomings.

Those are precisely the main reasons as to why one must combine efforts and incorporate cyber threat intelligence (CTI) readily into analysis. This approach sits between the continuous outputs of smart systems and modelling/analysis efforts and tools, bringing together technicians, domain experts, and managers into addressing cybersecurity problems together. These professionals, whilst working together, could enormously enrich analysis procedures through complementing cyber-attacks with context and relevant events that belongs to the timeline of malicious incursions that were gathered in outside sources. With this body of contextual information gathered not only in specific systems but elsewhere, on the Internet, may clarify and produce a systematic analysis panorama of cyber-attacks.

CTI has the potential of assisting cybersecurity officers making timely decisions on available data and help towards improving the cybersecurity posture and defenses of organizations. For instance, they might employ CTI-related knowledge to anticipate attacks, recover from attacks, highlight weaknesses, understand 'under attack' situations, and prepare for malicious incursions before they are propagated in sub-systems. Intelligence, in smart contexts, also accommodates accountability, non-repudiation, forensic analysis, and privacy preservation concerns.

Undoubtedly, in smart infrastructure, there is a trade-off on the use of cybersecurity measures, personal liberties, and convenience. The chapter will overview Smart Infrastructure concepts, CTI and threat hunting, and an introduction to modelling using standardized models. It will discuss how to map modelling primitives concerning a setting under observation and then addressing how to incorporate relevant data directly into models. Once defined, analysts may share those models with trustful counterparts (Burger et al., 2014) fostering discussions about the how adding intelligence features into complex analysis scenarios may help cyber-attack prevention.

Intelligence is of interest not only to companies but also to governments. For instance, the UK government is vouching threat hunting combined with CTI with the publication of a booklet detailing how organizations of any size could profit from its features (Digital, Data & Technology – UK, 2022). The author has identified the need for an integrated approach that enjoys the synergy of combining ideas from CTI altogether is still missing. This chapter aims to bridge this gap and offer cybersecurity analysts and managers a comprehensive vision on how, when, and where to employ CTI and enriched STIX™ models for comprehensive analysis sessions. The author will outline the current research on the topic of CTI in smart contexts and discuss the inherent trade-offs, concerns, future research, and perspectives.

SMART INFRASTRUCTURE

There is a wealth of opportunities in research to tackle any smart device belonging to smart infrastructure, i.e., cyber-physical systems (CPS), smart grid (SG), and smart buildings (SB) within smart cities (SC). These 'smartness'-related capabilities are fundamentally dependent upon Internet-of-Things (IoT) apparatuses normally installed at end-customers that enables remote communication of statuses and effective command execution to respond to events. They are sustained by various technologies for communication (e.g., wired, wireless, among other).

Smart Devices and Basic Ecosystem Overview

The core of any smart framework is telecommunications, usually enabled by IoT attached to equipment worth monitoring. It is rather common for companies to adopt device heterogeneity in efforts to enhance cybersecurity protections. However, it presents difficulties to cope, track, and update numerous devices requiring software patches to prevent the exploitation of vulnerabilities and damage to defenses.

Figure 1. Basic ecosystem overview encompassing the smart grid, smart home, and smart office
Source: Author (2022)

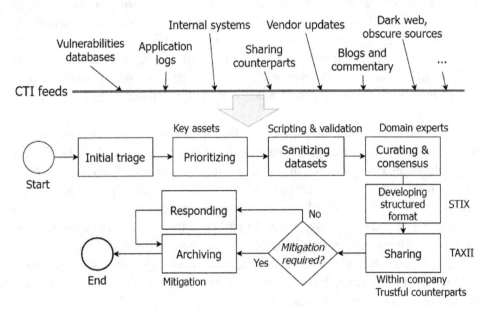

Figure 1 depicts an overview of the smart devices that could potentially encompass smart homes or offices as well as auxiliary components that assist in remote management and comfort regulation attached to information and security systems. The author will focus attention on cybersecurity as applied to smart components pertaining to an infrastructure worth protecting. In this regard one is interested in any device present in smart homes such as (broadly), the smart grid, smart meters, smart chargers (either to plug electric vehicles or battery-operated appliances), smart plugs (or light bulbs), smart phones, and personal voice assistants, where they are sustained by the overspread use of IoT capabilities attached to their physical counterparts.

Cybersecurity is obviously a concern and literature on this subject has produced interesting results to many aspects of such components. For instance, Pillitteri and Brewer (2014) discussed protections in the smart grid whereas Leszczyna (2018) assessed standards and cybersecurity for the smart grid. Humayed et al. (2017) analysed CPS with discussions on challenges and opportunities and Al-Fuqaha et al. (2015) and Yang et al. (2017) addressed issues in IoT.

In a broader context one might consider smart cities encompassing the smart grid which are in turn connected to the smart meters on each household or commercial enterprise, varying in load and size. It is worth commenting that many smart devices are of small processing power and limited capacity, which pose some cybersecurity concerns as security requirements are not necessarily embedded into the solution. One could classify those smart home or office components into smart appliances in general, having IoT capabilities for communicating status and exert commands when required by management in an automated or manual fashion.

Smart infrastructure is not a novel concept, and it has been subjected to extensive research and definition throughout the year (Ota et al., 2017; Mehmood et al., 2020). It is out of the scope of this work to discuss architectural internals or design decisions on how to best interconnect components. The author is interested in relating the feedback structures that might feed CTI systems and how they could be leveraged to deter and combat criminal activity.

CYBERSECURITY AND CYBER THREAT INTELLIGENCE

Protective measures to enhance the cybersecurity posture of any organizational infrastructure are crucial elements to deter and thwart potential cyber-attacks. A plethora of work detailing how to control access, protect, defend, and mitigate malicious actions has been proposed to ensure cybersecurity practices encompass systems and services. For instance, renown institutes in US and Europe such as *National Institute of Standards and Technology* (NIST) and the *European Union Agency for Network and Information* (ENISA) offer best practices and compile reports governing all aspects of safety and cybersecurity. In terms of protecting the critical infrastructure permeating society, the UK has the *Centre for the Protection of National Infrastructure* (CPNI) whereas in Europe there is the *European Programme for Critical Infrastructure Protection* (EPCIP), to mention a few as there are certainly other equally relevant institutes around the world.

Dushyant et al. (2022) have employed Machine Learning and Deep Learning in cybersecurity where they have incorporated cyber threat into the analysis with significant success. For tackling cybersecurity during the COVID-19 crisis, Gupta et al. (2022) investigated the use of Convolutional Neural Network models to help prediction of mask in image processing. These studies may complement the generation of actionable intelligence to attach to further analysis when developing a sensible snapshot of remarkable occurrences. Pradhan et al. (2022) have considered cybersecurity in the context of modern 5G networks, discussing the implications of the technologies for users, consumers, and organizations.

Liberati et al. (2021) compiled a comprehensive list of cyber-attacks in the smart grid, discussing the myriad of threats, exploit opportunities, and mitigation. Arnaboldi et al. (2020) modelled *Load Changing Attacks*, i.e., malicious incursions aiming to install malware into high-wattage devices and synchronize actions turning on or off a massive number of appliances to imbalance frequency. The authors have used *Continuous Time Markov Chains* and they analyzed the impact of these attacks on mixes of different power plants. In terms of preparedness, risk management and risk assessment methodologies and threat modelling, the author direct readers to vast literature on this topic (Gritzalis et al., 2018; Vallant et al., 2021; Abbas et al., 2021).

Cyber Threat Intelligence

There are three notions that needs clarification differentiating data, information, and intelligence. The first is any raw component describing a value whereas the second is about extracting its meaning. Intelligence is when information is curated, analyzed, scrutinized, and vetted so it can be used and shared. Relevant literature lists the following aspects, i.e., Data, Information, Knowledge, Intelligence, Wisdom (DIKIW) as discussed in Liew (2013).

Complementary to cybersecurity, Cyber Threat Intelligence (CTI) (Abu et al., 2018; Tounsi and Rais, 2018; Samtani et al., 2020) is an evidence-based approach that considers multiple data sources to discover potential cybersecurity issues arising in systems and networks. The chief idea behind CTI is to enrich analysis with contextual information for enabling better decisions with available data. Intelligence pieces are curated and vetted by domain experts with expertise in cybersecurity and management. CTI has been successfully used to drive protective measures and mitigations as cybersecurity officers are able to reason about circumstantial elements that could turn into active attacks requiring focused attention.

Over the years, research in CTI discussed how to represent data using standardized formats such as the intrusion detection message exchange format (IDMEF) by Debar et al. (2007), the incident object description exchange format (IODEF) proposed by Takahashi et al. (2014), or the structured threat information expression (STIX™) described by Barnum (2012), to mention a few. There is a sheer interest to map and delineate attributes related to noticeable security events worth considering in any cyber-attack for enacting prevention capabilities (Steinberger et al., 2015). Other example is the common attack pattern enumeration and classification (CAPEC) (Roberts, 2021), the real-time inter-network defense (RID), and OpenIoC (Liao et al., 2016). There are many sources, formats, frameworks, and languages devoted to CTI research and attempts to foster larger use by different audiences, as discussed in Ramsdale et al. (2020) and in Mavroeidis and Bromander (2017).

Besides different formats, another recurrent problem in CTI is due to the host of data sources that could be used in modelling that cover the most significant components pertaining any critical smart infrastructure. Examples are data from logging, sensing, movement, video and audio streams, collaborative feeds (from equipment vendors or vulnerabilities reports), blog sources of reputable cybersecurity experts, dark web forums, and so forth.

Understanding and Mapping Malicious Incursions

As cyber-attacks became increasingly sophisticated throughout the years, previous detection approaches such as anomaly-based or signature-based proved to be insufficient. One major downside of such approaches was due to simple changes in adversarial patterns and attack signatures that were easily established and successfully circumvented protections. Nowadays, cybersecurity analysis might use these techniques in conjunction with reasoning as to the *'why'* and the *'how'* of perpetrating attacks by considering most likely Tactics, Techniques, and Procedures (TTP).

TTPs allow officers to devise better protections and faster mitigations as they cope with the reasons and attack vectors behind any malicious incursion. They are the backbone of CTI as they promote reasoning on the clear motivations behind attacks to shed light into the required protective measures. Nowadays one witness a shy adoption of CTI's practices, features, and tools lacking overspread application in industry and academia. This fact could corroborate that organizations do not want to recognize they were subjected to successful attacks as well as be liable for damages or data loss in a large scale.

The Adversarial Tactics, Techniques, and Common Knowledge (ATT&CK®) maintained by the MITRE corporation (Strom et al., 2018) lists most usual TTPs based on organizations' documentation of successful cyber-attacks that happened. The framework maps and details most likely TTPs performed by adversaries using as input actual incursions documented by companies that sustained attacks. It scrutinizes cyber-attacks and list ways on how adversaries have accessed internal networks, installed malware, and established footholds to exploit in the future. In the defense side, cybersecurity officers may use this information to mitigate attacks by closing systems and reducing exposure to weaknesses.

All personnel involved in cybersecurity must take all these components into account when identifying and combating malicious incursions, however, they must factor false positives, misinformation campaigns, and *Advanced Persistent Threats* (APT) that lurks in smart networks waiting for opportunities to deliver the highest amount of damage. It is thus imperative to use the full arsenal of protective measures against threat actors, in a combined cybersecurity approach that leverages CTI produced by organizations and shared amongst trustful partners and cooperating entities with interest in thwarting cyber-attacks as soon as possible. CTI undoubtedly poses several challenges and opportunities for research (Conti et al., 2018) due to its benefits for enhancing the analysis landscape for stakeholders to anticipate actions and thwart criminal activities.

Threat Hunting, Sharing, and Data Approaches to CTI

The work of Daszczyszak et al. (2019) draws insights from threat hunting and its shared concerns with CTI, where they explain three axes to observe: i) the 'terrain' (e.g., the operating systems, the microkernels, etc.) that run in the myriad of systems belonging to an infrastructure; ii) the timeline of noticeable events taking place during the system's execution; and iii) the actions and motives behind cyber-attacks in the form of TTPs. It is worth explaining that all the TTPs depicted in the figure are exhaustively discussed in the literature on the subject. The TTPs differs from 'classic' Cyber Kill Chain® (CKC) – developed by Lockheed Martin – mappings by understanding that any cyber-attack does not follow a particular order, i.e., threat actors may abuse systems and networks in any order. They could wait for some previous footholds become available through bad configurations or incompetence by system administrators, for example. The ATT&CK framework cover all these elements in the Attack Matrix as shown in their website, where cybersecurity officers may consult any tactic, technique, procedure, and mitigation.

Figure 2 depicts the threat hunting effort and exemplifies the three axes. In one axis, it lists the TTPs as described in the ATT&CK framework, then it shows the technology that the threat-agents may target, and finally, an axis is used to provide the timeline of noticeable cybersecurity events as the cyber-attack progresses over time. The dots in the figure represent the type of TTP and the targeted technology used in each cyber-attack, as well as their positioning that represents 'when' the TTP has happened. This abstract representation of a cyber-attack provides a comprehensive snapshot of the potential attack surface, the action perpetrated by the attacker, and when it happened, so one may understand the sequences of events leading to the incursion.

CTI is intrinsically related to *threat hunting* practices (Bhardwaj & Goundar, 2019; Berady et al., 2021) capabilities and effective deployment in organizations (Gao et al., 2021). In similar direction, Agarwal et al. (2021) devised a *Cyber Security Model* to quantify the effectiveness of threat hunting whereas Shu et al. (2018) proposed a platform for experimenting with threats and discussed *Threat Intelligence Computing*. Their proposed methodology reframes the threat hunting problem by using graph computation to cope with threat discovery.

In terms of environments to foster intelligence gathering, the Malware Information Sharing Platform (MISP) was an attempt to propose a collaborative platform to increase cybersecurity engagement and threat intelligence sharing (Wagner et al., 2016). It focused on Indicators of Compromise (IoC) of targeted attacks, vulnerabilities reports, and financial information. Wagner et al. (2019) surveyed the literature on sharing intelligence on technical and non-technical literature. The Trusted Automated eXchange of Indicator Information (TAXII™) offers a framework for sharing CTI effectively (Connolly et al., 2014).

Figure 2. Threat hunting effort and axes to consider, i.e., TTP, technology (some examples), and time as malicious incursions unfolds in systems and networks
Source: Adapted from Daszczyszak et al. (2019)

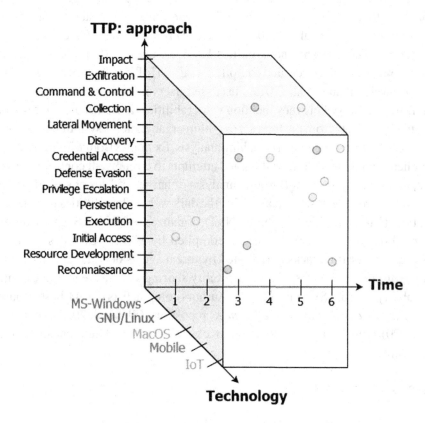

Research in CTI has combined efforts to understand and categorize data within multiple data sources, discussing drawbacks and trade-offs (Li et al., 2019). It is a known fact that CTI feeds are heterogeneous in essence and thus they require further quality analysis before entering databases. Previous work has focused on determining data quality (Griffioen et al., 2020) over 14 months of open-source CTI related feeds.

Afzaliseresht et al. (2020) used data mining to propose a human-centered approach that uses novel storytelling techniques from security logs to enhance CTI efforts. In a similar venue, de Boer et al. (2019) used text mining applied to cybersecurity and developed a scraper tool to analyze potential threats arising in the cyber domain. CTI could profit from artificial intelligence (AI) and machine learning (ML) as discussed by Dutta and Kant (2020).

Potential Data Sources for Use in CTI

There is a wealth of research on extracting intelligence from various sources. For example, Mittal et al. (2016) developed *Cybertwitter*, an intelligence gathering mechanism to compile Twitter posts for generating alerts about threats and vulnerabilities. Zhao et al. (2020) proposed *TIMiner*, a tool for extracting and categorizing CTI from social media outlets. Koloveas et al. (2019) proposed a crawler infrastructure to extract, track, and compile social and IoT intelligence using the Dark Web. Horawalavithana et al. (2019) discussed users in platforms such as Reddit, Twitter, and GitHub where they mention vulnerabilities (and possible exploitation).

Virtually any data from the Internet or within organization's systems are potential CTI sources with the potential of enriching analysis. Examples from within enterprises are application logs, IDS/Firewall logged attempts to circumvent controls, network traffic, malware deployment (through analysis of hashes of files or shared e-mail). Exterior data are blog posts, social media, the dark web, vulnerabilities reports (e.g., the National Vulnerabilities Database – NVD, organized by NIST/US or the Common Vulnerabilities and Exposures – CVE, compiled by MITRE/US), description of TTPs (i.e., successful attacks perpetrated by threat agents documented in detail by victims), discussion forums, and vulnerability scoring systems (e.g., the Common Vulnerability Scoring System – CVSS). Authors compile lists of CTI-based sources such as the *"awesome-threat-intelligence"* repository (Slatman, 2022). Stojanovic et al. (2020) presented a survey about attack techniques and automated detection mechanisms.

Issues, and Problems

A significant problem in CTI concerns extracting valuable information from unstructured sources (Liao et al., 2016; Zhao et al., 2020) also called *intelligence gathering*. This information should be not only extracted but also curated by domain experts. Mavroeidis and Bromander (2017) discussed a modelling taxonomy and ontology to deal with CTI whereas other previous research has tackled automated means for extracting contextual information such as the TTPDrill tool presented by Husari et al. (2017). This problem persists as the information is not readily available in known sources.

The difficulty of effectively employing CTI resides on reconciling massive datasets into one coherent analysis snapshot to understand cyber-attacks. CTI has some impending trade-offs as explained by Abu et al. (2018) whereas Menges et al. (2019) discussed a unified format. The authors argue the need for tackling two domains: 1) consistent understanding employing standardized formats and structured mapping of potential intelligence pieces; and 2) consider cross-compatibility issues when dealing with multiple datasets and platforms and how any structure description language could be leveraged to fulfil its capabilities. De Melo e Silva et al. (2020) discussed a methodology for evaluating standards and platforms.

Other recurrent problems of CTI when modelling cybersecurity are directed towards automation and abstraction. The former concentrates efforts on how to generate actionable pieces of standardized models that may be joined to form a model with sharing capabilities that holds value to stakeholders and enable them to make timely decisions. The latter tackles issues about how to best create models that convey the right amount of information without losing intrinsic details that if left out of analysis would signify a catastrophic loss of relevant contextual data.

LEVERAGING CTI IN SMART INFRASTRUCTURE

Preoccupation with intelligence comes after the usual cybersecurity measures are in place and operational. A functional and effective *Security Operations Center* (SOC) aggregates measurement and control data from distributed assets using the telecommunications network to evaluate statuses and health of components and devices observed in the attack surface. In this section, the author will discuss the basic process of CTI, input for intelligence, tools and methods, and a trade-off comparison for leveraging intelligence in smart devices.

For the explanation that follows here in this work the STIX framework was selected among other formats due to standardized approach to map and document CTI in a seamless manner, a characteristic that if fundamental for any sharing capability. STIX has been successfully used by academia and industry to represent cyber-attacks and noticeable events requiring immediate attention by cybersecurity officers.

Process

Figure 3 shows the basic process of a CTI initiative deployed by any given organization. It shows how multiple sources feed information systems with application logs, latest vulnerabilities and exposures data, measurements from internal systems and Internet-based information such as blogs or expert opinions.

Figure 3. Basic process for working with CTI in smart infrastructure and multiple feeds
Source: Author (2022)

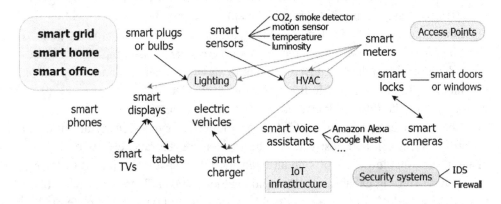

The next stage of the process is to triage massive amounts of data and prioritize which data comes from key assets that should be protected at all costs to prevent further propagation of cyber-attacks. Then, the data is sanitized to conform to semi-structured representations that could ease posterior phases and accelerate analysis features. These elements pass curation and consensus mechanisms performed by domain experts with the help of cybersecurity analysts, where they could use tools to help the creation of standardized security models (such as STIX) for sharing (using the precepts established by the TAXII framework, for instance). Specialized tools that work with STIX models (in the case of this example, other formats could be used as well) decide whether mitigation is required. Case affirmative, they are directed to respond teams that act on the cybersecurity breach or identified shortcoming at once; otherwise, this model is archived for later consultation, ending the CTI process. This process listed here is open to specific tailoring as dictated by organizations, where they may change some tasks to adhere to their internal processes.

All tasks demand cybersecurity officers of performing activities that treat data and submit to other modules until an actionable model emerges. It all starts with one or more data sources that are responsible for a device, equipment, application, or information system that stores cybersecurity related logs. Each task of Figure 3 is explained next:

- **Initial triage:** given the multitude of possibilities with respect to potential data sources to be incorporated into this type of analysis, it is crucial to determine the ones with the highest yield in terms of practical outcomes that could emerge. Usual data selection encompasses application and network related logs, information systems, sensing data from IoT deployed across the smart infrastructure, and so on;

- **Prioritizing:** this phase will take selected datasets and prioritize its consumption within the process by determining the list of key assets under protection making use of Asset Management concepts and approaches;
- **Sanitizing datasets:** here, a lot of scripting tasks as well as validation takes place for a myriad of components that use previous prioritization to treat data streams and correct potential errors in datasets or missing data that could impair future analysis. All corrections and misrepresentations are documented for further consultation;
- **Curating & consensus:** at this point domain experts may consult the deluge of data produced and curated in previous phases to determine importance, comment on specific data according to their expertise or 'feel' given previous cyber-attack incursions, and also re-prioritizing some attributes or assets' data;
- **Developing structured format:** after data is sufficiently curated by domain experts it is possible to build software that takes these data points and devise a STIX model given the smart infrastructure (that is somewhat static), and assign specific SDO/SCO, potential threat actors, malware analysis, and other relevant objects that are supported by the data;
- **Sharing:** depending on the objective of the analysis, it may be interesting to share the investigation among the network of trustful counterparts, so they may consider mitigations before the cyber-attack reaches their networks. In this phase, the STIX model employs the TAXII framework to share intelligence across these partners;
- **Responding:** if the analysts perceive that a threat is imminent, they should adjust their responses accordingly by devising mitigative actions to combat the cyber-attack as observed and supported by the data;
- **Archiving:** this is the latest action where the models are archived for future consultation (if required). The idea is to store a database of previous incursions, incidents, and cybersecurity events that may provide insights to future similar incursions.

Modelling and Data Prospects

The author is using the STIX modelling primitives in this chapter. Figure 4 shows the available STIX Domain Objects (SDO) for abstracting significant cybersecurity events.

Figure 4. modelling primitives in STIX (grouping suggestion by the author)
Source: Developed by the author, based on the STIX documentation (2022)

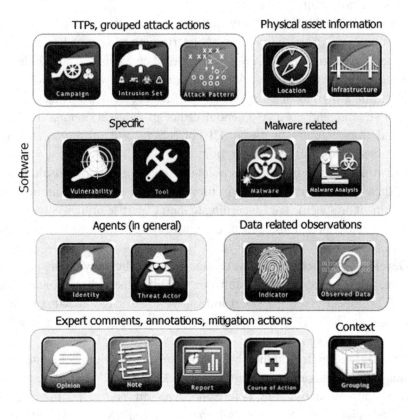

There are two other STIX Relationship Objects (SRO) namely "Relationship" that connects any two SDO altogether, and "Sighting" that conveys a 'belief' that something has occurred. Finally, various STIX Cyber-observable Objects (SCO) are available for assigning data into STIX models. It is worth noting that according to the researchers that proposed STIX, those elements are the minimum requirements for tackling cybersecurity incidents, the ones that have the potential of representing complex cyber-attack situations that could be easily understood by various stakeholders.

Tools for Modelling with STIX

Using STIX involves selecting pieces of intelligence worth creating and then choosing the SDO/SRO/SCO and parameters involved in the analysis by checking the extensive project documentation. These elements then generate a textual file (in

JSON format) that bundles all objects together and they could be shared or stored in appropriate places for later consultation.

The complexity of STIX demands visual and user friendly front-ends that ease the modelling process. Addressing this problem, Czekster et al. (2022a) implemented *cyberACTIve*, a tool for describing cybersecurity incidents using the STIX notation. The authors used JSON internally to represent the required parameters demanded by each STIX object, offering a friendly front-end for enriching models with intelligence.

There are other initiatives for visualizing STIX models, and the author mentions the official STIX Visualizer[1] (provided by the authors), stixview[2], or stix2-viz[3], to mention a few. These tools employ different visual strategies for representing STIX models with user-friendly features for organizing objects and interact with them in a seamless fashion.

Enriching Analysis with CTI

Table 1 shows the most likely STIX objects to consider for tackling cybersecurity in smart devices. The author is using STIX for this exemplification, however other formats could be employed without loss of generality. In the domain of Smart Devices those STIX objects are meant to be employed by analysts wanting to map malicious incursions and mitigation tasks.

A lot of the required work in the cybersecurity incident modelling effort will depend on the priorities dictated by the organization in line with its Risk Management process and framework as well as considering the key assets. The table has shown some STIX elements to use in mapping CTI to drive analysis and sharing. It is urged for administrators and cybersecurity officers to employ the usual protective mechanisms and monitoring, mixing with CTI to model cyber-attacks as they unfold in network and systems.

The *Note*, *Opinion*, and *Report* SDOs could be used to map to external sources with valuable information as of cyber-attacks or vulnerabilities discovery as advertised by equipment vendors. These elements are crucial for capturing multiple data sources as well as opinions and remarks from analysis, consultants, and domain experts so they can express their concerns to reach consensus or vet intelligence in a timely manner.

The SCOs are key to enrich the CTI models and use the information to better understand the cyber-threats. Objects in this class of STIX elements are for example: Domain Name, Email, File, IPv4/IPv6 Address, Process, User Account, Software, URL. They describe useful information related to the systems and services under protection. Any CTI representation must employ these constructs to enrich the modelling and help analysis with contextual information so they might make better decisions. For smart devices, these SCOs are key to map technologies and telecommunication streams (i.e., running *sniffers* and collecting packets traversing telecommunication networks) usually associated to cyber-attacks.

Table 1. Suggested STIX objects to use whilst devising cybersecurity in smart devices

STIX domain	STIX object(s)	Parameters and observations
SRO	Relationship	This object connects any two SDO or SCO altogether, so it will be used throughout the model.
SDO	Infrastructure, Location	These two objects are used to physically map assets so they could be reached if any problem surfaces. As parameters, one might use infrastructure_types, aliases, first_seen/last_seen (for Infrastructure), and country, city, lat/lon (for Location)
	Vulnerability	This object details a vulnerability in a component, and it is linked to other SCO through the external_references parameter.
	Threat Actor	It maps a threat actor and its skill level and threat considerations. Parameters to use are threat_actor_types, aliases, goals, sophistication, primary_motivation
	Campaign	Describes a group of malicious behaviors occurring over duration. Useful to describe so called 'waves' of cyber-attacks. Parameters to use are description, objective. This object connects to other actions as observed in systems and networks.
	Identity	This object could be used to represent any actor involved in the CTI effort, namely individuals, organizations, or groups. Parameters to use are sector, roles, contact_information.
	Note, Opinion, Report	These three objects contain descriptions with detailed analysis and information in the form of unstructured texts. They are often used to explain something important or point out to other literature involving the malicious incursions.
	Course of Action	Correspond to actions taken to thwart cyber-attacks. It could describe responses, patches, firewall configurations, etc. Parameters are description, action.
	Malware, Malware Analysis	They represent the execution of any malicious code and the mechanisms in place to mitigate. These objects are key for the analysis and several parameters are observed to use them in a proper fashion.
	Tool	Description of legitimate software to employ.
SCO	Observed Data	This object is used across the model (more details next).

Source: Author (2022), based on the STIX documentation

In terms of modelling effort, scalability issues, and tackling complexity for large attack surfaces, there are some specific constructs that are rather static (e.g., buildings and large equipment), while others are dynamic in nature. Examples are adversaries changing attack strategies or mobile electric cars changing position within a smart city landscape, so the use of tools is mandatory for all these cases.

The cybersecurity model will have a template with basic parameters that are seldom subjected to changes whereas other elements will require constant updates (e.g., telecommunication streams, phishing attack attempts, malware signatures and so on) and near real-time analysis to either confirm or refute cyber-attacks as they unfold in the networks under supervision. In this sense, multiple integrated teams will have to join efforts and collaborate to increase preparedness and pro-actively tackle any system deficiency across the organization. They must engage in the cybersecurity effort and commit to all defenses, mitigations, and responses.

Discussion

Despite recent efforts in tackling protections targeted at critical infrastructure, a small number of preoccupations has been directed at the intricacies of appending cybersecurity measures to smart devices. Companies have adopted an abundance of smart components without considering the security requirements and protections behind the chosen technology. In the one hand they solve problems and are used to increase the feedback loops for timely analysis, however, on the other hand, these devices may pose weaknesses that could be exploited by malicious threat actors. Massive external and internal data sources are open for interpretation, and CTI could balance these concerns by aggregating expert domain opinions substantiated by reports sanctioned by trustful organizations to meet analysis expectations.

In terms of case studies, STIX have been used with success in many contexts. For instance, when modelling cybersecurity for Active Buildings, a smart infrastructure consisting of Smart Buildings capable of energizing local power distribution networks, Czekster et al. (2022b) have demonstrated how physical elements could be intertwined with CTI. The objective of the work was to promote the use of STIX based modelling in a real-world setting where analysts could better understand the cyber-attack surface to protect and share their discoveries and ideas across their trusted network of contacts.

In such gigantic attack surfaces cybersecurity must encompass the whole portfolio of products, systems, and services behind organizations. In this sense, to meet such protective demand, higher investment is required to train personnel, maintain systems operating at reasonable levels of risk, and purchasing equipment bearing minimal cybersecurity prospects.

FUTURE RESEARCH DIRECTIONS

A clear indication of the future of CTI lies on its overspread use and adoption throughout organizations. The author envisions stakeholders focused on cybersecurity sharing and disseminating intelligence among sectors, enhancing preparedness, and allowing fast establishing fast protective measures in a timely fashion.

There is a clear trend in cybersecurity analysis to devise ways of fostering and incentivizing stakeholder's participation in the protective effort by sharing intelligence across organizations in an organic and scalable fashion. Companies are withholding information because they could be liable for admitting successful cyber-attacks. However, on the other hand, sharing the ways employed by adversaries may help preventing attacks from taking place elsewhere. Organizations must recognize the value of CTI and devise ways of obfuscating data to focus only on the TTPs employed by threat actors.

The author considers that automation will be significantly addressed when generating STIX (or other format) as events are captured in networks and systems. The idea is to either detect abnormalities and then generating the STIX model or after alarms reach pre-configured thresholds that could affect the cybersecurity and protective measures. After analysts created the models, they could be shared in platforms using TAXII. Cybersecurity offices must enact a network of trusted contacts to be able to produce and respond in a timely fashion.

An interesting venue for future research concerns employing the created STIX models in simulations, to help cybersecurity officers consider "what-if" scenarios and tackle preparedness by understanding most likely attack venues. This is an open research problem that could intertwine concepts arising in *Digital Twins* research where logs from the actual smart infrastructure are used to populate parameters in simulation models with digital and physical counterparts operating side by side. The idea is to allow faster decision making in close to real-world environments, offering cyber-attack detection in a timely fashion. Another similar approach is to combine CTI with attack graphs as discussed by Gylling et al. (2021), where the authors have developed a comprehensive framework to investigate the Time to Compromise (TTC) metric employing simulations.

A pillar of future research will have to devote attention to misinformation and 'fake news' attempts to undermine the CTI provision and reduce trust among counterparts. In a post-truth world, actual happenstances are increasingly difficult to verify and confirm. Research on how to best tackle such problems will have to accompany any CTI solution, perhaps with better moderation and vetting, or applying certifiable consensus mechanisms among domain experts.

Another issue is about the sheer scale of current attack surfaces of varying sized organizations. Analysts oversighting the infrastructure are interested in impactful events on resources happening across timescales, where analysts may inspect, confirm, refute, reach consensus, and share pieces of intelligence among trustful networks. Such mechanisms are needed for cases where threat agents act disruptively to counter-act intelligence gathering by planting falsehoods and misinformation into data sources.

These approaches are not new, they have been covered in the counter-intelligence field where adversaries insert seemingly accredited data so wrong actions may take place in mitigation efforts. The core concept of the process underlying here is to come up with a layer that accepts unstructured data, treats it, and outputs structured data for consumption in other CTI-based tool for deeper analysis.

CONCLUSION

Threat actors and malicious individuals or groups of adversaries combine efforts and look for design flaws in systems, i.e., vulnerabilities (weaknesses), where they could promote and advance more serious cyber-attacks. They search for one single point of entry whereas systems analysts and cybersecurity officers must make sure that all attack surface is protected. There is a clear mismatch in this regard, as it is easier to find one single weakness to explore instead of overlooking a massive number of systems and services.

The overspread adoption of CTI brings forth a lot of considerations prior to its deployment. Suppose a given data source has been compromised (without one's knowledge) and thus all shared information is deemed invalid or even worst, prejudicial to your organization. Misinformation and misguided decisions could cause even more damage and financial loss, so trust is a key component that must be factor in during decision making processes.

On the other hand, a host of initiatives focused on representing, understanding, and reasoning about cyber-attacks. For instance, in recent years, one witnessed the emergence of structured modelling frameworks to describe cyber-attacks with a reasonable level of detail. The main problem of this approach is due to the sheer number of parameters to consider for even simple cybersecurity models. To tackle this, one could resort to tools that help collating, compiling, and organizing pieces of models altogether, as well as listing parameters and auxiliary information to fill them, so they can be shareable as feeds to other stakeholders. In organizations where the attack surface is frequently modified, the cybersecurity teams have additional layers of concern as the models will have to reflect modifications in a timely manner.

CTI could be incorporated into organizations and promoted as a valuable tool to identify insider threats, considered hard to trace and that pose significant damage due to access to privileged information. Intelligence gathering phases could employ mechanisms to prevent these malicious actors from defacing data or altering entries when re-directing attention and resources.

The incorporation of effective SOC within organizations will play a significant role in CTI, preparedness, and enhancement of the overall cybersecurity posture of organizations. These centers will congregate all data traversing networks and consult information systems within a cyber-attack timeline to understand the adversarial progression and then mitigate malicious incursions. The author suggests training and adherence to standards (in terms of modelling, for the direction taken in this chapter) as means to improve trust and to bring stakeholders to the center of combat against cyber threats. Managers overlooking smart infrastructure and protective measures operating on the edge of systems may profit from combining cybersecurity with CTI because it promotes preparedness as cyber-attacks unfolds in systems and networks.

ACKNOWLEDGMENT

This research received no specific grant from any funding agency in the public, commercial, or not-for-profit sectors.

REFERENCES

Abbas, S. G., Vaccari, I., Hussain, F., Zahid, S., Fayyaz, U. U., Shah, G. A., Bakhshi, T., & Cambiaso, E. (2021). Identifying and mitigating phishing attack threats in IoT use cases using a threat modelling approach. *Sensors (Basel)*, *21*(14), 4816. doi:10.339021144816 PMID:34300556

Abu, M. S., Selamat, S. R., Ariffin, A., & Yusof, R. (2018). Cyber threat intelligence – issue and challenges. *Indonesian Journal of Electrical Engineering and Computer Science*, *10*(1), 371–379. doi:10.11591/ijeecs.v10.i1.pp371-379

Afzaliseresht, N., Miao, Y., Michalska, S., Liu, Q., & Wang, H. (2020). From logs to stories: Human-centred data mining for cyber threat intelligence. *IEEE Access : Practical Innovations, Open Solutions*, *8*, 19089–19099. doi:10.1109/ACCESS.2020.2966760

Agarwal, A., Walia, H., & Gupta, H. (2021, September). Cyber Security Model for Threat Hunting. In *2021 9th International Conference on Reliability, Infocom Technologies and Optimization (Trends and Future Directions)(ICRITO)* (pp. 1-8). IEEE. 10.1109/ICRITO51393.2021.9596199

Al-Fuqaha, A., Guizani, M., Mohammadi, M., Aledhari, M., & Ayyash, M. (2015). Internet of things: A survey on enabling technologies, protocols, and applications. *IEEE Communications Surveys and Tutorials*, *17*(4), 2347–2376. doi:10.1109/COMST.2015.2444095

Arnaboldi, L., Czekster, R. M., Morisset, C., & Metere, R. (2020). Modelling load-changing attacks in cyber-physical systems. *Electronic Notes in Theoretical Computer Science, 353*, 39–60. doi:10.1016/j.entcs.2020.09.018

Barnum, S. (2012). Standardizing cyber threat intelligence information with the Structured Threat Information eXpression (STIX). *Mitre Corporation, 11*, 1–22.

Berady, A., Jaume, M., Tong, V. V. T., & Guette, G. (2021). From TTP to IoC: Advanced persistent graphs for threat hunting. *IEEE eTransactions on Network and Service Management, 18*(2), 1321–1333. doi:10.1109/TNSM.2021.3056999

Bhardwaj, A., & Goundar, S. (2019). A framework for effective threat hunting. *Network Security, 2019*(6), 15–19. doi:10.1016/S1353-4858(19)30074-1

Burger, E. W., Goodman, M. D., Kampanakis, P., & Zhu, K. A. (2014, November). Taxonomy model for cyber threat intelligence information exchange technologies. In *Proceedings of the 2014 ACM Workshop on Information Sharing & Collaborative Security* (pp. 51-60). ACM. 10.1145/2663876.2663883

Connolly, J., Davidson, M., & Schmidt, C. (2014). The Trusted Automated eXchange of Indicator Information (TAXII), 1-20. The MITRE Corporation.

Conti, M., Dargahi, T., & Dehghantanha, A. (2018). Cyber threat intelligence: challenges and opportunities. In *Cyber Threat Intelligence* (pp. 1–6). Springer. doi:10.1007/978-3-319-73951-9_1

Czekster, R. M., Metere, R., & Morisset, C. (2022a). cyberaCTIve: a STIX-based Tool for Cyber Threat Intelligence in Complex Models. *arXiv preprint arXiv:2204.03676.*

Czekster, R. M., Metere, R., & Morisset, C. (2022b). Incorporating Cyber Threat Intelligence into Complex Cyber-Physical Systems: A STIX Model for Active Buildings. *Applied Sciences (Basel, Switzerland), 12*(10), 5005. doi:10.3390/app12105005

Daszczyszak, R., Ellis, D., Luke, S., & Whitley, S. (2019). *TTP-Based Hunting.* MITRE CORP MCLEAN VA.

de Boer, M. H., Bakker, B. J., Boertjes, E., Wilmer, M., Raaijmakers, S., & van der Kleij, R. (2019). Text mining in cybersecurity: Exploring threats and opportunities. *Multimodal Technologies and Interaction, 3*(3), 62. doi:10.3390/mti3030062

de Melo e Silva, A., Costa Gondim, J. J., de Oliveira Albuquerque, R., & García Villalba, L. J. (2020). A methodology to evaluate standards and platforms within cyber threat intelligence. *Future Internet, 12*(6), 108. doi:10.3390/fi12060108

Debar, H., Curry, D., & Feinstein, B. (2007). The intrusion detection message exchange format (IDMEF). *IETF Request for Comments, 4765.*

Digital, Data & Technology. (2022*). UK. Detecting the Unknown: A Guide to Threat Hunting.* HO Digital.. https://hodigital.blog.gov.uk/wp-content/uploads/sites/161/2020/03/Detecting-the-Unknown-A-Guide-to-Threat-Hunting-v2.0.pdf

Dushyant, K., & Muskan, G. Annu, Gupta, A. and Pramanik, S. (2022). Utilizing Machine Learning and Deep Learning in Cybesecurity: An Innovative Approach. In M. M. Ghonge, S. Pramanik, R. Mangrulkar and D.-N. Le (eds.) Cyber Security and Digital Forensics. doi:10.1002/9781119795667.ch12

Dutta, A., & Kant, S. (2020, December). An overview of cyber threat intelligence platform and role of artificial intelligence and machine learning. In *International Conference on Information Systems Security* (pp. 81-86). Springer, Cham. 10.1007/978-3-030-65610-2_5

Gao, P., Shao, F., Liu, X., Xiao, X., Qin, Z., Xu, F., Mittal, P., Kulkarni, S. R., & Song, D. (2021, April). Enabling efficient cyber threat hunting with cyber threat intelligence. In 2021 *IEEE 37th International Conference on Data Engineering (ICDE)* (pp. 193-204). IEEE. 10.1109/ICDE51399.2021.00024

Griffioen, H., Booij, T., & Doerr, C. (2020, October). Quality evaluation of cyber threat intelligence feeds. In *International Conference on Applied Cryptography and Network Security* (pp. 277-296). Springer, Cham. 10.1007/978-3-030-57878-7_14

Gritzalis, D., Iseppi, G., Mylonas, A., & Stavrou, V. (2018). Exiting the risk assessment maze: A meta-survey. [CSUR]. *ACM Computing Surveys*, *51*(1), 1–30. doi:10.1145/3145905

Gupta, A., Verma, A., & Pramanik, S. (2022). Advanced security system in video surveillance for COVID-19. In *An Interdisciplinary Approach to Modern Network Security* (pp. 131–151). CRC Press. doi:10.1201/9781003147176-8

Gylling, A., Ekstedt, M., Afzal, Z., & Eliasson, P. (2021, July). Mapping Cyber Threat Intelligence to Probabilistic Attack Graphs. In *2021 IEEE International Conference on Cyber Security and Resilience (CSR)* (pp. 304-311). IEEE. 10.1109/CSR51186.2021.9527970

Horawalavithana, S., Bhattacharjee, A., Liu, R., Choudhury, N. O., Hall, L., & Iamnitchi, A. (2019, October). Mentions of security vulnerabilities on reddit, twitter and github. In *IEEE/WIC/ACM International Conference on Web Intelligence* (pp. 200-207). IEEE. 10.1145/3350546.3352519

Humayed, A., Lin, J., Li, F., & Luo, B. (2017). Cyber-physical systems security – A survey. *IEEE Internet of Things Journal, 4*(6), 1802–1831. doi:10.1109/JIOT.2017.2703172

Husari, G., Al-Shaer, E., Ahmed, M., Chu, B., & Niu, X. (2017, December). TTPDrill: Automatic and accurate extraction of threat actions from unstructured text of CTI sources. In *Proceedings of the 33rd Annual Computer Security Applications Conference* (pp. 103-115). ACM. 10.1145/3134600.3134646

Koloveas, P., Chantzios, T., Tryfonopoulos, C., & Skiadopoulos, S. (2019, July). A crawler architecture for harvesting the clear, social, and dark web for IoT-related cyber-threat intelligence. In *2019 IEEE World Congress on Services (SERVICES)* (Vol. 2642, pp. 3-8). IEEE. 10.1109/SERVICES.2019.00016

Leszczyna, R. (2018). A review of standards with cybersecurity requirements for smart grid. *Computers & Security, 77*, 262–276. doi:10.1016/j.cose.2018.03.011

Li, V. G., Dunn, M., Pearce, P., McCoy, D., Voelker, G. M., & Savage, S. (2019). Reading the tea leaves: A comparative analysis of threat intelligence. In 28th USENIX Security Symposium (USENIX Security 19) (pp. 851-867).

Liao, X., Yuan, K., Wang, X., Li, Z., Xing, L., & Beyah, R. (2016, October). Acing the IoC game: Toward automatic discovery and analysis of open-source cyber threat intelligence. In *Proceedings of the 2016 ACM SIGSAC Conference on Computer and Communications Security* (pp. 755-766). ACM. 10.1145/2976749.2978315

Liberati, F., Garone, E., & Di Giorgio, A. (2021). Review of Cyber-Physical Attacks in Smart Grids: A System-Theoretic Perspective. *Electronics (Basel), 10*(10), 1153. doi:10.3390/electronics10101153

Liew, A. (2013). DIKIW: Data, information, knowledge, intelligence, wisdom and their interrelationships. *Business Management Dynamics, 2*(10), 49.

Mavroeidis, V., & Bromander, S. (2017, September). Cyber threat intelligence model: an evaluation of taxonomies, sharing standards, and ontologies within cyber threat intelligence. In *2017 European Intelligence and Security Informatics Conference (EISIC)* (pp. 91-98). IEEE. 10.1109/EISIC.2017.20

Mehmood, R., Katib, S. S. I., & Chlamtac, I. (2020). *Smart infrastructure and applications*. Springer International Publishing. doi:10.1007/978-3-030-13705-2

Menges, F., Sperl, C., & Pernul, G. (2019, August). Unifying cyber threat intelligence. In *International Conference on Trust and Privacy in Digital Business* (pp. 161-175). Springer, Cham.

Mittal, S., Das, P. K., Mulwad, V., Joshi, A., & Finin, T. (2016, August). Cybertwitter: Using twitter to generate alerts for cybersecurity threats and vulnerabilities. In *2016 IEEE/ACM International Conference on Advances in Social Networks Analysis and Mining (ASONAM)* (pp. 860-867). IEEE. 10.1109/ASONAM.2016.7752338

Moriarty, K. (2012). *Real-time Inter-network defense (RID) (RFC6545)*. Tools. https://tools.ietf.org/html/rfc6545

Ota, K., Kumrai, T., Dong, M., Kishigami, J., & Guo, M. (2017). Smart infrastructure design for smart cities. *IT Professional*, *19*(5), 42–49. doi:10.1109/MITP.2017.3680957

Pillitteri, V., & Brewer, T. (2014). *Guidelines for Smart Grid Cybersecurity, NIST Interagency/Internal Report (NISTIR)*. National Institute of Standards and Technology. doi:10.6028/NIST.IR.7628r1

Pradhan, D., Sahu, P. K., Goje, N. S., Ghonge, M. M., Tun, H. M., Rajeswari, R., & Pramanik, S. (2022). Security, Privacy, Risk, and Safety Toward 5G Green Network (5G-GN). *Cyber Security and Network Security*, 193-216.

Ramsdale, A., Shiaeles, S., & Kolokotronis, N. (2020). A comparative analysis of cyber-threat intelligence sources, formats and languages. *Electronics (Basel)*, *9*(5), 824. doi:10.3390/electronics9050824

Roberts, A. (2021). *Cyber threat intelligence: The no-nonsense guide for CISOs and security managers*. Apress. doi:10.1007/978-1-4842-7220-6

Samtani, S., Abate, M., Benjamin, V., & Li, W. (2020). Cybersecurity as an industry: A cyber threat intelligence perspective. The Palgrave Handbook of International Cybercrime and Cyberdeviance, 135-154.

Shu, X., Araujo, F., Schales, D. L., Stoecklin, M. P., Jang, J., Huang, H., & Rao, J. R. (2018, October). Threat intelligence computing. In *Proceedings of the 2018 ACM SIGSAC Conference on Computer and Communications Security* (pp. 1883-1898). ACM. 10.1145/3243734.3243829

Slatman, H. (2022, April 26). hslatman/awesome-threat-intelligence. General format. https://github.com/hslatman/awesome-threat-intelligence

Steinberger, J., Sperotto, A., Golling, M., & Baier, H. (2015, May). How to exchange security events? overview and evaluation of formats and protocols. In *2015 IFIP/IEEE International Symposium on Integrated Network Management (IM)* (pp. 261-269). IEEE. 10.1109/INM.2015.7140300

Stojanović, B., Hofer-Schmitz, K., & Kleb, U. (2020). APT datasets and attack modeling for automated detection methods: A review. *Computers & Security*, *92*, 101734. doi:10.1016/j.cose.2020.101734

Strom, B. E., Applebaum, A., Miller, D. P., Nickels, K. C., Pennington, A. G., & Thomas, C. B. (2018). *MITRE ATT&CK: Design and philosophy*. Technical report.

Takahashi, T., Landfield, K., & Kadobayashi, Y. (2014). *RFC 7203: An Incident Object Description Exchange Format (IODEF) Extension for Structured Cybersecurity Information. Internet Engineering Task Force*. IETF.

Tounsi, W., & Rais, H. (2018). A survey on technical threat intelligence in the age of sophisticated cyber attacks. *Computers & Security*, *72*, 212–233. doi:10.1016/j. cose.2017.09.001

Vallant, H., Stojanović, B., Božić, J., & Hofer-Schmitz, K. (2021). Threat Modelling and Beyond-Novel Approaches to Cyber Secure the Smart Energy System. *Applied Sciences (Basel, Switzerland)*, *11*(11), 5149. doi:10.3390/app11115149

Wagner, C., Dulaunoy, A., Wagener, G., & Iklody, A. (2016, October). MISP: The design and implementation of a collaborative threat intelligence sharing platform. In *Proceedings of the 2016 ACM on Workshop on Information Sharing and Collaborative Security* (pp. 49-56). ACM. 10.1145/2994539.2994542

Wagner, T. D., Mahbub, K., Palomar, E., & Abdallah, A. E. (2019). Cyber threat intelligence sharing: Survey and research directions. *Computers & Security*, *87*, 101589. doi:10.1016/j.cose.2019.101589

Yang, Y., Wu, L., Yin, G., Li, L., & Zhao, H. (2017). A survey on security and privacy issues in Internet-of-Things. *IEEE Internet of Things Journal*, *4*(5), 1250–1258. doi:10.1109/JIOT.2017.2694844

Zhao, J., Yan, Q., Li, J., Shao, M., He, Z., & Li, B. (2020). TIMiner: Automatically extracting and analyzing categorized cyber threat intelligence from social data. *Computers & Security*, *95*, 101867. doi:10.1016/j.cose.2020.101867

ENDNOTES

[1]   Available at: https://github.com/oasis-open/cti-stix-visualization
[2]   Available at: https://www.npmjs.com/package/stixview
[3]   Available at: https://pypi.org/project/stix2-viz/

Chapter 4
Automotive Controller Area Network Intrusion Detection Systems

Luis da Bernarda
ESTG, Polytechnic of Leiria, Portugal

Leonel Santos
iD https://orcid.org/0000-0002-6883-7996
CIIC, ESTG, Polytechnic of Leiria, Portugal

Rogério L. C. Costa
iD https://orcid.org/0000-0003-2306-7585
CIIC, Polytechnic of Leiria, Portugal

Carlos Rabadão
iD https://orcid.org/0000-0001-7332-4397
CIIC, ESTG, Polytechnic of Leiria, Portugal

ABSTRACT

The technological development observed in recent years has led to the expansion of automotive systems communication capabilities. Consequently, several security vulnerabilities and additional attack surfaces that a threat agent can potentially exploit are increased. The most employed communication protocol in a vehicle is the controller area network (CAN) serial bus protocol, designed with robust fault tolerance in mind, but little to no concern for security. This chapter offers a primer on the controller area network typical architecture, what messages are used in communication, its error management system, and its vulnerabilities. Possible CAN attack surfaces and attack methods are also presented, followed by an exposition on intrusion detection systems (IDS) as a potential solution to the security concerns raised by CAN bus vulnerabilities. Several case studies on IDS implementations for secure CAN bus systems are also presented, including a recently proposed framework to facilitate further development in this field of study.

DOI: 10.4018/978-1-6684-5991-1.ch004

INTRODUCTION

The technological development and evolution witnessed in the last decades have led to significant transformations in all areas of society, including the automotive industry. These technological innovations boosted the change of automotive vehicles from purely mechanical system platforms into complex multisystem platforms that integrate computerized systems with mechanical ones. Such new complex systems often contain many sensors, actuators, and embedded computers, as well as interfaces to communicate with the outside world (Le et al., 2018). With the increasing computerization of automotive systems, the number of devices present in vehicles rises as functionalities and improved. Currently, many high-end cars have advanced functionalities that might require over one hundred embedded computers (Wu et al., 2020). These components and functionalities are often enhanced via the use of specialized software applications to expand the system's efficiency, safety, usability, and comfort (Le et al., 2018).

The continued integration of mechanical and computerized technologies is convenient but also exposes several vectors of attack from a security standpoint and, as such, motivates the need for robust automotive security of the cyber-physical systems of vehicles. With the likely future emergence of fully autonomous vehicles, the potential damage of a security breach could result in catastrophic consequences, from significant financial and material damage to the loss of human life (Young et al., 2019). Several attacks were already successfully tested in controlled environments, initially with physical access to the vehicle. Since 2015, wireless controller area network attacks have proven viable against many vehicles, which resulted in a recall of 1.4 million units (Miller & Valasek, 2015). As vehicle manufacturers continue improving the security of their products, more and more research is required on the vulnerabilities of controller area network systems. Recently, a similar attack was successfully tested and resulted in a consistent shutdown of CAN electronic control units (ECU), indicating that more research into CAN vulnerabilities, security, and mitigation is necessary (Kulandaivel et al., 2021).

Nowadays, it is possible to categorize existing automotive applications into three core areas: control systems that handle the physical functions of the vehicle, such as the engine, chassis, body and passive safety functions; telematics systems that are responsible for generating information and support entertainment functionality, as well as financial transactions; the last core area of automotive applications is advanced driver assistance systems (ADAS), these systems serve the purpose of turning vehicles into intelligent systems, thereby improving safety and driving experience (Le et al., 2018). Although these advancements and improvements to vehicle functionality and safety are significant, they have also introduced a slew of different security vulnerabilities that need to be addressed (Jo & Choi, 2021).

The remainder of the chapter is organized as follows: the following section introduces the background of Controller Area Networks (CAN) and Intrusion Detection Systems (IDS). Section 3 reviews the exposition of attack surfaces in CAN and several attack methods. Then, Section 4 describes different IDS methodologies and solutions for CAN. Section 5 concludes the chapter.

BACKGROUND

This section introduces the concept of Controller Area Networks, presenting a brief history of the protocol, followed by an introduction to its architecture, message frame format, error management system, and CAN security vulnerabilities. It concludes by presenting the concept of Intrusion Detection Systems.

Controller Area Network

The concept of controller area networks was formalized in 1986 at the SAE congress in Detroit, and it was motivated by the need of adding new functionalities and reducing the wiring harnesses in already existing similar serial bus systems. Having been in development since 1983 by engineers from Bosch, specifically for the automotive industry, the CAN serial bus was rapidly adopted in other applications, from elevators to trains, being nowadays one of the most employed serial bus communication protocols (*History of the CAN Technology*, n.d.). This communication protocol underwent more development, ultimately being standardized in several ISO documents: ISO 11898-1 (ISO/TC 22/SC 31, 2015), which describes the protocol data link layer, ISO 11898-2 (ISO/TC 22/SC 31, 2016) refers to the protocols non-fault tolerant physical layer, and ISO 11898-3 (ISO/TC 22/SC 31, 2006, 2015) standardizes the fault-tolerant physical layer. Other standards exist for more specialized applications, from farming and forestry equipment and vehicles (ISO 11783) to truck and trailer interfaces (ISO 11992). But due to some differences in the physical layer specifications, they aren't compatible between them (*History of the CAN Technology*, n.d.).

The following subsections present the CAN architecture, the message frame formats, and the CAN network protocol error types and verification.

CAN Architecture

CAN is a message-based communication protocol, where several ECUs are interconnected through a common bus, so that the devices can communicate with each other without a communication host. Although there are a multitude of implementations, a typical CAN system architecture usually contains the following elements:

- **CAN BUS**: communication network where all nodes are reached by passive links which allow for bidirectional transmission (ISO/TC 2/SC 31, 2006).
- **CAN Transceiver**: Device that connects a CAN controller to the CAN bus, whose purpose is to translate the logic-level bits from the device to CAN bus voltages (Lynch et al., 2016).
- **CAN Controller (HW)**: Hardware component that is responsible for the physical access to the transmission medium via the transceiver (di Natale et al., 2012).
- **CAN Driver**: Software component responsible for tasks related to the transmission of CAN message frames. Many drivers also extend controller capabilities via message queuing or similar (di Natale et al., 2012).
- **Transport Layer**: Manages message segmentation and recombination when message sizes are large (in excess of 8 bytes). Furthermore, it serves as a mechanism to control message flow and reception acknowledgement (di Natale et al., 2012).
- **Interaction Layer**: This layer offers APIs to the application for data operations according to the application specifications. Moreover, it serves to perform several operations such as byte order conversion and message interpretation (di Natale et al., 2012).
- **Diagnostic and Network Management layers**: These layers handle network management and monitoring for all active nodes. They also manage synchronized transitions to sleep mode when necessary and manage all virtual subnetworks or network working modes (di Natale et al., 2012).
- **Calibration Layer**: This layer supports features for the development and testing phases as well as end–of–line flash programming into ECU memory for parameter calibration and measurement (di Natale et al., 2012).

With the technological development observed in the past decades, there was a necessity to expand CAN functionalities to accommodate for increased data rates when necessary. To solve this problem, an expanded standard was proposed in 2011 that allows for flexible data rate transmission, termed CAN FD, this new standard, is very similar to the standard CAN, and is retro-compatible in most scenarios. CAN FD is standardized in ISO 11898-1 (*History of the CAN Technology*, n.d.).

In recent years, the communication capabilities of automotive vehicles have been on the rise, from simple ECUs, all connected through a CAN bus, to multiple connected buses via a gateway (e.g., FlexRay, MOST, LIN) and interfaces allowing the vehicle to communicate between themselves (V2V - Vehicle to Vehicle) or with the outside world (V2I - Vehicle to Infrastructure) via wireless communication technologies such as Wi-Fi or Bluetooth as seen in Figure 1 (Lokman et al., 2019). These communication features, although increasing the convenience and usability of the vehicle, also open up additional attack surfaces from a security standpoint.

Figure 1. Communication systems in a modern car

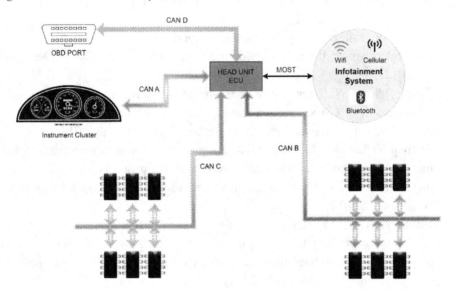

CAN Message Frame Formats

CAN has four different types of message frames, defined by their function and payload (di Natale et al., 2012).

- **Data frame**: These frames contain information from a source to one or more receivers.
- **Remote Frame**: These frames are employed to request the transmission of a Data Frame with the same identifier.
- **Error Frame**: Sent whenever a node on the network detects an error.
- **Overload Frame**: These frames are used for flow control and requesting delays on the transmission of a Data or Remote frame.

A data frame is composed of several elements as seen in Figure 2, these components are: Arbitration, Control, Data, CRC, ACK, ending delimiter, idle space and interframe bits (di Natale et al., 2012).

Figure 2. CAN Data Frame format

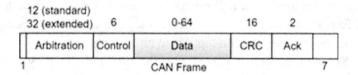

An identifier is employed in the control portion of a message frame to define both the priority of the message and the identification of the data content of the message stream. The identifier size varies if the frame is standard (11 bits) or extended (29 bits) as observed in Figure 3 (di Natale et al., 2012).

Figure 3. CAN identifier component

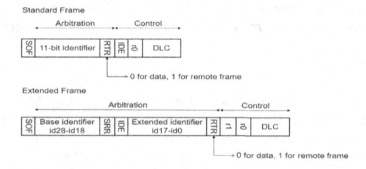

CAN Error Management

Although the CAN protocol was designed for serial bus communications in automotive applications, the designers kept robustness in mind, designing the protocol with mechanisms for fault detection and mitigation, and containment. The protocol is designed so that any message that is flagged as erroneous is discarded and retransmitted automatically (di Natale et al., 2012). The protocol resorts to CRC checks and acknowledgement flags in the message frame components to verify message validity. When an error is detected, an error message frame is generated that is comprised of a superimposition of the error flags, hence not being considered a true message frame.

There are several error types identified in the protocol, each with their management and response process (di Natale et al., 2012):

- **Bit Error**: When a node transmits a message, it monitors both the bits sent and the bits on the bus. If a discrepancy is detected, it will signal a bit error.
- **Stuff Error**: A stuff error is detected at the sixth consecutive occurrence of the same bit in a message susceptible to bit stuffing.
- **CRC Error**: This error is generated if the CRC computed by the receiving node is different from the CRC stored in the message frame.
- **Form Error**: This error occurs when a fixed-form bit field contains one or more illegal bits.
- **Acknowledgement Error**: This error occurs when a transmitter node detects a recessive bit in the message frame ACK field.

The CAN protocol uses all the information mentioned above for its fault confinement mechanism, which moves to shut down an ECU unit if a certain number of errors are detected in the unit during either its receive or transmit phases (di Natale et al., 2012). Some attacks on CAN solutions rely on this fault containment system to generate enough errors in a particular node to shut it down intentionally.

CAN Vulnerabilities

Several critical security vulnerabilities have been noted in the CAN bus system (Carsten et al., 2015). These vulnerabilities include CAN message frames not including any form of addressing, making it impossible to determine the origin and destination of a particular message. The fact that in CAN bus architecture, the standard implementation for message flow means that every node will receive a message transmitted on the CAN bus, coupled with the lack of addressing in the message structure makes it so that an attacker could potentially compromise one or more ECU units, and send fake packets on the CAN bus. This problem compounds with the lack of a message authentication system, resulting in a vulnerable CAN system (Lokman et al., 2019).

There are several methods to mitigate or manage this security problem, this chapter focuses on enumerating the advantages and disadvantages of the deployment of Intrusion Detection System based approaches.

Intrusion Detection Systems

With the growing complexity of modern networks, systems that autonomously detect and respond to security problems have become vital. One approach for problem detection is an Intrusion Detection System (IDS), which can be comprised of software or hardware elements with the express purpose of automatically monitoring and handling any problems occurring in the system being analysed (Bace & Mell, 2001).

An intrusion in a computer system can be defined as any attempt to compromise the confidentiality, integrity, or accessibility (CIA) of data, or to bypass the system security mechanisms (Bace & Mell, 2001).

IDS Standard Components

Most of IDS systems employ three fundamental components (Bace & Mell, 2001).

- **Information Sources**: The various sources of event information that are employed to determine if an intrusion has occurred. These sources can feed the IDS information from practically all levels of the system, from network and host to the application level.
- **Analysis**: The component of the IDS that is responsible for the organization of the information gathered and, through analysis, detecting if an intrusion is ongoing or has already occurred. The most common analysis methods are misuse detection and anomaly detection.
- **Response**: This component refers to the set of actions the system will execute once an intrusion is detected. These are normally grouped into passive and active actions, where active measures usually employ automated responses from the system and passive action involves reporting the occurrence to human personnel, who are expected to manually take action to address the detected problem.

There are many types of IDS deployments: they can be centralized, partially distributed, or fully distributed. They can also employ many sources of information, from the network level to the application or host levels. A more comprehensive primer on IDS types is out of scope for this chapter, but can be consulted in the following NIST documentation (Bace & Mell, 2001).

IDS Analysis Approaches

As mentioned before, the most common IDS analysis categories are misuse detection and anomaly detection, although a number of more recent works challenge this categorization and propose other categories (Lokman et al., 2019; Liao et al., 2013). An introduction to IDS analysis approaches as documented by NIST will be presented, focusing on each of the categories' advantages and disadvantages. Other analysis methods will be approached on a case–by–case basis when presenting specific solutions for CAN systems.

According to NIST, there are two approaches to analysing events in IDS systems:

- **Misuse Detection**: This method analyses events or sets of events in a system that match a known pattern. These patterns that correspond to known attacks are termed signatures, hence misuse detection is also termed signature–based detection (Bace & Mell, 2001)[13]. An advantage of this approach is that misuse detectors tend to excel at detecting attacks without generating large numbers of false alarms. Another advantage is that this approach can reliably detect the use of a specific attack methodology, which facilitates the selection of optimal countermeasures. A disadvantage of this method is, since it relies on the signatures of known attacks, it requires constant updating with new signatures (Bace & Mell, 2001).

- **Anomaly Detection**: This approach focuses on detecting unusual behaviour in a system, approaching the problem with the assumption that attacks will generate activity outside of the standard expected behaviour, and therefore can be detected by comparing the difference between the actual system state with the expected state (Bace & Mell, 2001). Some of the advantages of this approach is that since it detects anomalies in the expected behaviour, it does not need regular updates, facilitating the deployment of long– term solutions employing this method. Another advantage pertains to the fact that anomalies detected using this approach can be categorized and employed in defining signatures to be used in solutions employing the previous method. Some disadvantages of this method are that it tends to generate a large number of false alarms, and that it requires a large data set of event records to categorize what is normal operating behaviour (Bace & Mell, 2001).

ATTACKS ON CONTROLLER AREA NETWORKS

As mentioned beforehand, the automotive industry has, in recent years, witnessed an expansion of sensors and communication equipment deployed in modern vehicles. This deployment of new equipment is a source of many benefits and usability improvements, and it would have an even higher impact with the rise of V2V and V2I communication applications. These advancements are not without consequences, as more functionality and communication capabilities invariably mean additional security vulnerabilities and attack surfaces that a threat actor may exploit.

In this section, the potential attack surfaces that a threat actor can target will be explored, followed by an introduction to the types of attacks that can target CAN systems. This section concludes with the presentation of a few CAN attack case studies.

CAN Attack Surfaces

The CAN protocol was designed with fault tolerance in mind, but it has significant security vulnerabilities, as mentioned previously. In terms of attack surfaces, there are several in a modern automotive vehicle, varying if the attacker has physical access to the vehicle. Figure 4 presents some of potential surfaces an attacker may exploit.

Figure 4. Attack surfaces in a modern vehicle

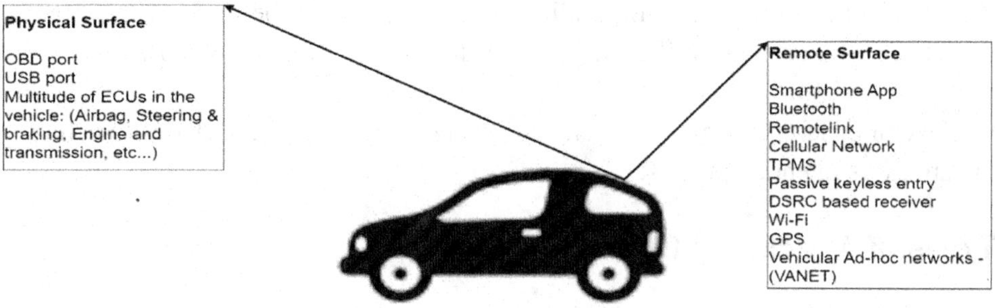

These attacks can be further categorized into their approach method, physical or remote.

- **Physical attack surfaces**: Physical attacks are termed as such due to their requirement of direct or indirect physical access to the vehicle CAN bus network. Regarding direct physical attacks, they can be divided into two major attack surfaces: exploiting the On-Board Diagnostics (OBD) port, which, due to the design behind CAN bus networks, has access to all nodes even if network segmentation is employed. Another direct attack surface lies in compromising an ECU node in the CAN bus system, which is termed a malicious node. Again, due to CAN bus design, any node in the system can transmit and receiving message frames from and to any other node in the system. The other major attack surface is the indirect approach, which requires a physical object to be inserted in the vehicle, but not necessarily access to the CAN network itself (Bozdal et al., 2020). Due to the nature of these physical attack surfaces, many experts tend to deem most of these attacks as impractical in real world conditions, hence most research is focused on remote attack surfaces (Bozdal et al., 2020).
- **Remote attack surfaces**: With the increasing integration of vehicle systems and communication technologies, and V2I and V2V communications,

the possibility of remote attacks on an automotive system has increased significantly. Nowadays, vehicles can be equipped with a multitude of communication technologies, from Bluetooth to Wi-Fi or GPS, which opens several surfaces for remote attacks. As with physical surfaces, remote attack surfaces can be categorized in two major categories: The short range, remote attack surface, which is comprised of Bluetooth, Wi-Fi, keyless entry, immobilizer, Automatic tyre pressure monitoring system (TPMS), or vehicular ad-hoc networks (VANETs). The last major attack surface for remote attacks is the long-range surface. This surface contains the cellular network, the GPS, and the radio channel, which can be divided into Radio Data systems and Traffic Message Channels (Bozdal et al., 2020).

Several different forms of attack can be deployed on these surfaces to achieve the attackers intended purpose.

Types of Attacks on CAN

Classical security in computerized systems tends to be based on a few pillars: Confidentiality, Integrity, Authentication, Availability/Reliability and Non-Repudiation. These pillars of computer security also apply to automotive systems since the system will be required to address attacks such as unauthorized entry via exploiting the keyless entry system or similar data collection by capturing traffic between CAN nodes or V2V and V2I communication among others.

Generally, there are two types of attack scenarios in CAN systems, the masquerade attack, and the Denial of Service (DoS) attack (Jo & Choi, 2021).

- **Masquerade Attacks**: These attacks attempt to fake CAN identifiers, mentioned beforehand, to gain unauthorized access to a vehicle system by impersonating compromised ECUs. These attacks generally employ message replay or message fabrication to affect the controls of the vehicle. In replay attacks, messages are simply sent repeatedly without any modification. In fabrication attacks, messages are sent with their identifier fields spoofed (Jo & Choi, 2021).
- **DoS Attacks**: These attacks attempt to stall the network by depleting the network bandwidth via message flooding or target a specific ECU with a suspension attack. In message flooding attacks, the threat actor repeatedly sends numerous message frames with altered identifiers (The lowest identifier values have transmission priority), since CAN bus employs CSMA/CD (Carrier Sense MultipleAccess with Collision Detection) with bitwise arbitration in case of collision (Sharma & Bhargav, 2016), by flooding the

network with high priority messages, it becomes possible to stall the network. This attack could lead to unpredictable events while operating the vehicle. In a suspension attack, the goal is to disable a specific ECU from performing their normal operations. There are several reasons why a threat attacker may seek to employ suspension attacks, some of which relate to combined attack approaches (Jo & Choi, 2021).

- **Combined Attacks**: For more sophisticated attacks that compromise safety-critical ECUs, a threat actor may need to employ both masquerade and DoS attacks. Some of the most successful attacks in the literature employed both types of attack, for example, in the 2015 work that proved the viability of remote attacks (Miller & Valasek, 2015), access to the vehicle system was only achieved after blocking the transmission of Anti-lock Braking System (ABS) CAN message frames by employing suspension attacks, after these messages were stalled, it was possible to bypass the fault verification that particular ECU was executing and send messages with false data to the CAN ECUs (Jo & Choi, 2021).

In the following subsection, some literature on case studies for attacks will be presented.

CAN Attack Case Studies

The case studies that will be presented are considered important to demonstrate the potential consequences of a CAN system breach, and as a result, the importance of robust security measures, with a focus on Intrusion Detection System solutions.

- **Remote Exploitation of an Unaltered Passenger Vehicle**: The first case study to be introduced was already mentioned beforehand in this chapter, constituting the first fully remote attack on the CAN bus. The Miller & Valasek (2015) research followed a previous research line that managed to disrupt CAN bus systems with physical approaches, first directly in 2010 (Koscher et al., 2010) and subsequently indirectly via software deployed to the MP3 parser on the radio, the Bluetooth stack of the car and the telematics unit. Once the malicious code was running in the system, the researchers could attack the car from anywhere (Checkoway et al., 2011). The response from the automotive industry at the time was that since physical access to the vehicle was required at least one point in time, the industry believed the attacks impractical, considering only fully remote attacks problematic (Miller & Valasek, 2015). The case study that is presented derived from the studies realized in the previously mentioned works, and was the first known successful, fully remote breach of CAN bus security. This attack impacted both the steering system and the braking system and was responsible for the FCA recalling 1.4 million vehicles (Miller & Valasek, 2015). The attack target described in this case study was a 2014 Jeep Cherokee, and the adversary mainly used the attack surface of the LTE network to carry out the long-range nature of the attack. A summary of the steps required to carry out the attack is given below:

○ **Identify Target:** The IP address of the target vehicle is required. This address can be obtained by simply picking a random IP address from known IP address blocks that car manufacturers deploy in their vehicles, or via secondary attacks to determine the intended target vehicle IP address. If the adversary knows the VIN (Vehicle Identification Number) or GPS Identifier, it would be possible to scan the LTE network until a match has been found (Miller & Valasek, 2015).

○ **Exploit the OMAP chip of the head unit:** The OMAP chip is responsible for most of the infotainment system in the target vehicle and was relatively common within automotive systems circa 2015. Code can be run anonymously employing several vulnerabilities in the D-Bus service, which is typically used for inter-process communication, since it is exposed to the LTE network on port 6667 in this particular vehicle. Using several D-Bus services functions, files can be uploaded to the OMAP chip, allowing the upload of an SSH public key and a configuration file. After uploading the SSH files and key, the SSH service can be started, which allows remote root access (Miller & Valasek, 2015).

○ **Control the Uconnect (Infotainment) system:** With access to the D-Bus service and the remote SSH command line, several scripts can be run that allow control and acquisition of radio, HVAC, GPS location, and other non-CAN related attacks. If these are all the adversary needs, the attack may be concluded with this step. If malicious CAN messages are required for the adversary, further steps are necessary. In fact, it is possible to control many of the vehicle functionalities simply with D-Bus functions, without requiring remote code execution (Miller & Valasek, 2015).

○ **Flash the v850 with modified firmware:** Should the adversary require the ability to send CAN messages, this step is necessary. The v850 chip must be flashed with custom firmware, using techniques presented by the authors of this case study. However, flashing of this chip requires an automated reboot of the system, which may alert the driver that something has occurred (Miller & Valasek, 2015).

- ○ **Perform cyber-physical actions:** With the modified firmware deployed, it is possible to send a CAN message to provoke a physical action in the vehicle, by sending messages from the OMAP chip (which cannot directly send CAN messages to the BUS) to the modified firmware on the v850 chip using SPI (Miller & Valasek, 2015). This step requires specific research depending on the implementation used, similar to the research carried out by the authors of the following paper: (Valasek & Miller, 2013).

Although this case study focused on a particular car (Jeep Cherokee from 2014), many of the underlying systems and hardware (Infotainment system, v850 chip, OMAP chip) can be found in other vehicles from other manufacturers, as the chips can be the same between manufacturers (Miller & Valasek, 2015). However, even if the implementation is different, systems such as LTE connections, head units with infotainment systems that are connected to every CAN bus in the vehicle, are all potentially vulnerable to a targeted attack of the sophistication presented in the case study.

- **CANnon - Reliable and Stealthy Remote Shutdown Attacks**: The attack described in this work was published in 2021 and introduces a new way to exploit the CAN bus, by employing vulnerabilities in the clock gating mechanism of microcontroller units (MCUs) to gain unauthorized access to the CAN bus. This attack was successfully tested on two lines of MCU brands used in automotive vehicles and was successful in executing remote shutdown attacks (Kulandaivel et al., 2021). This attack involves using the *Peripheral Clock Gating* functionality, which is accessible via software control in most modern automotive MCUs for performance optimization reasons. This allows a remote adversary to employ the CAN peripheral clock to bypass the hardware-based CAN protocol compliance and manipulate the ECU output (Kulandaivel et al., 2021). This feature enables the adversary to inject *arbitrary* bits and signals, where previous attacks were usually required to inject complete CAN compliant frames, giving this attack the ability to shape the signals very precisely on the CAN bus with bit-level accuracy. The authors demonstrate the capabilities of their novel approach to attacking the CAN bus by shutting down several well-known and common MCUs used by the automotive industry in a laboratory setting, and successfully shutting down two cars (2017 Ford Focus and 2009 Toyota Prius) (Kulandaivel et al., 2021). The authors state that the main insight to be drawn from this work is the ability to *control* the peripheral's clock signal to *pause* the ECU state in the middle of a transmission or between state transitions. Leveraging the ability to pause and resume an ECU's transmission enables the insertion of arbitrary bits for a duration and time instance of the adversary's choice. This fine control over malicious bit insertion makes detection of CANnon attacks very difficult for current implementations of IDS systems where entire messages are typically analysed for signs of malicious activity (Kulandaivel et al., 2021). The attack described in this case study was focused on precise control of malicious bit injection to be as stealthy as possible, ideally not detected by any of the modern IDS security solutions used in the automotive industry (Kulandaivel et al., 2021). Due to this, the authors did not execute the initial remote exploitation step of the attack and initiated their attack assuming that an ECU had already been compromised, citing a number of previous case studies where remote attacks were carried out where the initial breach of ECUs was conducted (Keen Security Lab, n.d.-b, n.d.-a; Miller & Valasek, 2015; Nie et al., n.d.).

Figure 5. Two part approach to the CANnon attack

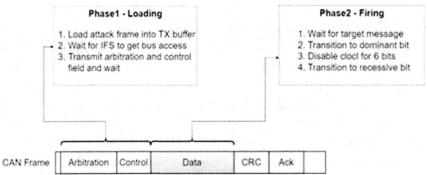

The attack detailed in this case study consists of two phases, the *Loading* phase, and the *Firing* phase. A representation of these two phases is depicted in Figure 5. An explanation of the two phases of the attack follows:

- **Loading Phase:** The main objective of the loading phase is to trick the compromised ECU into thinking that it is allowed to transmit on the bus in preparation for the firing phase. After loading an attack frame into the compromised ECU peripheral transmit buffer, the adversary must wait for the compromised ECU to win the bus. In this attack, the adversary waits for the conclusion of the arbitration phase and the transmission of the control bits, before pausing the clock during the first payload bit. At this point, the adversary is ready to start the firing phase (Kulandaivel et al., 2021).

- **Firing Phase**: The main objective of this phase is to convert a single dominant bit into an active error flag, which will overwrite the recessive bits of the victim message. After waiting for a victim message to appear on the network and for the next periodic transmission, the adversary wins bus arbitration. After bus arbitration is won, the adversary may overwrite the recessive bit, which causes the victim to detect an error, which increments the error counter by 8. After an error is detected, the victim will attempt to retransmit the failed frame, whereby the adversary repeats the firing phase until the error counter reaches the shutdown threshold (256) and enters the bus-off state (Kulandaivel et al., 2021).

The presented case studies do not especially propose any countermeasures for the vulnerabilities they exploit, merely serving as a proof-of-concept as to what is possible to execute in CAN bus systems and suggesting that additional research for defending the CAN bus system is necessary. The authors of the first case study suggested a form of TLS for message encryption and authentication, but the automotive industry responded that it was impractical since they had not been able to successfully implement a TCP stack on their systems (Kulandaivel et al., 2021).

To solve the problems presented by these case studies and other attacks, several solutions were introduced, among which specialized IDS for CAN bus systems.

INTRUSION DETECTION SYSTEMS IN AUTOMOTIVE CAN

As alluded previously, the CAN bus system is one of the most widely used protocols in automotive vehicles, but it has some security vulnerabilities. One of the most effective methods of addressing this problem is the deployment of IDS solutions (Lokman et al., 2019).

IDS solutions are implemented in CAN bus systems to attempt to address any attacks described in the previous section, employing methods of detection that will be expanded in the following subsection.

Types of IDS

The IDS deployed in automotive systems could be grouped in a few categories based on the detection methods employed (Tomlinson et al., 2018a).

- **Signature Based**: This method relies on detecting known attacks, the attack pattern is stored in a database and used to monitor the messages in the system. If they match a known pattern of attack, they are handled by the IDS as configured. This method has several advantages such as the relatively low requirement of processing power and low false positive rates. A major disadvantage of this method is that, since it relies on known signatures, any new attack or modification of a known attack may be enough to bypass it (Tomlinson et al., 2018a). Some examples of this method are Jin et al. (2021) and Studnia et al. (2018).

- **Statistical**: This method employs comparisons of the current statistical state to known baselines such as the mean, median and mode. The method can employ both univariate and multivariate techniques, depending on the implementation. Some of the advantages of this method are that the memory requirements are low, and it requires no prior knowledge of the systems normal activity, and it can also identify long-term attacks. The disadvantages are that this method is susceptible to being retrained by the attacker and setting the baselines themselves can be difficult (Tomlinson et al., 2018a). Some examples of this method can be found in Ling & Feng (2012) and Gmiden et al. (2017).

- **Knowledge Based**: This method deduces a set of rules from the data set that is studied. Events are then classified against these rules, if the data set is comprehensive enough, this method has an excellent capture rate and a very low number of false positives. Some disadvantages of this method lie in the difficulty of developing the knowledge base itself, and the IDS maintenance required (Tomlinson et al., 2018a). Some examples of this method are Marchetti & Stabili (2017) and Studnia et al. (2018).

- **Clustering or Density Based**: A machine learning approach, this method employs clustering of machine learning (ML) techniques that assume that instances of a data class can be profiled into clusters around an archetype. Each new instance can be then compared to the archetype. Some advantages of this method are that it is rather simple and understandable for machine learning deployments. Some disadvantages are that it can be very processing and memory intensive, and the time for classification operations may increase significantly with the number of neighbours (Tomlinson et al., 2018a). Some examples of this method can be consulted in Martinelli et al. (2017) and Tomlinson et al. (2018b).

- **Support Vector Machines**: Another ML approach, where Support Vector Machines (SVMs) separate classes using a hyperplane that follows the centre of the largest margin between classes, the instances on the edge of each class become support vectors. This method has the advantage of not being memory intensive, and that it can deal with high dimensional data and small samples. Some disadvantages of this method are the resource hungry training required, and that this method is prone to false positives (Tomlinson et al., 2018a). An example of this method can be observed in Taylor, Japkowicz, and Leblanc (2016).

- **Neural Networks**: Another ML approach, this method was inspired in the neural networks of the brain, and it consists of multiple nodes processing data until a decision is reached based on collective output. The functioning of this method is determined by the structure and the approach the solution the implementation decides to take. Advantages of this method are the high adaptability to environment changes and the ability to ignore potential noise occurring in the system. Some disadvantages are the high processing requirements, it being prone to false positives, and the lack of a descriptive model accounting for the decisions that are taken (Tomlinson et al., 2018a). Some examples of this method can be consulted in Kang & Kang (2016) and Taylor, Leblanc, Japkowicz (2016).

- **Hidden Markov Models**: Another ML approach, this method attempts to predict the future state of a system considering its current state, although they cannot be applied in a situation where the future state of a system is independent of the actual state, they can be effective in CAN bus scenarios. Advantages of this approach lie in it being used extensively in IDS already and its relatively low memory requirement. A disadvantage of this method is that the results of this method depend on assumptions about the system behaviour (Tomlinson et al., 2018a). An example of this method can be seen in Narayanan et al. (2016).

IDS Deployment in CAN

The types of IDS mentioned in the previous subsection can be deployed in many locations of the CAN bus system.

In the architecture seen in Figure 6, there are three locations for possible IDS implementations. Location A is on a bus shared by multiple gateways, in location B, the IDS are built-in on an already deployed gateway, and in location C, the IDS is deployed in a distributed manner, across several small modules in the network (Studnia et al., 2018). Although the example refers to an architecture example, these implementation locations can be applied across a multitude of CAN solutions.

Figure 6. Possible IDS implementation locations

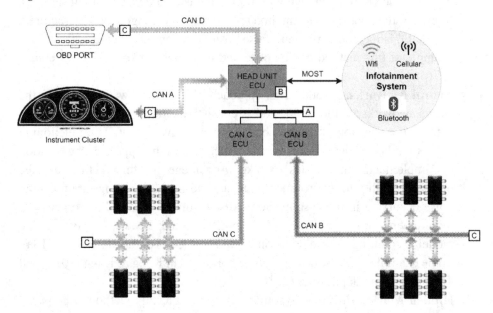

Case Studies

This subsection presents some case studies of IDS solutions, starting with a proposed framework for IDS implementation, followed by a few proposed solutions in academic environments.

Framework Proposal

The first case study presented is a framework proposal for CAN bus attack detection, CANADF, that was published in 2020. This framework serves as a comprehensive anomaly generation, detection, and evaluation system for a CAN bus (Tariq, Lee, Kim, et al., 2020). To achieve this purpose, the authors of this framework developed new approaches to detecting attacks on the CAN bus that are ensemble-based. These methods allow for combining several base models to produce one optimal predictive model. The authors also built a visualization tool to allow both drivers and operators to be informed about the state of the system.

This framework was not tested in real-world conditions but was evaluated on datasets from real-world sources, namely, KIA and Hyundai automotive data. The reported experimental results the authors achieved with their approach were promising, namely 99.45% accuracy rating, which is a substantial increase compared to the OTIDS method (Lee et al., 2018), which has an accuracy rating of 83.3%.

This method employs mainly signature-based detection and Recurrent Neural Networks (RNN) to detect any attacks on the CAN bus. Regarding signature-based detection, the framework author's proposed methods to detect a number of attacks which use different CAN packet characteristics:

- **DoS Attack:** To detect DoS attacks, the authors focus on capturing the features of inter-arrival time of the packet, since an attacker who intends to execute a DoS attack usually has to inject high priority packets in a short time frame. The implementation stored IDs that were sent at a higher rate than normal in a suspicious ID list and continued to monitor them. Should the behaviour persist for a certain time, it is considered a DoS attack.
- **Fuzzing Attack:** To detect fuzzing attacks the authors store the last few messages from each node ID and use those messages stored to calculate the similarity and distance between new data and the data in the stored message queue. If the message payload is larger than a certain distance, the ID is stored in a list of suspicious IDs. Should the behaviour persist, it is classified as a fuzzing attack.
- **Replay Attack:** Replay attacks tend to be more difficult to detect, since the message structure is very similar to normal packets and behaviours. The authors propose a method that considers two factors to add an ID to a suspicious ID list. The first factor leverages the fact that, in replay attacks, the replay attack packets and the normal packets will have the same IDs, which will cause some packet IDs to be adjacent to each other, which is a strong indication of the execution of a replay attack. The second factor measures the dissimilarity of the adjacent packets mentioned above, and, should the message payload distance be greater than a certain threshold, it is also considered an indicator of a replay attack. If both conditions are verified, the IDs are stored in a suspicious ID list, and should the behaviour persist or happen across a number of IDs, it is then considered to be a replay attack.

Regarding RNN detection, the authors developed a RNN in which the input is CAN packet sequences. The features selected in the input packets are time interval between packets, ID, DLC, and data payload. The network takes 40 consecutive CAN packets as a sequence with 11 features each. The output consists of five classes that can classify an attack from normal behaviour, DoS, fuzzing, replay, and other class (Tariq, Lee, Kim, et al., 2020).

The results generated by both methods are then used in an ensemble method to combine and choose the best result from two different detection methods. This was considered advantageous due to the authors' assumption that both approaches would be better at detecting different types of attack classes (Tariq, Lee, Kim, et al., 2020).

IDS Implementations

- **Simple intrusion detection method for CAN**: The Boudguiga et al. (2016) work, published in 2016, proposes a detection method where legitimate ECUs detect attacks on the CAN bus. The work authors assume that each ECU will be fitted with a Hardware Security Module (HSM), which serves as a security processor, dedicated for cryptographic computation and secure key storage. The authors also state that the reason for their assumption is that virtually any modern ECU already contains an HSM. The proposed method works by capitalizing on HSM features to extend CAN message frames to allow for ECU authentication with trusted keys, which defeats many of the known attacks on the CAN bus. The intrusion detection method proposed by the authors of this paper uses their proposed extended CAN frame, where each ECU checks that the received data frame contains one of its produced frame identifiers. If a data frame does not contain the required fields, the ECU detects a malicious entity on the network. The ECU erases the attacker frame with an Error frame, and subsequently sends a Domain_Violation frame, part of their expanded CAN message frames to the network. These Domain_Violation frames contain a counter value that is verified against a certain threshold. Should the counter value exceed the threshold, measures are taken to limit attempts at unauthorized access on the ECUs and the driver is notified that the vehicle has been attacked and should be driven to a garage so the origin of the intrusion can be determined (Boudguiga et al., 2016).

- **An entropy-based IDS for CAN in vehicles**: Wang et al. (2019) proposed an IDS methodology that leverages the CAN arbitration protocol where bit 0 is dominant and bit 1 is recessive, hence bit 0 will have greater priority. The authors approach the problem by analysing for entropy changes at the bit level, which enabled the development of a fast algorithm to detect malicious identifiers in CAN message frames. Upon detection of these malicious frames, the system discards them. The first step in the entropy detection scheme that the authors propose is the collection of data during normal driving to generate a template of normal behaviour. Most messages on the CAN bus are periodic, hence the distribution of entropy should be steady during normal driving. The authors proposed a binary entropy vector with 11 bits, where the golden template is calculated by averaging 35 measurements from diverse driving behaviours. For detection, the binary entropy is compared with the template bit by bit, if the bit change is above a certain threshold, the CAN bus can be considered to be under attack, and the system will send an alert signal to the driver

- **SAIDuCANT**: Olufowobi et al. (2020) proposes intrusion detection methods that extract real-time model parameters by monitoring the message behaviour on CAN bus, without prior knowledge, and a specification-based detection method based on real-time response time of the CAN bus. This paper is an extension of the authors previous work and seeks to improve classification accuracy. The implementation of this IDS works by monitoring the bus and calculating an interval of possible values that bounds the valid completion time of each message instance. This calculation is based on a number of factors, such as learned parameters, the RTA model as a specification, and on the history of observations of messages that have been transmitted on the bus since it was last idle. A message is considered anomalous if the completion time violates the acceptable interval defined by the specification of its real--time parameters (Olufowobi et al., 2020).

- **CANTransfer**: Tariq, Lee, & Woo (2020) proposes an IDS solution that employs convolution LSTM models to accurately classify network intrusions in the CAN bus. This method also accounts for previously unknown attacks by employing one–shot transfer learning methods to retrain the model to detect new attacks. According to the authors, the reported accuracy of this method for known attacks is 95.25% and for previously unknown attacks 88.47%, both of which were superior to the baseline models the authors used for control. The core component of the IDS approach proposed by the authors uses multivariate Convolutional LSTM (ConvLSTM). By learning from both normal and abnormal data, it is possible to predict normal and abnormal sequences effectively through transfer learning. The model used by this approach is initially trained with known intrusions, and then transfer learns to new intrusions, in the experimental results section of this case study, the authors initially introduced DoS attacks, and then used transfer learning to detect both fuzzing and replay attacks. The core parameters behind the detection of anomalous behaviour in the network are packet--arrival timeline, IDs, DLC, and Data values.

CONCLUSION

Controller Area Networks revolutionized how communication in vehicles was conducted, but they were designed with fault–tolerance in mind, not security. With the increasing communication capabilities of modern automotive systems, robust security is vital to prevent potential catastrophic consequences to material and human resources.

Deploying IDS is an efficient method of addressing the problem, but with the ever-growing computerization of vehicles, so do the potential attack surfaces and vulnerabilities in their systems. This chapter describes this problem and reviews ongoing research. But as the advent of the fully autonomous vehicle approaches, new security challenges will arrive, and more research and investment will be required both academically and industrially.

ACKNOWLEDGMENT

This work was funded by Portuguese national funds through FCT (Foundation for Science and Technology) under the Scientific Employment Stimulus Institutional Call CEECINST/00051/2018 and in the context of the project UIDB/04524/2020.

REFERENCES

Bace, R., & Mell, P. (2001). NIST special publication on intrusion detection systems. In Nist Special Publication.

Boudguiga, A., Klaudel, W., Boulanger, A., & Chiron, P. (2016). A simple intrusion detection method for controller area network. *2016 IEEE International Conference on Communications, ICC 2016*. IEEE. 10.1109/ICC.2016.7511098

Bozdal, M., Samie, M., Aslam, S., & Jennions, I. (2020). Evaluation of can bus security challenges. In Sensors (Switzerland), 30(8). doi:10.339020082364

Carsten, P., Andel, T. R., Yampolskiy, M., & McDonald, J. T. (2015). In-Vehicle Networks. *Proceedings of the 10th Annual Cyber and Information Security Research Conference*, (pp. 1–8). ACM. doi:10.1145/2746266.2746267

Checkoway, S., McCoy, D., Kantor, B., Anderson, D., Shacham, H., Savage, S., Koscher, K., Czeskis, A., Roesner, F., & Kohno, T. (2011). Comprehensive experimental analyses of automotive attack surfaces. *Proceedings of the 20th USENIX Security Symposium*. USENIX.

di Natale, M., Zeng, H., Giusto, P., & Ghosal, A. (2012). Understanding and using the controller area network communication protocol: Theory and practice. In *Understanding and Using the Controller Area Network Communication Protocol. Theory and Practice.*, doi:10.1007/978-1-4614-0314-2

Gmiden, M., Gmiden, M. H., & Trabelsi, H. (2017). An intrusion detection method for securing in-vehicle CAN bus. *2016 17th International Conference on Sciences and Techniques of Automatic Control and Computer Engineering, STA 2016 - Proceedings*. IEEE. doi:10.1109/STA.2016.7952095

History of the CAN technology. (n.d.). CAN. Https://Www.Can-Cia.Org/Can-Knowledge/Can/Can-History/

ISO/TC 22/SC 31. (2006). *ISO 11898-3:2006: Road vehicles — Controller area network (CAN) — Part 3: Low-speed, fault-tolerant, medium-dependent interface*. ISO 11898-3:2006.

ISO/TC 22/SC 31. (2015). *ISO 11898-1:2015: Road vehicles -- Controller area network (CAN) -- Part 1: Data link layer and physical signaling*. In ISO 11898-1:2015.

ISO/TC 22/SC 31. (2016). *ISO 11898-2:2016: Road vehicles — Controller area network (CAN) — Part 2: High-speed medium access unit*. ISO 11898-2:2016.

Jin, S., Chung, J. G., & Xu, Y. (2021). Signature-based intrusion detection system (IDS) for in-vehicle CAN bus network. *Proceedings - IEEE International Symposium on Circuits and Systems, 2021-May*. IEEE. doi:10.1109/ISCAS51556.2021.9401087

Jo, H. J., & Choi, W. (2021). A Survey of Attacks on Controller Area Networks and Corresponding Countermeasures. *IEEE Transactions on Intelligent Transportation Systems*. doi:10.1109/TITS.2021.3078740

Kang, M. J., & Kang, J. W. (2016). Intrusion detection system using deep neural network for in-vehicle network security. *PLoS One*, *11*(6), e0155781. doi:10.1371/journal.pone.0155781 PMID:27271802

Koscher, K., Czeskis, A., Roesner, F., Patel, S., Kohno, T., Checkoway, S., McCoy, D., Kantor, B., Anderson, D., Snachám, H., & Savage, S. (2010). Experimental security analysis of a modern automobile. *Proceedings - IEEE Symposium on Security and Privacy*. IEEE. 10.1109/SP.2010.34

Kulandaivel, S., Jain, S., Guajardo, J., & Sekar, V. (2021). CANNON: Reliable and stealthy remote shutdown attacks via unaltered automotive microcontrollers. *Proceedings – IEEE Symposium on Security and Privacy, 2021-May*. IEEE. doi:10.1109/SP40001.2021.00122

Le, V. H., den Hartog, J., & Zannone, N. (2018). Security and privacy for innovative automotive applications: A survey. *Computer Communications*, *132*, 17–41. doi:10.1016/j.comcom.2018.09.010

Lee, H., Jeong, S. H., & Kim, H. K. (2018). OTIDS: A novel intrusion detection system for in-vehicle network by using remote frame. *Proceedings - 2017 15th Annual Conference on Privacy, Security and Trust, PST 2017*. IEEE. doi:10.1109/PST.2017.00017

Liao, H. J., Richard Lin, C. H., Lin, Y. C., & Tung, K. Y. (2013). Intrusion detection system: A comprehensive review. In Journal of Network and Computer Applications, 36(1). doi:10.1016/j.jnca.2012.09.004

Ling, C., & Feng, D. (2012). An algorithm for detection of malicious messages on CAN buses. *Proceedings of the 2012 National Conference on Information Technology and Computer Science, CITCS 2012*. Springer. 10.2991/citcs.2012.161

Lokman, S.-F., Othman, A. T., & Abu-Bakar, M.-H. (2019). Intrusion detection system for automotive Controller Area Network (CAN) bus system: A review. *EURASIP Journal on Wireless Communications and Networking*, *2019*(1), 184. doi:10.118613638-019-1484-3

Lynch, K. M., Marchuk, N., & Elwin, M. L. (2016). Chapter 21. Sensors. Embedded Computing and Mechatronics with the PIC32.

Marchetti, M., & Stabili, D. (2017). Anomaly detection of CAN bus messages through analysis of ID sequences. *IEEE Intelligent Vehicles Symposium, Proceedings*. IEEE. 10.1109/IVS.2017.7995934

Martinelli, F., Mercaldo, F., Nardone, V., & Santone, A. (2017). Car hacking identification through fuzzy logic algorithms. *IEEE International Conference on Fuzzy Systems*. IEEE. 10.1109/FUZZ-IEEE.2017.8015464

Matvej Yli-Olli. (2019). *Machine Learning for Secure Vehicular Communication: an Empirical Study*. Aalto University.

Miller, C., & Valasek, C. (2015). Remote Exploitation of an Unaltered Passenger Vehicle. *Defcon*, *23*, 2015.

Narayanan, S. N., Mittal, S., & Joshi, A. (2016). OBD-SecureAlert: An Anomaly Detection System for Vehicles. *2016 IEEE International Conference on Smart Computing, SMARTCOMP 2016*. IEEE. 10.1109/SMARTCOMP.2016.7501710

Olufowobi, H., Young, C., Zambreno, J., & Bloom, G. (2020). SAIDuCANT: Specification-Based Automotive Intrusion Detection Using Controller Area Network (CAN) Timing. *IEEE Transactions on Vehicular Technology*, *69*(2), 1484–1494. doi:10.1109/TVT.2019.2961344

Sharma, O., & Bhargav, P. A. (n.d.). *Controller area network*.

Studnia, I., Alata, E., Nicomette, V., Kaâniche, M., & Laarouchi, Y. (2018). A language-based intrusion detection approach for automotive embedded networks. *International Journal of Embedded Systems, 10*(1), 89430. doi:10.1504/IJES.2018.089430

Tariq, S., Lee, S., Kim, H. K., & Woo, S. S. (2020). CAN-ADF: The controller area network attack detection framework. *Computers & Security, 94*, 101857. Advance online publication. doi:10.1016/j.cose.2020.101857

Tariq, S., Lee, S., & Woo, S. S. (2020). CANTransfer: Transfer learning based intrusion detection on a controller area network using convolutional LSTM network. *Proceedings of the ACM Symposium on Applied Computing.* ACM. 10.1145/3341105.3373868

Taylor, A., Japkowicz, N., & Leblanc, S. (2016). Frequency-based anomaly detection for the automotive CAN bus. *2015 World Congress on Industrial Control Systems Security, WCICSS 2015.* IEEE. doi:10.1109/WCICSS.2015.7420322

Taylor, A., Leblanc, S., & Japkowicz, N. (2016). Anomaly detection in automobile control network data with long short-term memory networks. *Proceedings - 3rd IEEE International Conference on Data Science and Advanced Analytics, DSAA 2016.* IEEE. 10.1109/DSAA.2016.20

Tomlinson, A., Bryans, J., & Shaikh, S. A. (2018a). Towards Viable Intrusion Detection Methods For The Automotive Controller Area Network. *Proceedings of the 2nd ACM Computer Science in Cars Symposium,* 9. ACM.

Tomlinson, A., Bryans, J., & Shaikh, S. A. (2018b). Using a one-class compound classifier to detect in-vehicle network attacks. *GECCO 2018 Companion - Proceedings of the 2018 Genetic and Evolutionary Computation Conference Companion.* doi:10.1145/3205651.3208223

Wang, Q., Lu, Z., & Qu, G. (2019). An Entropy Analysis Based Intrusion Detection System for Controller Area Network in Vehicles. *International System on Chip Conference, 2018-September.* doi:10.1109/SOCC.2018.8618564

Wu, W., Li, R., Xie, G., An, J., Bai, Y., Zhou, J., & Li, K. (2020). A Survey of Intrusion Detection for In-Vehicle Networks. *IEEE Transactions on Intelligent Transportation Systems, 21*(3), 919–933. doi:10.1109/TITS.2019.2908074

Young, C., Zambreno, J., Olufowobi, H., & Bloom, G. (2019). Survey of Automotive Controller Area Network Intrusion Detection Systems. *IEEE Design & Test, 36*(6), 48–55. doi:10.1109/MDAT.2019.2899062

Chapter 5
Intelligent Transportation Systems Security and Privacy

Guilherme Santo
ESTG, Polytechnic of Leiria, Portugal

Leonel Santos
https://orcid.org/0000-0002-6883-7996
CIIC, ESTG, Polytechnic of Leiria, Portugal

Rogério L. C. Costa
https://orcid.org/0000-0003-2306-7585
CIIC, Polytechnic of Leiria, Portugal

Carlos Rabadão
https://orcid.org/0000-0001-7332-4397
CIIC, ESTG, Polytechnic of Leiria, Portugal

ABSTRACT

Intelligent transportation systems are an area that have been in discussion for a lot of time, more precisely since in the 90's. With the advances in technology, it has been possible to start implementing this type of system, which brings a lot of benefits to people's lives; like, for example, making their road trips more secure and efficient. It also helps the environment, due to people spending less time in transit, and is a system that complements the emerging industry of smart cities. It all sounds good, except when it comes to security and privacy. This chapter will present these systems and their security and privacy concerns, including vulnerabilities that can be exploited if the due measures are not considered and implemented, which are even harder to obey because of privacy regulations like the general data protection regulation (GDPR).

DOI: 10.4018/978-1-6684-5991-1.ch005

INTRODUCTION

Intelligent transportation systems (ITS) strive to improve mobility, comfort, safety and efficiency by integrating sensing, control, analysis and communication technologies into travel infrastructure and transportation. Automobile makers are always developing new models. The sensation of travel, like accident warning, best route calculation, trip efficiency and comfort are changing because vehicles, roadways and infrastructures are starting to become more connected and exchange data in real-time between each other due to the use of ITS technology. With a variety of unique technologies and ITS research and development, travel is becoming more efficient and reliable. Every year, safer vehicles are developed with greater regard for passenger and pedestrian safety; nonetheless, the new technology and increased connectivity in ITS provide malicious actors with unique attack vectors. The data generated about passengers and their travel habits in smart cities with connected public transportation systems raises significant privacy concerns.

As transportation systems become more integrated with loosely secured devices and apps, attackers will have more opportunity to exploit them. Attacks on ITS have physical consequences, including infrastructure damage, delays in emergency response, casualties, and even concerns to national security. Risk assessments for ITS (Krivolapova, 2017) have been carried out and risk models have been constructed (Inkoom et al., 2020) due to the likelihood of substantial physical and personal damage. However, many of these models still contain unanswered problems, necessitating further research. With such dangers, the creation of a secure and privacy conscious ITS framework is required to secure the safety and privacy of people around the world.

This chapter starts off by giving an overview on what ITS are, so that further information can be given in the topic, making the context easier to understand, which makes up for the following section. In the third section, many security issues on the various layers of the network are presented, besides attacker models and types of attacks that can occur. The following section refers to the importance of privacy and how it can be corrupted in the current ITS. The fifth section points out some challenges that cannot be ignored when trying to solve current security problems. Some examples of solutions will be illustrated in the sixth section. Then, the final section concludes the chapter.

INTELLIGENT TRANSPORTATION SYSTEMS

Intelligent transportation system (ITS) is a sophisticated system that aims to provide revolutionary services related to various modes of transportation and traffic management, allowing users to be better informed and make safer, more coordinated, and 'smarter' use of transportation networks. Some of these technologies include emergency callouts in the event of an accident, the use of cameras to police traffic laws, and signs that indicate speed limit changes based on conditions (Dimitrakopoulos & Demestichas, 2010).

Types of ITS

ITS applications are broadly classified into three categories (Lishchenko, 2021), those being Mobility, Safety, and Environment.

Firstly, the Mobility ITS try to give the shortest route between origin-destination pairings in a data-rich travel environment, considering aspects such as distance, time, energy consumption, and so on. By altering traffic signals, dynamically regulating transit operations, or summoning emergency maintenance services, these programs can help monitor and manage transportation system performance (Mangiaracina et al., 2017).

When it comes to Safety ITS, they offer advice and warnings, safety applications help to reduce collisions. Vehicle safety applications and emergency management are examples of these uses. For example, a safety Intelligent Transport System can issue a speed warning on a slick (Janušová & Čičmancová, 2016).

The Environment ITS provide instant traffic data which can assist in making informed decisions, reducing the environmental effect of day-to-day trips. It is feasible to avoid traffic congestion by taking different routes or rescheduling journeys, making them more environmental (Balasubramaniam et al., 2017).

Intelligent Transportation Systems are also classed based on where they are located. As a result, Intelligent Transportation Systems can be found both outside and indoors. Indoor systems are those that are installed within the vehicle and transmit information to the driver. Most outdoor systems are positioned above the road.

Why ITS are Needed

To improve their transportation networks, many countries choose to deploy Intelligent Transport Systems. India, for instance, is one of the largest countries in the world and has mobility problems and issues in urban areas, so it can benefit largely on having an ITS implemented (Chand & Karthikeyan, 2018). An Intelligent Transportation System is required for a variety of reasons (Lishchenko, 2021), as discussed in the next paragraphs.

For starters, an Intelligent Transport System allows us to track and manage the performance of the road network in real time. Furthermore, data traditionally collected by expensive physical infrastructure can now be delivered via new data sources such as webcams. Intelligent Transportation Systems can conduct analysis based on historical data using real-time data analytics for Intelligent Transportation Systems. Road users' decisions can increasingly be impacted by a variety of media, including mobile devices and in-car systems. Intelligent Transportation Systems can also benefit a variety of stakeholders.

Traffic congestion is one of the main issues that Intelligent Transportation Systems aim to solve. According to Cheng et al. (2020), the United States deployed a large federally supported ITS between the years of 1994 and 2014 and the results estimate that the adoption of 511 Systems is linked to a substantial reduction in traffic congestion, resulting in yearly savings of approximately $4.7 billion and 175 million hours of travel time in U.S. cities. With this we can conclude that ITS play a crucial role in reducing road traffic.

Furthermore, in terms of accessibility of transportation, not only the elderly but also people with disabilities such as visual loss and audio impairment can struggle to access public transportation. In accordance with a report published by the United States Department of Transportation (Greer et al., 2018), there are several examples of the success of ITS in enhancing the accessibility of transportation. For example, in Williamsport, Pennsylvania, River Valley Transit (provider of public bus transportation) provides client information in real-time at its transit hub. With the purpose of giving customers real-time in-terminal information, River Valley Transit combines Automated Vehicle Location (AVL) with mobile data terminal technologies. Customers can see and hear the 10 loading bays that buses will be arriving and departing from thanks to the Traveler Information System (TIS). Additionally, it alerts clients 20 seconds before buses leave for their subsequent trip. The system even alerts drivers when they enter the incorrect bus bay. The TIS's successful implementation indicated a variety of advantages for clients. The transit agency improved accessibility for people with disabilities, including to the customer information systems, which feature visual and auditory announcements. The research team also found a number of benefits beyond those that are directly related to technology, namely increased community confidence (ITS deployments have the ability to increase community trust in the agency's capacity to run a reliable transportation network) and potential for increased ridership and revenue (ITS makes the transit service more appealing, which may lead to an increase in ridership and farebox revenue).

In the next subsection, a handful of real-world examples are provided, which further prove the point of why ITS are needed by showing the benefits of the implementation of those ITS's.

Real-World Examples

In this subsection, a couple more examples of real-world applications of ITS are provided (What Is ITS, 2019) (*City Circle Line*, 2022), in addition to the ones mentioned in the previous subsection:

- The Intelligent Transport System in Glasgow, Scotland, provides daily commuters with information about public buses, timings, seat availability, the current location of the bus, the time taken to reach a specific destination, the next location of the bus, and the density of passengers inside the bus on a regular basis.
- The Seoul government based the routes of its new night bus services on an examination of mobile phone location data collected at night. The city collaborated with private telecom providers to evaluate calls made between midnight and 5 a.m., then matched this data anonymously and in aggregate with invoicing addresses to estimate which routes would have higher demand for overnight services.
- The city of New Orleans has optimized the locations of its ambulances on standby, based on patterns of emergency calls.
- The highly anticipated Sydney Metro, Australia's biggest public transport project, is the first and currently the only city in Australia with a fully automated (driverless) rapid transit metro system.
- The Cityringen project in Copenhagen is a huge undertaking. It is the most advanced public transport system in Europe. Cityringen is a new circular urban line around the very center of the city. The new metro line that will help the city in its bid to become the greenest capital in the world. The new fully automated line is a driverless system operating 24/7 (non-stop) and has a peak frequency between trains of 100 seconds. It can be accessed by approximately 240,000 passengers a day. The trains on the line travel at an average speed of 40km/h.

SECURITY

ITS providers must be prepared for all types of attacks because an ITS has a variety of users who can produce data, send messages, and receive alarms. The following list of security threats and attacks existing in it is based on its model and security needs, which is similar to the 5-Layer Network model (Physical, Data Link, Network, Transport and Application), as well as the multiple-layer stacks in communication view of its (Ming et al., 2018):

- **Application layer**: message replay attacks, message modification attacks, malicious message attacks, and other attack methods such as man-in-the-middle, spoofing, sniffing, and denial of service should all be taken into account. The adversary uses a message replay attack to resend old messages that were originally sent by normal users in order to increase network traffic and generate congestion. The adversary, acting as a man-in-the-middle, modifies the communications and then sends them out to cause problems or mislead users. Malicious message attacks include malicious message attacks in Vehicle to Vehicle (V2V) and Road-side Units (RSU) to Vehicle (R2V) communication, in which the adversary delivers fake information to other nodes in the network, confusing users and perhaps causing chaos.

- **Transport and network layers**: the following communication-related threats should be considered: RSU forging, denial of service, foundational keys leak, and other communication disrupting attacks are all possible. Forging RSU attacks are used to obtain car node information and then disrupt vehicle networking connection. The goal of denial of service in the transport and network layers is to make network resources unavailable to their intended users by temporarily or permanently interrupting services in nodes connected to vehicle networking. Because master keys used in V2V, communication can be sniffed and manipulated by attackers, foundational keys leak is a threat.

- **Data link layer and physical layer**: physical damage, building obstruction, and energy disturbance should all be evaluated as signal and physical foundation dangers. Physical damage causes the RSU or sensors in the car to be physically broken or disorganized. Setting up an impediment, such as a structure or a wall, to block wireless signal communication of vehicle networking is known as creating an obstacle. The term "energy disturbing" refers to the use of energy and power control to disrupt wireless vehicle networking connectivity.

Man-in-the-middle attacks may compromise the confidentiality of ITS in the cases mentioned above. Sniffing may also jeopardize the integrity of its messages. Sniffing and spoofing may also affect its message non-repudiation. And its availability may be threatened by denial of service, physical attack, signal interruption, and energy disruption.

Aside from technical dangers, it faces numerous security management concerns, such as operation failure, personal security setting failure, key leakage due to vehicle loss, rental car exploitation, and so on.

With that said, in order to better protect these systems and increase their security, it is critical to understand the actual architecture of a typical ITS (Mangiaracina et al., 2017), which can be seen in Figure 1 (Mangiaracina et al., 2017).

Figure 1. Architecture of an Intelligent Transportation System

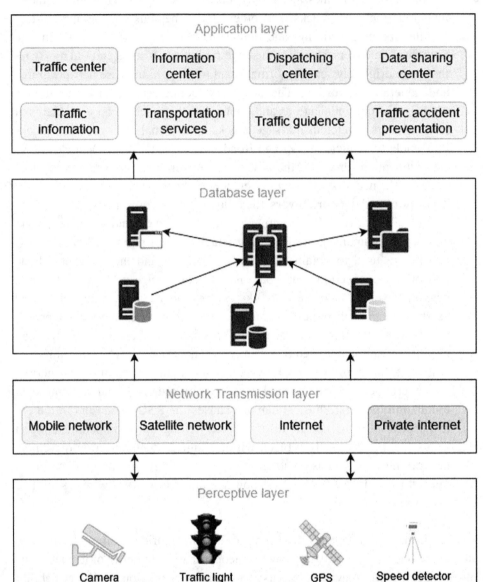

The Perceptive layer is the base layer. To achieve real-time capture of traffic information elements, car detectors, video, GPS, and other information collecting technologies are used. The ITS is built on it.

Then, there is the Network Transmission layer, which sends system and control management instructions as well as the upload of perceptual data using specialized equipment, such as base stations and public networks. It is responsible for the exchange of data between the Perceptive and Database layers.

Speaking of Database layer, this one is responsible for classifying, storing, and analyzing the underlying data and provides analytical results to the application layer.

Finally, there is the Application layer. It uses traffic information aggregation, fusion, intelligent disposal, information analysis and extraction, and distribution to analyze and process multi-source heterogeneous data. It also establishes perceptual linkage relationships between people and objects, and recognize the functions of vehicle dynamic guidance, path planning, and road network traffic management and control.

Attacker Models

Without the need for human involvement, ITS activities are totally managed by integrated software in the vehicle. If an attacker succeeds in remotely infiltrating the system, they will be able to operate the car. As a result, comprehending attack models is a prerequisite for developing effective schemes to forecast attacker behavior and fight their destructive activities. By examining probable attack characteristics (e.g., attack method and scope) and interactions of attackers with the system under attack, attackers are grouped into different classes (Lamssaggad et al., 2021) which are the following:

- **Active vs Passive:** Active attackers create malicious packets that are sent to other nodes, causing network disruption. These attackers typically have permission to operate within the network, allowing them to carry out nearly any type of attack, including DoS attacks, Sybil attacks (Yu, 2021), and blackhole wormholes. The features of passive attackers are the polar opposite of active attackers. They try to stealthily monitor and eavesdrop on network traffic in order to extract important information that may be used to plan future attacks; these attackers are usually outsiders who do not cause any immediate network damage, making them difficult to identify.
- **External vs Internal**: External or outsider attackers attack from the outside of the network; they are not authorized to operate within it. In general, they are restricted in the types of attacks they may carry out. To operate within the network, they must effectively evade system defenses such as firewalls and Intrusion Detection Systems (IDS). Internal attackers, on the other hand, are mostly legitimate users or members of the network; as a result, they have access to basic network resources based on their access privilege. Due to their capacity to carry out nearly any type of assault aimed at the

system's confidentiality, availability, and integrity, these attackers can inflict significant damage.

- **Local vs. Extended**: Local attackers operate on a small scale, only attacking adjacent vehicles or RSUs. Extended attackers broaden the reach of their attacks, which can be carried out from any location via the internet; in this scenario, the attackers' physical location is unimportant.
- **Malicious vs. Rational**: Malicious attackers' primary purpose is to disrupt and harm the network without regard for the repercussions. Typically, these kinds of attackers aren't looking for any personal gain from their attacks. Rational attackers, on the other hand, can be more harmful by launching attacks against specific victims in order to draw attention and maximize their gains.

Types of Attacks

It is important to identify threat actors for ITS. Intelligence from other nations, criminal gangs, hacktivists, cyberterrorists, insiders, unscrupulous operators, and natural disasters are all described as potential attackers to ITS. The following paragraphs reference the most common attacks.

A typical type of attack on most systems are the DDoS attacks (Haydari & Yilmaz, 2018), and in ITS they are no exceptions. This attack causes systems to crash and cause chaos. It can also be used to convey political messages, protests, or pranks. This could harm the company's reputation as well as cause financial loss. If a fake V2V communication is sent, it might cause traffic pandemonium. This attack has the potential to cause V2V information poisoning. Location transmitters, GPS receivers, and GPS signal spoofing can all be hacked using map hacking.

One of the most deadly and serious type of attacks in ITS are classified as Revenge and Terrorism (Huq et al., 2017). The ability to drive can be hacked and utilized as a weapon. It is extremely difficult to predict and fight against these types of attacks. By dumping sensitive data online, traffic flow management mechanisms can be interrupted, ITS safety systems can be disabled, roadside emergency alert systems can be triggered, and a company's operations and employees' privacy can be jeopardized. Hacking ITS systems is usually done with the intention of leveraging it as a point of entry into the ITS ecosystem. An attack on the ITS system that is connected via the internet or Virtual Private Networks (VPN) grants access to the ITS ecosystem. With minimal effort, you can gain access to the deepest parts of the network. Attacks can be launched from inside the network when an attacker has access to the network.

Another common type of attack is System Gaming and Theft (Harvey & Kumar, 2020), which involves stealing items from inside vehicles or stealing the vehicle in its entirety. It is also possible to avoid paying fees and service charges by using ITS systems. Autonomous vehicles can be hacked and rerouted to a remote place, or they can be utilized to covertly convey contraband. Autonomous automobiles can be hacked and sent to a distant location, where valuables, vehicle parts, or the entire vehicle can be stolen or abducted. Using an ITS system to avoid paying service costs is possible. Using a remote activator, Mobile Infrared Transmitters (MIRT) can modify a traffic signal controlled by a computer. To disrupt competition and make vehicles inaccessible, a competitor's car might be hacked. A situation could arise in which autonomous vehicles must make way for a hacked vehicle with a high priority. It is possible to place fictitious ridesharing orders in order to defraud unwary clients.

The ITS infrastructure is exposed on the roadways, which leads to Physical attacks (van der Heijden et al., 2018) being easily conducted. Physical connections can be made to exposed ports. Using brute force or guessing credentials, a device can be accessed. Scanning a secured or closed network might reveal topology. Deleted files can jeopardize an ITS device or system. To recover credentials and configurations, firmware can be installed. Man-in-the-middle attacks use exposed wiring or cables to intercept traffic and relay bogus data to backend systems. Data can be stolen or compromised by tampering with a device. Malware can be installed from a removable storage device. Incorrect commands can be transmitted to the controller and backend systems. By using an ITS device as a trusted entry point, the corporate network can be accessed. Software flaws can be taken advantage of. Trusted operators' abuse of authority can also compromise or tamper with devices.

Wireless Networks attacks (Buinevich & Vladyko, 2019) pose a major IT security threat to an ITS infrastructure. Spoofing messages, sniffing wireless transmissions, remotely transmitting and installing malicious firmware, electronically jamming wireless transmissions and vehicle safety systems, man-in-the-middle attacks to intercept and modify data, vulnerabilities can be exploited, and Wi-Fi can be used to gain access to the Controller Area Network (CAN) bus and the on-board diagnostics, infotainment, and telematics control Remote hijacking of the CAN bus is possible, and malicious third-party software can be loaded.

Besides Wireless attacks, Wired Network attacks may also occur (Buinevich & Vladyko, 2019). These attacks are a risk because ITS systems are exposed to the Internet and discoverable on IoT search engines making them vulnerable to cyberattacks. Misconfigurations of devices are discovered and exploited. Software and hardware flaws are taken advantage of. The system can be detected and abused from afar. On systems, malware and/or spyware can be installed. State-sponsored targeted attacks and advanced persistent threats are both plausible. It is possible to upload and install malicious firmware. On the ITS infrastructure and backend servers that are open to the internet, Distributed Denial of Service (DDoS) assaults can be launched. Advertisements can be injected with malicious script. Cross-site Scripting (XSS), in which a malicious script is introduced into the network, is one of the threats to ITS. In the corporate network, ITS devices can be reconfigured as trusted access points. Trusted operators have the potential to abuse their power and compromise systems or devices. A third-party contractor's computer can be hacked and used to get access to the corporate network.

Finally, the VANET Attacks (Zheng et al., 2017). Vehicular Ad hoc Networks (VANETs) are vulnerable to attacks that can affect roadway safety. Sybil attacks are one of the most damaging and hardest attacks to detect. They involve a vehicle that appears to have multiple identities. It is impossible to tell whether the data received from this car is from a single vehicle or numerous vehicles. Attackers exploit this to reshape the network to suit their objectives. A DDoS attack occurs when a system receives more requests than it can manage, overloading and crashing it. When communications are collected and held to be broadcasted later to deceive other cars in the network when the message is no longer valid or genuine, this is known as a replay attack. This form of attack mimics and exploits the circumstances that existed at the time the original communication was received. When an attacker monitors the network to track vehicular movement or listen to communications in automobiles, this is known as passive eavesdropping. Messages are intercepted and analyzed by attacker vehicles. In order to be employed in future attacks, information about the vehicles and communication patterns is obtained.

PRIVACY

Like security, one of the key human rights is privacy that needs to be preserved. Privacy of a user in ITS is a crucial issue (Ali et al., 2018). Vehicle theft, life threats, and other damages, such as stealing at home or at work, can all be linked to the privacy issue in ITS. Identity is used in ITS to achieve communication authenticity. If genuine identities are utilized, however, the attacker can trace the user's path, including the start and end points of their drive. As a result, an attacker can gather a user's daily routine information. If the opponent has its user confidential information, he or she will be able to determine the user's schedule. For example, when the user is at home, at work, or somewhere else. An adversary can accuse fraud/theft or even put a user's life at stake by storing this information. As a result, privacy-preserving solutions must be developed in order to ensure that the private information of its users does not fall into the hands of an enemy.

For ITS, privacy is a critical factor to consider. Privacy concerns are divided into three areas (Hahn et al., 2021) in this section: identity privacy, behavioral privacy, and location privacy (Ometov et al., 2019).

Identity Privacy

The privacy of a driver, traveler, passenger, pedestrian, or participant's real-world identification is referred to as identity privacy in the context of ITS. This could be their first and last name, driver's license number, or vehicle identification number, for example. Recent research in VANETs has pushed for the use of pseudonyms, also known as pseudo-IDs, as a substitute for tying real-world identities to VANET vehicles. The potential of pseudonyms to protect the link between message broadcasts in VANETs that include safety information, such as vehicle position, and the identity of the sender of these messages has been demonstrated in research. However, research has revealed that when employing basic pseudonym implementations, hostile actors can still track specific automobiles. As a result, pseudonym research in VANETs has progressed to include more innovative methods to when and how a vehicle's pseudonym should be changed.

Attribute-based credentials have been offered as an alternative to utilizing pseudonyms for privacy-preserving identification. Users can authenticate to verifiers using privacy enhancing attribute-based credentials, which ensure that users are not linked between authentication events and only reveal the qualities from their credentials that are relevant to the verifier. However, attributed-based credentials have high resource requirements and also necessitate creation of shared secrets/ attributes for all desired services. In short, there exists a tradeoff between preserving privacy of ITS participants and providing security service of non-repudiation, which is needed to correctly identify users of the system in cases of vehicular accidents and/or crimes.

Behavioral Privacy

With so much precise information about users in ITS, ranging from financial information to location information to user habits within the system, there is a huge risk of invading people's behavioral privacy. Behavioral privacy in the context of ITS refers to the protection of data that characterizes various elements of a group or individual, as well as their actions within ITS. To maintain behavioral privacy, a system must be able to anonymize and protect gathered user data from disclosure, as well as disguise prevalent ITS user behavioral patterns.

To prevent attackers from tracking and inferring on specific individuals within the system, the privacy of ITS users' actions must be protected. Because ITS collects information on travelers' routing patterns in order to make routes safer and more efficient, individual travelers' movement patterns are also logged in the system, and their analysis can yield inferences about their habits. Individual travelers' origin and destination points, for example, can cause privacy concerns because they allow a malicious actor to deduce a traveler's residence or employment.

Differential privacy can be utilized to protect ITS users' privacy. The purpose of differential privacy is to protect information privacy by providing strategies to improve the accuracy of statistical database searches while lowering the likelihood of identifying the database's records. Differential privacy, on the other hand, poses difficulties when applied to recurrent or time-series data.

Essentially, the question of privacy boils down to the disclosure of undesirable information: Consider the following scenarios: a person leaving the house empty for a long trip by car or boat (which may enable house burglaries); how often an employee, who is supposed to be at work, is visiting places by car (which may lead to social reputation loss); how often a spouse is visiting places that he or she has never mentioned to his or her relatives (which may cause family crises) and so on.

Location Privacy

Within ITS, location privacy is defined as "privacy of location and space," or a user's right to roam or move around the system without fear of his or her location information being exposed. While accurate location information is useful for ITS to provide location-aware services, it can also be exploited to intrude on people's privacy. Attackers can use this location information to perform targeted attacks on a specific person. It is incredibly difficult for GPS-based navigation systems to deliver service while maintaining user privacy.

As a result, it is critical to strike a balance between providing users with useful and accurate services while also protecting their privacy. Location obfuscation, also known as location cloaking, is a technique used in location-based services to protect users' privacy. Location cloaking preserves a user's privacy by subtly modifying or generalizing the user's location in order to prevent revelation of the user's true location.

SOLUTIONS

Protecting the complex ITS environment completely is a difficult endeavor. Cyberattacks and breaches are unavoidable, but ITS operators should incorporate preventative and recovery techniques into their regular operations. Data should be able to be transmitted in a timely manner. This should be accomplished with low overhead and lightweight cryptographic techniques. For ITS ecosystems, confidentiality and authentication are critical security aspects. Security flaws must be recognized swiftly and reacted to on a regular basis. Security flaws must be contained, and sensitive data must not be lost. All weaknesses must be secured to avoid attacks. Following an attack on the ITS environment, defenses must be enhanced, and recurrence events avoided. Security recommendations include network segmentation, the use of firewalls and next-generation firewalls, and Unified Threat Management (UTM) gateways to solve the security-related concerns and requirements discussed in preceding sections. Encryption, anti-malware, anti-phishing, and Breach Detection Systems (BDS) are all options. Intrusion Protection Systems (IPS) and Intrusion Detection Systems (IDS), Shodan scanning, vulnerability scanning, and patch management are some of the other security options available (physical or virtual) (Harvey & Kumar, 2020).

- **Network segmentation**: divides a network into subnetworks, which reduces traffic, improves security, and limits failures. When ITS controllers are put on a network separate from corporate networks, lateral movement concerns are decreased, and overall security is increased.
- **Firewalls**: are used to control both incoming and outgoing traffic. This control is based on a set of rules that the monitor is subjected to. Applications and endpoints that may be creating or requesting harmful traffic are discovered.
- **Next-generation firewalls and UTM gateways**: multiple systems and services are brought together as a single engine or appliance. Devices with lower traffic are analyzed using network traffic at line speed.
- **Anti-malware**: software that scans files looking for malicious content. Malware can be found, prevented, and eliminated. Heuristics, specific and generic signatures are used to detect known and undiscovered malware. Spear phishing is one of the most common vectors for infection, hence anti-phishing technologies are essential.
- **Anti-phishing solutions**: scan email for incoming spam and phishing emails and block these emails. Malicious attachments pose a potential risk and can be screened using message sandboxes as part of anti-phishing solutions.
- **Breach detection systems (BDS)**: detect targeted attacks and threaten to harvest information from the targeted system. BDS analyzes and detects complex attacks, but it cannot prevent them. Various protocols can be used to study network traffic patterns. Domains that are malicious can be recognized. Emulation-sandboxing can be used to imitate harmful file behavior and impact.
- **IPS and IDS**: monitor the entire network, looking for traffic deemed suspicious. They undertake deep pocket inspections and evaluate protocols. An IDS is a passive device that generates a report after an attack. When an IPS detects a negative event, the packet is rejected.
- **Digital signature algorithms**: can be used to overcome the majority of attacks on ITS applications and systems. Encryption can be used to defend against

assaults that aren't mitigated by digital signatures. Data can be encrypted and decrypted using encryption technologies. Using encrypted network traffic, man-in-the-middle (MitM) attacks can be defeated.

- **Physical and virtual patch management software**: updates endpoints, servers, and remote computers. Security patches and updates are applied to the system. A security enforcement layer can prevent malicious traffic by screening away traffic that attempts to exploit known vulnerabilities.

- **Vulnerability scanner**: scan for vulnerabilities in endpoints, servers, networks, and applications. The system is examined for vulnerabilities that have not yet been patched. When a vulnerability is discovered, the IT administrator can apply a patch.

- **Shodan scanning**: this is used for internet-connected devices. This solution conducts Open-Source Intelligence (OSINT) gatherings. Shodan's information can be used to identify unpatched vulnerabilities in exposed cyber assets. Shodan can be used by ITS operators to ensure that their devices and systems are not exposed to the internet.

- **Data fusion**: software on a vehicle can identify the true state of the vehicle. It can also provide information on the surroundings of the vehicle. Data is compiled and reported from a variety of sources. Based on the information that is still available in the vehicle, attacks can be discovered and countered. Cooperative nearby cars and infrastructure pieces may be able to confirm or deny observations made by a compromised vehicle. Additional sources of data can help in the detection of assaults. These data fusion systems have the potential to help in the detection of unusual inputs resulting from cyberattacks.

- **Biometrics**: is an authentication technique that measures physiological and individual characteristics. These features are then checked automatically. Biometric technology will become increasingly important in the future of security. An automated system is a biometric system. Information regarding certain attributes is collected by the system. Within the system, the data is subsequently distributed, stored, and processed. It is decided whether the user should be authorized. The inclusion of biometrics improves the security of the entire ITS system while lowering the possibility of impersonation. With the use of biometrics, the overall security of the ITS system may be improved, and dangers can be reduced.

- **Policy recommendations can improve security protection for ITS**: Instead of attempting to combine incompatible ITS frameworks, countries sharing land borders should coordinate so that their ITS frameworks can work together. Greater cross-border collaboration, information sharing, and cyber security knowledge will aid in the development and implementation of awareness for teaching end-users about the potential threats in ITS environments. Cyber threat and attack information and responses can be exchanged. To secure the ITS ecosystem, cybersecurity rules should be required. To save money, existing communication protocols should be updated rather than establishing new communication protocols. In ITS, multiple protocols are required to handle communications. The ITS ecosystem generates a vast amount of everyday user data. Data storage must be secure, and data access and usage regulations must be tight. For the protection of privacy and the rights of road users, these policies must be defined and enforced. Legislation is needed to specify the boundaries of authorized autonomous vehicle operation. Before new ITS applications and systems are approved for use on the roadways, minimum security standards should be defined in legislation.

As seen in the previous list, there are great security recommendations that should be implemented in order to minimize de probability and impact of a security attack. However, these security recommendations are not enough to prevent every possible attack and vulnerability, so the next section makes emphasis on the importance of researching problems and overcoming challenges in the ITS field.

FUTURE CHALLENGES

Considering the current limitations on ITS, many challenges will arise in implementing solutions. Furthermore, a few decades of research in this area, only in recent years have there been real world implementations of large intelligent transportation systems, which leads to security and privacy issues being relatively common to be exploited. Overall, there are challenges that need to be faced in order to improve these systems (Pop et al., 2020).

The overload of wireless networks due to the increased number of devices used for traffic monitoring and control is likely to be the most significant identified communication difficulty. As the number of devices grows, so will the requirement for an adaptive routing protocol for resource allocation and prioritization, as well as a system for storing and managing large volumes of road traffic data.

Other problems will include Vehicle-to-Vehicle (V2V) communication. To maintain the privacy, safety, and security of infrastructure communication networks, new certificate management systems must be established. Transmission interferences or other attacks, such as gaining vehicle control or manipulating data sent to other mobile hosts, might cause V2V messages to be intercepted, resulting in accidents.

Different technologies can be applied in complex sensor networks integrated in road infrastructure, traffic signal systems, and vehicle-to-vehicle communication. As a result, the future of ITS must have a single platform which can support a wide range of technologies and architectures. The availability of autonomous networks and good integration between them and ITS will be required in the future for autonomous driving. Furthermore, these systems must be dependable and capable of self-recovery in the event of a breakdown.

Another issue to be addressed is cost reduction through the use of low-cost sensors, deployment services, and energy conservation. The orientation to eco-friendly solutions, which can be achieved by employing software and hardware solutions to cut consumption, develop a system based on renewable energy, send information only when required, and so on, is a big problem that can address a part of cost-saving.

Because of the exponential growth of ITS data, the future of ITS faces general IoT difficulties such as scalability, durability, and latency, which are crucial in real-time data transmission and processing. Many of the issues discussed are interconnected and can be addressed in part by implementing suitable policies and regulations. Due to the legal permissions granted to future ITS systems, this will play a significant role in data storage and consumption.

Finally, another point that should be taken to account is the slow process of migrating legacy Intelligent Transportation Systems into new connected systems (Harvey & Kumar, 2020). When communication and information trade isn't viable, security is weakened. Knowledge of the run of cyber dangers and being able to secure ITS can be challenging. Cybersecurity can be implemented, but on the off chance that there's restricted information on how to use the software, it isn't as successful because it seems be. Countermeasures can be a successful way to avoid and resolve cyber assaults, but in case there's resistance to security adoption the ITS is at expanded hazard as assaults are evolving and entering the ITS biological system.

CONCLUSION

Although the emerging revolution of Intelligent Transportation Systems (ITS) offers lots of new advantages, including improved comfort and safety, increased energy efficiency, reduced pollution, reduced noise, and reduced traffic congestion, it also raises serious security and privacy concerns if these are not factored into the design of ITS. To maintain a safe and secure ITS, security and privacy must be considered in the design of individual ITS agents as well as the entire ITS. This report offers a thorough classification of security and privacy issues and vulnerabilities that must be addressed.

ITS ecosystems are often changing, and dangers to these systems are adapting as well, because as these systems become more common and technologically complex, attacks on security and privacy also increasingly become more sophisticated. There is a lot that can be done to enhance things in several areas. It is necessary to improve security by focusing it more narrowly on attack prevention and resolution.

ACKNOWLEDGMENT

This work was funded by Portuguese national funds through FCT (Foundation for Science and Technology) under the Scientific Employment Stimulus Institutional Call CEECINST/00051/2018 and in the context of the project UIDB/04524/2020.

REFERENCES

Ali, Q. E., Ahmad, N., Malik, A. H., Ali, G., & ur Rehman, W. (2018). Issues, challenges, and research opportunities in intelligent transport system for security and privacy. In *Applied Sciences (Switzerland)*, *8*(10). doi:10.3390/app8101964

Balasubramaniam, A., Paul, A., Hong, W. H., Seo, H., & Kim, J. (2017). Comparative Analysis of Intelligent Transportation Systems for Sustainable Environment in Smart Cities. *Sustainability*, *9*(7), 1120. doi:10.3390u9071120

Buinevich, M., & Vladyko, A. (2019). Forecasting Issues of Wireless Communication Networks' Cyber Resilience for An Intelligent Transportation System: An Overview of Cyber Attacks. *Information (Basel)*, *10*(1), 27. doi:10.3390/info10010027

Chand, H. V., & Karthikeyan, J. (2018). Survey on the role of IoT in intelligent transportation system. *Indonesian Journal of Electrical Engineering and Computer Science*, *11*(3), 936–941. doi:10.11591/ijeecs.v11.i3.pp936-941

Cheng, Z., Pang, M.-S., & Pavlou, P. A. (2020). Mitigating Traffic Congestion: The Role of Intelligent Transportation Systems. *Information Systems Research*, *31*(3), 653–674. doi:10.1287/isre.2019.0894

City Circle Line. (2022, June).

Dimitrakopoulos, G., & Demestichas, P. (2010). Intelligent Transportation Systems. *IEEE Vehicular Technology Magazine*, *5*(1), 77–84. doi:10.1109/MVT.2009.935537

Greer, L., Fraser, J. L., Hicks, D., Mercer, M., & Thompson, K. (2018). *Intelligent transportation systems benefits, costs, and lessons learned: 2018 update report*. DT.

Hahn, D., Munir, A., & Behzadan, V. (2021). Security and privacy issues in intelligent transportation systems: Classification and challenges. *IEEE Intelligent Transportation Systems Magazine*, *13*(1), 181–196. doi:10.1109/MITS.2019.2898973

Harvey, J., & Kumar, S. (2020). A Survey of Intelligent Transportation Systems Security: Challenges and Solutions. *Proceedings - 2020 IEEE 6th Intl Conference on Big Data Security on Cloud, BigDataSecurity 2020, 2020 IEEE Intl Conference on High Performance and Smart Computing, HPSC 2020 and 2020 IEEE Intl Conference on Intelligent Data and Security, IDS 2020*. IEEE. 10.1109/BigDataSecurity-HPSC-IDS49724.2020.00055

Haydari, A., & Yilmaz, Y. (2018). Real-Time Detection and Mitigation of DDoS Attacks in Intelligent Transportation Systems. *2018 21st International Conference on Intelligent Transportation Systems (ITSC)*, 157–163. 10.1109/ITSC.2018.8569698

Huq, N., Vosseler, R., & Swimmer, M. (2017). Cyberattacks against intelligent transportation systems. *TrendLabs Research Paper*.

Inkoom, S., Sobanjo, J., & Chicken, E. (2020). Competing Risks Models for the Assessment of Intelligent Transportation Systems Devices: A Case Study for Connected and Autonomous Vehicle Applications. *Infrastructures*, 5(3), 30. doi:10.3390/infrastructures5030030

Janušová, L., & Čičmancová, S. (2016). Improving Safety of Transportation by Using Intelligent Transport Systems. *Procedia Engineering*, *134*, 14–22. doi:10.1016/j.proeng.2016.01.031

Krivolapova, O. (2017). Algorithm for Risk Assessment in the Introduction of Intelligent Transport Systems Facilities. *Transportation Research Procedia*, *20*, 373–377. doi:10.1016/j.trpro.2017.01.056

Lamssaggad, A., Benamar, N., Hafid, A. S., & Msahli, M. (2021). A Survey on the Current Security Landscape of Intelligent Transportation Systems. In IEEE Access (Vol. 9). IEEE doi:10.1109/ACCESS.2021.3050038

Lishchenko, T. (2021, January 14). *Intelligent Transport System: Trends, best practices, success stories*.

Mangiaracina, R., Perego, A., Salvadori, G., & Tumino, A. (2017). A comprehensive view of intelligent transport systems for urban smart mobility. *International Journal of Logistics Research and Applications*, *20*(1), 39–52. doi:10.1080/13675567.201 6.1241220

Ming, L., Zhao, G., Huang, M., Kuang, X., Li, H., & Zhang, M. (2018). Security analysis of intelligent transportation systems based on simulation data. *Proceedings - 2018 1st International Conference on Data Intelligence and Security, ICDIS 2018*. IEEE. 10.1109/ICDIS.2018.00037

Ometov, A., Bezzateev, S., Davydov, V., Shchesniak, A., Masek, P., Lohan, E. S., & Koucheryavy, Y. (2019). Positioning information privacy in intelligent transportation systems: An overview and future perspective. *Sensors (Switzerland)*, *19*(7), 1603. doi:10.339019071603 PMID:30987097

Pop, M. D., Pandey, J., & Ramasamy, V. (2020). Future Networks 2030: Challenges in Intelligent Transportation Systems. *ICRITO 2020 - IEEE 8th International Conference on Reliability, Infocom Technologies and Optimization (Trends and Future Directions)*. IEEE. 10.1109/ICRITO48877.2020.9197951

Tech Target. (2019) What is Intelligent transportation system (ITS): Applications and Examples. *Tech Target*.

van der Heijden, R. W., Dietzel, S., Leinmüller, T., & Kargl, F. (2018). Survey on misbehavior detection in cooperative intelligent transportation systems. *IEEE Communications Surveys and Tutorials*, *21*(1), 779–811. doi:10.1109/COMST.2018.2873088

Yu, J. J. Q. (2021). Sybil Attack Identification for Crowdsourced Navigation: A Self-Supervised Deep Learning Approach. *IEEE Transactions on Intelligent Transportation Systems*, *22*(7), 4622–4634. doi:10.1109/TITS.2020.3036085

Zheng, B., Sayin, M. O., Lin, C.-W., Shiraishi, S., & Zhu, Q. (2017). Timing and security analysis of VANET-based intelligent transportation systems: (Invited paper). *2017 IEEE/ACM International Conference on Computer-Aided Design (ICCAD)*, (pp. 984–991). IEEE. 10.1109/ICCAD.2017.8203888

Chapter 6
A Comprehensive Review of Privacy Preserving Data Publishing (PPDP) Algorithms for Multiple Sensitive Attributes (MSA)

Veena Gadad

(iD) https://orcid.org/0000-0002-3396-1719
RV College of Engineering, India

Sowmyarani C. N.
RV College of Engineering, India

ABSTRACT

Privacy preserving data publishing (PPDP) provides a suite of anonymization algorithms and tools that aim to balance the privacy of sensitive attributes and utility of the published data. In this domain, extensive work has been carried out to preserve the privacy of single sensitive attributes. Since most of the data obtained from any domain includes multiple sensitive attributes (MSAs), there is a greater need to preserve it. The data sets with multiple sensitive attributes allow one to perform effective data analysis, research, and predictions. Hence, it is important to investigate privacy preserving algorithms for multiple sensitive attributes, which leads to higher utilization of the data. This chapter presents the effectiveness and comparative analysis of PPDP algorithms for MSAs. Specifically, the chapter focuses on privacy and utility goals and illustrates implications of the overall study, which promotes the development of effective privacy preservation techniques for MSAs.

DOI: 10.4018/978-1-6684-5991-1.ch006

INTRODUCTION

Privacy preserving is main concern when it comes to the personal data, which is collected at various places such as hospitals, banks, government organizations etc. Privacy preservation can be achieved by methods like cryptography (de Capitani et al., 2018a; Benaloh et al., 2009; Chase & Chow, 2009; Goyal et al., 2006), access control (Can, 2018; Seol et al., 2018; Ruj et al., 2012; Peleg et al., 2008; Takabi, 2014) and Homomorphic Encryption (Kundalwal et al., 2019; Naehrig et al., 2011). But these techniques do not provide data utility but prevent only the privacy leaks (Brickell & Shmatikov, 2008). Personal data is either information that relates to any identifiable living individual or the pieces of information collected together that can lead to identification of a particular person. Examples of the former case is a name and surname, home address, personal email address, identification card number, any location, Internet Protocol (IP) address, cookie ID, location data etc., examples of latter case are the data held by hospital or doctor, Transport data, census data and data that is provided at the workplace. Figure 1 shows the A Process of Data collection, data publishing and data utilization.

The collected data is published in the websites or it is outsourced to third party and is utilized by data scientist to perform data analytics, research or it may be used by an intruder to cause privacy threats (de Capitani et al., 2018a). Privacy preservation has also becomes a concern in technologies like Deep Learning, Artificial Intelligence (Jajodia, 1996; Liu et al., 2021), Cloud, Fog computing and Edge Computing (Tang et al., 2016; Zhang et al., 2020; de Capitani et al., 2018b, 2019) Federated learning (Yin et al., 2021l; Yuan et al., 2021), Mixed reality (de Guzman et al., 2020), blockchain (de Aguiar et al., 2020) and cyber security (Toch et al., 2018), which are driving force for smart health (Ding et al., 2021), smart cities, digital economy, robust surveillance system etc. According to GDPR (EU Commission Website., n.d.) the personal data is allowed to for processing only with the consent of the data owner and the hence processing should be done only on anonymized data with great care (Gruschka et al., 2018).

In figure 1, the individual data gets collected at Hospitals, Government organization, e-commerce sites and Banks. The data is published in Internet, sold or given to some third party to carry out some analysis (Yüksel et al., 2017; Gardiyawasam Pussewalage & Oleshchuk, 2016). Thus, the data is utilized by wide community of users effectively to make some decisions. But there could be an intruder also who utilizes the data and may cause privacy threat to the individual. The aim of any privacy preserving data publishing algorithm is to balance between privacy preservation and data utilization (Loukides & Shao, 2007; Li & Li, 2009).

Figure 1. A Process of Data collection, data publishing and data utilization

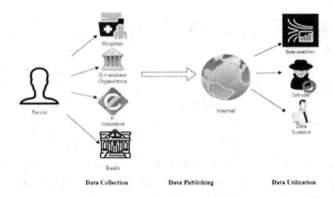

Table 1. Sample healthcare data with multiple sensitive attributes

ID	ZIP code	Age	Gender	Occupation	Salary	Physician
1	54677	39	M	Nurse	2000+	John
2	54602	32	M	Nurse	3000+	Bob
3	54678	40	F	Police	4000+	Jercy
4	54905	53	M	Cook	8000+	Alice
5	54909	62	F	Actor	10000+	Tom
6	54906	57	M	Actor	10000+	Lucy
7	54605	52	F	Clerk	6000+	Bob
8	54673	55	M	Clerk	6000+	Leo
9	54607	40	F	Teacher	7000+	Lucy

Most of the existing anonymization algorithms preserve privacy of single sensitive attributes but majority of the data sets such as healthcare, census, transactional and crowdsourced data contain Multiple Sensitive Attributes (MSA) (Ghinita et al., 2011; Prasdika & Sugiantoro, 2013; Ram Mohan Rao et al., 2018; Wang et al., 2018).For example, consider the healthcare data in Table 1, the multiple sensitive attributes are: Salary, Disease and Physician all of which are sensitive information that needs to be preserved.

The data sets with MSA provide better insights hence are used to perform effective data investigations, research and predictions (Fang et al., 2011).

BACKGROUND

This section discusses some general concepts and definitions that are used throughout the paper. A microdata table is the information obtained at the level of individual respondents(Fung et al., 2010) (de Capitani et al., 2018b; Ciriani et al., n.d.; Can, 2018). Let T_{mn} be a microdata table, $r_1, r_2 \ldots \ldots r_m$ represents a row that corresponds to individual's information and $a_1, a_2 \ldots a_n$ represents specific attribute. Depending upon handling of various attributes $a_1, a_2 \ldots a_n$ they can be classified as follows:

1. Identifier attributes (ID): This attribute values directly identify the respondent. For example, Name, social security number and roll number. These values are removed before the microdata is published to the public.
2. Quasi Identifier attributes (QID): This attribute values can indirectly identify the respondent when two or more microdata tables are combined. For example, Zip Code, Age and Date of birth. The QID's are treated and altered with various anonymization methods to prevent disclosures.
3. Sensitive Attributes (SA): This attribute values are the personal information/ sensitive information, that the respondent doesn't want public to know. For example, Disease, Salary and Occupation.

In the process of anonymization, the first step is removal of all IDs from the collected data. Since the intruder may already know some of the QID's through background knowledge or by referring other datasets (Martin et al., 2007), these are treated and altered with various anonymization methods such as generalization, suppression, anatomization, slicing and perturbation. A detail discussion of these techniques is provided in the next sections. It must be noted that the sensitive attributes values are not altered, and they are published in their original form because they carry wealth of information and are used in various research or analysis.

Privacy and Utility Goals of Anonymization Algorithms

Anonymization algorithms are designed with some privacy and utility goal. The anonymization algorithms are designed with privacy goal such that it is difficult for the intruder to identify and disclose the individual's information and prevent privacy threats and utility goal such that a researcher or an analyst is able to obtain valuable information from the published data (Fung et al., 2019; Iyengar, 2002).

Privacy Goal

An intruder who has a good background information obtained from neighbor/ colleague/friend or using the external released data obtains the QID's and cause a privacy threat (Loukides & Shao, 2007; Lee & Lee, 2017). The threat occurs when the intruder knows three individual details of a respondent (I):

- The presence of individual(I) in the other published tables.
- The list QID's associated with I.
- Some of the SA associated with I.

Anonymization algorithms are applied on the QID values to prevent the intruder from causing privacy threat. Therefore, the privacy goal of any anonymization algorithms is to prevent the privacy threats.

Utility Goal

With data anonymization there is difference between the original data and the anonymized data, this is called as information loss. To prevent privacy threats, the data is anonymized and there is an information loss, but it should be minimal to have greater utility of the published data. There must be balance between the privacy preservation and information loss (Martin et al., 2007).

In this paper the privacy and utility goals of fifteen algorithms is discussed.

Definitions

Let T be the original microdata table, in the published microdata the identifiers are removed and anonymization methods are applied on Quasi-Identifier's. The resulting table is of the form: T` (QID's, SA's).

- Definition 1: Equivalence Class (EQ)- An EQ is a set of anonymized records that have same QID attribute values. The records in an EQ are all identical with respect to their QID values.
- Definition 2: k-anonymity (Ciriani et al., n.d.)- A table satisfies k-anonymity if the records in an EQ are indistinguishable from other (k-1) records with reference to QID attributes.
- Definition 3: l-diversity (Machanavajjhala et al., 2007; Xiao et al., 2010; Kifer & Gehrke, 2006a)- An EQ is said to satisfy l-diversity if there are at least l "well represented" values for SA's.

- Definition 4: t-closeness (Li, 2007)- A EQ is said to satisfy t-closeness if the distance between the distribution of a SA within any EQ and the distribution of the same attribute in the entire table is not more than the predefined threshold 't'.
- Definition 5: Privacy Threat (Sowmyarani and Dayananda, n.d.)- A threat that is caused by an intruder after gaining access to the published data and is able to link the record of the respondent with his sensitive attribute. The threat may be in physical or informational.

Consider Table 2, it contains the single SA i.e., disease. Table 3 is anonymized version of Table 2.

Table 2. Original data

ID	ZIP code	Age	Gender	Disease
1	54677	39	M	Heart Disease
2	54602	32	M	Gastritis
3	54678	40	F	Bronchitis
4	54905	53	M	Gastritis
5	54909	62	F	Heart Disease
6	54906	57	M	Cancer
7	54605	40	F	Flu
8	54673	46	M	HIV
9	54607	40	F	Cancer

Table 3. 3 Anonymous Table

ID	ZIP	Age	Gender	Disease
123	546**546**546**	[30-40][30-40] [30-40]	M/FM/FM/F	Heart DiseaseGastritis Bronchitis
456	549**549**549**	>=50>=50>=50	M/FM/FM/F	GastritisHeart DiseaseCancer
789	546**546**546**	4*4*4*	M/FM/FM/F	FluHIVCancer

k-anonymity is applied to the original data. Here k=3, indicates number of records grouped into one EQ where, QID values are same in all three records.

Even though the k-anonymity overcame the attribute and record linking attack (Sweeney, 2002a), it failed to prevent other privacy attacks such as homogeneity attack, background knowledge attack (Machanavajjhala et al., 2007) skewness attacks and similarity attack (Chase & Chow, 2009). Also, k- anonymity was designed to preserve privacy of only one SA. Various techniques (Wang et al., 2018) (Truta & Vinay, 2006)(Sun, Wang, Li, et al., 2008; Sun, Wang, and Truta, 2008; Rahimi et al., 2015; Sun, Sun, and Wang, 2011)(Sowmyarani & Srinivasan, 2015; Sowmyarani et al., 2021) were proposed to preserve privacy of single sensitive attribute and were difficult to extend the algorithms to the data set that contained more than one SA.

Privacy Threats

A thorough study of various privacy threats is presented in (Sowmyarani & Dayananda, n.d.). These privacy threats can be broadly classified into four types membership disclosure, identity disclosure (Fung et al., n.d.), attribute disclosure (Chi-Wing et al., 2006) and association disclosure.

- *Membership disclosure* threat occurs when an intruder is able to find out the individual's record from the large published data. For example, the adversary learns the presence of records belonging to Peter, John, Prerana in the table.
- *Identity disclosure* occurs when the individual's record can be linked to a particular record of the published data based on the background knowledge of the adversary. For example, the adversary who has the background knowledge of the ZIP code of an individual is 54602 and his gender as male with age 32, can identify a particular person. This is a serious type of attack as it may lead to legal consequences for data owners (Li et al., 2012; Sweeney, 2002a). By identity disclosure the attacker can learn almost all sensitive data of the individual.
- *Attribute disclosure* occurs when the adversary learns additional information from the published data that the individual doesn't want others to know but are of special interest to the attacker. The attacker with the help of other published data learns other attributes of a person. Usually identity disclosure leads to attribute disclosure(F. Liu et al., 2012)(Chi-Wing et al., 2006). Table 4 shows these various types of privacy threats.

Association disclosure occurs when there is more than one sensitive attribute that need to be preserved. If there exist a logical association among MSA disclosing one sensitive attribute will reveal other sensitive attribute correspondingly, this is called association disclosure. There are two types of association disclosures- positive and

Table 4. Types of privacy threats

Name	ZIP code	Age	Gender	Disease
Peter	54677	39	M	Colon cancer
John	54602	32	M	Prostate cancer
Prerana	54678	37	F	Breast Cancer
Michael	54905	53	F	Breast Cancer
Suman	54909	62	F	Breast Cancer

negative disclosures (Wu et al., 2010). To overcome such disclosures it is essential to distribute the SA's statically (Iyengar, 2002; Brickell & Shmatikov, 2008; Wang et al., 2008).

CONTRIBUTION OF THE PAPER

The paper discusses fifteen different algorithms for privacy preserving data publishing for MSA. The main contributions of the paper are:

- Discussion of various anonymization approaches.
- Information loss and Privacy leak measures.
- Privacy threats and the Utility goals of each MSA algorithm.
- Implications of the study.
- Research directions in the domain of PPDP for multiple sensitive attributes.

ORGANIZATION OF THE PAPER

The next section presents the approaches of Data Anonymization. This section is followed by discussion of the information loss and Privacy leak measures. PPDP algorithms for MSA are presented next. Later part of the chapter presents the implications of the study. Finally, the research directions in the domain of PPDP for MSA is discussed. The chapter concludes with the conclusion and future work.

APPROACHES FOR DATA ANONYMIZATION

Plethora of anonymization algorithms are available in the literature. These algorithms can be classified and studied based on the anonymization operations applied on the data. This section discusses these approaches.

Generalization and Suppression

Generalization replaces the QID values into broader domain values(Samarati & Sweeney, 1998). For example: For the categorical attribute Occupation if the original value is Cardiologist, it is generalized to Doctor. Similarly, for numerical attribute Age, if the value is 30 it is generalized to range of values as 20-40. This approach is used in various algorithms (LeFevre, DeWitt, Ramakrishnan, 2005; Sweeney, 2002a; Machanavajjhala et al., 2007; Li, 2007; Truta & Vinay, 2006; Sun et al., 2008). Generalization is also known as recoding and there are two types of recoding: Local recoding and global recoding (Truta, Campan & Abrinica, 2008) depending upon the nature of generalizations (Xu et al., 2006). Recently, cell level generalization was performed to prevent composition attack (Hasan et al., 2018a) for personalized privacy preservation (Xiao & Tao, 2006b).

Suppression replaces some attribute values with a special symbolic character like *, # (T. Li & Li, 2008) to anonymize the data. In most of the anonymization algorithms generalization and suppressions are combined to anonymize the data (Xu et al., 2014; LeFevre, DeWitt, Ramakrishnan, 2005; Lefevre et al., 2009)(V & K.P, 2012; Ghinita et al., 2007; Sweeney, 2002b).

Anatomization and Slicing

In these approaches original values of the attributes are retained and separate tables of SA and QID's are generated. The main advantage is that these is less information loss and also, they perform better with high dimensional data.

Anatomy (Xiao & Tao, 2006a) releases the QID and SA as a separate table and both the tables have one common attribute called the group identifier. The tables can combine using grouping mechanism hence captures the correlation among various attributes. To understand the algorithm, consider the anatomized Table 5 and Table 6 obtained from vertical partitioning of Table 2.

The algorithm preserves the privacy because the QIT does not reveal the sensitive attributes of any records. In order to determine the sensitive values, the SAT must be referred. For example, consider an intruder who has age 39, and zip code 54677 of Alice. From QIT the intruder gets to know that the record belongs to group 1 and does not get to know any information about the disease. From SAT, the intruder learns that 4 records out of 9 belong to group 1 and Alice might have any of the three disease- Heart, Gastritis or Cancer. Therefore, anatomy algorithm is believed to have high data quality when compared to generalization.

Slicing (Li et al., 2012) partitions the dataset both horizontally and vertically. The vertical partitions are called as attribute partitioning and horizontal portioning is called as tuple partitioning. The tuple partition when done leads to creation of buckets. Each bucket is further observed to satisfy l-diversity property (Machanavajjhala et al., 2007). Now, within each buckets the values are permuted, and the sliced table is published by combining all the partitions.

To understand the slicing approach, consider the original data table, Table 1. The attribute partition is represented as {{Zip code},{Age},{Gender},{Disease}}. The buckets satisfying 3-diversity are {{t1,t2,t3},{t4,t5,t5},{t7,t8,t9}}. The tuple values are permuted, and the sliced table is published as shown in Table 7.

Table 5. Quasi Identifier Table (QIT)

ZIP code	Age	Gender	Group ID
54677	39	M	1
54602	32	M	1
54905	53	M	1
54906	57	M	1
54673	46	M	1
54678	40	F	2
54909	62	F	2
54605	40	F	2
54607	40	F	2

Table 6. Sensitive Attribute Table (SAT)

GroupID	Disease	Count
1	Heart Disease	1
1	Gastritis	2
1	Cancer	1
1	HIV	1
2	Heart Disease	1
2	Bronchitis	1
2	Flu	1
2	Cancer	1

Table 7. Sliced Table

Age, Gender	ZIP code, Disease
(39,F)	(54677, Gastritis)
(40,M)	(54602,Heart Disease)
(32,M)	(54678, Bronchitis)
(53,F)	(54905,Gastritics)
(57,M)	(54909,Cancer)
(62,)M)	(54906,Heartdisease)
(40,F)	(54673,HIV)
(46,F)	(54605,Flu)
(40,M)	(54607,Cancer

Since the slicing method partitions the attributes into more than two columns, it prevents the membership attack. When compared with anatomy, it is easy to find out whether the record of an individual is present in the published data or not. For example, if the data is published only of patients having diabetes, the intruder must not be able to find out whether a particular individual's record is present in the published table.

The anonymization algorithm in (Susan & Christopher, 2016) combines both slicing and anatomy to preserve privacy of multiple sensitive attributes while obeying the principles of k-anonymity, l-diversity and t-closeness.

Permutation

Permutation follows the same approach as that of anatomization i.e., it disassociates the relationship between the QID and SA and groups the records, shuffles the sensitive values within each group (Zhang et al., 2007; Li et al., 2016).

Consider Table 8 and Table 9, in table 9 the sensitive attributes are permuted, that prevents the intruder to determine the sensitive attribute directly.

Permutation anonymization (Li et al., 2016; He et al., 2012) partitions the original table into groups to satisfy l-diversity.

In (Bahrami & Singhal, 2015) a lightweight data privacy algorithm that uses a pseudo random permutation to scramble the original data is proposed. There are techniques that combine anatomy and permutations (Ye et al., 2017).

Table 8. Anatomized QID table

ZIP code	Age	Gender	Group_ID
54677	39	M	
54602	32	M	1
54905	53	M	
54678	40	F	
54909	62	F	2
54605	40	F	
54906	57	M	
54607	40	F	3
54673	46	M	

Table 9. Permuted SAT table

Disease	Group_ID
Gastritis	
Heart Disease	1
Gastritis	
Flu	
Heart Disease	2
Bronchitis	
Cancer	
HIV	3
Cancer	

Perturbation

These operations are applied on the dataset to distort the data so as to protect the privacy by preserving the statistical properties (Xiao et al., 2009; Agrawal & Aggarwal, 2001; Kargupta et al., 2005; Agrawal & Aggarwal, 2001; Muralidhar & Sarathy, 1999). Perturbation is achieved by adding noise (Rahimi et al., 2015; Hasan et al., 2018b; Xiao et al., 2009; Brand, 2002) swapping the data (Dalenius & Reiss, 1982; Reiss, 1984) or by micro aggregation (Domingo-Ferrer & Mateo-Sanz, 2002). Differential privacy (Taylor et al., 2018; Li et al., 2012) incorporates random noises into the data so that an intruder receives an imprecise data and becomes difficult to breach privacy.

Microaggregation

Microaggregation (Domingo-Ferrer & Mateo-Sanz, 2002) is basically grouping the records satisfying the k-anonymity or l-diversity and then replacing the records in a group by an aggregate value such as mean, median or standard deviation(Shi et al., 2018)(Domingo-Ferrer & Soria-Comas, 2017). Synthetic data generation replaces the original data points with sample data points that are from a pre-defined statistical model (Pascual et al., 2021)

Many algorithms have been proposed for single sensitive attributes and the mainly used anonymization approaches here are generalization, suppression or both. As discussed, when such operations are applied on the dataset, (Xiao & Tao, 2006a) information loss (Xiao & Tao, 2006a; Li et al., 2012; Ninghui Li et al., 2010). Also, when there are a greater number of sensitive attributes, these algorithms cannot be easily extended to MSA (Iyengar, 2002; Liu et al., 2012). Hence there is a need for separate algorithms for preserving privacy of MSA.

Commonly used anonymization operations to preserve privacy of MSA are Anatomy, slicing, permutation and perturbation. In these techniques most of the QID and SA values are retained as they are and hence these methods have proven to achieve good data utility when compared with algorithms that use generalization or suppression techniques.

INFORMATION LOSS AND PRIVACY LEAK MEASURES

The existing techniques for single sensitive attributes use generalization or suppression approaches to anonymize the data. In the resulting published data, there is always the information loss. Various information (Wagner & Eckhoff, 2018) ed in (Wagner & Eckhoff, 2018; Mendes & Vilela, 2017). However, since Anatomy, Slicing and Permutation approaches that are predominantly used for MSA, there is no information loss measures but we can measure the Privacy Leaks.

Information Loss Measures

Loss Metric (Iyengar, 2002; Fung et al., 2019), Generalized Loss Measure (Gadad & Sowmyarani, 2019), Suppression Ratio (Liu et al., 2012) etc., are commonly used metrices for to measure information loss that happens when generalization and suppression techniques are used for anonymization.

Loss Metric (LM)

The LM determines the amount of information loss that has occurs with data anonymization. The metric is designed for both numeric and categorical QID's. For each tuple of numeric data, the information loss is computed using equation (1) and for categorical data the loss is computed using equation (2). For entire table the loss is computed using the equation (3).

$$LM_i = \frac{(p_i - q_i)}{Domain\_max - Domain\_min} \qquad (1)$$

For tuple i, pi and qi denote the generalized interval and the Domain_max, Domain_min indicates the maximum and minimum values in the domain.

$$LM_i = \frac{l_p - 1}{l - 1} \qquad (2)$$

For tuple i, when the categorical values are generalized using the taxonomy tree, l denotes total number of leaf nodes in the tree and the lp denotes number of leaf nods rooted at P.

$$LM(Y) = \sum_{i=1}^{|Y|} LM_i \qquad (3)$$

Generalized Loss Measure (GM)

For the tuples that are generalized using greater than or less than operators, the GM is used to compute the information loss.

$$G_i = \frac{DomainValue - ActualValue}{DomainValue} \qquad (4)$$

Where Gi denotes each tuple in the anonymized table, DomainValue denotes the maximum value of the domain and the ActualValue indicates the generalized value.

Suppression Ratio (SR)

This measures the loss by comparing the number of tuples suppressed to tuples in the tables. If T denotes number of records in the table and ts denotes number of suppressed records the SR is computed using the equation (5)

$$SuppRatio(SR) = \frac{t_s}{T} \tag{5}$$

Consider Table 2, it the anonymized version of Table 1. The information loss in EQ1 with respect to 'age' attribute can be computed using LM(10/99+10/99+10/99= 0.30). For the same attribute, in EQ2 the loss can be computed using equation 4 (0.49+0.49+.49=1.48). In EQ3 the loss is (3/9=0.33). The total loss incurred by generalizing the age attribute is 23.48%.

Privacy Leak Measures

As discussed, in anatomy and slicing approaches, there is no such information loss since the data is published in its original form. In such tables it is necessary to measure the probability of Privacy leak(Ye et al., n.d.)'P' determined using equation 6.

$$P(t.s_i = v) = \frac{c(v)}{|t.s_i = v|} \quad (1 \le i \le m) \tag{6}$$

Where v is a value of sensitive attribute i, $c(v)$ is number of tuples with value v. |t.si=v| denotes total number of tuples with value v.

Consider the table (anatomy), for group id 1,c(v)= 2, when QID table and SAT table are linked using group_id, |t.si=v| value is 5. P(t.si=Gastritis)= 2/5= 0.4

Combining anatomy with permutation, each QID values are selected from the permutation set, the probability of privacy leak can be calculated using equation 7.

$$P(t.s_i = v) = \frac{c(v)}{\prod_{i=1}^{d} QI_i.s_i} \quad (1 \le i \le m) \tag{7}$$

Where |QIi.si| is the product of number of tuples that value si is v and different values of QID's. In group 1 of Table(permutation) there are three different values for QID's and 2 different values for SA's. The number of tuples with Heart Disease is 1 and Gastritis is 2. The leaking probability for Gastritis is 2/ (2*3)+(1*3)= 2/9 = 0.22 which is much lesser than 2/5.

PRIVACY PRESERVING ALGORITHMS FOR MULTIPLE SENSITIVE ATTRIBUTES

Many Privacy preserving data publishing algorithms for single sensitive attributes have been proposed fundamental among them were k-anonymity (Sweeney, 2002a), l- diversity (Machanavajjhala et al., 2007), t- closeness (Li, 2007), p sensitive k-anonymity (Truta & Vinay, 2006), (p+,α) sensitive(Sun, Wang, Truta, et al., 2008) and (p+, α, t)-Anonymity (Sowmyarani et al., 2021). When it was observed that there is requirement for MSA, the approach of researchers was to extend these algorithms for data set which had two to three sensitive attributes. In this section we discuss about 15 different techniques that have been proposed to preserve privacy of multiple sensitive attributes.

Privacy Protection for MSA with Column Wise Constraints

This was the first technique that was proposed to preserve privacy of medical data that had two sensitive attributes (disease and treatment) (Gal et al., 2008). It was observed that on applying k- anonymity and l-diversity on the data with multiple sensitive attributes, the adversary can easily apply elimination attack on one of the attributes and determine the other sensitive value. Therefore, the authors proposed the technique that extends the k-anonymity and l-diversity to preserve privacy of multiple sensitive attributes. When multiple sensitive attributes are considered, some of them have fewer distinct values while others have many. In this model, different diversity is applied for sensitive attributes depending on its diversity.

Consider the original microdata shown in Table 10. The first four records are displayed. Table 11 shows the k-anonymous data with k=4.

Table 10. Original microdata

Patient ID	Age	Disease Type	Treatment
1	42	Heart Disease	Medicine
2	41	Heart Disease	Surgery
3	49	Flu	Intravenous
4	43	Stomach Ache	Intravenous
...	...	...	...

Table 11. 4 anonymous table

Patient ID	Age	Disease Type	Treatment
1	[41-50]	Heart Disease	Medicine
2	[41-50]	Heart Disease	Surgery
3	[41-50]	Flu	Intravenous
4	[41-50]	Stomach Ache	Intravenous
...	...	...	...

Here, age is the quasi-identifier, sensitive attributes are- disease and treatment. Though the k- anonymity technique prevents the linking attack it fails to prevent the elimination attack (Gal et al., 2008). In Table 11, if k=3 and the adversary with some background knowledge knows that the patient is unlikely to have a heart disease, then he can conclude that the patient is suffering from flu. l-diversity which states that there must be diversity among the sensitive attributes, in the group shown in table 2 for Disease type and treatment attribute the value of l is 3. Now if the adversary knows that the patient is unlikely to have heart disease, then two attribute values for treatment can be eliminated and he can conclude easily that the patient can is taking Intravenous treatment.

Table 12. Column wise constraints for SA

Disease Type	Treatment
D1	T1
D2	T1
D3	T2
D4	T2
D5	T3
D6	T3

To overcome this attack, the authors propose to apply column wise constraints. The l- diversity requirement is chosen different for different columns depending on number of distinct values. For example, consider the Table 12. Let L1 and L2 be the diversity constraint for disease type and treatment attributes respectively. The distinct values for disease type are 6 and Distinct values for the treatment types are.

Now, if L1 is set to 4 and L2 is set to 2, minimum of 4 records needs to be deleted to prevent the elimination attack. The privacy goal of this model is to prevent elimination and linking attack that happens when there are MSA. The technique provides privacy considering two sensitive attributes and prevents the linking and elimination attack by applying the column wise constraints. In this model since the generalization and suppression are used to anonymize, the information loss increases with the value of 'k' and 'l'. Authors have used discernability metric (Bayardo & Agrawal, n.d.) to measure the distortion of the data and to determine the information loss.

P Cover K- Anonymity

This algorithm (Wu et al., 2010) extends the p-sensitive, k- anonymity algorithm (Truta & Vinay, 2006) that was designed for single sensitive attribute. When there are two sensitive attributes and the p- sensitive k- anonymity is applied, there is disclosure if the intruder is able to eliminate one sensitive value with high confidence and other sensitive value lacks diversity.

For example consider Table 13 after removal of identifiers. Here the two sensitive attributes are Marital Status and Disease. Table 14 is constructed by applying p-sensitive k anonymity algorithm, where value of p=3 and k=4. A table T is said to satisfy MSA p-cover property, if it is not possible for the adversary to eliminate p-1 records from the equivalence class confidently. Further, to prevent the disclosure risks, the authors propose the condition that the number of identical values in SG are not less than p. Table satisfying p cover k- anonymity is shown in Table 15.

As observed the tuples 1,3,5,6 form one EQ class and the tuples 2,4,7 8 forms another EQ. The sensitive attribute group (SG) is combination of both sensitive attribute and each EQ class has 3 identical SG's. Like {(Single, Asthma), (Married, Cancer), (Divorced, Cancer)}, {(Single, Asthma), (Married, Obesity),(Divorced, Cancer)}.

Consider the background knowledge attack on Table 11. Suppose that the attacker aware that Bob is in EQ1(using QID values) and he is not single. The attacker can eliminate the tuples 1 and 3. He can easily figure out that Bob is suffering from cancer. Hence, the requirement is not only satisfying p-sensitivity on single sensitive attribute but also make the diversity between multiple sensitive attributes satisfy p-sensitive.

To prove the efficiency of the model authors have used the quality metric proposed in (Byun et al., 2006) based on taxonomy tree.

A table T is said to satisfy MSA p-cover property, if it is not possible for the adversary to eliminate p-1 records from the equivalence class confidently. Further, to prevent the disclosure risks, the authors propose the condition that the number of identical values in SG are not less than p. Table satisfying p cover k- anonymity is shown in Table 15.

Table 13. Sample microdata

ZIP code	Age	Gender	Marital Status	Disease
54677	21	M	Single	Asthma
54902	32	F	Single	Asthma
54678	26	M	Single	Obesity
54906	35	M	Married	Obesity
54675	25	M	Married	Cancer
54676	28	M	Divorced	Cancer
54905	36	F	Divorced	Obesity
54973	38	F	Divorced	Cancer

Table 14. 3- sensitive 4 anonymity

ZIP code	Age	Gender	Marital Status	Disease
546**	[21-28]	M/F	Single	Asthma
549**	[32-38]	M/F	Single	Asthma
546**	[21-28]	M/F	Single	Obesity
549**	[32-38]	M/F	Married	Obesity
546**	[21-28]	M/F	Married	Cancer
546**	[21-28]	M/F	Divorced	Cancer
549**	[32-38]	M/F	Divorced	Obesity
549**	[32-38]	M/F	Divorced	Cancer

Table 15. 3 Cover 4 Anonymity

ZIP code	Age	Gender	Marital Status	Disease
54***	[21-35]	M/F	Single	Asthma
54***	[25-38]	M/F	Single	Asthma
54***	[21-35]	M/F	Single	Obesity
54***	[21-35]	M/F	Married	Obesity
54***	[25-28]	M/F	Married	Cancer
54***	[21-35]	M/F	Divorced	Cancer
54***	[25-38]	M/F	Divorced	Obesity
549**	[25-38]	M/F	Divorced	Cancer

As a privacy goal the algorithm overcomes background knowledge attack very efficiently. To achieve this since the algorithm uses generalization and suppression techniques on QID's the information loss is more. Also, the algorithm is difficult to extend to numerical attributes.

Rating: Privacy Preservation for MSA with Different Sensitive Requirements.

The Rating algorithm (Liu et al., n.d.) sets different sensitivity coefficients for the attributes and generates the Attribute Table(AT) and ID table(IDT). The algorithm is useful in the scenarios where it is difficult to classify the attributes into QID's and SA (Brickell & Shmatikov, 2008). Sensitivity Coefficient (SC) is set for each attribute and higher the SC value indicates that the data owner wants to preserve the attribute with high confidence. For example, SC value for Disease and Education attributes when set to 4 and 2 respectively indicates that Disease must not be linked by the adversary with ¼ confidence and Education should not be linked with ½ confidence.

Due to curse of dimensionality (Aggarwal, 2005; Ghinita et al., 2008), using k- anonymity or l-diversity may not be feasible since the information loss will be more. In this algorithm multiple attributes with different sensitivity requirements are addressed hence overcomes the problem of curse of dimensionality.

To understand the Rating algorithm, consider the microdata as shown in Table 13. With the SC(3,3,3,2,2) assigned for the attributes (zip code, age, gender, marital status and disease) the AT and IDT are shown in Table 16 and Table 17 respectively.

The algorithm uses average relative error as the information measure metric (Xiao & Tao, 2006a).

Table 16. Attribute table

ZIP code	Age	Gender	Marital Status	Disease
A1ID1	A2ID1	A3ID1	A4ID1	A5ID1
A1ID1	A2ID1	A3ID1	A4ID2	A5ID2
A1ID1	A2ID1	A3ID1	A4ID4	A5ID1
A1ID2	A2ID2	A3ID2	A4ID1	A5ID3
A1ID2	A2ID2	A3ID2	A4ID3	A5ID2
A1ID2	A2ID2	A3ID3	A4ID2	A5ID3
A1ID3	A2ID3	A3ID2	A4ID3	A5ID4
A1ID3	A2ID3	A3ID3	A4ID4	A5ID4

Table 17. ID table

ID		Age	Gender	Marital Status	Disease
ID1	54,67,75,49,02,54,678	21,32,26	M,F,M	S,M	A,O
ID2	54,90,65,46,75,54,676	35,25,28	M,F,M	S,D	A,C
ID3	5,49,05,54,973	36,38	M,F	M,D	O,C
ID4				S,D	O,C

Depending upon the privacy requirement of the data owner, the SC are assigned, and the data is anonymized. The main objective of the algorithm is to handle high dimensional data and to preserve privacy of all types of attributes. As shown in the published tables, since there is no generalization/suppression there is no information loss.

Rating algorithm ignores the association between the sensitive attributes. An intruder with some background knowledge on the relationship between the sensitive attributes, may disclose the identity/attribute of the individual. This was over come in the Privacy protection method for MSA based on strong rule algorithm (Yi & Shi, 2015)

Decomposition for Privacy Preserving MSA

Anatomy as well as slicing algorithms were designed considering single sensitive attributes and it was difficult to extend the methods for more than one sensitive attributes. Decomposition(Ye et al., 2009)method considers two sensitive attributes and anonymizes the data. The algorithm resembles the Anatomy algorithm.

To understand the algorithm consider the dataset in Table 18 with two SA –Occupation and Salary (in LPA). The algorithm creates SA groups by using l-diversity method in creating the groups. One of the sensitive attributes is chosen as a primary SA and others as non-primary SA. Care is taken to for SA groups such a way that each SA will have its own l. The diversity of primary sensitive attribute is denoted as lpri. The choice of primary SA depends on the publisher and if the non-primary sensitive attribute does not satisfy l pri, then random noise is added to the attribute value.

For example, in Table 16, Occupation is chosen as primary SA and Salary as non-primary SA. The SA groups are formed on Occupation satisfying 3 diversities, as shown in Table 19. If any of the tuple of salary is duplicate, then the attribute value is replaced with the noise. The decomposed table, Table 20 and the sensitive table, Table 21 are published.

Table 18. Sample microdata with 2 SA

ID	ZIP code	Age	Gender	Occupation	Salary
1	54677	39	F	Nurse	1
2	54602	32	F	Nurse	4
3	54678	40	M	Police	8
4	54905	53	F	Cook	9
5	54909	62	F	Actor	2
6	54906	57	M	Actor	7
7	54605	52	M	Clerk	8
8	54673	55	F	Cook	2

Table 19. 3 Diversity table

ZIP code	Age	Gender	Occupation	Salary
54***	30-50	M/F	Nurse	1
54***	30-50	M/F	Nurse	4
54***	30-50	M/F	Police	8
54***	30-50	M/F	Cook	9
54***	50-70	M/F	Actor	2
54***	50-70	M/F	Actor	7
54***	50-70	M/F	Clerk	8
54***	50-70	M/F	Cook	2

Table 20. Decomposed table

Group ID	ZIP code	Age	Gender	Occupation	Salary
1	54677	39	F	PoliceActorNurseClerk	1284
	54909	62	F		
	54678	40	M		
	54605	52	M		
2	54602	32	F	NurseActorCookClerk	4792
	54906	57	M		
	54905	53	F		
	54673	55	F		

Table 21. Sensitive attribute table

Occupation	Salary	Group ID
Nurse	1	1
Actor	2	1
Police	8	1
Clerk	4	1
Nurse	4	2
Actor	7	2
Cook	9	2
Clerk	2	2

When there are more than one sensitive attributes in the original dataset and needs to be anonymized, with the help of correlation between SA and QID, the intruder may be able to find the values of other SA's.

To measure the data utility of the algorithm KL divergence (Kifer & Gehrke, 2006b) is used.

For example, consider an intruder who obtains the QI values {M, 54678,F, 39} from other published data set and wants to find the occupation of the data owner. In this case even though the table is generalized and diverse, the intruder gets to know the individual belongs to first group. Later on, with the common sense he may be able to find that Nurse is female's occupation and thus gets to know her salary earned. The algorithm overcome attributes linking attack and record linking attacks as its privacy goals.

Compared with generalization and suppression techniques, the information loss is pretty less as the values are published in the original form. However, with non-primary sensitive attributes since the random noise is added it leads to data distortion.

Decomposition +: Improving I-Diversity for MSA

Although Decomposition algorithm ensures distinct l-diversity in multiple sensitive attributes and the model overcomes record and attribute linking attacks it has following drawbacks:

1. L- diversity is applied only for primary sensitive attributes.
2. The algorithm adds noise values for non-primary sensitive attribute values which leads to information loss.

3.   The random noise addition works well if the non-primary sensitive attribute is numerical, and no discussion is provided for categorical non primary sensitive attributes.

Decomposition + (Das & Bhattacharyya, 2012) is an extension of the decomposition algorithm, where in the authors consider the continuous data release. For example, the hospital releases the data on a monthly basis and there are chances that an intruder may find the data owner in multiple data releases.

The privacy goal of this algorithm is to prevent disclosure risks when the data is published incrementally. However, the utility goal of the algorithm is not clearly discussed by the authors.

(α,β,k)- Anonymity

With two sensitive attributes, the (α,β,k)- Anonymity algorithm(Zhao et al., 2009) provides an extension to k-anonymity and l-diversity. An adversary who has background knowledge of an individual can easily determine the one of the SA, with the help of other SA. Consider the Table 22, with Disease and Salary as sensitive attributes, Gender, Age and Zip code as QID's. A three diverse table on QID- Age, Gender and ZIP code is shown in Table 23.

Table 22. Sample microdata with 2 SA

ID	ZIP code	Age	Gender	Salary	Disease
1	54677	39	F	6k	Headache
2	54602	32	F	4k	Depression
3	54678	40	M	2k	Depression
4	54905	53	F	6k	Flu
5	54909	62	F	5k	Catatonia
6	54906	57	M	2k	Flu
7	54605	52	M	6k	Catatonia
8	54673	55	F	2k	Insomnia

In this table two equivalence groups are created. On observation it is found that in each group there are three distinct values for salary and disease. The β parameter indicates the distinct values of the sensitive attributes in each group. A table T is said to satisfy (α,β,k)- Anonymity iff it satisfies k-anonymity and no. of distinct values for each sensitive attributes appear at least β times. Within each group $\alpha=$ No. of distinct values of sensitive attribute – Corresponding No. of distinct sensitive attribute values. In the first group

- Distinct values of salary=Distinct values of Disease=3.
- Distinct values of (Salary, Disease)=2. Therefore $\alpha=3-2=1$.

As per the analysis done by the authors in the paper, if value of $\alpha=1$, it leads to privacy leakage when an intruder has a background knowledge. This happens when there is lesser diversity between sensitive attributes.

For example, if the intruder gets to know the QID's {54600, 40,F} from external source and is very much confident with background knowledge that the salary is not 6000. Then, with the published table the intruder can easily figure out that the individual is suffering from depression.

Table 23. 3 Diverse table on two SA

ZIP code	Age	Gender	Salary	Disease
54***	30-50	M/F	6k	Headache
54***	30-50	M/F	4k	Depression
54***	30-50	M/F	2k	Depression
54***	30-50	M/F	6k	Flu
54***	50-70	M/F	5k	Catatonia
54***	50-70	M/F	2k	Flu
54***	50-70	M/F	6k	Catatonia
54***	50-70	M/F	2k	Insomnia

To overcome this attack, one of the duplicated SA is generalized using the taxonomy tree. In this case Depression is replaced with Affective disorder, to prevent privacy leakage.

When the Multiple Attributes having lesser diverse values are generalized using l-diversity, there are chances of background knowledge attack. To prevent this (α,β,k)-Anonymity, replaces one of the repeated SA values with its generalized value, this is the main privacy goal of the algorithm. Although the algorithm operates on two SA, due to generalization and suppressions of QID's there is information loss. Also, if the SA attribute values are less diverse then the attribute values are generalized, this again leads to information loss.

Slicing on Multiple Sensitive attributes (SLOMS)

Slicing, Anatomy deals with only one sensitive attribute, whereas decomposition operates with 2 sensitive attributes. SLOMS (Han et al., 2013) algorithm as well as ANGELMS proposed by same author (Luo et al., n.d.) considers more than 2 sensitive attributes and anonymizes the data.

Table 24. Sample microdata with more than 2 SA

ID	ZIP code	Age	Gender	Occupation	Salary	Physician	Disease
1	54677	39	M	Nurse	2000+	John	Heart Disease
2	54602	32	M	Nurse	3000+	Bob	Flu
3	54678	40	F	Police	4000+	Jercy	Asthma
4	54905	53	M	Cook	8000+	Alice	Gastritis
5	54909	62	F	Actor	10000+	Tom	Heart Disease
6	54906	57	M	Actor	10000+	Lucy	Cancer
7	54605	52	F	Clerk	6000+	Bob	Flu
8	54673	55	M	Clerk	6000+	Leo	Asthma
9	54607	40	F	Teacher	7000+	Lucy	Cancer

The basic idea of the algorithm is to vertically partition the original attribute table into several sensitive attribute tables and one quasi-identifier table. The tuples in the tables are partitioned into some equivalence groups. The quasi-identifier values in each group are generalized to obey k-anonymity. The sensitive values of the sensitive table are sliced and bucketized to obey l-diversity requirements. Consider a microdata Table 24 with multiple sensitive and quasi-identifiers.

The table consist of sensitive attributes- Occupation, Salary, Disease and Physician. The quasi-identifiers are- Age, Gender and Zip code. The algorithm partitions the original table into one quasi identifier table as shown in Table 27 and two sensitive attribute tables (Occupation- Salary) and (Physician –Disease) as shown in Table 25 and Table 26.

In the sensitive attribute tables the SA are grouped such that each group satisfies l-diversity and the Group_Id is assigned to each group. In the final anonymized table mapping is done to the QID table and the Group_IDs of the sensitive attributes. The final table after applying SLOMS is shown in table 28.

Two metrices are used to measure the distortion of anonymous data caused by generalization (Li et al., 2006) and anatomy (Yang et al., 2009)

Table 25. Occupation and salary sensitive table (O-S)

Group-ID	Tuple id	Occupation	Salary
1	t1	Nurse	2000+
1	t5	Actor	10000+
1	t3	Police	4000+
2	t4	Cook	8000+
2	t8	Clerk	6000+
2	t6	Actor	10000+
3	t7	Clerk	6000+
3	t2	Nurse	3000+
3	t9	Teacher	7000+

Table 26. Physician and disease sensitive table(P-D)

Group-ID	Tuple id	Physician	Disease
1	t1	John	Heart Disease
1	t2	Bob	flu
1	t9	Lucy	Cancer
2	t4	Alice	Gastritis
2	t8	Leo	Asthma
2	t6	Lucy	Cancer
3	t7	Bob	Flu
3	t5	Tom	Heart Disease
3	t3	Jercy	Asthma

Table 27. Quasi identifier table

ID	Zip Code	Gender	Age
1	560089	F	20
2	560090	M	33
3	560091	F	22
4	560092	M	34
5	560099	M	21
6	560098	F	28
7	520028	F	33
8	534263	M	20
9	540019	F	24

Table 28. Final published table using SLOMS

ZIP	Age	Gender	O-S	P-D
546**	[30-40]	M/F	1	1
546**	[30-40]	M/F	3	1
546**	[30-40]	M/F	1	3
549**	>=50	M/F	2	2
549**	>=50	M/F	1	3
549**	>=50	M/F	2	2
546**	4*	M/F	3	3
546**	4*	M/F	2	2
546**	4*	M/F	3	1

SLOMS overcomes membership disclosure, identity disclosure and attribute disclosure threats, this is because the SLOMS conforms the k-anonymity, l-diversity property.

SLOMS uses means square contingency coefficient to measure the correlations between the SA's. Therefore, those SA that have high correlations are separated into single table. However, since there is generalization and suppressions on QID attribute values, there is information loss.

Anatomization with Slicing

Although SLOMS provides better privacy since suppressions and generalizations are incorporated, there is information loss. On basis of Anatomy and Slicing a method was proposed that integrates the benefits of both anatomy and slicing adhering to the principle of l-diversity and k- anonymity. This algorithm (Susan & Christopher, 2016) can also handle any number of sensitive attributes.

Consider Table 29, initially the sensitive attributes and the quasi-identifiers are identified and separated using anatomization. Later on, using slicing approach the anonymized table is generated as shown in Table 34. This approach reduces the information loss because of direct release of quasi-identifier attributes. Also using slicing vertical partitioning is done to group the corelated sensitive attributes. In the partitioned SA table, l-diversity is further applied to prevent attribute disclosures.

The dependency table shown in Table 30, discusses the correlation between various sensitive attributes. According to their dependencies the sensitive attributes are partitioned and grouped into buckets using l-diversity. Table 31 and 32 are sensitive attributes tables. Table 33 is a QID table and Table 34 is final anonymized table that is published.

Table 29. Sample table with many SA

Zip Code	Gender	Age	Symptoms	Occupation	Physician	Method used for diagnosis	Diagnosis	Salary (LPA)
560391	F	24	Stomach Ache	Doctor	P	Ultrasound Scan	Ovarian Cancer S1	32
560299	M	23	Chest Ache	Teacher	B	Sputum Culture	Acute Pneumonia	20
540119	F	26	Appetite loss	Doctor	J	Urine Culture	Uremia	8
534263	M	22	Legs inflammation	Business	A	DRE Analysis	Prostate Cancer S2	4
520128	F	35	Pelvic pain	Teacher	V	biopsy Test	Cervical Cancer S1	12
560398	F	30	Muscle pain	Business	E	ELISA Test	HIV	20
560192	M	36	Gasp	Teacher	R	spirometry Analysis	Asthma Acute	12
560290	M	35	Back Ache	Business	S	Blood test	Heart Disease	24
560189	F	22	Stomach Ache	Doctor	K	X-ray	UTI	12

Table 30. Dependency table between SA

SID	SA	Dependency
sa1	Symptoms	No
sa2	Occupation	No
sa3	Physician	sa1,sa4,sa5
sa4	Method used for diagnosis	sa1
sa5	Diagnosis	sa1
sa6	Salary	sa2

The privacy goal of Anatomization with slicing algorithm is to handle any number of sensitive attributes. It overcomes the background knowledge, attribute and record linking attacks.

All the information is published in the original form and since there is no suppression or generalization there is no information loss, however the algorithm leads to generation of many tables as discussed.

Table 31. Sensitive attribute table 1(ST1)

Occupation	Salary	Group Id
Teacher		
Business	8	G3
Doctor		
Doctor		
Teacher	24	G2
Business		
Doctor		
Business	16	G1
Teacher		

Table 32. Sensitive attribute table 2(ST2)

Symptoms	Physician	Method used for diagnosis	Diagnosis	Group Id
Legs inflammation	S	DRE Analysis	Prostate Cancer S2	
Appetite loss	K	Urine Culture	Uremia	G3
Stomach Ache	J	X-ray	UTI	
Muscle pain	R	ELISA Test	HIV	
Stomach Ache	V	Ultrasound Scan	Ovarian Cancer S1	G2
Pelvic pain	P	Biopsy Test	Cervical Cancer S1	
Chest Ache	E	Sputum Culture	Acute Pneumonia	
Gasp	B	Spirometry Analysis	Asthma Acute	G1
Back Ache	A	Blood test	Heart Disease	

Table 33. Quasi identifier table

Zip Code	Gender	Age
560189	F	22
560290	M	35
560391	F	24
560192	M	36
560299	M	23
560398	F	30
520128	F	35
534263	M	22
540119	F	26

Table 34. Anonymized table

(Gender, Age)	(ZIP code, ST1_GID1, ST2_GID)
(F,22)	(560189,1,3)
(M,35)	(560290,1,1)
(F,24)	(560391,2,2)
(M,36)	(560192,1,1)
(M,23)	(560299,2,1)
(F,30)	(560398,2,2)
(F,35)	(520128,3,2)
(M,22)	(534263,3,3)
(F,26)	(540119,3,3)

Anatomy with Permutation (APNE) Based on Naïve MSA Bucketization (NMBPA) and Closest Distance MSA Bucketization

Since anatomy releases the data in the original form, it does not overcome linking attacks. To overcome this, Anatomy with permutation (He et al., 2012) was proposed. This algorithm has two steps: 1. Anatomizing the data 2. Permuting the quasi-identifiers. Consider Table 17, after anatomizing the sensitive attributes and quasi-identifier tables are generated and later the attributes in quasi identifier are permuted. Table 35, shows the permuted quasi identifier values (Zip Code, Age and Gender) and the sensitive attributes are published as they are as shown in Table 36.

The process of grouping records via sensitive attributes is called bucketization. To achieve bucketization permutation method, multi-dimensional buckets are constructed. The bucketization process is achieved using Naïve multisensitive bucketization permutation algorithm (NMBPA). It consists of three stages: Building the buckets. Assigning the tuples and permutation. The groups/equivalence classes are constructed on QID's by measuring the distances using Closet distance multi-sensitive bucketization permutation algorithm (CDMBPA)

The main advantage of anatomizing with permutation is that the algorithm overcomes the linking attack, since the quasi-identifiers are permuted. Since, all the values are published in the original form hence there is no information loss when compared to generalization and suppression.

Table 35. QID table

ZIP code	Age	Gender	GID
54677	40	F	
54678	39	M	
54602	57	F	1
54906	32	M	
54909	52	F	
54605	62	M	
54905	55	F	2
54673	53	F	

Table 36. SA table

Salary	Disease	GID
6k	Headache	
2k	Depression	
4k	Depression	1
2k	Flu	
5k	Catatonia	
6k	Catatonia	
6k	Flu	2
2k	Insomnia	

KC Slice Algorithm

In this technique, multiple sensitive categorical attributes are considered. Here, K means the bucket size and C specifies the constant threshold for all sensitive attributes. The KC Slice algorithm (Onashoga et al., 2017) operates in three phases to generate the published table. In the first phase the SA's and the QID's are separated. One attribute value within each of the SA is considered as the High Sensitive Value (HSV) and other values treated as low sensitive values. In the next phase the buckets (EQ's) are created with K being the size of buckets and C being the threshold of the HSV of the SA. In the final phase, considering the correlations between the QID's, highly corelated QID's are concatenated with one of the Sensitive Identifiers. Also, the QID columns are randomly permuted to prevent linking attack. Consider the Table 37 with multiple SA (Occupation, Relationship, Disease, Education) and QID's (Hours of Work, Salary, Age, Gender and Zip Code). These are shown in Table 38 and Table 39.

Table 37. Sample microdata with many SA

ZIP code	Age	Gender	HrsOfWork	Salary	Occupation	Disease	Relationship	Education
54677	39	M	2	2000+	Nurse	Heart Disease	Other-Relative	Some-College
54602	32	M	3	3000+	Nurse	Flu	Wife	Pre School
54678	40	F	4	4000+	Police	Asthma	Husband	Some-College
54905	53	M	5	8000+	Clerk	Gastritis	Not-In Family	HS Grade
54909	62	F	6	10000+	Actor	Heart Disease	Unmarried	Some-College
54906	57	M	6	10000+	Actor	Cancer	Husband	Bachelors
54605	52	F	5	6000+	Clerk	Flu	Not-In Family	Some-College
54673	55	M	5	6000+	Clerk	Asthma	Not-In Family	HS Grade
54607	40	F	5	7000+	Teacher	Heart Disease	Wife	Pre School

Here, Clerk, Heart-Disease, Not in Family and Some College are considered as HSV of the Sensitive attributes, if the Threshold value is set to 2 then the resulting suppressed table of SA is shown in Table 40.

The algorithm considers only one sensitive value of each of the sensitive attributes even though there are other sensitive values. It doesn't consider the sensitiveness of the sensitive attribute. The threshold value (C) is same for all the sensitive attributes which may lead to similarity attack. Proper methodology is not used in creation of buckets.

Table 38. Sample microdata with many SA

HrsOfWork	Salary	Age	Gender	ZIP code
2	2000+	39	M	54677
3	3000+	32	M	54602
4	4000+	40	F	54678
5	8000+	53	M	54905
6	10000+	62	F	54909
6	10000+	57	M	54906
5	6000+	52	F	54605
5	6000+	55	M	54673
5	7000+	40	F	54607

Table 39. Sliced QID's and SID's

Hours of Work,/ Salary/ SID_ Education	Age/ SID_ Disease	Gender/ SID_ Relationship	ZIP code/ SID_Occupation
20, 2000+,41	39, 21	M, 31	54677, 11
3,3000+, 41	32, 21	M, 31	54602, 11
4, 4000+, 41	40, 21	F,31	54678, 11
5,8000+, 41	53, 21	M,31	54905, 11
6,10000+, 41	62, 21	F,31	54909, 11
6,10000+, 41	57, 21	M,31	54906, 11
5,6000+, 41	52, 21	F,31	54605, 11
5,60000+, 41	55, 21	M,31	54673, 11
5,7000+, 41	40, 21	F,31	54607, 11

Table 40. Assigning SID's to sensitive attributes

SID	Sensitive Attributes
11	***(1), Actor(2), Teacher(1), Clerk(2), Police(1), Nurse(2)
21	***(1), Heart Disease(2), Asthma(2), Gastritis(1), Flu(2), Cancer(1)
31	***(1) Not-In Family(2), Wife(2), Unmarried(2), Husband(2),
41	***(2), Some College(2), HS Grade(2), Bachelors(1), Pre School(2)

The technique overcomes the linking attacks, probabilistic attack, skewness and homogeneity attacks mainly because the sensitive attributes are separated from the quasi-identifiers and also the sensitive attributes and quasi identifiers are further sliced to provide better privacy. Other than the HSV that crosses the predefined threshold all other attribute values are retained in their original form, hence there is lesser information loss.

Enhanced and Optimal Dynamic KCi Slice Algorithm

There are various extensions to KC Slice model proposed by same author - KCi Slice (Raju et al., 2019a), Enhanced KC slice (Lakshmipathi Raju et al., 2018) and Optimal KC Slice (Raju et al., 2019b). These algorithms were proposed for dynamic data set.

The drawbacks of KC slice model were overcome in these techniques. The main features of these algorithms are:

1. The algorithms considers the sensitive levels of the SA.

2.   Different Thresholds are set for different SA values.
3.   The algorithms uses semantic l-diversity (Elabd et al., 2015) for bucketization.
4.   Since the thresholds are different for each of the sensitive attribute values, the utility is high.

Privacy Preserving Data Publishing with MSA Based on Overlapped Slicing

In this technique (Journal et al., n.d.) the sensitive values are distributed evenly in each created bucket. The distribution is done by maintaining the correlation between the QID's and SA's. Since the technique doesn't use generalization and suppression methods, the information loss is less. This technique overcomes the elimination attack, association disclosure attack and full functional dependency attack.

The overlapped slicing is an extension of slicing method. The idea is to duplicate the sensitive attribute column into more than one column. One of the sensitive attributes is considered as Primary Sensitive Attribute (PSA) and the high sensitive values are chosen from the PSA. Other sensitive attribute is considered as Contributary Sensitive Attribute (CSA) and the sensitive attributes are also chosen from the CSA. For example, consider the Table 41, here disease is chosen as PSA with Heart disease, Cancer and HIV being the highly sensitive values. Occupation is CSA with cook and driver being the highly sensitive attributes.

Buckets are created such that the buckets satisfy k anonymity and p-sensitivity (on PSA), values of k=3 and p=2. The resulting table is shown in Table 42.

In the next step, the table is sliced vertically for attribute partitioning. The partitions- (Age, Gender) and (Zip Code, Disease, Occupation) are created.

Table 41. Sample microdata table

Age	Gender	Zip Code	Disease	Occupation
39	F	54677	Flu	Cook
40	M	54602	Heart Disease	Nurse
32	M	54678	Bronchitis	Police
53	F	54905	Gastritis	Teacher
57	M	54909	Cancer	Cook
62	M	54906	Heart Disease	Police
40	F	54673	HIV	Driver
46	F	54605	Flu	Teacher
40	M	54607	Cancer	Teacher

Table 42. 2 sensitive 3 anonymous table

Group Id	Age	Gender	Zip Code	Disease	Occupation
1	39	F	54677	Flu	Cook
1	40	M	54602	Heart Disease	Nurse
1	40	F	54673	HIV	Driver
2	32	M	54678	Bronchitis	Police
2	53	F	54905	Gastritis	Teacher
2	57	M	54909	Cancer	Cook
3	62	M	54906	Heart Disease	Police
3	46	F	54605	Flu	Teacher
3	40	M	54607	Cancer	Teacher

The PSA is overlapped with the Age, Gender partition.

Finally, the group values are permuted to avoid any type of linking attacks. The sliced table is shown in Table 43 and the final permuted table is shown in Table 44. The author claims that such approach increases the utility since there is more attribute correlation.

Table 43. Sliced table

(Age, Gender, Disease)	(Zip Code, Disease, Occupation)
(39,F,Flu)	(54677,Flu,Cook)
(40,M,Heart Disease)	(54602, Heart Disease, Nurse)
(40,F,HIV)	(54673, HIV, Driver)
(32,M,Bronchitis)	(54678, Bronchitis, Police)
(53,F,Gastritics)	(54905, Gastritis, Teacher)
(57,M,Cancer)	(54909, Cancer, Cook)
(62,M,Heart Disease)	(54906, Heart Disease, Police)
(46,F, Flu)	(54605, Flu, Teacher)
(40,M,Cancer)	(54607, Cancer, Teacher)

The technique guarantees against elimination attack, association disclosure attack and full functional dependency attack. Suppose the attacker knows the age, gender and one of the sensitive attributes (disease or Occupation), he will not be able to map the other sensitive attribute since the attributes are all permuted.

Table 44. Overlapped table

(Age, Gender, Disease)	(Zip Code, Disease, Occupation)
(39,F,Flu)	(54677,Flu,Nurse)
(40,M,Heart Disease)	(54602, Heart Disease, Cook)
(40,F,HIV)	(54673, HIV, Driver)
(32,M,Bronchitis)	(54678, Bronchitis, Cook)
(53,F,Gastritics)	(54905, Gastritis, Teacher
(57,M,Cancer)	(54909, Cancer, Police)
(62,M,Heart Disease)	(54906, Heart Disease, Police)
(46,F, Flu)	(54605, Flu, Teacher)
(40,M,Cancer)	(54607, Cancer, Teacher)

When compared with techniques that employ generalization and suppression which has much information loss, this technique provides better utility.

1:M Anonymization Algorithms

Recently few algorithms were designed to preserve the privacy of 1: M datasets. In these datasets the individual can have multiple records. (p,k) angelization (Anjum et al., 2018) algorithm is designed to overcome background knowledge, non-membership and demographic attack that occur in the data set with multiple sensitive attributes(Han et al., 2013).It publishes two tables: Generalized table and Sensitive Batch table. The algorithm uses two techniques internally Angelization(Yufei Tao et al., 2009) and Extended (p,k) Anonymity (Sun et al., 2011). In Angelization, batches and buckets are created from the original table. A batch partitioning is performed on the sensitive attributes such that each batch satisfies pre-defined l-diversity requirements. A bucket partitioning is performed on the generalized quasi-identifiers such that each buckets satisfies k-anonymity. Although this technique is similar to Anatomy (Xiao & Tao, 2006a), it different because in Anatomy the attributes are published in the original form but in Angelization, the QID's are generalized. With the batch table and the bucket table, angelization generates Sensitive Batch Table (SBT) and Generalized Table(GT). The SBT has three columns: Batch_Id, Sensitive Attribute, Count. The GT has all QID's along with the batch id. (p,k) Angelization – If a batch partitioning table and a bucket partitioning table of a microdata are given, (p,k) Angelization produces an anonymized sensitive and generalized table. The main privacy goal of the algorithm demographic knowledge attack. The algorithm is designed to provide 1:M anonymity. Compared to SLOMS the algorithm produces better utility, but there is privacy breach that happens due to association attacks that happens because of MSA.

(c,k) diversity (Khan et al., 2020) is an improved version of (p,k) angelization. The algorithm is designed to overcome fingerprint correlation attack (Khan et al., 2020) that occurs when there are more than one records belonging to an individual. The authors of the algorithm proves that angel algorithm cannot be extended for MSA and the invalidations that occurs in (p,k) angelization when done.

On similar grounds (p,l) diversity algorithm is designed to overcome identity and attribute disclosure attack in 1: M datasets. It is an extension of balanced p+ sensitive k- anonymity and balance (p,α) anonymity algorithms that were proposed to preserve single sensitive attributes (Sun et al., 2011). Since most of our algorithms were discussed with single records in the data set, not much explanation is provided for these algorithms.

IMPLICATION OF THE RESEARCH AND RESEARCH DIRECTIONS

The algorithms are designed for MSA are designed with different privacy and utility goals as discussed in Section 6 The summary of all these algorithms is presented in Table 45. The implications of this study are:

- The algorithms designed for single sensitive attributes cannot be easily extended to MSA.
- Different algorithms and privacy/information loss measures are needed for MSA.
- The correlation between the SA's leads to association disclosure therefore the attributes must be partitioned/sliced to the privacy leaks.
- Most of the privacy preserving MSA algorithms are combined with Anatomy and Slicing to achieve better results.

With these observations there is a scope for research in these directions:

- Most of the existing privacy preserving algorithms for MSA do not consider the sensitivity levels of the SA. There is a need for algorithms that takes care of the correlations and the sensitivity levels of multiple sensitive attributes.
- The equivalence class are mostly created to satisfy L-diversity requirement; however, l-diversity leads to privacy threats, hence the equivalence class may be created to satisfy t-closeness.

Table 45. Summary of PPDP algorithms

SI.no	Algorithm Name	Year	Observations	Type and No. Of SA	Anonymization Methods	Privacy Goal	Utility Goal
1.	(p,l) diversity	2021	Designed for 1: M anonymization	Mixed/>2	Anatomy and Generalization	Overcome attribute and identity disclosures in 1:M datasets	The information loss is less since most of the data is published in the original form only.
2.	(c,k) Anonymization	2020	Designed for 1: M anonymization	Mixed/>2	Anatomy and Generalization	Overcomes Fingerprint Correlation(Fcorr) attack, prevents attribute disclosure attack.	The utility is high since all data is published in the original form only.
3.	Overlapped Slicing	2019	Works well with categorical data but not feasible with categorical and numerical attributes.	Categorical/2	Anatomy and slicing	Overcomes elimination attack, association disclosure attack and full functional dependency attack.	The information is published in the original form with no generalization or suppression, hence no information loss.
4.	(p,k) Angelization	2018	Designed for 1: M anonymization	Mixed/>2	Anatomy and Generalization	overcomes demographic attack.	The information loss is less since most of the data is published in the original form only.
5.	Novel KCi slice	2019	Designed for dynamic data publishing by giving equal priority for all the sensitive attribute values.	Mixed/>2	Anatomy and Permutations	Overcomes sensitivity attacks	Utility is high since only few attributes are suppressed.
6.	Enhanced Dynamic KC Slice model	2018	Designed for dynamic data publishing by choosing different thresholds for various SA based on their sensitiveness. The model takes care of only one value of SA's.	Categorical/2	Anatomy and Permutations	Overcomes similarity attack, Linkage attacks and identity disclosure attacks	Utility is enhanced by reducing cell suppressions.
7.	KC Slice	2017	Designed for Dynamic Data publishing and a constant sensitivity level is considered for all sensitive attributes.	Categorical/2	Anatomy and Permutation	Overcomes Linkage, Probabilistic, Skewness,, minimality, Correspondence Homogeneity attacks	Information loss is caused by few attributes cell suppressions
8.	Anatomy with permutation	2016	Handles both numerical and categorical data, no generalization or suppression methods are used	Mixed/>2	Anatomy and Permutation	overcomes the background knowledge, attribute and record linking attacks	All the information is published in the original form and since there is no suppression or generalization there is no information loss.
9.	Anatomization with Slicing	2016	Handles both numerical and categorical data, no generalization or suppression methods are used	Mixed/>2	Anatomy and slicing	overcomes the background knowledge, attribute and record linking attacks	All the information is published in the original form and since there is no suppression or generalization there is no information loss.
10.	Rating based on Strong Association Rules	2015	Extension of Rating Algorithm- designed to prevent association attack that occurs when MSA are associated	Mixed/>2	Permutation	Overcomes association attacks	The information loss is minimal since the all data values are published in the original form
11.	ANGELMS	2013	Overcomes the drawback of Multiple Sensitive Bucketization approach, that leads to more information loss.	Mixed/>2	Anatomy and generalization	membership disclosure, identity disclosure and attribute disclosure threats	uses means square contingency coefficient to measure the correlations between the SA's. Therefore, those SA that have high correlations are separated into single table. However, since there is generalization and suppressions on QID attribute values, there is information loss

continued on following page

Table 45. *Continued*

SLno	Algorithm Name	Year	Observations	Type and No. Of SA	Anonymization Methods	Privacy Goal	Utility Goal
12.	SLOMS	2013	First algorithm to consider MSA and Anatomize the SA considering their dependency. The algorithm generates anonymous tables with less generalization and suppression ratio.	Mixed/>2	Anatomy, generalization and suppression	membership disclosure, identity disclosure and attribute disclosure threats	uses means square contingency coefficient[ ] to measure the correlations between the SA's. Therefore, those SA that have high correlations are separated into single table. However, since there is generalization and suppressions on QID attribute values, there is information loss
13.	Decomposition +	2012	Extension of Decomposition algorithm designed to protect privacy for incremental data sets	Categorical and Numerical/2	Anatomy, Permutation	Overcomes Attribute and Record Linking attacks	Addition of noise leads to data distortion
14.	Rating	2011	Applies sensitivity coefficient to all the attributes (QID and MSA) suitable for high dimensional data.	Categorical and Numerical/2	Permutation	Attribute disclosure and Identity disclosure attacks	The utility is high since the data is published in the original form in two tables- Attribute Table and Identity Table
15.	P cover k- anonymity	2010	Extending the algorithm to numerical data is difficult.	Categorical/ 2	Generalization and Suppression	The algorithm overcomes background knowledge attack very efficiently	Observing the QID's they are all generalized, leading to heavy information loss. It can also be observed that the algorithm is difficult to apply on the combination of Numerical and categorical attributes.
16.	(α,β,k)- Anonymity	2009	Works well with categorical data but not feasible with categorical and numerical attributes.	Categorical/2	Generalization and Suppression	When the Multiple Attributes having lesser diverse values are generalized using l-diversity, there are chances of background knowledge attack. To prevent this (α,β,k)-Anonymity, replaces one of the repeated SA values with its generalized value. (α,β,k)-Anonymity, replaces one of the repeated SA values with its generalized value.	Although the algorithm operates on two SA, due to generalization and suppressions of QID's there is information loss. Also, if the SA attribute values are less diverse then the attribute values are generalized, this again leads to information loss.
17.	Decomposition	2009	Noise is added to prevent similarity and linking attack, this leads to data distortion. Fails to consider the correlation between the attributes.	Categorical and Numerical/2	Anatomy	Overcomes Attribute and Record Linking attacks	Addition of noise leads to data distortion
18.	Privacy Protection model for patient data with multiple sensitive attributes.	2008	The technique applies the diversity constraint on all the sensitive attributes depending upon the distinct values, it is feasible for categorical values but difficult for numerical values.l –diversity and k-anonymity can be extended to maximum of 2 sensitive attributes but not more than that.	Categorical/ 2	Anatomy, Generalization and Suppression	The technique provides privacy considering two sensitive attributes and prevents the linking and elimination attack by applying the column wise constraints	generalization and suppression techniques are applied there is information loss.

- A highly sensitive attribute that is occurring at lower frequency is not handled by algorithms (KC slice and its variants).
- The method of determining the correlation between the sensitive attributes is not clearly described in previous work.
- Most of the algorithm consider either multiple categorical data or multiple numeric data. However, the data set has both numerical and categorical sensitive data that needs to be preserved.

CONCLUSION AND FUTURE WORK

Most of the data set consist of multiple sensitive attributes that needs to be preserved. Even though the authors claim that the algorithms designed for single sensitive attributes can be extended to multiple sensitive attributes it is not feasible. Mainly because these algorithms predominantly use suppression and generalization as anonymization operations. When these methods are applied on the data with multiple sensitive attributes, there is heavy information loss and balancing the privacy and utility becomes difficult. Also with high dimensional data, these algorithms are not efficient. The data sets with MSA allows researcher to perform effective investigations, predictions and make decisions. Therefore, it is a high time to understand the techniques for MSA to preserve the privacy. In this survey, about fifteen different techniques provided us better insights in this domain. As a part of future work, we would like to propose a robust technique for privacy preserving MSA.

REFERENCES

Aggarwal, C. C. (2005). *On k-Anonymity and the Curse of Dimensionality*. Academic Press.

Agrawal, D., & Aggarwal, C. C. (2001). On the design and quantification of privacy preserving data mining algorithms. *Proceedings of the Twentieth ACM SIGMOD-SIGACT-SIGART Symposium on Principles of Database Systems - PODS '01*, 247–255. 10.1145/375551.375602

Anjum, A., Ahmad, N., Malik, S. U. R., Zubair, S., & Shahzad, B. (2018). An efficient approach for publishing microdata for multiple sensitive attributes. *The Journal of Supercomputing, 74*(10), 5127–5155. doi:10.100711227-018-2390-x

Bahrami, M., & Singhal, M. (2015). A light-weight permutation based method for data privacy in mobile cloud computing. *Proceedings - 2015 3rd IEEE International Conference on Mobile Cloud Computing, Services, and Engineering, MobileCloud 2015*, 189–196. 10.1109/MobileCloud.2015.36

Bayardo, R. J., & Agrawal, R. (n.d.). Data Privacy through Optimal k-Anonymization. *21st International Conference on Data Engineering (ICDE'05)*, 217–228. 10.1109/ICDE.2005.42

Benaloh, J., Chase, M., Horvitz, E., & Lauter, K. (2009). Patient controlled encryption. *Proceedings of the 2009 ACM Workshop on Cloud Computing Security - CCSW '09*, 103. 10.1145/1655008.1655024

Brand, R. (2002). *Microdata Protection through Noise Addition*. 1 doi:0.1007/3-540-47804-3_8

Brickell, J., & Shmatikov, V. (2008). The cost of privacy: Destruction of data-mining utility in anonymized data publishing. *Proceedings of the ACM SIGKDD International Conference on Knowledge Discovery and Data Mining*, 70–78. 10.1145/1401890.1401904

Byun, J.-W., Sohn, Y., Bertino, E., & Li, N. (2006). *Secure Anonymization for Incremental Datasets*. 1 doi:0.1007/11844662_4

Can, O. (2018). Personalised anonymity for microdata release. *IET Information Security*, *12*(4), 341–347. doi:10.1049/iet-ifs.2016.0613

Chase, M., & Chow, S. S. M. (2009). Improving privacy and security in multi-authority attribute-based encryption. *Proceedings of the 16th ACM Conference on Computer and Communications Security - CCS '09*, 121. 10.1145/1653662.1653678

Chi-Wing, R., Li, J., Fu, A. W.-C., & Wang, K. (2006). (α, k)-anonymity. *Proceedings of the 12th ACM SIGKDD International Conference on Knowledge Discovery and Data Mining - KDD '06*, 754. 10.1145/1150402.1150499

Ciriani, V., Vimercati, S. D. C., Foresti, S., & Samarati, P. (n.d.). *k-Anonymity*. Academic Press.

Dalenius, T., & Reiss, S. P. (1982). Data-swapping: A technique for disclosure control. *Journal of Statistical Planning and Inference*, *6*(1), 73–85. doi:10.1016/0378-3758(82)90058-1

Das, D., & Bhattacharyya, D. K. (2012). Decomposition+: Improving ℓ-Diversity for Multiple Sensitive Attributes. In *International Conference on Computer Science and Information Technology* (pp. 403–412). 10.1007/978-3-642-27308-7_44 de Aguiar, E. J., Faiçal, B. S., Krishnamachari, B., & Ueyama, J. (2020). A Survey of Blockchain-Based Strategies for Healthcare. *ACM Computing Surveys*, *53*(2), 1–27. doi:10.1145/3376915

de Capitani di Vimercati, S., Foresti, S., Livraga, G., Paraboschi, S., & Samarati, P. (2018a). *Confidentiality Protection in Large Databases*. 1 doi:0.1007/978-3-319-61893-7_27

de Capitani di Vimercati, S., Foresti, S., Livraga, G., & Samarati, P. (2019). Data security and privacy in the cloud. In S. S. Agaian, S. P. DelMarco, & V. K. Asari (Eds.), *Mobile Multimedia/Image Processing, Security, and Applications 2019* (p. 15). SPIE. doi:10.1117/12.2523603

de Capitani di Vimercati, S., Foresti, S., Paraboschi, S., Pelosi, G., & Samarati, P. (2018b). *Access Privacy in the Cloud*. 1 doi:0.1007/978-3-030-04834-1_10

de Guzman, J. A., Thilakarathna, K., & Seneviratne, A. (2020). Security and Privacy Approaches in Mixed Reality. *ACM Computing Surveys*, *52*(6), 1–37. doi:10.1145/3359626

Ding, W., Nayak, J., Swapnarekha, H., Abraham, A., Naik, B., & Pelusi, D. (2021). Fusion of intelligent learning for COVID-19: A state-of-the-art review and analysis on real medical data. *Neurocomputing*, *457*, 40–66. doi:10.1016/j.neucom.2021.06.024 PMID:34149184

Domingo-Ferrer, J., & Mateo-Sanz, J. M. (2002). Practical data-oriented microaggregation for statistical disclosure control. *IEEE Transactions on Knowledge and Data Engineering*, *14*(1), 189–201. doi:10.1109/69.979982

Domingo-Ferrer, J., & Soria-Comas, J. (2017). Steered Microaggregation: A Unified Primitive for Anonymization of Data Sets and Data Streams. *2017 IEEE International Conference on Data Mining Workshops (ICDMW)*, 995–1002. 10.1109/ICDMW.2017.141

Elabd, E., Abdulkader, H., & Mubark, A. (2015). L–Diversity-Based Semantic Anonymaztion for Data Publishing. *International Journal of Information Technology and Computer Science*, *7*(10), 1–7. doi:10.5815/ijitcs.2015.10.01

EU Commission website. (n.d.). https://ec.europa.eu/commission/priorities/justice-and%02fundamental-rights/data-protection/2018-reform-eu-data-protection-rules_en.%0A

Fang, Y., Ashrafi, M. Z., & Ng, S. K. (2011). *Privacy beyond Single Sensitive Attribute*. 1 doi:0.1007/978-3-642-23088-2_13

Fung, B. C., Wang, K., Fu, A. W. C., & Philip, S. Y. (2010). *Introduction to privacy-preserving data publishing: Concepts and techniques.* Chapman and Hall/CRC. doi:10.1201/9781420091502

Fung, B. C. M., Wang, K., Chen, R., & Yu, P. S. (2010). Privacy-preserving data publishing: A survey of recent developments. *ACM Computing Surveys, 42*(4), 1–53. Advance online publication. doi:10.1145/1749603.1749605

Fung, B. C. M., Wang, K., & Yu, P. S. (n.d.). Top-Down Specialization for Information and Privacy Preservation. *21st International Conference on Data Engineering (ICDE'05)*, 205–216. 10.1109/ICDE.2005.143

Gadad, V., & Sowmyarani, C. N. (2019). A novel utility metric to measure information loss for generalization and suppression techniques in Privacy Preserving Data publishing. *CSITSS 2019 - 2019 4th International Conference on Computational Systems and Information Technology for Sustainable Solution Proceedings, 4*, 1–5. doi:10.1109/CSITSS47250.2019.9031014

Gadad, V., Sowmyarani, C. N., Kumar, R., & Dayananda, P. (2020). Role of privacy attacks and utility metrics in crowdsourcing for urban data analysis. *CEUR Workshop Proceedings, 2557*, 17–31.

Gal, T. S., Chen, Z., & Gangopadhyay, A. (2008). A Privacy Protection Model for Patient Data with Multiple Sensitive Attributes. *International Journal of Information Security and Privacy, 2*(3), 28–44. doi:10.4018/jisp.2008070103

Gardiyawasam Pussewalage, H. S., & Oleshchuk, V. A. (2016). Privacy preserving mechanisms for enforcing security and privacy requirements in E-health solutions. *International Journal of Information Management, 36*(6), 1161–1173. doi:10.1016/j.ijinfomgt.2016.07.006

Ghinita, G., Kalnis, P., & Tao, Y. (2011). Anonymous publication of sensitive transactional data. *IEEE Transactions on Knowledge and Data Engineering, 23*(2), 161–174. doi:10.1109/TKDE.2010.101

Ghinita, G., Karras, P., Kalnis, P., & Mamoulis, N. (2007). Fast data anonymization with low information loss. *33rd International Conference on Very Large Data Bases, VLDB 2007 - Conference Proceedings*, 758–769.

Ghinita, G., Tao, Y., & Kalnis, P. (2008). On the Anonymization of Sparse High-Dimensional Data. *2008 IEEE 24th International Conference on Data Engineering*, 715–724. 10.1109/ICDE.2008.4497480

Goyal, V., Pandey, O., Sahai, A., & Waters, B. (2006). Attribute-based encryption for fine-grained access control of encrypted data. *Proceedings of the 13th ACM Conference on Computer and Communications Security - CCS '06*, 89–98. 10.1145/1180405.1180418

Gruschka, N., Mavroeidis, V., Vishi, K., & Jensen, M. (2018). Privacy Issues and Data Protection in Big Data: A Case Study Analysis under GDPR. *2018 IEEE International Conference on Big Data (Big Data)*, 5027–5033. 10.1109/BigData.2018.8622621

Han, J., Luo, F., Lu, J., & Peng, H. (2013). SLOMS: A privacy preserving data publishing method for multiple sensitive attributes microdata. *Journal of Software*, *8*(12), 3096–3104. doi:10.4304/jsw.8.12.3096-3104

Hasan, A., Jiang, Q., Chen, H., & Wang, S. (2018a). A New Approach to Privacy-Preserving Multiple Independent Data Publishing. *Applied Sciences (Basel, Switzerland)*, *8*(5), 783. doi:10.3390/app8050783

Hasan, A. S. M. T., Jiang, Q., Chen, H., Wang, S., Liu, F., Jia, Y., Han, W., Science, C., Liao, W., He, J., Zhu, S., Chen, C., Guan, X., Maheshwarkar, N., Pathak, K., Choudhari, N. S., Xu, Y., Ma, T., Tang, M., ... Siva Kumar, A. P. (2018b). Anonymization and Analysis of Horizontally and Vertically Divided User Profile Databases with Multiple Sensitive Attributes. *Journal of Big Data*, *8*(10), 768–772. doi:10.1109/ICMLC.2017.8108955

He, X., Xiao, Y., Li, Y., Wang, Q., Wang, W., & Shi, B. (2012). *Permutation Anonymization: Improving Anatomy for Privacy Preservation in Data Publication*. 1 doi:0.1007/978-3-642-28320-8_10

Iyengar, V. S. (2002). Transforming data to satisfy privacy constraints. *Proceedings of the ACM SIGKDD International Conference on Knowledge Discovery and Data Mining*, 279–288. 10.1145/775047.775089

Jajodia, S. (1996). Managing security and privacy of information. *ACM Computing Surveys*, *28*(4es), 79. doi:10.1145/242224.242327

Journal, I., Giri, S. S., & Mukhopadhyay, N. (n.d.). *Overlapping Slicing with New Privacy Model A Novel Framework for Privacy Conserving Data Publishing and Handling High Dimensional Data*. Academic Press.

Kargupta, H., Datta, S., Wang, Q., & Sivakumar, K. (2005). Random-data perturbation techniques and privacy-preserving data mining. *Knowledge and Information Systems*, *7*(4), 387–414. doi:10.100710115-004-0173-6

Khan, R., Tao, X., Anjum, A., Sajjad, H., & Malik, S. (2020). ur R., Khan, A., & Amiri, F. (2020). Privacy Preserving for Multiple Sensitive Attributes against Fingerprint Correlation Attack Satisfying c -Diversity. *Wireless Communications and Mobile Computing*, 1–18. doi:10.1155/2020/8416823

Kifer, D., & Gehrke, J. (2006). Injecting utility into anonymized datasets. *Proceedings of the ACM SIGMOD International Conference on Management of Data*, 217–228. 10.1145/1142473.1142499

Kundalwal, M. K., Chatterjee, K., & Singh, A. (2019). An improved privacy preservation technique in health-cloud. *ICT Express*, 5(3), 167–172. doi:10.1016/j.icte.2018.10.002

Lakshmipathi Raju, N. V. S., Seetaramanath, M. N., & Srinivasa Rao, P. (2018). An enhanced dynamic KC-slice model for privacy preserving data publishing with multiple sensitive attributes by inducing sensitivity. *Journal of King Saud University - Computer and Information Sciences*. 1 doi:0.1016/j.jksuci.2018.09.013

Lee, Y. J., & Lee, K. H. (2017). Re-identification of medical records by optimum quasi-identifiers. *2017 19th International Conference on Advanced Communication Technology*, 428–435. 10.23919/ICACT.2017.7890125

Lefevre, K., Dewi, D. J., Ramakrishnan, R., & Boulos, G. W. (2009). *Mondrian Mul+dimensional K-Anonymity*. Academic Press.

LeFevre, K., DeWitt, D., & Ramakrishnan, R., I. (2005). Efficient Full-Domain Kanonymity. *ACM SIGMOD International Conference on Management of Data*.

Li, D., He, X., Cao, L., & Chen, H. (2016). Permutation anonymization. *Journal of Intelligent Information Systems*, 47(3), 427–445. doi:10.100710844-015-0373-4

Li, J., Wong, R. C.-W., Fu, A. W.-C., & Pei, J. (2006). *Achieving k-Anonymity by Clustering in Attribute Hierarchical Structures*. 1 doi:0.1007/11823728_39

Li, N., Li, T., & Venkatasubramanian, S. (2010). Closeness: A New Privacy Measure for Data Publishing. *IEEE Transactions on Knowledge and Data Engineering*, 22(7), 943–956. doi:10.1109/TKDE.2009.139

Li, N., Qardaji, W., & Su, D. (2012). On sampling, anonymization, and differential privacy or, k -anonymization meets differential privacy. *Proceedings of the 7th ACM Symposium on Information, Computer and Communications Security - ASIACCS '12*, 32. 10.1145/2414456.2414474

Li, T., & Li, N. (2008). Towards optimal k-anonymization. *Data & Knowledge Engineering*, 65(1), 22–39. doi:10.1016/j.datak.2007.06.015

Li, T., & Li, N. (2009). On the tradeoff between privacy and utility in data publishing. *Proceedings of the ACM SIGKDD International Conference on Knowledge Discovery and Data Mining*, 517–525. 10.1145/1557019.1557079

Li, T., Li, N., Zhang, J., & Molloy, I. (2012). Slicing: A new approach for privacy preserving data publishing. *IEEE Transactions on Knowledge and Data Engineering*, *24*(3), 561–574. doi:10.1109/TKDE.2010.236

Liu, B., Ding, M., Shaham, S., Rahayu, W., Farokhi, F., & Lin, Z. (2021). When Machine Learning Meets Privacy. *ACM Computing Surveys*, *54*(2), 1–36. doi:10.1145/3436755

Liu, F., Jia, Y., & Han, W. (2012). A new k-anonymity algorithm towards multiple sensitive attributes. *Proceedings - 2012 IEEE 12th International Conference on Computer and Information Technology, CIT 2012*, 768–772. 10.1109/CIT.2012.157

Liu, J., & Luo, J. (n.d.). *Rating: Privacy preservation for multiple attributes with different sensitivity requirements*. Retrieved July 20, 2021, from https://ieeexplore.ieee.org/abstract/document/6137444/

Loukides, G., & Shao, J. (2007). Capturing data usefulness and privacy protection in K-anonymisation. *Proceedings of the ACM Symposium on Applied Computing*, 370–374. 10.1145/1244002.1244091

Luo, F., Han, J., & Lu, J. (n.d.). *ANGELMS: A privacy preserving data publishing framework for microdata with multiple sensitive attributes*. Retrieved July 20, 2021, from https://ieeexplore.ieee.org/abstract/document/6747576/

Machanavajjhala, A., Kifer, D., Gehrke, J., & Venkitasubramaniam, M. (2007). ℓ-diversity: Privacy beyond k-anonymity. *ACM Transactions on Knowledge Discovery from Data*, *1*(1), 3. Advance online publication. doi:10.1145/1217299.1217302

Martin, D. J., Kifer, D., Machanavajjhala, A., Gehrke, J., & Halpern, J. Y. (2007). Worst-case background knowledge for privacy-preserving data publishing. *Proceedings - International Conference on Data Engineering*, 126–135. 10.1109/ICDE.2007.367858

Mendes, R., & Vilela, J. P. (2017). Privacy-Preserving Data Mining: Methods, Metrics, and Applications. *IEEE Access: Practical Innovations, Open Solutions*, *5*, 10562–10582. doi:10.1109/ACCESS.2017.2706947

Muralidhar, K., & Sarathy, R. (1999). Security of random data perturbation methods. *ACM Transactions on Database Systems*, *24*(4), 487–493. doi:10.1145/331983.331986

Naehrig, M., Lauter, K., & Vaikuntanathan, V. (2011). Can homomorphic encryption be practical? *Proceedings of the 3rd ACM Workshop on Cloud Computing Security Workshop - CCSW '11*, 113. 10.1145/2046660.2046682

Onashoga, S., & Bamiro, B. (2017). *KC-Slice: A dynamic privacy-preserving data publishing technique for multisensitive attributes.* Taylor & Francis. 1 doi:0.1080/19393555.2017.1319522

Pascual, D., Amirshahi, A., Aminifar, A., Atienza, D., Ryvlin, P., & Wattenhofer, R. (2021). EpilepsyGAN: Synthetic Epileptic Brain Activities With Privacy Preservation. *IEEE Transactions on Biomedical Engineering, 68*(8), 2435–2446. doi:10.1109/TBME.2020.3042574 PMID:33275573

Peleg, M., Beimel, D., Dori, D., & Denekamp, Y. (2008). Situation-Based Access Control: Privacy management via modeling of patient data access scenarios. *Journal of Biomedical Informatics, 41*(6), 1028–1040. doi:10.1016/j.jbi.2008.03.014 PMID:18511349

Prasdika, & Sugiantoro, B. (2013). A Review Paper On Big Data And Data Mining. *International Journal on Informatics for Development, 7*(1), 33–35.

Rahimi, M., Bateni, M., & Mohammadinejad, H. (2015). Extended K-Anonymity Model for Privacy Preserving on Micro Data. *International Journal of Computer Network and Information Security, 7*(12), 42–51. doi:10.5815/ijcnis.2015.12.05

Raju, N. V. S. L., Seetaramanath, M. N., & Rao, P. S. (2019a). A Novel Dynamic KCi - Slice Publishing Prototype for Retaining Privacy and Utility of Multiple Sensitive Attributes. *International Journal of Information Technology and Computer Science, 11*(4), 18–32. doi:10.5815/ijitcs.2019.04.03

Raju, N. V. S. L., Seetaramanath, M. N., & Rao, P. S. (2019b). An optimal dynamic KC<SUB align="right">i-slice model for privacy preserving data publishing of multiple sensitive attributes adopting various sensitivity thresholds. *International Journal of Data Science, 4*(4), 320. doi:10.1504/IJDS.2019.105264

Ram Mohan Rao, P., Murali Krishna, S., & Siva Kumar, A. P. (2018). Privacy preservation techniques in big data analytics: A survey. *Journal of Big Data, 5*(1), 33. doi:10.118640537-018-0141-8

Reiss, S. P. (1984). Practical data-swapping: The first steps. *ACM Transactions on Database Systems, 9*(1), 20–37. doi:10.1145/348.349

Ruj, S., Stojmenovic, M., & Nayak, A. (2012). Privacy Preserving Access Control with Authentication for Securing Data in Clouds. *2012 12th IEEE/ACM International Symposium on Cluster, Cloud and Grid Computing (Ccgrid 2012)*, 556–563. 10.1109/CCGrid.2012.92

Samarati, P., & Sweeney, L. (1998). Generalizing data to provide anonymity when disclosing information (abstract). *Proceedings of the Seventeenth ACM SIGACT-SIGMOD-SIGART Symposium on Principles of Database Systems - PODS '98*, 188. 10.1145/275487.275508

Seol, K., Kim, Y.-G., Lee, E., Seo, Y.-D., & Baik, D.-K. (2018). Privacy-Preserving Attribute-Based Access Control Model for XML-Based Electronic Health Record System. *IEEE Access: Practical Innovations, Open Solutions*, 6, 9114–9128. doi:10.1109/ACCESS.2018.2800288

Shi, Y., Zhang, Z., Chao, H.-C., & Shen, B. (2018). Data Privacy Protection Based on Micro Aggregation with Dynamic Sensitive Attribute Updating. *Sensors (Basel)*, 18(7), 2307. doi:10.339018072307 PMID:30013012

Sowmyarani C. N., & Dayananda P. (n.d.). *Analytical Study on Privacy Attack Models in Privacy Preserving Data Publishing*. 1 doi:0.4018/978-1-5225-1829-7.ch006

Sowmyarani, C. N., Gadad, V., & Dayananda, P. (2021). (P+, A, T)-Anonymity Technique Against Privacy Attacks. *International Journal of Information Security and Privacy*, 15(2), 68–86. doi:10.4018/IJISP.2021040104

Sowmyarani, C. N., & Srinivasan, G. N. (2015). A robust privacy preserving model for data publishing. *2015 International Conference on Computer Communication and Informatics (ICCCI)*, 1–6. 10.1109/ICCCI.2015.7218095

Sun, X., Sun, L., & Wang, H. (2011). Extended k-anonymity models against sensitive attribute disclosure. *Computer Communications*, 34(4), 526–535. doi:10.1016/j.comcom.2010.03.020

Sun, X., Wang, H., Li, J., & Truta, T. M. (2008). Enhanced P-Sensitive K-Anonymity Models for Privacy Preserving Data Publishing. *Health (San Francisco)*, 1, 53–66.

Sun, X., Wang, H., Truta, T. M., Li, J., & Li, P. (2008). (p+, α)-sensitive k-anonymity: A new enhanced privacy protection model. *Proceedings - 2008 IEEE 8th International Conference on Computer and Information Technology, CIT 2008*, 59–64. 10.1109/CIT.2008.4594650

Susan, V. S., & Christopher, T. (2016). Anatomisation with slicing: A new privacy preservation approach for multiple sensitive attributes. *SpringerPlus, 5*(1), 964. Advance online publication. doi:10.118640064-016-2490-0 PMID:27429874

Sweeney, L. (2002a). A model for protecting privacy. *IEEE Security and Privacy, 10*(5), 1–14.

Sweeney, L. (2002b). Privacy protection using generalization and suppression 1. *IEEE Security and Privacy, 10*(5), 1–18.

Takabi, H. (2014). Privacy aware access control for data sharing in cloud computing environments. *Proceedings of the 2nd International Workshop on Security in Cloud Computing - SCC '14*, 27–34. 10.1145/2600075.2600076

Tang, J., Cui, Y., Li, Q., Ren, K., Liu, J., & Buyya, R. (2016). Ensuring Security and Privacy Preservation for Cloud Data Services. *ACM Computing Surveys, 49*(1), 1–39. doi:10.1145/2906153

Tao, Y., Chen, H., Xiao, X., Zhou, S., & Zhang, D. (2009). ANGEL: Enhancing the Utility of Generalization for Privacy Preserving Publication. *IEEE Transactions on Knowledge and Data Engineering, 21*(7), 1073–1087. doi:10.1109/TKDE.2009.65

Taylor, L., Zhou, X. H., & Rise, P. (2018). A tutorial in assessing disclosure risk in microdata. *Statistics in Medicine, 37*(25), 3693–3706. doi:10.1002im.7667 PMID:29931695

Toch, E., Bettini, C., Shmueli, E., Radaelli, L., Lanzi, A., Riboni, D., & Lepri, B. (2018). The Privacy Implications of Cyber Security Systems. *ACM Computing Surveys, 51*(2), 1–27. doi:10.1145/3172869

Truta, T. M., Campan, A., Abrinica, M., & Miller, J. (2008). A comparison between local and global recoding algorithms for achieving microdata-sensitive-anonymity. *Acta Universitatis Apulensis. Mathematics-Informatics, 15*, 213–233.

Truta, T. M., & Vinay, B. (2006). Privacy Protection: p-Sensitive k-Anonymity Property. *22nd International Conference on Data Engineering Workshops (ICDEW'06)*, 94–94. 10.1109/ICDEW.2006.116

V, K., & K.P, T. (2012). Protecting Privacy When Disclosing Information: K Anonymity and its Enforcement through Suppression. *International Journal of Computing Algorithm, 1*(1), 19–22. 1 doi:0.20894/ijcoa.101.001.001.004

Wagner, I., & Eckhoff, D. (2018). Technical Privacy Metrics. *ACM Computing Surveys, 51*(3), 1–38. doi:10.1145/3168389

Wang, G., Zhu, Z., Du, W., & Teng, Z. (2008). Inference analysis in privacy-preserving data re-publishing. *Proceedings - IEEE International Conference on Data Mining, ICDM*, 1079–1084. 10.1109/ICDM.2008.118

Wang, M., Jiang, Z., Zhang, Y., & Yang, H. (2018). T-Closeness slicing: A new privacy-preserving approach for transactional data publishing. *INFORMS Journal on Computing*, *30*(3), 438–453. doi:10.1287/ijoc.2017.0791

Wang, R., Zhu, Y., Chen, T.-S., & Chang, C.-C. (2018). Privacy-Preserving Algorithms for Multiple Sensitive Attributes Satisfying t-Closeness. *Journal of Computer Science and Technology*, *33*(6), 1231–1242. doi:10.100711390-018-1884-6

Wu, Y., Ruan, X., Liao, S., & Wang, X. (2010). P-cover k-anonymity model for protecting multiple sensitive attributes. *ICCSE 2010 - 5th International Conference on Computer Science and Education, Final Program and Book of Abstracts*, 179–183. 10.1109/ICCSE.2010.5593663

Xiao, X., & Tao, Y. (2006a). Anatomy: Simple and effective privacy preservation. *VLDB 2006 - Proceedings of the 32nd International Conference on Very Large Data Bases*, 139–150.

Xiao, X., & Tao, Y. (2006b). Personalized privacy preservation. *Proceedings of the 2006 ACM SIGMOD International Conference on Management of Data - SIGMOD '06*, 229. 10.1145/1142473.1142500

Xiao, X., Tao, Y., & Chen, M. (2009). Optimal random perturbation at multiple privacy levels. *Proceedings of the VLDB Endowment International Conference on Very Large Data Bases*, *2*(1), 814–825. doi:10.14778/1687627.1687719

Xiao, X., Yi, K., & Tao, Y. (2010). The hardness and approximation algorithms for L-diversity. *Advances in Database Technology - EDBT 2010 - 13th International Conference on Extending Database Technology, Proceedings*, 135–146. 10.1145/1739041.1739060

Xu, J., Wang, W., Pei, J., Wang, X., Shi, B., & Fu, A. W.-C. (2006). Utility-based anonymization using local recoding. *Proceedings of the 12th ACM SIGKDD International Conference on Knowledge Discovery and Data Mining - KDD '06*, 785. 10.1145/1150402.1150504

Xu, Y., Ma, T., Tang, M., & Tian, W. (2014). A Survey of Privacy Preserving Data Publishing using Generalization and Suppression. *Applied Mathematics & Information Sciences*, *8*(3), 1103–1116. doi:10.12785/amis/080321

Yang, X.-C., Wang, Y.-Z., Wang, B., & Yu, G. (2009). Privacy Preserving Approaches for Multiple Sensitive Attributes in Data Publishing. *Chinese Journal of Computers, 31*(4), 574–587. doi:10.3724/SP.J.1016.2008.00574

Ye, Y., Liu, Y., Wang, C., & Lv, D. (2009). Decomposition: privacy preservation for multiple sensitive attributes. *Springer, 5463,* 486–490. 1 doi:0.1007/978-3-642-00887-0_42

Ye, Y., Wang, L., & Han, J. (n.d.). *An anonymization method combining anatomy and permutation for protecting privacy in microdata with multiple sensitive attributes.* Retrieved July 20, 2021, from https://ieeexplore.ieee.org/abstract/document/8108955/

Ye, Y., Wang, L., Han, J., Qiu, S., & Luo, F. (2017). An anonymization method combining anatomy and permutation for protecting privacy in microdata with multiple sensitive attributes. *2017 International Conference on Machine Learning and Cybernetics (ICMLC),* 404–411. 10.1109/ICMLC.2017.8108955

Yi, T., & Shi, M. (2015). *Privacy Protection Method for Multiple Sensitive Attributes Based on Strong Rule.* 1 doi:0.1155/2015/464731

Yin, X., Zhu, Y., & Hu, J. (2021). A Comprehensive Survey of Privacy-preserving Federated Learning. *ACM Computing Surveys, 54*(6), 1–36. doi:10.1145/3460427

Yuan, X., Ma, X., Zhang, L., Fang, Y., & Wu, D. (2021). Beyond Class-Level Privacy Leakage: Breaking Record-Level Privacy in Federated Learning. *IEEE Internet of Things Journal.* 1 doi:0.1109/JIOT.2021.3089713

Yüksel, B., Küpçü, A., & Özkasap, Ö. (2017). Research issues for privacy and security of electronic health services. *Future Generation Computer Systems, 68,* 1–13. doi:10.1016/j.future.2016.08.011

Zhang, P., Jin, H., Dong, H., Song, W., & Bouguettaya, A. (2020). Privacy-Preserving QoS Forecasting in Mobile Edge Environments. *IEEE Transactions on Services Computing,* 1–1. doi:10.1109/TSC.2020.2977018

Zhang, Q., Koudas, N., Srivastava, D., & Yu, T. (2007). Aggregate Query Answering on Anonymized Tables. *2007 IEEE 23rd International Conference on Data Engineering,* 116–125. 10.1109/ICDE.2007.367857

Zhao, Y., Wang, J., Luo, Y., & Le, J. (2009). (α,β,κ)-anonymity: An effective privacy preserving model for databases. *Proceedings of the International Symposium on Test and Measurement, 1,* 412–415. 10.1109/ICTM.2009.5412903

Chapter 7

A Comprehensive Consent Management System for Electronic Health Records in the Healthcare Ecosystem

Swapnil Shrivastava
iD https://orcid.org/0000-0001-6673-0426
The International Institute of Information Technology, Bangalore, India

T. K. Srikanth
The International Institute of Information Technology, Bangalore, India

ABSTRACT

The recent trends in the healthcare sector have catalyzed the emergence of several healthcare ecosystems. The inevitable and innate health data exchange amongst ecosystem components for provisioning of healthcare services as well as secondary use has raised several trust issues. The consent is a predominant mechanism to ensure privacy preserving, secure and ethical exchange, as well as sharing of health records of a patient by establishments. The proposed consent management system supports the life cycle of consent given by the patient or their authorized entity as well as validation and delegation of consent by a provider for health records requested by a user in an ecosystem. It reinforces different types as well as flavors of consent to strike a balance between privacy protection, ease of use, and patient safety. It supports the simple, flexible, and efficient management of consent at different granularity of health resource, user, and purpose. This is enabled by embedding consent structure in tree representation of EHR and a tree traversal algorithm for conflict resolution.

DOI: 10.4018/978-1-6684-5991-1.ch007

INTRODUCTION

The emerging Healthcare Ecosystems (Shrivastava, Srikanth, & Dileep, 2020) comprise various healthcare establishments spread across different geographic locations as ecosystem components. Hospitals, pathology labs, clinics, blood banks and pharmacy stores are examples of healthcare establishments. In the ecosystem, they could play the role of either a health records user or a health records provider. The user is a healthcare establishment or healthcare professional (e.g. doctor, surgeon) at an establishment who wants to access health records of a patient in the custody of other establishments. In contrast, a provider is the establishment with whom the health records requested by the user reside. These components would dynamically interact amongst each other to support delivery of healthcare services e.g., consultation and therapy to a patient by a user. The service delivery process may require sharing of a patient's health records in the custody of one or more providers with the user. The exchange of health records enables unprecedented medical history generation, patient control, and coordinated care to the patient. The health records could also be shared with external entities for secondary use such as public health statistics, clinical research and insurance claims. This is enabled by Electronic Health Records (EHR) (Iakovidis,1998), a longitudinal view of health records of a patient that are generated as a result of clinical encounters undergone by them or clinical events that occur for them in different healthcare establishments during their lifetime.

In recent times, medical devices such as X-Ray machines and ultrasound devices are made online for fast sharing of patient's health records. Smart devices like fitness bands and insulin pumps are direct and continuous sources of a patient's vital parameters. This increasing connectivity of establishments and devices supports easy access to health records as well as providing timely healthcare to anyone from anywhere. On the flip side, this real time open environment has raised several security challenges that could compromise privacy and integrity of health records. The virtual collapse of organizational boundaries and plugging of devices to the internet has expanded the attack surface by manifolds (Ahmed, Naqvi & Josephs, 2019). Over the past few years, cyber security incidents e.g., massive scale targeted attacks (Padmanabhan, 2017), data breaches (Davies, 2018) and insider attacks (Spanakis et al., 2020) are on the rise in the healthcare sector. They are believed to have adverse effects on patient safety as well as functioning and reputation of establishments. Hence there is need for novel security controls for the distributed setting of the ecosystem that could block unauthorized access and update of health records.

In this chapter the authors have discussed fortification of the healthcare ecosystem based on the concept of consent i.e. the agreement of the owner on sharing of their health records amongst ecosystem components. As per various privacy guidelines, the patient is the owner of their health records and healthcare establishments are the custodian of these records (GDPR, 2016). The proposed dynamic, online, fine-grained and comprehensive Consent Management System supports collection, updating, revocation, retrieval, storage, delegation and validation of patient's Informed Consent on their EHR in the purview of the healthcare ecosystem. The Informed Consent is specific and bounded in terms of provider, user, health resource, purpose, operation, access right and validity. In some exceptional scenarios where a patient is unable to express preferences, the consent is given on their behalf by an Authorized Entity. The authors believe that seamless design and implementation of Consent Management System in a Healthcare Ecosystem should be an amalgamation of building foolproof privacy protection measures, minimizing laborious consent collection and validation for clinical activities and ensuring patient safety. These three dimensions of the proposed system are explained below.

- **Privacy Protection:** a wide-ranging system that manages the patient's consent in the healthcare ecosystem. The system supports different types (explicit, implicit, derived and proxy) as well as different forms of consent (allow, deny and combination of both). It also supports consent validation, delegation, revocation and breach detection for privacy preservation.
- **Ease of Use:** the implicit and derived consent offered by the system would minimize expressed consent collection from the owner. The tree representation of consent that matches with the underlying EHR structure makes the consent validation flexible, efficient and effective.
- **Patient Safety:** the system ensures with the help of mechanisms such as conflict resolution that patient safety is not endangered, or clinical work is not impeded in the scenarios or context where consent to a registered professional is indeterminate, unavailable or denied.

The proposed system provides separate interfaces for Owner, User and Provider to help them perform their corresponding functionalities. The **Owner** interface allows the patient and authorized entity to have direct access to the patient's health records stored in the custody of various healthcare establishments. They can give informed consent as well as view access history of a patient's health records. The **User** interface is utilized whenever a healthcare professional at a healthcare establishment needs to view health records of a patient stored with one or more providers. Whereas **Provider** interface would enable automatic validation and delegation of consent for providing health records of a patient to a user in the ecosystem. The Consent Repository stores the informed consent artifact in an appropriate model that supports flexible, effective and efficient validation of consent. The Electronic Health Record (EHR), Privacy Policies, Audit Log and Identity System are auxiliary repositories that provide supporting information for Consent Management. The authors have conceptualized an EHR-Consent tree structure that helps in providing a comprehensive view of all the consents given by a patient for different granularity of health resources, users and purposes. A tree traversal algorithm is designed for performing flexible and efficient consent management operations in the ecosystem. The fusion of Consent Management System with conventional security controls viz authentication, access control and auditing are believed to curtail cyber security incidents as well as generate cyber threat intelligence (Bhuyan et al., 2020).

CONSENT MANAGEMENT SYSTEM-A REVIEW

The health data is sensitive personal data, and any form of unauthorized disclosure, update or denial of access could cause severe harms to both patient and healthcare establishments inclusive of physical, financial, reputational and social (Matthan, 2017). Several countries have defined privacy regulations and guidelines to ensure privacy protection of their citizen's health data (Galpottage & Norris, 2005; GDPR, 2016). Moreover, ethically, the Hippocratic Oath (Agrawal, Kiernan, & Srikant, 2002) is taken by young physicians to uphold specific standards including medical confidentiality and non-maleficence for patients. There have been numerous reviews and studies conducted around security and privacy of digital health data (Fernandez-Aleman et al., 2013; Ghazvini & Shukur, 2013). For instance, privacy awareness (Tsai, 2010), privacy measures with built in access control (Win, 2005), data integrity for patient safety (Onuiri, Sunday, & Komolafe, 2015), overriding personal preference for public good (Harman, Flite, & Bond, 2012), monitoring audit trails for breach detection (Miron-Shatz & Elwyn, 2011) and patient's control over health data (Shah, Murtaza, & Opara, 2014).

The electronic consent from an owner is an efficient and effective mechanism to collect their privacy preferences for privacy compliance by the custodian to ensure confidentiality of their sensitive data (health records). A gap has been noticed (Asghar et al., 2017) between the health data privacy legislations and consent management in healthcare solutions that have been implemented across the world. Since the 20th century, the usage of term consent, namely Informed Consent has been prevalent in several fields including Ethical Theory (Faden & Beauchamp, 1986) and Politics (Monbiot, 2004). The importance of consent for building trust and privacy protection in the online environment of World Wide Web (Bonnici & Coles-Kemp, 2010) and e-Commerce applications (Clarke, 2002) were emphasized later. The prevalent but not the only way for consent collection from users of various web based and mobile based applications is the Notice and Consent mechanism (Cate & Mayer-Schonberger, 2015). Since it gives users the option to either consent or abandon use of requested service, it doesn't really ensure privacy protection. It is also called Opt-in and General Consent. On the contrary, Opt-out is a general denial of access to a patient's health data that requires a new consent from the owner for each access request by the custodian. Due to stark tradeoff between ease of use and privacy protection both Opt-in and Opt-out are not appropriate for practical applications. Hence the support for implied and implicit consent types as well as combination of Consent and Denial of Consent would cater to several practical requirements with ease (Coiera & Clarke, 2004).

Informed Consent is the choice or preference of the owner, in terms of context and purposes, given to the provider, for creation and subsequent usage of their health records by a user in the purview of privacy regulations. The design guidelines for Informed Consent in an online environment are discussed in (Friedman, Felten, & Millett, 2000). The owner's consent should be stored digitally and validated as and when access is made by an end user to their personal data for a certain purpose. Hence consent is linked with both privacy policies and access enforcement mechanisms (Russello, Dong & Dulay, 2008). An online consent model and demonstrator are enabled by privacy preserving transfer protocols (O'Keefe, Greenfield, & Goodchild, 2005) to ensure that access to the health records by the users is governed by the patient's consent.

Though the concept of consent is relevant in several fields, not much attention has been given in literature to the Consent Management System. The Consent Management System provides a collection of processes, policies and mechanisms for managing consent. The consent management system is a way of establishing trust of an individual that an organization respects their interest and personal data. The authors (Bonnici & Coles-Kemp, 2010) have categorized the existing Consent Management System into first generation, ex-post and principled. The principled Consent Management with consent theory, norms and norms manifestation as key components is believed to be a way forward to consent management. The Consent Management Suite (Heinze et al., 2011), Authorization model for e-consent (Ruan & Varadharajan, 2003) and Automatic creation and lifecycle management of authorization policies (ACTORS) (Asghar & Russello, 2015) are some of the Consent Management System available in the literature. A Consent Management System (Asghar & Russello, 2012) supports capture, storage, evaluation and revocation of consent which captures contextual information like requester name, requester role, request time, request location and combination of these for validation.

In a conventional healthcare application with Role Based Access Control (Ferraiolo & Kuhn,1992; Sandhu et al. 1996; Ferraiolo et al., 2001) or recent Attribute Based Access Control (Hu et al 2014; XACML, 2022) as a security control, the security policy would be defined to check only the role of the end users performing this activity. The Purpose Based Access Control (Byun, Bertino, & Li, 2005), Condition Purpose

Based Access Control (Kabir & Wang, 2011), Privacy Aware RBAC (PRBAC) (Ni et al., 2007), Multi-domain Privacy aware RBAC (Martino et al., 2008) and Noisy Views (Chaudhari et al., 2011), Consent Based Access Control (Zhang, Bacchus, & Lin, 2016) and more (Ghani, Selamat, & Sidek, 2012) are access controls that takes care of patient's privacy at the time of user request processing. While a huge body of work is known about access control to prevent unauthorized access, very little work exists to determine how an individual's consent to view their personal data is safeguarded in a distributed environment.

In the context of healthcare applications, consent (Hathaliya et al., 2019) is about agreement of a patient on sharing of their health records. The decentralized and immutable Blockchain ledger is believed to bring a paradigm shift in implementation of the Consent Management System for health data exchange in a distributed setting (Esmaeilzadeh & Mirzaei, 2019). The consent artifact is a formal agreement between the owner and custodian. Its non-reputability and non-forgeability characteristics could be met by innate properties of Blockchain. A Consent Management System (Tith et al., 2020) using Hyperledger Fabric provides a secure channel among participating establishments for writing consent artifacts, metadata about consented health records physically stored in EHR and hash values. The other Consent Management Systems using Blockchain are offered for fitness tracking ecosystem (Alhajri, Salehi, & Rudolph, 2022), efficient health data sharing (Hu et al., 2022), privacy regulation compliance (Vargas, 2019) and Internet of Things (Nathaniel, Baal, & Broda, 2019).

The recent development from social, technology and regulatory aspects in the healthcare landscape has caused the emergence of Healthcare Ecosystems (Gunter & Terry, 2005; Nadhamuni et al., 2021) across the globe. The OpenNCP (Fonseca et al., 2015) recommended and promoted by the European Commission connects National Health Systems across European countries. The protection of health data in an ecosystem cannot be provided by just deploying conventional security controls but there is a hard-pressed requirement for building privacy measures as well. Several security and privacy challenges were identified (Shrivastava, Srikanth & Dileep, 2020) that need to be addressed for seamless implementation of a healthcare ecosystem. The lack of accessibility, lack of awareness and digital exclusion challenges were identified from societal perspective, whereas, consent management, patient portal, unique identity, breach detection, data anonymization, data integrity and consent-based access control were identified from technology perspective. The Healthcare Industry 4.0 reference architecture (Larrucea et al., 2020) manages security and privacy during health data exchange in OpenNCP as per GDPR. The Consent Manager uses a data hiding tool and data sensitivity analyzer tool to share only consented data. To create a comprehensive view of health records, the ecosystem (Mandl, Szolovits, & Kohane, 2001) should be developed as per the privacy and technology standards as well as controlled by the patient. The exhaustive list of Consent Management

System requirements identified by the authors for the healthcare ecosystem using EHR to make a tradeoff between triad of privacy protection, ease of use, and patient safety while complying with privacy regulations is discussed in the next section.

CONSENT MANAGEMENT SYSTEM REQUIREMENTS FOR HEALTHCARE ECOSYSTEM

The Consent Management System for EHR in the healthcare ecosystem is envisaged to manage consent in a comprehensive, online, flexible and fine-grained manner. The low level functional and nonfunctional requirements that need to be catered for seamless design and implementation of proposed Consent Management System are listed in table 1.

Table 1. Requirement analysis of the proposed consent management system from privacy protection, ease of use and patient safety perspectives

Requirement	Description
Ecosystem Component Role	An establishment could be termed as either provider or user of health records depending upon the role played by them for the healthcare service delivery process in the healthcare ecosystem.
Persistence	The consent collected from the owner on their EHR should be stored in the Consent Repository of corresponding ecosystem components. This is to support consent validation for record creation and subsequent requests to view these records.
Fine grained	The management and validation of consent should be done at different levels of health resources (EHR), user and purpose in the distributed setting.
Informed Consent	The consent artifact stored in the Consent Repository captures the context in terms of who gave the consent, on which health resources, for what purpose, to whom and for what time period.
Denial of Consent	The proposed system should support the ability to deny access explicitly or implicitly at different levels of granularity.
Types of Consent	The system should support Informed Consent generation by explicit consent as well as by implicit consent, inferred consent and proxy consent.
Flavors of Consent	The system should support varying degrees of consent and denial of consent on health resources for different users and purposes.
Authorized Entity	The consent collected from legally capacitated person in case of patient being minor, incapacitated, critically ill or emergency.
Patient Safety	The indeterminate state at the time of access request processing is a serious concern in the health sector where patient wellness and safety is of utmost importance. For example, a doctor may not be able to access a patient's EHR at the time of emergency due to lack of consent and thus endangering the patient's wellbeing is an additional challenge that needs to be addressed.
Conflict Resolution	To resolve the situations where clashes between Consents, Denial of Consents or their combinations on a health resource could result in indeterminate response for access requests.

continues on following page

Table 1. Continued

Requirement	Description
Authorization	The consent validation functionality of the proposed system should be integrated with the access control mechanism of ecosystem components to ensure both security and privacy for health records of a patient in the healthcare ecosystem.
Revocation	The system should not only provide functionality for consent creation but also for revocation of an existing consent. The revoked consent is no longer valid.
Delegation	The system should provide the functionality to a healthcare professional to delegate the consent given to them by the owner to another healthcare professional.
Verify the Identity	The consent collection as well as revocation, update and delegation of existing consent would require authentication of the owner or their authorized entity.
Non repudiability	The Proof of Authentication support to affirm that the consent artifact is created by the Owner or their Authorized Entity.
Non forgeability	The tampering of consent and any kind of abnormal access to health records needs to be prevented.
Transparency	The owner should be provided a complete picture of all the consents given by them across different ecosystem components, their health records and access history.
Dynamic	The User should have access to the different levels of patient EHR mapped to different establishments depending upon their clinical requirements, the state of the service delivery process, and patient's consent.
Validity	The consent cannot be indefinite. It should have some validity that could be in terms of time and location.

The external entities like government agencies, judiciary, research centers and insurance agencies would also be termed as users of health records. The ecosystem should ensure the patient's privacy by maintaining confidentiality of a patient's health records at the time of access request made by healthcare professionals or any other external entities.

DESIGN AND IMPLEMENTATION OF PROPOSED SOLUTION

The authors have conceptualized consent as a proof of agreement with specific time validity that the patient or their authorized entity has granted or denied permission to healthcare resource users to perform operations for intended purpose(s) on their health resources in the custody of a health resource provider. The proposed Consent Management System is a collection of processes, methods and policies with the aim to support secure, privacy preserving, and ethical sharing of health records organized as EHR in the healthcare ecosystem. The proposed consent management system is intended to assist the triad of Privacy Protection, Ease of Use and Patient Safety. It comprises Consent Repository, Interfaces for Owner, User and Provider as well as Auxiliary Repositories (Privacy Policies, EHR, Identity System and Audit Logs) as building blocks. The high-level block diagram of the proposed system that enables these key functionalities are shown in figure 1 and briefly described as follows:

Figure 1. Block diagram of proposed Consent Management System

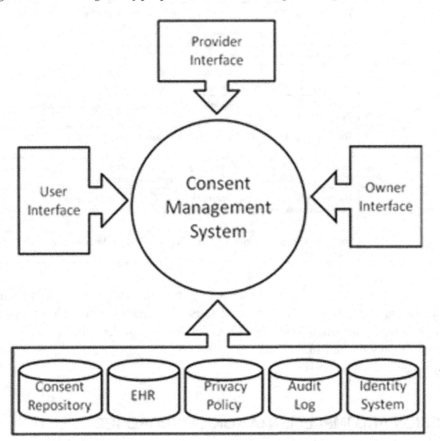

Consent Repository

In a healthcare ecosystem, consent could be managed in a centralized repository or in repositories distributed across ecosystem components. In the proposed system we have considered the later approach i.e., consent repository local to each ecosystem component. The consent collected from the owner or authorized entity is stored in the form of consent artifact (discussed in the subsequent section) in the repository. The consent should be validated for any future provisioning of healthcare service or secondary use of a patient's health data. The repository stores the collected consent artifact in an appropriate model that supports flexible, effective and efficient validation of consent. This repository assists in storing and managing different types of consent in a non-forgeable and non-repudiable manner. The Consent Repository also supports automated lifecycle management of different types of consent.

Owner Interface

An interface is provided to the owner, i.e., patient, to have direct access to their health records stored in the custody of various healthcare establishments. They could control the creation and usage of their health records by healthcare professionals working in a healthcare establishment or external entities by providing their choices in the form of consent. In some exceptional scenarios where a patient is unable to express their preferences, the consent is given by an authorized entity on behalf of the patient. This interface provides consent collection, consent revocation, consent updation and consent retrieval functionalities. 1) The Consent Collection feature is invoked to collect the explicit consent and proxy consent from a patient and authorized entity respectively as well as store them in the form of a consent artifact.2) The Consent Revocation functionality would help the patient or authorized entity to revoke their existing consent. This operation doesn't literally remove the artifact of consent chosen for revocation from the Consent Repository. It rather updates the status of this consent artifact to inactive. 3) Consent Updation functionality helps the owner to make changes to an existing consent. For instance, change in validity as well as addition or deletion of a purpose to the intended purpose list. 4) The Consent Retrieval is the functionality that would help the owner to view existing consent or search for existing consents using certain keywords. This feature is typically invoked before performing any of the above three operations. The efficient and flexible management of consent by the owner with the help of these functionalities is supported by tree representation of consent that is discussed in the later half of the chapter.

Provider Interface

It enables automatic validation and delegation of consent for providing health records of a patient to a user in the healthcare ecosystem. The provider is the healthcare establishment which holds the health records as well as maintains the consents for these records. Consent Validation is the functionality that checks the effectiveness of consent every time a healthcare professional views, creates and deletes the health records of an individual. In addition to security policies in terms of roles and responsibilities, the access enforcement mechanism should also validate the consent for the accessed purpose. Every time the system intercepts an access request made by a user for remote health records, that in turn should trigger the provider to allow sharing of required fields of consent artifact for validation. This includes validation of consent of both Allow and Deny type from multiple components, given at different granularity of health resource, user and purpose. The access purpose of the user's access request should be a subset of intended purposes of this consent. The health resources requested by the user should also be a subset of health resources for which consent is given. The user requesting the resource should be contained in the set of users who are consented to use it. The consent validity should also be checked i.e., consent status should be active and valid for the time at which the request is made. Only if all these conditions are true then the provider grants permission to user's access request else request is denied. A healthcare professional at the provider side can delegate consent to another healthcare professional at the user side. Consent Delegation function helps in delegation of consent from one healthcare professional to another healthcare professional. For example, when a doctor working in a hospital refers the patient to a specialist associated with another hospital.

User Interface

This interface is used whenever a healthcare professional at a healthcare establishment needs to view health records of a patient stored with one or more healthcare establishments (provider). For example, a pharmacist working at a pharmacy store needs to view the doctor's prescription stored in a hospital for dispensing medicine to the patient. The consent is given to a provider by the patient for allowing access to users on their health resources for intended purposes. The user may request for health records from one or multiple ecosystem components. For example, a doctor wants to view the medical history of a patient that can be created by aggregating a patient's health records from two hospitals and a pathology lab. In such a scenario, the consent given by the patient to the doctor should be validated at each of these components. Only after successful validation using tree representation of consent, requested health records are sent to the user. This interface should aggregate these health records in a chronological order prior to sending it to the user.

Auxiliary Repositories

There are the data repositories that provide supporting information for consent management. These auxiliary repositories are data stores for Electronic Health Record (EHR), Privacy Policies, Audit Log and Identity System.

Electronic Health Record (EHR)

The Patient EHR structure that the authors have considered for the proposed system is inspired by the OpenEHR (OpenEHR, 2022) Information Model. It can be represented by an ordered nary tree composed of three types of nodes viz. Patient EHR summary node, episode / encounter node and event node. It captures chronological order amongst various clinical encounters from timestamps in the health records. These nodes are described as follows: 1) Patient EHR summary node: This is the root node of the tree that comprises the unique patient id assigned to the individual along with the summary information like immunization chart and demographic details. The node also stores status information like whether the patient is alive. This node would be created at the time of the registration of an individual or first clinical encounter. 2) Episode / Encounter node: This is the internal node of the patient EHR tree. The encounter node would be created as a child node to the root node or an episode node. The series of encounters of an individual as part of long term clinical care would get organized under an episode and the episode would be accordingly modeled as a child to the root node in the EHR structure. 3) Event node: It is the leaf node of the tree that captures the details of the event generated at the time of execution of healthcare service (encounter) delivery activities. The node also points to the actual health record physically stored in the health record repository of ecosystem components.

Audit Logs

The ecosystem components perform various healthcare related activities (Shrivastava & Srikanth, 2021). The events executed as part of these activities are recorded in Audit Logs. The events recorded by Audit Logs have a context that comprises who performed the operation (actor), when the operation was performed, where the operation was performed and why the operation was performed. The different Audit Logs are used to come up with Proof of Authentication, Policy Compliance and Transparency methods. For advanced analysis, machine learning could be applied on log records to detect unauthorized access in near real time if some insider circumvents the consent management system for viewing health records of a patient.

Privacy Policies

For privacy compliance, the system should define privacy policies in addition to security policies (Karat et al., 2009). The Privacy Policies repository would be a collection of privacy policies that are overlaid with the policies of the establishment and privacy regulations. These privacy policies would be applicable on activities of healthcare service delivery that involve creation, viewing, processing, storing, update, deletion and sharing of health resources of a patient by healthcare professionals within or across healthcare establishments in an ecosystem.

Identity System

It would facilitate unique identity generation for a patient or their authorized entity and maintain their personally identifiable information e.g., demographic details, fingerprint and iris scan. They support fast and paperless identity verification and assertion of the identity holder in a distributed environment by means of Authentication service. The Authentication Service is used to verify whether the consent is given by the person who they claim to be. This service is used for identity verification at the time of updation, revocation and delegation of consent also.

CONSENT: STRUCTURE, LIFE CYCLE AND VALIDITY

Consent is the means by which the patient or their Authorized Entity can give permission to a Provider on the collection as well as usage of their EHR for Intended Purpose(s) by a User with specific time validity. A consent artifact follows a well-defined life cycle in the system. According to its current stage in the life cycle the status of consent could be active, inactive or archived. The newly created consent artifact is said to be in an active state. An existing consent artifact after any kind of update continues to stay in active state. The state of an existing consent in case of deletion or revocation would be changed from active to inactive. The state of an existing consent would also change from active to inactive after the end of its validity. After certain time duration, consent artifacts in active or inactive state are permanently archived for record purpose.

$(o, r, f, u, s, p, v, a^*, d^*, c^*)$

   The superscript "*" depicts that the parameters a, d and c are optional.

- Owner (o): the patient is the owner and gives consent for the collection, storage or use of their health resource. The unique id assigned to the patient is stored in this parameter. Here $o \in O$ where O is the collection of unique ids assigned to all the patients registered to the ecosystem.
- Health Resource (r): the health records of an owner from different healthcare establishments are modeled in the form of a comprehensive EHR structure. The health resource could have granularity ranging from coarse grained

to fine grained in the form of complete patient's EHR i.e. "all", summary information, encounter(s), episode(s) and event(s). If EHR R is represented by an ordered tree, then r signifies its sub tree. The health records of different granularity are fetched by traversal of R. The size of r would decrease as granularity is changed from coarse grained to fine grained.

- Operation (f): the consent also captures the permission given by the patient on their health records. The health records are immutable. Hence they are created once and viewed multiple times. In case of Consultation purpose, the patient can give "create" permission to the Health Resource User. Whereas, if the end user needs to view past history then the patient would give consent with "view" permission only. The permission $f \in F$ where $F = \{create, view\}$

- Health Resource User (u): The Health Resource User is either a healthcare establishment, or a role/department of healthcare professional in the establishment or the identity of a healthcare professional working in an establishment. Similarly for an external entity, user is either an organization or role or an individual. Hence u is represented as combinations of establishment/ organization identity (e), role/department identity (l) and individual identity (i). Here $e \in E$ where E is the set of all the establishments in the ecosystem as well as trusted apps, l belongs to the set of all the roles or departments in the establishment e and i is the identity of an individual working in the establishment e. If the consent is given to a healthcare establishment or external organization then user u would hold e. The consent given to a particular role/department would specify a user as (e, l). Whereas if consent is given to an individual the user u is an ordered collection represented as (e, l, i). This flexibility of user selection is facilitated by a user hierarchy with "all" as root node followed by establishment/organization as child nodes. Each establishment/organization would have the roles/departments as child nodes. The individuals playing a role/working in a department in the establishment would have that role/department as parent node.

- Access Right (s): this parameter captures the access right of the user that could either be "allow" or "deny". For example, the owner may give explicit consent (allow) to a Health Resource User on their Health Resource for intended purpose(s). On the contrary, a patient may give Denial of Consent i.e. deny access to a Health Resource User on their Health Resource for intended purpose(s). So the access right $s \in S$ where $S = \{allow, deny\}$

- Purpose (p): this field would hold one or more intended purposes for which the consent is given. The intended purpose here means the purpose for which the health resource of an owner could be created and used in the future. Healthcare services such as coordinated care, surgery and consultation as well as secondary use such as clinical research and insurance are examples of purpose. All the intended purposes could be represented in the form of a tree structure with "all" as the root node. If P represents the purpose tree, then p is the collection of all the intended purpose subtrees $p_1, p_2,....p_n$ for which the consent is given.

- Validity (v): consent can have different levels of validity. A consent can be permanent i.e. it doesn't have a validity end date. Here the consent is persistent and would be invalidated only when it is revoked. Another type is temporal validity i.e. time based and could be expressed in terms of number of days or time duration. The consent with temporal validity would have a field that represents number of days or consent validity end date. The third type of validity is event based validity also known as One Time Consent. Such a consent is given explicitly for an event for example correction of demographic details. The consent becomes invalid after successful execution of this event. The validity v is represented in terms of type (t), time duration (m_1,m_2), event (n) and status (q). The validity type $t \in T$ where $T = \{$permanent, temporal, one-time$\}$. If t is permanent then m1 is the consent creation date but m2 is not specified. For t as temporal both m_1 and m_2 are specified. m_2 could be either the number of days from date of consent creation or validity end date. For one-time consent, only the event n is specified. The status $q \in Q$ where $Q = \{$active, inactive, archived$\}$ is also maintained for all the consent artifacts.

- Authorized Entity (a): is the one who gives consent on behalf of the patient. For example parent or guardian is an authorized entity in case of the patient being minor. Whereas, caretaker and doctor are authorized entities in case of incapacitated patient and emergency situation respectively. The value in parameter a is the unique id of the authorized entity for owner o. This relationship can be represented by (o,a) where $o \in O$ and $a \in A$. Here A is the set of unique ids of all the Authorized Entity.

- Delegated (d): This parameter captures the Health Resource User who delegates the existing consent to another Health Resource User. This would be done as part of activity that involves data sharing between healthcare professionals. The d here would store the Health Resource User u who has delegated the consent. This is done for the traceability purpose. The delegated consent would always have permission as "view".

- Health Resource Provider (c): The provider is the healthcare establishment where the patient's health records are created and stored. It also stores the consent given by the patient on these health records. So, the provider $c \in E$ where E is the set of all the healthcare establishments onboarded to the ecosystem as well as trusted apps.

Consent: Types and Flavors

The healthcare service delivery process consists of a set of activities and each activity may be performed by different end users. For instance, Consultation starts with Registration by Front Office followed by Vital Parameter Measurement by on-duty Nurse then Consultation by Doctor and Medication by On duty nurse. It would be laborious to give consent to each and every end user for activity performed by them. Hence for ease of use the proposed system supports different types of consents for minimizing the need for expressed consent for different end users to perform different activities. The system also supports different flavors of consent to meet real world requirements.

Types of Consent

The proposed system supports creation and management of different types of consent viz informed consent, implicit consent, derived consent and proxy consent. This is to incorporate different healthcare service scenarios as well as support efficient delivery of time critical healthcare services. The explicit consent and proxy consent are directly collected from the owner and authorized entity respectively in the form of consent artifact. Whereas, implicit consent and derived consent are collected indirectly as part of execution of healthcare service. The consent artifacts of explicit consent, proxy consent and implicit consent have long term usage. Whereas derived consent has one time validity and is active for a very short span. These different types of consent are described as follows:

1. **Explicit Consent:** The explicit consent is the expressed consent given by the owner o to health resource user u to perform operation f for purpose p on health resource r having certain validity v. The consent can have either allow or deny access right. For instance, a patient with unique id 123 has allowed the health resource user Hospital A to create their health records with name "ResourceName" for intended purpose Consultation. These specifications are captured in the form of following consent artifact:

(o:"123", r:"ResourceName", f:create, u:(e:"Hospital A"), s:allow, p:["Consultation"], v=(t:permanent, q:active))

Let us take another example as the same patient visiting Hospital B for the purpose of a second opinion. The patient gives consent to the doctor with id 222 to view health records that were created at Hospital A. This consent is temporal and has an end date with value validity-end-date. The corresponding consent structure is:

(o:"123", r:"ResourceName", f:view, u:(e:"Hospital B", l: "doctor", i: 222), s: allow, p:["Second Opinion"], v=(t:temporal, m_1: timestamp, m_2: validity-end-date, q:active), c: "Hospital A")

2. **Proxy Consent:** The proxy consent is also an expressed consent that is given by an authorized person on behalf of the patient. The authorized entity here could be parent, guardian, caretaker, doctor and so on. The consent given by a parent on behalf of their child who is a minor is an example of proxy consent. The proxy consent would have the same artifact as explicit consent with an additional authorized entity parameter. For example, a patient with id 123 is a minor and visits the hospital accompanied with parents for consultation with a General Physician. The consent artifact for proxy consent given by the parent with unique id: 345 and authorized entity for the patient is

(o:"123", r: "ResourceName", f:create, u:(e:"Hospital B", l: "General Physician"), s: allow, p:["Consultation"], v=(t:temporal, m_1: timestamp, m_2: validity-end-date, q:active), a: "345")

The validity of authorized entity and proxy consent should be managed automatically by the system. For instance as the patient turns adult, the system wouldn't allow the authorized entity to give consent on behalf of the patient.

3. **Implicit Consent:** The implicit consent is generated for the patient's health record as part of execution of some healthcare related task or activity. There are many support apps that perform operations on patient's health records. For example there are apps that keep track of a patient's visit to an establishment and accordingly sends reminders for follow up consultation. These trusted apps require the patient's consent to perform their time bound activities/ tasks. In order to provide ease of use these consents are implicitly generated by the system. PatientApp is another example of a trusted app that maintains a summary of a patient's EHR. The consent is generated as part of execution of adding EHR context from a healthcare establishment. It is validated while performing operations like viewing health records from the app. The structure of implicit consent for this example would allow capturing the PatientApp as a health resource user is as follows:

(o:"123", r: "ResourceName", f:view, u:(e: "Patient App"), s: allow, p:["All"], v=(t:permanent, q:active), c: "Hospital A")

Only read operation could be performed by the Health Resource User to whom implicit consent is given. Another example of implicit consent is Consent Delegation.

a. **Consent Delegation:** It is the transfer of an expressed consent for a patient from one healthcare professional to another healthcare professional as part of performing some healthcare activity. For example the patient with unique id 123 gives consent to a doctor at Hospital A for consultation. At the time of consultation, the doctor diagnoses the patient with some serious disease and wants to seek the opinion of a Specialist. The doctor refers the patient to a specialist with id 111 at Hospital B. As part of this activity, the consent given by the patient to the doctor is delegated to the Specialist for viewing the patient's health records. The consent delegation is implicit creation of a new consent artifact.

(o:"123", r: "ResourceName", f:view, u:(e:"Hospital B", l: "Surgeon", i: 111), s: allow, p:["Consultation"], v=(t:temporal, m_1: timestamp, m_2: validity-end-date, q:active), d: (e:"Hospital A", l: "Doctor", i: 121), c: "Hospital A")

Here d captures the consent identifier to keep reference of the original expressed consent given by the patient and c is the health resource provider,

4. **Derived Consent:** This consent is derived or inferred from the expressed consent given for the patient. Derived consent is implicitly granted for a certain activity that is being executed as part of healthcare service for which the patient gave expressed consent. For example, a patient gives expressed consent for Consultation purposes to the Hospital A. This healthcare service is performed by the receptionist, on duty nurse and doctor. The derived consent is inferred from this expressed consent for all the end users. It has short term validity and is deactivated after the activity is executed successfully. This derived consent reduces the frequency of consent collection from patients and at the same time enables validation of access for each step of the healthcare service process, thus helping comply with the privacy policies of the organization.

Flavors of Consent

The proposed system supports coarse grained to fine grained consents. The General Consent (Opt-In) and General Denial (Opt-Out) are the simplest form of consent. In both these approaches there is a tradeoff between ease of use and privacy protection. Also, the real-world requirements of consent are not that straight forward. The consent can be given for different granularities of health records, purpose and user. The consent could be 1) General Allow, 2) General Denial, 3) General Denial and Expressed Allow, 4) General Allow and Expressed Denial and 5) Both Expressed Allow and Expressed Denial.

In order to understand different flavors of consent, let us consider the patientEHR of a patient with patient id 123. This EHR has two encounter nodes viz. "Consultation" and "Therapy". The "Consultation" encounter happened in Hospital A and has "Vital Parameters" and "Diagnosis Report" event nodes as children. Whereas therapy "Therapy" was given to the patient in Hospital B and has "Observation" and "Procedure" events as children. This EHR structure is shown in figure 2.

Figure 2. Patient EHR for patient with id 123

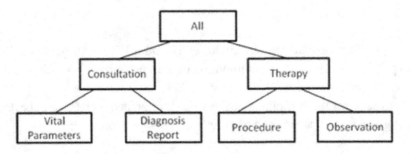

1.   **General Allow:** General Consent or Allow is a blanket consent that is given by the patient on their health records. The custodians can use and share these records with anyone for current as well as any future purposes. For example, the owner with patient id 123 gives consent with Allow access right to all health resource users to perform all operations for all purposes on all health resources. This consent would have permanent validity. The consent artifact for this form of consent is as follows:

(o:"123", r:all, f:create, u:all, s: allow, p:all, v=(t:permanent, q:active)) (1)

This consent artifact would result in fetching of the entire patientEHR shown in fig 2 for all purposes and all health resource users.

2.   **General Denial:** Whereas General Denial to a patient's health data requires new consent from the owner for each access request by the custodian. For example, the owner with patient id 123 gives consent with a Deny access right to all health resource users to perform all operations for all purposes on all health resources. This consent would have permanent validity. The consent artifact for this form of consent is as follows:

(o:"123", r:all, f:create, u:all, s: deny, p:all, v=(t:permanent, q:active)) (2)

This consent artifact alone would prevent fetching of patientEHR for any purpose and any health resource user. It is assumed that the owner would provide specific Allow consents where access is to be provided.

3.   **General Allow and Expressed Denial:** This is a variant of the General Allow. Expressed denial is the refusal from a patient for some health resource user to access some health data for some purpose. For instance, the patient denies consent to the Insurance Agent to view Therapy health records for the Insurance Claim purpose. The corresponding consent artifact is

(o:"123", r: "Therapy", f:view, u:(e: "Insurance Office"), s: deny, p:["Insurance Claim"], v=(t:permanent, q:active)) (3)

There could be scenarios where in addition to General Allow there could also be Explicit Denials. If we consider (1) and (3), the access request from Insurance Agent would be allowed access to only the Consultation health records.

4.   **General Denial and Expressed Allow:** In addition to General Denial, the Expressed Allow is gathered from an owner for some health data, for some purpose and for some end user. For instance, a patient with id 123 gave consent to the General Physician to create Health Records for intended purpose Consultation. The corresponding consent artifact is

(o:"123", r: "ResourceName", f:create, u:(e: "Hospital A", l: "General Physician"), s: allow p:["Consultation"], v=(t:permanent, q:active)) (4)

Combination of (2) and (4) could be interpreted as that there is a General Denial for any health record access request on PatientEHR from any health resource user except for this Expressed Allow given by the patient to the General Physician to create a new Encounter.

5.   **Expressed Denial and Expressed Allow:** This is combination of both i.e., Expressed Allow and Expressed Denial. In this case for the same end user there could be Expressed Allow for a set of health records for one set of purposes and Expressed Denial for another set of health records for another set of purposes. There could be overlap between these different sets of health records and purposes. For example, the patient 123 who gave Expressed Allow using (4) wants the Diagnosis Report generated out of the Consultation hidden from all. The consent artifact for this would be

(o:"123", r:"Diagnostics Report", f:view, u:all, s: deny, p:all, v=(t:permanent, q:active)) (5)

In such a scenario the user has Allow on all the Consultation health records of patient 123 created as per (4) except Diagnostic Reports. The flavors that are discussed from (3) to (5) require conflict resolution amongst multiple consents at the time of consent validation to avoid indeterminate state.

Consent Validation

In order to comply with healthcare privacy rules in the healthcare ecosystem, it is not sufficient that consent is collected and stored for record purpose and later archived. The access of health records in the ecosystem components should be done as per the patient's consent and privacy guidelines. The access here includes creation and viewing of health resources by various healthcare establishments. Hence the intercepting of access requests by access enforcement mechanisms for the ecosystem should also invoke consent validation functionality of the proposed system for privacy protection. So if there is a request to view the medical history of a patient that spans across three different hospitals, then the consent given by the patient for these three establishments should be individually validated by the provider interface. The validation of consent depends upon the type of consent.

1. **Explicit Consent:** In case of explicit consent the consent status should be verified. Only consent with Active status is valid i.e consent with q as active are valid. The status is set automatically by the system by verifying various validity parameters. In case of validity type as temporal for a consent, q is set as inactive if m_2 is less than system date and time. Whereas for validity type as permanent, only create date i.e. m_1 is captured. There is no value assigned for the validity end date m_2. For the validity type as an event, the consent is active only till the execution of the task is not completed. After successful execution of the task, the consent is marked as inactive. The access purpose p_a should belong to the intended purpose p_i mentioned in the consent artifact. For any purpose belonging to the intended purpose list, p_a should be a subset of p_i. The access request should be from the end user who belongs to the health resource user in the consent. The validation rules for access requests from an end user w.r.t. health resource user in the consent is explained in the conflict resolution sub section. The requested health resource should be a member of the health resource on which the consent is given.

2. **Proxy Consent:** In case of proxy consent all the aforementioned conditions are applicable. Along with them the Authorized Entity field value would also be validated. Whether the value in this field matches with the Authorized Entity nominated by the patient. The authorized entity value a_a sent in access request

for patient o_a health records is valid if there exist $(o_a, a_a) \in R$ where $R = \{(o_i, a_i) \mid o_i \in O$ and $a_i \in A$ and a_i is an Authorized Entity of o_i $\}$.

3. **Implicit Consent:** The implicit consent though captured indirectly are validated in the same way as the explicit and proxy consent. However, the validation of implicit consents that are given for support apps are triggered automatically without any human intervention. For example, reminders for follow up or regular checkup are sent at a stipulated time. The sending of these reminders are scheduled as jobs. The implicit consent of concerned patients is automatically validated at the time of execution of these jobs. Only for patients whose consent is valid, the required actions are performed. In case of consent delegation using implicit consent, the validation is initiated in the same way as the validation of explicit or proxy consent.

4. **Derived Consent:** The derived consent is validated automatically as part of execution of the activities of a healthcare service by different end users. The expressed consent is given by a patient for healthcare service they wish to avail at a healthcare establishment. The derived consent is inferred from this expressed consent for all the end users who are involved in delivery of healthcare service. The derived consent is validated as the precondition for execution of an activity by an end user. Only if there is a valid derived consent, the end user is allowed to perform the activity else not. The end users in establishments are on move and the activities are assigned dynamically to individuals or teams. Hence instead of organizational roles or individuals, the derived consent is generated for functional roles and teams.

Tree Representation of Consent

The health resource could have varied granularity ranging from the entire EHR to a single health record depending upon the purpose. These resources may be physically stored in one or many ecosystem components. The consents given by a patient for these health resources over a period of time are stored in the consent repository of corresponding ecosystem components. The owner interface should provide a complete picture of all the consents given by them across different ecosystem components. This would help them to decide on creation, updation and revocation of consent. Whereas the user interface should have access to the patient's EHR at different levels depending upon their consents. In order to meet these requirements, the owner and user interface would have to explicitly discover and make calls to all the providers of the patient's health records. For example, if the medical history of a patient is available with n establishments, then location of these n providers needs to be discovered for sending request for health records. The authors conjecture that the tree representation of patient's active consents leveraging on patient EHR would cater to different consent flavors in a distributed environment and user's request for various levels of health resources, purposes and users in a uniform and efficient manner. The ordered tree representation of consent anchored by patient EHR is shown in figure 3. This helps in providing a comprehensive view of all the consents given by a patient for different granularity of health resources, users and purposes. A tree traversal algorithm is designed to enable flexible and efficient consent validation in an ecosystem. The EHR-Consent Tree Structure and Tree Traversal algorithm are discussed in this section.

EHR-Consent Tree Structure

The EHR-Consent tree structure differs from conventional ordered tree structure as it contains nodes of different types viz root node, summary node, encounter node, episode node and event node. Each of these node types holds different forms of health information. A generic structure is defined for the Node of the PatientEHR Tree as shown in figure 4. Each node has a pointer to its Parent node and also connects to children's nodes in lexicographic order. Each node has a health resource name, health resource type and a consent structure. The node structure can be customized depending upon the characteristics of the above-mentioned types of node. For example, a root node would have resource name as all, health resource type as root, patient id and also contains a summary node. The structure of each of these nodes which are nothing, but variants of generic node structure are described as follows.

Figure 3. Patient EHR Tree

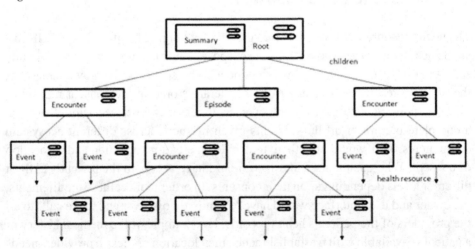

- **Root Node:** this node is the entry point into the patientEHR. It holds the unique patient id, demographic details, contains the summary node as well as is parent to various encounter and episode nodes.
- **Summary Node:** it holds a summary of the patient's chronology of health-related encounters and events. For instance, immunization charts and vital parameter statistics of the patient are stored in the summary node.
- **Encounter Node:** it contains the list of all the events that were performed as part of delivery of healthcare service to the patient. Consultation, Treatment and Surgery are examples of encounters.
- **Episode Node:** this node is parent to all the encounter nodes that were generated as part of prolonged medical care imparted to the patient. Pregnancy and childbirth, fracture and co-morbidities related treatment are examples of an episode.
- **Event Node:** it contains the details of the event that is performed at a healthcare ecosystem as part of healthcare service delivery. Encounter node is parent to an event node. The Event Nodes are leaf nodes of the tree and have pointers to actual health records.

Consent Structure

This structure is contained in all the nodes irrespective of their health resource type. The purpose of this structure is to hold relevant details about all the active consents that are given by the patient for a particular health resource. To support different flavors of consent, this structure is composed of two collections viz Agree List and Deny List. This list captures whether a patient has either allowed or denied access to the users on a health resource.

- **Agree List:** it is an ordered collection that stores details of the patient's consents given on the health resource that contains this list. Only consents that are of "Agree"type would be part of this list.
- **Deny List:** it is an ordered collection that stores details of the patient's consents given on the health resource that contains this list. Only consents that are of "Deny"type would be part of this list.

Each element of this collection would be a key value pair where the key is the "Health Data User" and value is the "Purpose" for which access is Allowed or Denied as well as timestamp of actual consent creation.

The EHR-Consent tree is a single window for all the patient's consents to help in dynamic and effective validation of different flavors of consent as well as different granularity of health resources, users and purposes.

Figure 4. Generic PatientEHR node with embedded Consent Structure

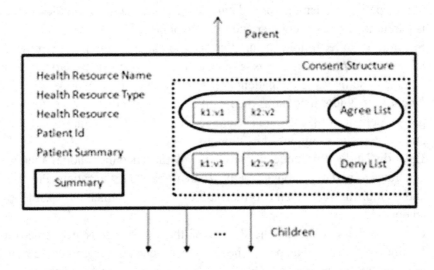

Tree Traversal Algorithm

The Tree Traversal algorithm has multiple applications that are a single window for all the patient's consents and return of medical history from multiple establishments depending upon the patient's consents. This structure would help in dynamic and effective validation of different flavors of consent as well as different granularity of health resources, users and purposes. This algorithm would traverse the PatientEHR Tree and depending upon the chosen application would do something. Here "to do something" could be some action like returning all consent, pointers to the allowed resources or only the names of the allowed resources.

The pseudo code of the tree traversal algorithm takes the patient id, health resource name, user details and purpose requested by the user as input. The algorithm would first verify whether a patientEHR exists for the patient with specified patientId. If the patientEHR with specific patientId is not found then it means that EHR for that patient doesn't exist and algorithm execution would terminate. If PatientEHR exists then starting from root node search for the requested health resource in the tree structure is done. As part of heath resource search, details of all the consents given by the patient to the requesting user and for the requested purpose on path starting from root node to the requested node in the tree are collected. A queue structure is used to traverse the requested health resource sub tree. The requested health resource is added to the queue structure. The resource from the queue is removed and consent for the requesting user for the requested purpose is searched in the consent structure. If the consent is of allow type, then do something else continue with the traversal. Now find the children of the resource and add them to the queue. Repeat the steps 5 to 20 i.e., dequeuing the health resource, consent validating and enqueuing the children of the health resource for all the nodes in the subtree of the requested resource. The consent validation done at the time of tree traversal isn't a straightforward matching of parameters. There could be instances where there are multiple consents given by a patient for a health resource or consent not given for requested purpose but for its parent consent and so on. The tree traversal in such situations may result in indeterminate output. Hence to deal with such ambiguous scenarios conflict resolution mechanism is required for consent. The various Conflict Resolution rules that are invoked in this algorithm to handle indeterminate situations are explained in the next section.

Algorithm TraverseConsentStructure(patientId, health resource, user, purpose)

1. Traverse to the requested resource node in the Patient EHR Tree
2. Collect the relevant patient's consent on the traversed path
3. Add the health resource node in a queue Q
4. Until Q is not empty
5. Remove health resource R from Q
6. f consent to user U for purpose P in consent structure of R
7. if consent is of allow type after conflict resolution
8. do something
9. else
10. create "consent of allow type doesn't exist" state
11. if consent is of deny type after conflict resolution
12. continue
13. else
14. create "consent of deny type doesn't exist" state
15. if both the state exists
16. return "consent doesn't exist" message
17. if consent is given for both allow type and deny type
18. conflict resolution
19. if allow type after conflict resolution do something
20. Add children of resource R to the queue

For example, the patient has given consent to all to view his entire medical history for all purposes on PatientEHR shown in figure 1. The patient visits Hospital C for some treatment, where the consulting doctor wants to view the medical history of the patient. The consent structure in the patientEHR tree is populated accordingly. The medical history generation would execute the tree traversal algorithm on the patient's EHR. The algorithm would do something e.g., return pointers to health records from both the encounters. What if the patient denies consent to everyone on the DiagnosisReport event to not disclose his disease to anyone. For this scenario, the tree traversal algorithm would do something for all the events and return all the health records except DiagnosisReport. The same patientEHR tree can be used by the patient to manage their consent. Taking the above scenario with two consents further, the patient while giving the consent to Hospital C would be shown an alert that there is a Deny for Diagnosis Report. The patient can choose to override this by One Time Consent to the doctor in Hospital C or maintain status quo. For the former choice, the doctor in Hospital C would be able to view all the health records from both the encounters. This scenario along with many other scenarios to show the robustness and completeness of the tree traversal algorithm are also depicted in the Result section.

Conflict Resolution

The patient's safety is ensured by the proposed system in the form of conflict resolution and consent overriding mechanisms. There are certain scenarios where multiple consents are given by a patient at different granularity that is applicable on requested health resources. There could also be situations where consent is not given for requested health resources but at a higher granularity. Such instances may cause indetermination or ambiguity at the time of consent validation while processing access requests made to an activity. The conflict resolution algorithms come in handy to resolve such vague state of affairs and take appropriate decisions for picking consent. The decision-making rules are defined to resolve conflicts and pick the most appropriate action in the scenario. These rules would be defined based on the privacy policies. The conflict resolution mechanisms developed in this work can be broadly classified into user conflict resolution, purpose conflict resolution and multiple consent conflict resolution.

- **User Conflict Resolution:** The Health Resource User in the consent would be specified at either healthcare establishment level or healthcare professional role level or individual healthcare professional level. However, the access request is made by a healthcare professional. The consent validation would require rule formulation for mapping requesting healthcare professionals to different user levels in the consent. The healthcare professional would be allowed access if consent is given for healthcare establishment where they work or healthcare professional role same as that of the requester or for the same individual, However the reverse won't be allowed i.e., consent given to an individual and access request coming from healthcare establishment or healthcare professional role. Also consent given to a healthcare professional role doesn't mean that the healthcare establishment would also get access. If the consent is given for "All" users on a health resource then an access request from any healthcare establishment, healthcare professional role and individual healthcare professional should be allowed.

- **Purpose Conflict Resolution:** The purpose is the reason for which the consent is given by the patient. OP consultation, surgery and therapy are some of the examples of purpose. All the healthcare purposes could be organized in the form of a purpose tree. For example, consultation and surgery purposes are children of OP node and IP node respectively. There could be situations where consent is given for a parent purpose, but the access request is sent for child purpose. In such a case the purpose conflict resolution would validate the appropriate rules to decide on the grant or deny of access request. As in, grant access request if the intended purpose in consent is a parent node to the access purpose. On the contrary if the intended purpose in the consent is child to the access purpose, then the access request should be denied. This would hold true assuming that the requester is the one to whom consent is given and the explicit consent is still active. If the consent is given for "All" purposes to a user on a health resource, then an access request from that user for any purpose for that resource should be allowed.

- **Multiple Consent Conflict Resolution:** There could be some scenarios where multiple consents are given by the patients that are applicable on the requested health resource. For instance, deny type consent is given to a user at the requested health resource. Whereas, allow type consent is given to the same healthcare professional on the parent node of request resource i.e. at a higher granularity. The conflict resolution for multiple consents could be done in different ways like time based, purpose based and user-based conflict resolution.

  ◦ Time based multiple consent resolution: The rule could be defined as in choose the latest consent amongst the two. For example, the Allow type consent on parent node was given prior to the Deny type consent given on the requested health resource. As per this rule, for this example the Deny type consent is the latest and would be picked over the Allow type consent that was created earlier.

  ◦ Purpose based multiple consent resolution: There could be situations where a patient would have given Allow consent to a parent purpose and Deny consent to one or more child purpose(s). In such a scenario if the access request is for the parent purpose, then for all the health resources where there is a denied consent for children's purposes, the access would be prohibited.

◦ User based multiple consent resolution: In the role hierarchy, the access may be given to the parent role but explicitly denied to one or more children nodes in the form of consents for the same health resource. In such a scenario any access request by a user with a parent role, for health resource would be denied for those children's nodes.

The key features of Consent Tree Structure and Traversal Algorithm are 1) It reduces the complexity of searching each provider system, sending the request and processing the response. 2) The tree structure provides a comprehensive view of consents and thus facilitates medical history creation from more than one HIPs. 3) The consent chronology is available with HIP only. Hence it is easier for them to resolve the conflict and send the allowed resources.

Result

The table 2 shows examples of six different consent flavors on the patient EHR-Consent structure for patient with id 123 discussed in earlier section. It also depicts the output of the tree traversal algorithm for the access requests from a user with identity number 12 and working in an establishment named Org A. The "ip" in consent represents intended purpose and "ap" in request stands for access purpose. In the first example, the patient has given consent to a user with id as 12 to view his entire medical history for the consultation purpose. Hence this consent would be stored in the consent structure of patientEHR's root node. The patient visits Hospital C for consultation, where the consulting doctor wants to view the medical history of the patient. As part of a medical history generation request from user (doctor) with id 12 and for purpose Consultation would execute the tree traversal algorithm on the patient's EHR and do something for health records marked in gray. The nodes marked in gray are selected as output of the tree traversal algorithm.

However, in the second example, the patient has given consent to all to view his entire medical history for all purposes. In this case the output remains the same, but the tree traversal algorithm would invoke conflict resolution mechanism to resolve purpose and user conflicts. In example 3, in addition to the previous consent given to the user 12 for consultation purpose, the patient denies consent to everyone on the DiagnosisReport event to not disclose his disease to anyone. For this scenario, the tree traversal algorithm would do something for all the events and return all the health records except DiagnosisReport. In addition to user and purpose conflict resolution, multiple time-based consent resolution would also be invoked. In example 4, first consent is given to a user with id 12 on the entire EHR for all purposes. Later Org A is given consent on the Therapy subtree of EHR for the consultation purpose. The tree traversal algorithm would do something for Procedure and Observation

Table 2. Owner consents and tree traversal algorithm output for different granularity of health resource, user and purpose

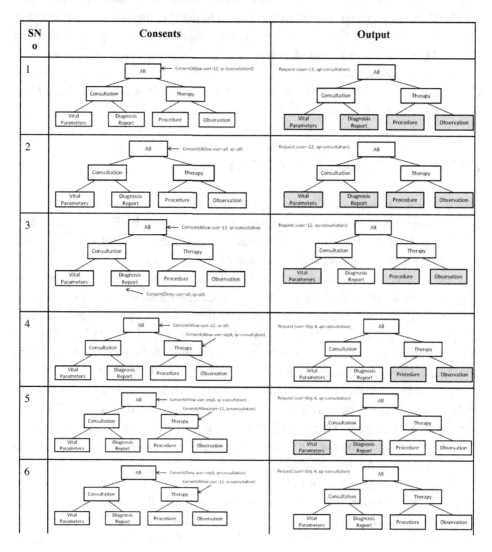

health records when a user request is sent by Org A for the consultation purpose. In example 5 the consent is given to user org A on the entire EHR for consultation purpose, whereas user with id 12 is given consent on the Therapy subtree of EHR for the same consultation purpose. The tree traversal algorithm in this case would do something for Vital Parameters and Diagnosis Report health records when a user request is sent by Org A for the consultation purpose. In the last example, the consent is denied to user org A on the entire EHR for consultation purpose. Later a user with id 12 is given consent on the Therapy subtree of EHR for the same purpose. The tree traversal algorithm in this scenario would return no health records for Org A user.

The Consent Tree can be used by the patient to manage their consent. Taking the above scenario with two consents further, the patient while giving the consent to Hospital C would be shown an alert that there is a Deny for Diagnosis Report. The patient can choose to override this by One Time Consent to the doctor in Hospital C or maintain status quo. For the former choice, the doctor in Hospital C would be able to view all the health records from both the encounters.

FUTURE RESEARCH DIRECTIONS

The Consent Management System discussed in this chapter is about managing consent from a patient or their authorized entity on patient EHR. The health data can have different types other than EHR such as real time vital parameters, advance directive, genome sequencing, health statistics and so on. There is a need for a Consent Management System to provide different degrees of consent depending upon the sensitivity level of the health data type. The backend support of different types of authentications is one possibility that could be explored for extending the proposed system for different health data types. The classification of health data depending upon their sensitivity level is another challenge that needs to be addressed. The consent collection in the Big Data era where future purposes are unknown at the time of data collection is a laborious and next to impossible task. In such a scenario the privacy risk analysis should be performed in terms of activity performed on the sensitive personal data and the extent of harm that they could cause should be analyzed. The consent collection should be restricted only for activities with unacceptable degree of harm.

The proposed system is an online solution that requires uninterrupted internet connectivity. However, there are several pockets across the world that have zero to very low to ad hoc internet connectivity. This could cause hindrance in consent collection and its real time validation in such regions. The alternate means of consent collection and validation such as using SMS service in such stringent circumstances needs to be explored. The consent artifact is a critical document and thus requires support for non-forgeability and non-reputability. The role of Blockchain to support these characteristics of consent in a distributed environment requires a thorough investigation. The Breach Detection algorithm using machine learning techniques could be another area of interest to detect unauthorized access in near real time. For example, insider circumventing the consent management system for malicious access to health records of patients.

The emergence of online consent management systems is believed to have an intrusive effect on conventional security controls viz authentication, access control and auditing. The incorporation of these privacy preserving features in the security controls would help in adoption of Consent Management System to its full potential. While a huge body of work is known about access control to prevent unauthorized access, very little work exists to determine how an individual's consent to view their personal data is safeguarded in a distributed environment. There is a need to explore integration of the proposed consent management system with access control to ensure both security and privacy while using health records of a patient in the healthcare ecosystem.

CONCLUSION

The Consent Management System deals with the collection of consent in the form of consent artifact, storage of consent artifact and validation of this consent. The consent in the healthcare domain is managed for sharing of health records. The authors have proposed a Consent Management System that supports the life cycle of consent, its validation and delegation for sharing of EHR in the healthcare ecosystem. The EHR facilitates creation of a holistic longitudinal view from health records of a patient that are physically stored in various healthcare establishments. The foreseen advantages of EHR has catalyzed the world over emergence of large scale, distributed healthcare ecosystems. The Consent artifact explicitly captures privacy choices given voluntarily by a patient/authorized entity to a health resource user after understanding the criticality and consequence of the healthcare service they are willing to avail. The key characteristics of the proposed Consent Management System are:

- The system collects, stores, delegates and manages the entire life cycle of consent in the healthcare ecosystem component.
- The system supports different types (explicit, implicit, derived and proxy), different forms of consent (allow, deny and combination of both) and breach detection for privacy preservation.
- The tree representation of consent that matches with the underlying EHR structure makes the consent management flexible, efficient and effective.
- The consent conflict resolution mechanism to ensure patient safety in exceptional and indeterminate scenarios.

In addition to security policies validation, the futuristic Consent Based Access Control would invoke consent validation functionality of the proposed Consent Management System to authorize a Health Resource User to access health resources of a patient distributed across different Health Service Providers (ecosystem components). The Identity and Authentication system enables maintaining a unique patient id across the entire healthcare ecosystem. This facilitates linking of patient's health records from different establishments as well as verifying identity of patient or their authorized entity for secured and non-repudiable management of consent. The consent management requires auditing to also support the compliance of privacy regulations. The monitoring of events recorded in distributed audit logs support Proof of Authentication, Privacy Compliance and Transparency. The breach detection could thus help in providing security measures for cyber threat intelligence. The seamless adoption of Consent Management System thus requires amalgamation with conventional security controls viz authentication, access control and auditing.

REFERENCES

Agrawal, R., Kiernan, J., & Srikant, R. (2002). *Hippocratic Database*. In *28th International Conference on Very Large Data Bases*, Hong Kong, China.

Ahmed, Y., Naqvi, S., & Josephs, M. (2019). Cybersecurity Metrics for Enhanced Protection of Healthcare IT Systems. *13th International Symposium on Medical Information and Communication Technology (ISMICT)*, 1-9. 10.1109/ISMICT.2019.8744003

Alhajri, M., Salehi, A., & Rudolph, C. (2022). Privacy of Fitness Applications and Consent Management in Blockchain. In *Australasian Computer Science Week 2022 (ACSW 2022)*. ACM. 10.1145/3511616.3513100

Asghar, M., & Russello, G. (2012). Flexible and Dynamic Consent Capturing. In J. Camenisch & D. Kesdogan (Eds.), Lecture Notes in Computer Science: Vol. 7039. *Open Problems in Network Security. iNetSec 2011*. Springer. doi:10.1007/978-3-642-27585-2_10

Asghar, M., & Russello, G. (2015). Automating Consent Management Lifecycle for Electronic Healthcare Systems. In A. Gkoulalas-Divanis & G. Loukides (Eds.), *Medical Data Privacy Handbook*. Springer. doi:10.1007/978-3-319-23633-9_14

Asghar, M. R., Lee, T., Baig, M. M., Ullah, E., Russello, G., & Dobbie, G. (2017). A Review of Privacy and Consent Management in Healthcare: A Focus on Emerging Data Sources. *IEEE 13th International Conference on e-Science (e-Science)*, 518-522. 10.1109/eScience.2017.84

Bhuyan, S.S., Kabir, U.Y., Escareno, J.M., Ector, K., Palakodeti, S., Wyant, D., Kumar, S., Levy, M., Kedia, S., Dasgupta, D., & Dobalian, A. (2020). Transforming Healthcare Cybersecurity from Reactive to Proactive: Current Status and Future Recommendations. *Journal of Medical Systems, 44*(5), 98. doi:10.1007/s10916-019-1507-y

Bonnici, C. J., & Coles-Kemp, L. (2010). Principled Electronic Consent Management A Preliminary Research Framework. *2010 International Conference on Emerging Security Technologies*, 119-123. 10.1109/EST.2010.21

Byun, J. W., Bertino, E., & Li, N. (2005). Purpose Based Access Control of Complex Data for Privacy Protection. In *Proceedings of the tenth ACM symposium on Access control models and technologies (SACMAT '05)*. Association for Computing Machinery. 10.1145/1063979.1063998

Cate, F. H., & Mayer-Schonberger, V. (2013). Notice and consent in a world of Big Data, Tomorrow's Privacy. *International Data Privacy Law, 3*(2), 2013. doi:10.1093/idpl/ipt005

Chauduri, S., Kaushik, R., & Ramamurthy, R. (2011). *Database Access Control & Privacy: Is there a Commom Ground.* 5th Biennial Conference on Innovative Data Systems Research (CIDR '11), Asilomar, CA.

Clarke, R. (2002). eConsent: A critical element of trust in ebusiness. *Proceedings of the 15th Bled Electronic Commerce Conference*, 338-360.

Coiera, E., & Clarke, R. (2004, March-April). e-Consent: The Design and Implementation of Consumer Consent Mechanisms in an Electronic Environment. *Journal of the American Medical Informatics Association, 11*(2), 129–140. doi:10.1197/jamia.M1480 PMID:14662803

Davies, J. (2018). *The 10 biggest U.S. healthcare data breaches of 2018.* Retrieved from https://healthitsecurity.com/news/the-10-biggest-u.s.-healthcaredata-breaches-of-2018

Esmaeilzadeh, P., & Mirzaei, T. (2019, June 20). The Potential of Blockchain Technology for Health Information Exchange: Experimental Study From Patients' Perspectives. *Journal of Medical Internet Research, 21*(6), e14184. doi:10.2196/14184 PMID:31223119

Faden, R. R., & Beauchamp, T. L. (1986). *A History and Theory of Informed Consent*. Oxford University Press.

Fernández-Alemán, J. L., Señor, I. C., Lozoya, P. Á., & Toval, A. (2013, June). Security and privacy in electronic health records: A systematic literature review. *Journal of Biomedical Informatics, 46*(3), 541–562. doi:10.1016/j.jbi.2012.12.003 PMID:23305810

Ferraiolo, D. F., & Kuhn, D. R. (1992). Role-Based Access Controls. *15th National Computer Security Conference*, 554–563.

Ferraiolo, D. F., Sandhu, R., Gavrila, S., Kuhn, D. R., & Chandramouli, R. (2001). Proposed NIST Standard for Role-Based Access Control. *ACM Transactions on Information and System Security, 4*(3), 222–274. doi:10.1145/501978.501980

Fonseca, M., Karkaletsis, K., Cruz, I. A., Berler, A., & Oliveira, I. C. (2015). OpenNCP: A novel framework to foster cross-border e-Health services. *Studies in Health Technology and Informatics, 210*, 617–621. PMID:25991222

Friedman, B., Felten, E., & Millett, L.I. (2000). *Informed Consent Online: A Conceptual Model and Design Principles*. CSE Technical Report.

Galpottage, P. A. B., & Norris, A. C. (2005). Patient consent principles and guidelines for e-consent: A New Zealand perspective. *Health Informatics Journal, 11*(1), 5–18. doi:10.1177/1460458205050681

GDPR. (2016). *The European Parliament and of the council. 2016. Directive 95/46/EC (General data protection regulation)*. Retrieved from https://eur-lex.europa.eu/legal-content/EN/TXT/PDF/?uri=CELEX:32016R0679

Ghani, N.A., Selamat, H., & Sidek, Z.M. (2012). Analysis of Existing Privacy-Aware Access Control for Ecommerce Application. *Global Journal of Computer Science and Technology, 12*(4).

Ghazvini, A., & Shukur, Z. (2013). Security challenges and success factors of electronic healthcare system. *4th International Conference of Electrical Engineering and Informatics (ICEEI)*. 10.1016/j.protcy.2013.12.183

Gunter, T. D., & Terry, N. P. (2005). The Emergence of National Electronic Health Record Architectures in the United States and Australia: Models, Costs, and Questions. *Journal of Medical Internet Research, 7*(1), e3. doi:10.2196/jmir.7.1.e3 PMID:15829475

Harman, L. B., Flite, C. A., & Bond, K. (2012). Electronic Health Records: Privacy, Confidentiality and Security. *The Virtual Mentor, 14*. PMID:23351350

Hathaliya, J.J., Tanwar, S., Tyagi, S., & Kumar, N. (2019) Securing electronics healthcare records in Healthcare 4.0: a biometric-based approach, *Comput. Electr. Eng., 76*, 398–410. 1.2019.04.017 doi:0.1016/j.compeleceng

Heinze, O., Birkle, M., Köster, L., & Bergh, B. (2011). Architecture of a consent management suite and integration into IHE-based regional health information networks. *BMC Medical Informatics and Decision Making, 11*(1), 58. doi:10.1186/1472-6947-11-58 PMID:21970788

Hu, C., Li, C., Zhang, G., Lei, Z., Shah, M., Zhang, Y., Xing, C., Jiang, J., & Bao, R. (2022). CrowdMed-II: A blockchain-based framework for efficient consent management in health data sharing. *World Wide Web (Bussum), 25*(3), 1489–1515. doi:10.100711280-021-00923-1 PMID:35002477

Hu, V. C., Ferraiolo, D., Kuhn, R., Schnitzer, A., Sandlin, K., Miller, R., & Scarfone, K. (2014) *Guide to Attribute Based Access Control (ABAC) Definition and Considerations.* NIST Special Publication 800-162.

Iakovidis, I. (1998). Towards Personal Health Record: Current situation, obstacles and trends in implementation of Electronic Healthcare Records in Europe. *International Journal of Medical Informatics, 52*(128), 105–117. doi:10.1016/S1386-5056(98)00129-4 PMID:9848407

Kabir, M. E., & Wang, H. (2009) Conditional Purpose Based Access Control Model for Privacy Protection. *20th Australasian Database Conference (ADC 2009),* Wellington, New Zealand.

Karat, J., Karat, C.M., Bertino, E., Li, N., Ni, Q., Brodie, C., Lobo, J., Calo, S.B., Cranor, L.F., Kumaraguru, P., & Reeder, R.W. (2009). Policy framework for security and privacy management. *IBM J. Res. Dev., 53*(2). 1 doi:0.1147/JRD.2009.5429046

Larrucea, X., Moffie, M., Asaf, S., & Santamaria, I. (2020). Towards a GDPR compliant way to secure European cross border Healthcare Industry 4.0. *Computer Standards & Interfaces, 69.* doi:10.1016/j.csi.2019.103408

Mandl, K. D., Szolovits, P., & Kohane, I. S. (2001, February 3). Public standards and patients' control: How to keep electronic medical records accessible but private. *BMJ (Clinical Research Ed.), 322*(7281), 283–287. doi:10.1136/bmj.322.7281.283 PMID:11157533

Martino, L. D., Ni, Q., Lin, D., & Bertino, E. (2008). Multi-domain and Privacy-aware Role Based Access Control in eHealth. *Second International Conference on Pervasive Computing Technologies for Healthcare,* 131-134. doi: 10.1109/PCTHEALTH.2008.4571050

Matthan, R. (2017). *Beyond Consent: A new paradigm for data protection.* Discussion Document 2017-2003.

Miron-Shatz, T., & Elwyn, G. (2011). To serve and protect? Electronic health records pose challenges for privacy, autonomy and person-centered medicine. *International Journal of Person Centered Medicine, 1*(2), 405–409.

Monbiot, G. (2004). *The Age of Consent- A Manifesto For A New World Order.* Harper Perennial.

Nadhamuni, S., John, O., Kulkarni, M., Nanda, E., Venkatraman, S., Varma, D., Balsari, S., Gudi, N., Samantaray, S., Reddy, H., & Sheel, V. (2021). Driving digital transformation of comprehensive primary health services at scale in India: An enterprise architecture framework. *BMJ Global Health, 6*(Suppl 5), e005242. doi:10.1136/bmjgh-2021-005242 PMID:34312149

Nathaniel, A., Baal, L., & Broda, G. (2019). Design and Implementation of a Blockchain-Based Consent Management System. *Computing Research Repository.* 1. doi:0.48550/ARXIV.1912.09882

Ni, Q., Trombetta, A., Bertino, E., & Lobo, J. (2007). Privacy-aware role based access control. *Proceedings of the 12th ACM symposium on Access control models and technologies*, 41-50. 10.1145/1266840.1266848

O'Keefe, C. M., Greenfield, P., & Goodchild, A. (2005). A Decentralised Approach to Electronic Consent and Health Information Access Control. *Journal of Research and Practice in Information Technology, 37*(2).

Onuiri, E., Sunday, I., & Komolafe, O. (2015). Electronic Health Record Systems and Cyber Security Challenges. *International Conference on African Development Issues*, 98–105.

openEHR. (2022). *openEHR - EHR Information Model.* Retrieved from https://specifications.openehr.org/releases/RM/latest/ehr.html

Padmanabhan, P. (2017). *The NHS ransomware event and security challenges for the U.S. healthcare system.* Retrieved from https://www.cio.com/article/3196706/cyber-attacks-espionage/thenhs-ransomware-event-and-security-challenges-for-the-u-s-healthcaresystem.html

Ruan, C., & Varadharajan, V. (2003). An Authorization Model for E-consent Requirement in a Health Care Application. In J. Zhou, M. Yung, & Y. Han (Eds.), Lecture Notes in Computer Science: Vol. 2846. *Applied Cryptography and Network Security. ACNS 2003.* Springer. doi:10.1007/978-3-540-45203-4_15

Russello, G., Dong, C., & Dulay, N. (2008). Consent-Based Workflows for Healthcare Management. *IEEE Workshop on Policies for Distributed Systems and Networks*, 153-161. 10.1109/POLICY.2008.22

Sandhu, R. S., Coyne, E. J., Feinstein, H. L., & Youman, C. E. (1996). Role-Based Access Control Models. *IEEE Computer*, *29*(2), 38–47. doi:10.1109/2.485845

Shah, J. R., Murtaza, M. B., & Opara, E. (2014). Electronic Health Records: Challenges and Opportunities. *Journal of International Technology and Information Management*, *23*(3), 10. doi:10.58729/1941-6679.1082

Shrivastava, S., & Srikanth, T. K. (2021). A Dynamic Access Control Policy for Healthcare Service Delivery in Healthcare Ecosystem using Electronic Health Records. *International Conference on COMmunication Systems & NETworkS (COMSNETS)*, 662-667. 10.1109/COMSNETS51098.2021.9352812

Shrivastava, S., Srikanth, T. K., & Dileep, V. S. (2020). e-Governance for healthcare service delivery in India: challenges and opportunities in security and privacy. In *Proceedings of the 13th International Conference on Theory and Practice of Electronic Governance (ICEGOV 2020)*. ACM. 10.1145/3428502.3428527

Spanakis, E. G., Bonomi, S., Sfakianakis, S., Santucci, G., Lenti, S., Sorella, M., . . . Magalini, S. (2020, July). Cyber-attacks and threats for healthcare–a multi-layer thread analysis. In *2020 42nd Annual International Conference of the IEEE Engineering in Medicine & Biology Society (EMBC)* (pp. 5705-5708). IEEE. 10.1109/EMBC44109.2020.9176698

Tith, D., Lee, J., Suzuki, H., Wijesundara, W. M. A. B., Taira, N., Obi, T., & Ohyama, N. (2020). Patient Consent Management by a Purpose-Based Consent Model for Electronic Health Record Based on Blockchain Technology. *Health Information Research*, *26*(4), 265-273. 1 doi:0.4258/hir.2020.26.4.265

Tsai, F. S. (2010). Security Issues in e-Healthcare. *Journal of Medical and Biological Engineering*, *30*(4), 209–214. doi:10.5405/jmbe.30.4.04

Vargas, J. C. (2019). Blockchain Cyber-attacks and threats for healthcare – a multi-layer thread analysis -based consent manager for GDPR compliance. In Open Identity Summit 2019, Lecture Notes in Informatics (LNI). Gesellschaft für Informatik.

Win, K. T. (2005). A review of security of electronic health records. *Health Information Management*, *34*(1), 13-18.

XACML. (2022). *OASIS eXtensible Access Control Markup Language (XACML)*. Retrieved from https://www.oasis-open.org/committees/tc_home.php?wg_abbrev=xacml

Zhang, A., Bacchus, A., & Lin, X. (2016). Consent-based access control for secure and privacy-preserving health information exchange. *Security and Communication Networks*, 9(16), 3496–3508. doi:10.1002ec.1556

ADDITIONAL READING

Math, S. B., Manjunatha, N., Kumar, C. N., Dinakaran, D., Gowda, G. S., Rao, G. N., Parthasarathy, R., Srikanth, T. K., & Gangadhar, B. N. (2021, March). Mental healthcare management system (e-MANAS) to implement India's Mental Healthcare Act, 2017: Methodological design, components, and its implications. *Asian Journal of Psychiatry*, 57, 102391. doi:10.1016/j.ajp.2020.102391 PMID:33187888

Shrivastava, S., & Srikanth, T. K. (2022). A Framework for Secure and Privacy Preserving Health Data Exchange across Health Information Systems using a Digital Identity System. In *15th International Conference on Theory and Practice of Electronic Governance (ICEGOV 2022)*. ACM. 10.1145/3560107.3560115

KEY TERMS AND DEFINITIONS

Electronic Health Records (EHR): It is the longitudinal collection of the health records of a patient that are physically stored in healthcare establishments they visited to avail healthcare services.

Health Resource Provider (HRP): The healthcare establishment where the health records of a patient are created and stored. It is also known as Health Information Provider.

Health Resource User (HRU): The healthcare professional, role, department at an establishment or establishment itself requesting for past health records of a patient stored in another establishment. It is also called as Health Information User.

Healthcare Ecosystem: It comprises healthcare establishments as ecosystem components that dynamically interconnect at the time of healthcare service delivery to an individual that requires health data exchange.

Healthcare Establishment: It is an entity that offers healthcare services such as consultation and surgery to the individuals. A hospital, pathology lab and clinic are examples of health establishments.

Informed Consent: It is the expressed agreement given by the patient or their authorized entity to HRP on sharing of specified health records with a HRU that includes contextual information like operation, intended purpose(s) and validity of consent.

Purpose: The reason for which the user can perform operations on health records of a patient. The healthcare services like Consultation and Surgery are examples of purpose.

Chapter 8
Mobile Text Misinformation Detection Using Effective Information Retrieval Methods

Sanjaikanth E. Vadakkethil Somanathan Pillai

 https://orcid.org/0000-0003-3264-9923
University of North Dakota, USA

Wen-Chen Hu
University of North Dakota, USA

ABSTRACT

Misinformation is always a serious problem for the general public, especially during a pandemic. People constantly receive text messages of related coronavirus news and its cures from their smartphones, which have become major devices for communication these days. These health text messages help people update their coronavirus knowledge repeatedly and better manage their health, but some of the messages may mislead people and may even cause a fatal result. This research tries to identify mobile health text misinformation by using various effective information retrieval methods including lexical analysis, stopword removal, stemming, synonym discovery, various message similarity measurements, and data fusion. Readers will learn various information retrieval methods applied to contemporary research: mobile misinformation detection. Experiment results show the accuracy of the proposed method meets the expectation but still has room for improvement because misinformation detection is intrinsically difficult, and no satisfactory methods have been found yet.

DOI: 10.4018/978-1-6684-5991-1.ch008

INTRODUCTION

By October 2022, coronavirus had infected more than 610 million people and killed more than 6 million human beings in the world according to the US CDC (Centers for Disease Control and Prevention). It has completely changed our lives. Amid pandemic, people are becoming more aware of their health and well-being. They check the health and coronavirus news constantly, especially via their smartphones which have become indispensable devices for people. Other than useful and true health information, these devices also deliver misinformation or fake news, which not only misleads people, but also may cause fatal results. For example, many people refuse to take COVID-19 vaccines because of the concerns of safety and effectiveness. Much of the information they receive may come from mobile text messages from their relatives, friends, subscribed news, etc. This research tries to help relieve the problem by using various information retrieval technologies to identify mobile health text misinformation. Therefore, users can take appropriate actions like ignoring the fake messages or referring other sources such as the Internet to verify the misinformation according to the recommendations.

This research tries to classify a mobile message as one of the five classes (true, fake, misinformative, disinformative, and neutral) and notify the mobile user about its finding, so the user can take an appropriate action like ignoring the message or forwarding it to others. Each message will go through a series of steps: (i) preprocessing (including lexical analysis, stopword removal, stemming, and synonym discovery), (ii) indexing and storage, (iii) classification by using four message similarity measurements (keyword, phrase, LCS (longest common subsequence), and LACS (longest approximate common subsequence) matching), and (iv) finally a final class recommended from a function of data fusion taking accounts of the four similarity scores. Experiment results show the accuracy of the proposed method meets the expectation, but still has room for improvement. An explanation for this may be because the short messages do not provide much information and small deviation may cause a great impact on the results. Further refinements are needed before it is put into effective use.

The rest of this chapter is organized as follows. Section 2 shows the background information about this research and related works on misinformation detection. The flow diagram and the pre-processing components (including syntax analysis, stopword removal, stemming, and synonym discovery), and indexing and storage of the proposed system are given in Section 3. Section 4 discusses the data fusion function and the four message similarity measurements for detecting health text misinformation. The experiment results and evaluations are given in Section 5, followed by a conclusion and references.

BACKGROUND AND RELATED LITERATURE

This section gives the background information of this research and related research in case readers are interested in finding more relevant publications. Misinformation detection is critical and popular in these days because information can be created and sent by everyone, not just news agencies, and some may distribute misinformation unintentionally or intentionally. Many methods are used to detect all kinds of misinformation like politics, businesses, text messages, emails, or news. This research places the focus on mobile health text misinformation identification. If the results are favorable, the method may be extended to other kinds of information. Generic misinformation detection can be found from the articles (Sharma et al., 2019; Zhou & Zafarani, 2020; Khan, Michalas, & Akhunzada, 2021; Savage, 2021).

Brennen, Simon, & Nielsen (2021) analyze visual content in misinformation concerning COVID-19. They use a mixed-method analysis of ninety-six examples of visuals in misinformation rated false or misleading by independent professionals. It shows the value in both attending to visual content in misinformation and unnecessity of a concern with only the representational aspects and functions of misinformation. Another study by Gupta et al. (2020) identifies social media as a potential source of misinformation on COVID-19 and a perceived high risk of plagiarism. More stringent peer review and skilled post-publication promotion are advisable. They recommend editors should play a more active role in streamlining publication and promoting trustworthy information on COVID-19. Gisondi et al. (2022) examine the social media companies play in the COVID-19 infodemic by showing how fake news about the virus developed on social media and acknowledging the initially muted response by the scientific community to counteract misinformation. The authors then describe legal and ethical imperatives to challenge social media companies to better mitigate the COVID-19 infodemic. Finally, they close with recommendations for social media companies to better partner with community influencers and implementation scientists. Related research about coronavirus misinformation identification can be found from the articles (Mian & Khan, 2020; Fleming, 2020; Ball & Maxmen, 2020; Vuong et al., 2022; Roozenbeek et al., 2020).

The media targeted by this research is short text messages. Sinha, Sakshi, and Sharma (2021) classify a tweet as real or fake. The complexity of natural language constructs along with variegated languages makes this task very challenging. In this work, a deep learning model to learn semantic word embeddings is proposed to handle this complexity. The evaluations on the benchmark dataset show that the proposed methods are superior to traditional natural language processing algorithms. Ahmed, Ali, Hussain, Baseer, and Ahmed (2021) analyze the performance of a fake news detection model based on neural networks using three feature extractors: TD-IDF vectorizer, Glove embeddings, and BERT embeddings. It was found that BERT embeddings for text transformation delivered the best performance. TD-IDF has been performed far better than Glove and competed the BERT as well at some stages. Other misinformation from social media can be found from the articles (Aldwairi & Alwahedi, 2018; Sitaula et al., 2020; Collins et al., 2021; Guo et al., 2020).

Kula et al. (2020) present an innovative solution for fake news detection that utilizes deep learning methods. Their experiments prove that the proposed approach is effective. Isha Priyavamtha, Vishnu Vardhan Reddy, Devisri, & Manek (2021) propose a model to detect fake news that includes three main phases: preprocessing, feature extraction, and classification. Input is first preprocessed to extract features using clustering algorithms. Subsequently, a model is developed to detect fake news. The proposed neural networks and linear support vector clustering algorithms resulted in 99.90% and 97.5% accuracy respectively. Another research using deep learning to identify misinformation can be found from the article (Islam et al., 2020).

Misinformation detection is not an easy topic to tackle because the detection is usually subjective. In addition, a variety of misinformation exists which requires a great amount of data to be stored. Research of misinformation detection has been studied extensively, and this research does not intend to solve all the misinformation problems at once. Instead, it focuses on two themes: short text messages and health-related misinformation, especially the COVID-19. Interested readers can refer to other misinformation identification methods from the articles (Visser, Lawrence, & Reed, 2020; Reddy et al., 2020; Schuster et al., 2020; Sethi, Rangaraju, & Shurts, 2019).

THE PROPOSED SYSTEM

The proposed system includes several components. In order to help readers better understand it, this chapter tries to introduce it by using two sections. The pre-processing functions (including lexical analysis, stopword removal, stemming, and synonym discovery) and indexing and storage are explained in this section. The four message similarity measurements (including keyword, phrase, LCS, LACS matching) and data fusion function will be given in the next section.

The Five Mobile Health Text Message Classes

When users receive a mobile health text message, several kinds of content the message may carry. This research is to classify the message as one of the following five classes:

- *True*, which is true information and is without a doubt. For example, it is true that a vaccine to prevent COVID-19 is available because COVID-19 vaccines have been authorized by the U.S. Food and Drug Administration (FDA) and vaccine programs have begun across the country.

- *Misinformative*, which is false or out-of-context information that is intentionally or unintentionally presented as fact to deceive. For example, it is misinformative that the COVID-19 vaccines are mandatory because they are strongly recommended, but not mandatory.
- *Disinformative*, which is a type of misinformation that is intentionally delivered the false or misleading information to deceive or mislead readers. For example, it is disinformation that the COVID-19 vaccines were not properly tested or developed since they were tested legitimately.
- *Fake*, which could be either misinformation or disinformation. For example, it is an obviously fake news that the COVID-19 vaccines contain microchips for government tracking because the current technology has not been this advanced yet.
- *Neutral*, which cannot be decided by the proposed method. For example, our method is not able to decide whether Coronavirus is from labs since even the societies have controversy about this in these days, let alone software.

The System Structure

This research is to identify mobile health text misinformation. Figure 1 shows the work flow of this research which takes the following steps:

1. Five kinds of messages (true, fake, misinformative, idsinformative, and neutral) are collected from the Internet initially.
2. Preprocess the test and collected messages by using the following four steps:
    a. Lexical analysis, which finds the keywords from the message,
    b. Stopword removal, which removes stopwords from the message,
    c. Stemming, which locates the stem of a word, and
    d. Synonym discovery, which finds the relevant terms.
3. Index and save the processed messages in a database, or test (classify) the message by using the four message similarity measurements consisting of
    a. Keyword matching,
    b. Phrase matching,
    c. LCS matching, and
    d. LACS matching.
4. Combine all four similarity scores by using a data fusion method.

Figure 1. A workflow of the proposed system

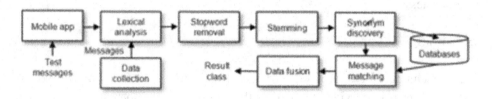

The System Components

This part of the chapter discusses various components of the proposed system except the four message matching methods, which will be detailed in the next section.

Lexical Analysis

Lexical analysis is the process of converting an input stream of characters into a stream of words or tokens, which are groups of characters with collective significance. It is the first stage of automatic indexing which is the process of algorithmically examining information items to generate lists of index terms. The lexical analysis phase produces candidate index terms that may be further processed, and eventually added to indexes. It also helps split the longer sentences into smaller chunks of the dataset to perform algorithms with better accuracy.

Stopword Removal

English stopwords such as "is," "has," "an," "the," etc. do not signify any importance as index terms when analyzing the dataset for information. It is crucial to remove the stopwords from the dataset as they do not help us find the true meaning of a sentence and can be removed without any negative consequences. Also, eliminating such words from consideration early in automatic indexing speeds processing, saves huge amounts of space in indexes. It has been recognized since the earliest days of information retrieval that many of the most frequently occurring words in English (like "the," "of," "and," "to," etc.) are worthless as index terms. A search using one of these terms is likely to retrieve almost every item in a database regardless of its relevance, so their discrimination value is low. Furthermore, these words make up a large fraction of the text of most documents: the ten most frequently occurring words in English typically account for 20 to 30 percent of the tokens in a document. Eliminating such words from consideration early in automatic indexing speeds processing, saves huge amounts of space in indexes, and does not damage retrieval effectiveness.

Stemming

It is a technique for improving retrieval effectiveness and reducing the size of indexing files is to provide searchers with ways of finding morphological variants of search terms. If, for example, a searcher enters the term stemming as part of a query, it is likely that he or she will also be interested in such variants as stemmed and stem. Since a single stem typically corresponds to several full terms, by storing stems instead of terms, compression factors of over 50 percent can be achieved. The stem need not be identical to the morphological root of the word; it is usually sufficient that related words map to the same stem, even if this stem is not in itself a valid root. It is a method for casting words into their original form which aims to the removal of inflectional endings from words. It performs morphological analysis on the words by returning the words into its dictionary meaning. For example, the stemming converts caring into care, troubled into trouble, geese into goose, etc.

Synonym Discovery

Many times, common terms like coronavirus, COVID-19, Omicron, and Delta virus could be treated the same while measuring the message similarity. Instead of building a thesaurus, which is not a trivial task, this research stores synonyms of a set of popular words such as COVID-19, vaccine, and message in a database. The database is checked whenever a similarity measurement runs. However, this approach is a temporary fix because it misses many words. On the other hand, saving all synonyms in a database is not feasible since it would take much space from a database. Other than building a thesaurus yourself, WordNet (n.d.) could be used to facilitate synonym matching. It is a lexical database of semantic relations between words, and has become one of the most popular dictionaries for use in natural language processing (NLP). Future research will also consider taking advantage of online services like Synonym.com (https://www.synonym.com/), which provides a list of synonyms of a word, but it slows down the execution tremendously. More investigation needs to be conducted for this matter.

Databases

Databases are critical for all data research. It is no exception that database is essential for this research. It is used to store the messages and other data. The database includes three tables: (a) keyword table, which saves the keywords of messages, (b) message table, which stores the message classes, and (c) message-keyword table, which saves the messages by using linked lists. Figure 2 shows sample values of database, of which "kid," "mid," and "mkid" are the primary keys of the tables keyword, message, and message-keyword, respectively. The "mkid" is the foreign key of the table message, and "mid" and "kid" are the foreign keys of the table message-keyword. In the keyword table, the "count" column is the number of the occurrences of the keyword in the messages. The messages are saved in the database by using a structure similar to linked lists as shown in message-keyword table, where the "next" column points to the next keyword in the message, and it is not needed at this moment, but is saved in case. Since a structure of linked lists is used in this database, the message heads are saved in the "mkid" column of the table message.

Figure 2. Database tables used: (a) keyword table, (b) message table, and (c) message-keyword table

kid	keyword	count
1	covid-19	116
2	cdc	28
3	vaccine	41
...	...	...
k	sign up	9

(a)

mid	mkid (start)	result (class)
1	103	misinformative
2	26	true
3	52	disinformative
...	...	...
m	94	fake

(b)

mkid	mid	kid	next
1	4	3	2
2	4	21	28
3	4	122	--
4	10	30	6
5	46	32	49
6	10	8	7
7	10	21	118
8	122	30	--
9	55	8	72
10	41	3	61
...	...	...	...
n	87	138	9

(c)

MESSAGE SIMILARITY MEASUREMENTS FOR MISINFORMATION DETECTION

The measurements of message similarity will be used to classify the message as one of the five information classes (true, fake, misinformative, disinformative, and neutral). The following four similarity measurements are used in this research:

- (Keyword matching) Number of keywords matched,
- (Phrase matching) Phrases matched,
- (LCS matching) Longest common subsequence, and
- (LACS matching) Longest approximate common subsequence.

The measurements give similarity scores, which show the degree of association between two messages. After the four similarity scores are found, the recommended class is generated by a data fusion function, which is the process of integrating the four measurement scores to produce more consistent, accurate, and useful information than that provided by any individual measurement.

Number of Keywords Matched (Keyword Matching)

This is the simplest method used. It counts the number of keywords matched between the testing message and each of the saved messages in the database. The class of the testing message is the class of the saved message with the highest number of keywords matched. For example, the similarity score of the following two messages is five:

m_1: center disease control prevention introduce oral tablet covid-19 vaccine effective no side effect
m_2: mask social distance coronavirus covid-19 vaccine symptom disease control prevention

because there are five keywords (disease, control, prevention, covid-19, and vaccine) matched according to the following equation:

similarity = # of keywords matched (1)

Figure 3 gives the algorithm used by this method. The running time is $O(kmn)$, where k is the number of messages in the database, m is the length of the testing message, and n is the length of the saved messages in the database. Figure 4 shows the result of executing the keyword matching. The accuracy is reaching to a plateau after the number of messages is over about 100.

Figure 3. The algorithm of finding the class of a message by using keyword matching

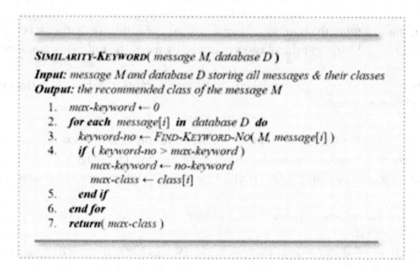

Figure 4. The accuracy of finding the class of a message by using the keyword matching

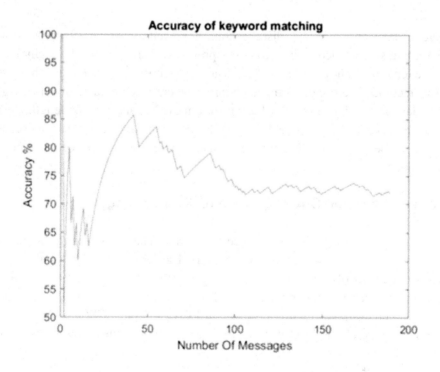

Phrases Matched (Phrase Matching)

Other than counting the number of keywords matched, this method also considers the number and length of the phrases matched by using the following equation:

similarity = (# of keywords matched) + 2×(# of phrases matched) + $\sum$(length of each phrase matched) (2)

The higher the similarity score is, the more resemblant the two messages are. The class of the testing message is the class of the saved message with the highest similarity scale. For example, the similarity score of the following two messages is 14:

m_1: center disease control prevention introduce oral tablet covid-19 vaccine effective no side effect

m_2: mask social distance coronavirus covid-19 vaccine symptom disease control prevention

because

similarity = 5 + 2×2 + 3 + 2 = 14

where the keywords matched (disease, control, prevention, covid-19, and vaccine) is 5, the phrases matched ("disease control prevention" and "covid-19 vaccine) is 2, and the lengths of phrases matched are 3 and 2. Figure 5 gives the algorithm used by this method. The running time is $O(km^2n)$, where k is the number of messages in the database, m is the length of the testing message, and n is the length of the saved messages in the database. Figure 6 shows the result of executing the phrase matching. The accuracy is reaching to a plateau after the number of messages is over about 50.

Longest Common Subsequence (LCS Matching)

Consider each message is a sequence of words. The LCS (longest common subsequence) used here is the longest common subsequence between two messages, where subsequence of a given sequence is a sequence that can be derived from the given sequence by deleting some or no elements without changing the order of the remaining elements. For example, Figure 7 shows an LCS example LCS(m_1,m_2)="disease control prevention" whose similarity score is 3 according to the following equation:

similarity = # of connections (3)

Figure 5. The algorithm of finding the class of a message by using phrase matching

SIMILARITY-PHRASE(*message M, database D*)

Input: *message M and database D storing all messages & their classes*
Output: *the recommended class of the message M*

```
1.   max-similarity ← 0
2.   max-class ← ε
3.   for each message[i] in database D do
4.       no-phrase ← 0
5.       phrase ← [ ]
6.       keyword-no ← FIND-KEYWORD-NO( M, message[i] )
7.       message ← message[i]
8.       while ( lcs ← FIND-LCS( M, message ) ) ≠ φ
9.           no-phrase ← no-phrase + 1
10.          phrase ← phrase + lcs
11.          M ← M – lcs
12.          message ← message – lcs
13.      end while
14.      similarity ← keyword-no + 2×no-phrase + |phrase|
15.      if max-similarity < similarity
16.          max-similarity ← similarity
17.          max-class ← class[i]
18.      end if
19.  end for
20.  return( max-class )
```

Figure 6. The accuracy of finding the class of a message by using the phrase matching

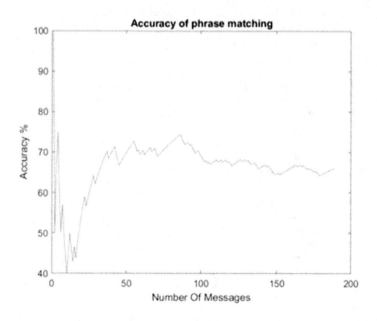

Figure 7. An example of a longest common subsequence between two messages

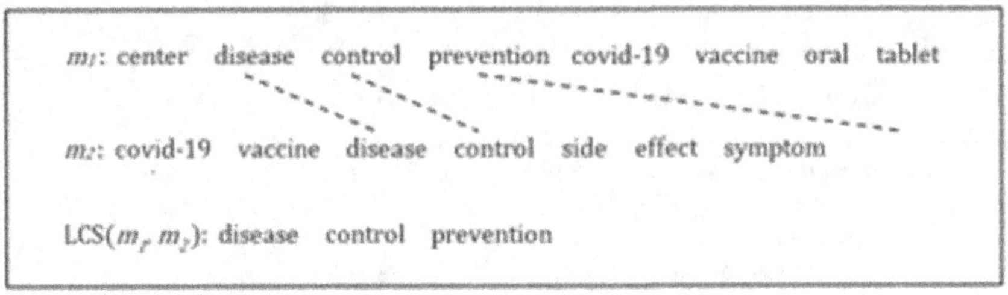

m_1: center   disease   control   prevention   covid-19   vaccine   oral   tablet

m_2: covid-19   vaccine   disease   control   side   effect   symptom

LCS(m_1, m_2): disease   control   prevention

Figure 8 gives the algorithm used by this method (Wikipedia, n.d.; Cormen et al., 2009). The running time is $O(kmn)$, where k is the number of messages in the database, m is the length of the testing message, and n is the length of the saved messages in the database. Figure 9 shows the result of executing the LCS matching, where the accuracy is reaching to a plateau after the number of messages is over about 100. The performance is similar to the one of the keyword matchings.

Figure 8. The algorithm of finding the class of a message by using the LCS matching

SIMILARITY-LCS(message X, database D)

Input: *message M and database D storing all messages & their classes*
Output: *the recommended class of the message M*

1. **for each** $Y[k]$ **in** database D **do**
2. $c \leftarrow array(0..|X|, 0..|Y[k]|)$
3.   **for** $i := 0 .. |X|$ **do**
4. $c[i, 0] \leftarrow 0$
5.   **end for**
6.   **for** $j := 0 .. |Y[k]|$ **do**
7. $c[0, j] \leftarrow 0$
8.   **end for**
9.   **for** $i := 1 .. |X|$ **do**
10.   **for** $j := 1 .. |Y[k]|$ **do**
11.   **if** $X = Y[j]$
12. $c[i, j] \leftarrow c[i-1, j-1] + 1$
13.   **else**
14. $c[i, j] \leftarrow max(c[i, j-1], c[i-1, j])$
15.   **end if**
16.   **end for**
17.   **end for**
18.   **return**($c[m, n]$)

Figure 9. The accuracy of finding the class of a message by using the LCS matching

Longest Approximate Common Subsequence (LACS)

However, the LCS method misses much information about the messages. For the example in Figure 10, the two messages s_1 and s_2 have five common words (covid-19, vaccine, disease, control, and prevention), but the LCS method only counts three words (disease, control, and prevention). The LACS method counts all five words, but has to take some weights from it like the following equation:

similarity = (# of connections) – (# of crossings) / (# of connections)   (4)

Figure 10. An example of a longest approximate common subsequence between two messages

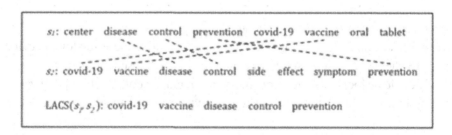

Figure 11 gives the algorithm used by this method. The running time is $O(k(m+n)^2)$, where k is the number of messages in the database, m is the length of the testing message, and n is the length of the saved messages in the database. The function *FIND-CROSSINGS* can be found from the article (Hu, Ritter, & Schmalz, 1998). Figure 12 shows the result of executing the LACS matching. The accuracy is better compared to other matchings, and it also drops after the number of messages is over about 100.

Figure 11. The algorithm of finding the class of a message by using the LACS matching

```
SIMILARITY-LACS( message M, database D )
Input: message M and database D storing all messages & their classes
Output: the recommended class of the message M
  1.    max-similarity ← 0
  2.    for each message[i] in database D do
  3.        no-comn ← SIMILARITY-LCS( M, message[i] )
  4.        no-cross ← FIND-CROSSINGS( M, message[i] )
  5.        similarity ← no-comn – no-cross / no-comn
  6.        if max-similarity < similarity
  7.           max-similarity ← similarity
  8.           max-class ← class[i]
  9.        end if
 10.    end for
 11.    return( max-class )
```

EXPERIMENT RESULTS

Experiment results are provided in this section to justify our research method. It includes two parts: the first part shows the experiment setup and screenshots, and the second part gives the evaluation data and discussions.

Experiments

A prototype system is built to validate the proposed method. Xamarin (n.d.), a cross-platform app development platform, helps to build a single app for all devices. Figure 13 shows the system setup for evaluating the proposed method. The system actually could be located at either client or server, but the construction is convenient if the system is held at the server. The prototype system can be found at GitHub

Figure 12. The accuracy of finding the class of a message by using the LACS matching

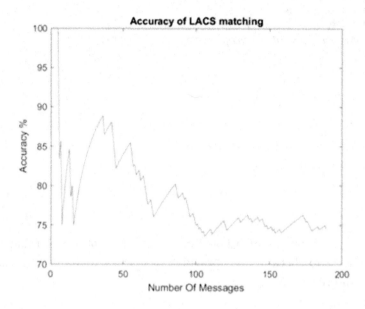

(E Vadakkethil Somanathan Pillai, 2022). The final recommendation takes the following steps:

1. A text message at the client (smartphone) is forwarded to the proposed system located at the server.
2. Match the incoming message to the five sets of messages (true, fake, misinformative, disinformative, or neutral), respectively.
3. The consolidated similarity score $similarity_{class}$ of the class could be found by using the formula (5):

$$similarity_{class} = similarity_{keyword} \times W_{keyword} + similarity_{phrase} \times W_{phrase} + similarity_{LCS} \times W_{LCS} + similarity_{LACS} \times W_{LACS} \tag{5}$$

where the similarity score $similarity_m$ is the highest similarity score from the similarity measurement method m, and the weight W_m could be adjusted accordingly based on users' needs.

4. The data fusion sends the user the recommended class (true, fake, misinformative, disinformative, or neutral), which is the class with the highest similarity score $similarity_{class}$.

5.   The user takes an appropriate action based on the recommendation.

Figure 13. An overview of the proposed system for experiments

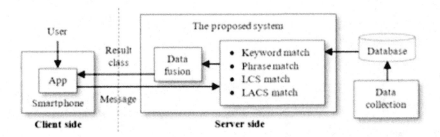

Figure 14 shows three screenshots from the experiment, where 14.a gives a list of text messages to check, a disinformative message is found in 14.b, and a true message is shown in 14.c.

Figure 14. The screenshots from the experiments: (a) selecting which message to check, (b) showing the message and its class, and (c) showing another message

Evaluations and Discussions

The experiment was described in the previous sub-section, and this sub-section gives and discusses the evaluation data. Individual accuracy of each matching method was given previously and Figure 15 shows all four accuracies together for easy comparison. From the figure, the LACS matching performs the best and the keyword matching comes next. The LCS matching performs better than the phrase matching when the number of messages is less around 50. After that, the phrase matching beats the LCS matching.

Figure 15. Experiment data of the four similarity measurements in a figure

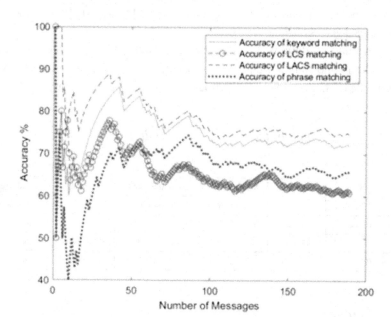

The experiment data is displayed by using not only figures, but also Table 1 which shows the experiment data of the four message similarity measurements. For example, the accuracy of keyword matching used for the class True is 10/24=46%, which means among 24 True test messages, 10 of them are correctly identified. The results are expected like the LACS matching having the highest accuracy, but it also shows some surprising findings like the accuracy of keyword matching being higher the ones of the phrase and LCS matchings. Identifying misinformation is intrinsically difficult. People are not able to tell whether the information is correct easily, let alone computers. The following observations are noticed:

- The accuracy is satisfactory because of greater than the threshold value 50%, but not optimal. It may be because the information provided by short messages is limited. To fix the problem, more information or knowledge needs to be discovered from the messages.

- The LACS method is supposed to beat other three methods because it considers more features in messages. The experiment data also supports the assumption.
- It is surprising to find that the accuracies of true messages are the lowest and the ones of fake messages are the highest. It may be because the vocabulary of true messages is broad and the one of fake messages is limited, so finding fake messages is easier.
- The evaluation data is less foolproof because the messages are filtered beforehand and may not be generic enough. To be fair, the proposed method should be compared to other methods, which will be considered in the future.

Table 1. Experiment data of the four message similarity measurements using 189 messages

	True	Fake	Misinformative	Disinformative	Neutral	Overall Accuracy
Keyword	11/24=46%	49/52=94%	24/35=69%	26/34=76%	26/44=59%	136/189=72%
Phrase	10/24=42%	46/52=88%	20/35=57%	23/34=68%	25/44=57%	124/189=66%
LCS	09/24=38%	43/52=83%	17/35=49%	18/34=53%	28/44=64%	115/189=61%
LACS	10/24=42%	50/52=96%	23/35=66%	27/34=79%	31/44=70%	141/189=75%

CONCLUSION

Smartphones are indispensable devices for people in these days, and tens or even hundreds of messages are sent to each device every day. All kinds of information can be found from the delivered messages such as news, greetings from family members or friends, advertisements, promotions, weather reports, etc. People are overwhelmed by the sheer amount of information and they spend much time trying to find a way to sort out the messages. Even worse is some messages give false or fake information and mislead the viewers consequently. The problem becomes more serious especially during the pandemic. This research tries to automatically classify the mobile health messages into one of the five classes: true, fake, misinformative, disinformative, and neutral by using various mobile information retrieval technologies, which include text preprocessing (consisting of lexical analysis, stopword elimination, stemming, and synonym discovery), indexing and storage using a database, message similarity measurements (consisting of keyword, phrase, LCS, and LACS matching), and data fusion. Experiment results show the proposed method is effective, but it still has room for improvement. This chapter not only gives practical methods for misinformation detection, but also provides great pedagogic values for readers who are interested in learning various information retrieval methods and misinformation research.

Future Research Directions

Experiment results show the proposed method works. However, there is still room for improvement. Using RNN (recurrent neural network) to handle the sequential data will be considered next. The ANNs (artificial neural networks) are considered because this problem has no definite answers. For example, a message may be considered true for some people, but others may think it is disinformative, especially if it is related to politics, and ANN is competent for this kind of ambivalence. However, DL (deep learning) will not be considered because the information provided by short messages is limited and DL is good at processing complicated and large data sets like images and speeches. In addition, other than using artificial neural networks to detect misinformation, statistical means will be considered too. The statistical means includes the methods of Bayesian classifiers and hidden Markov models. It is less innovative, but may be more effective. On the other end, this problem, mobile health misinformation identification, could be classified as one of the NLP (natural language processing) problems. We will consider a variety of NLP methods and adapt them to our problem, and see whether the problems are mitigated. Besides, there has been a rising interest in proactive intervention strategies to counter the spread of misinformation and its impact on society (van der Linden, 2022). Methods to mitigate the ill effects caused by misinformation will be investigated too.

REFERENCES

Ahmed, B., Ali, G., Hussain, A., Baseer, A., & Ahmed, J. (2021, April). Analysis of text feature extractors using deep learning on fake news. *Engineering, Technology, & Applied Scientific Research*, *11*(2), 7001–7005.

Aldwairi, M., & Alwahedi, A. (2018, November 5). Detecting fake news in social media networks. *Procedia Computer Science*, *141*, 215–222. doi:10.1016/j.procs.2018.10.171

Ball, P., & Maxmen, A. (2020). The epic battle against coronavirus misinformation and conspiracy theories. *Nature*, *581*(7809), 371–374. doi:10.1038/d41586-020-01452-z PMID:32461658

Brennen, J. S., Simon, F. M., & Nielsen, R. K. (2021). Beyond (mis) representation: Visuals in COVID-19 misinformation. *The International Journal of Press/Politics*, *26*(1), 277–299. doi:10.1177/1940161220964780

Collins, B., Hoang, D. T., Nguyen, N. T., & Hwang, D. (2021). Trends in combating fake news on social media – a survey. *Journal of Information and Telecommunication*, *5*(2), 247–266. doi:10.1080/24751839.2020.1847379

Cormen, T. H., Leiserson, C. E., Rivest, R. L., & Stein, C. (2009). *Introduction to algorithms* (3rd ed.). MIT Press and McGraw-Hill.

Fleming, N. (2020, June 17). Coronavirus misinformation, and how scientists can help to fight it. *Nature*, *583*(7814), 155–156. doi:10.1038/d41586-020-01834-3 PMID:32601491

Gisondi, M., Barber, R., Faust, J., Raja, A., Strehlow, M., Westafer, L., & Gottlieb, M. (2022, February). A deadly infodemic: Social media and the power of COVID-19 misinformation. *Journal of Medical Internet Research*, *24*(2), e35552. doi:10.2196/35552 PMID:35007204

Guo, B., Ding, Y., Yao, L., Liang, Y., & Yu, Z. (2020, September 4). The future of false information detection on social media: new perspectives and trends. *ACM Computing Surveys*, *53*(4), 1-36.

Gupta, L., Gasparyan, A. Y., Misra, D. P., Agarwal, V., Zimba, O., & Yessirkepov, M. (2020, July 13). Information and misinformation on COVID-19: A cross-sectional survey study. *Journal of Korean Medical Science*, *35*(27), e257. doi:10.3346/jkms.2020.35.e256 PMID:32657090

Hu, W.-C., Ritter, G. X., & Schmalz, M. S. (1998, April). Approximating the longest approximate common subsequence problem. *Proceedings of the 36th Annual ACM Southeast Conference*, 166-172. 10.1145/275295.283951

Isha Priyavamtha, U. J., Vishnu Vardhan Reddy, G., Devisri, P., & Manek, A. S. (2021). Fake news detection using artificial neural network algorithm. In Data Science and Computational Intelligence. ICInPro. Communications in Computer and Information Science. Springer. doi:10.1007/978-3-030-91244-4_26

Islam, M. R., Liu, S., Wang, X., & Xu, G. (2020). Deep learning for misinformation detection on online social networks: A survey and new perspectives. *Social Network Analysis and Mining*, *10*(1), 82. doi:10.100713278-020-00696-x PMID:33014173

Khan, T., Michalas, A., & Akhunzada, A. (2021, September 15). Fake news outbreak 2021: Can we stop the viral spread? *Journal of Network and Computer Applications*, *190*, 103112. doi:10.1016/j.jnca.2021.103112

Kula, S., Choraś, M., Kozik, R., Ksieniewicz, P., & Woźniak, M. (2020). Sentiment analysis for fake news detection by means of neural networks. In Lecture Notes in Computer Science (vol. 12140). Springer. doi:10.1007/978-3-030-50423-6_49

Mian, A. & Khan, S. (2020, March). Coronavirus: The spread of misinformation. *BMC Medinine*, *18*(89).

Reddy, H., Raj, N., Gala, M., & Basava, A. (2020, February 18). Text-mining-based fake news detection using ensemble methods. *International Journal of Automation and Computing*, *17*(2), 210–221. doi:10.100711633-019-1216-5

Roozenbeek, J., Schneider, C. R., Dryhurst, S., Kerr, J., Freeman, A. L. J., Recchia, G., van der Bles, A. M., & van der Linden, S. (2020, October 14). Susceptibility to misinformation about COVID-19 around the world. *Royal Society Open Science*, *7*(10), 201199. doi:10.1098/rsos.201199 PMID:33204475

Savage, N. (2021, March 12). Fact-finding mission. *Communications of the ACM*, *64*(3), 18–19. doi:10.1145/3446879

Schuster, T., Schuster, R., Shah, D. J., & Barzilay, R. (2020). The limitations of stylometry for detecting machine-generated fake news. *Computational Linguistics*, *46*(2), 499–510. doi:10.1162/coli_a_00380

Sethi, R. J., Rangaraju, R., & Shurts, B. (2019, May 30). Fact checking misinformation using recommendations from emotional pedagogical agents. Intelligent Tutoring Systems.

Sharma, K., Qian, F., Jiang, H., Ruchansky, N., Zhang, M., & Liu, Y. (2019, May). Combating fake news: a survey on identification and mitigation techniques. *ACM Transactions on Intelligent Systems and Technology*, *10*(3), 1-42.

Sinha, H. S., & Sharma, Y. (2021). Text-convolutional neural networks for fake news detection in Tweets. In Evolution in Computational Intelligence. Advances in Intelligent Systems and Computing. Springer.

Sitaula, N., Mohan, C. K., Grygiel, J., Zhou, X., & Zafarani, R. (2020). Credibility-based fake news detection. In K. Shu, S. Wang, D. Lee, & H. Liu (Eds.), *Disinformation, misinformation, and fake news in social media, Lecture Notes in Social Networks* (pp. 163–182). Springer. doi:10.1007/978-3-030-42699-6_9

Vadakkethil Somanathan Pilla, E. S. (2022). *LCS, LACS, and phrase match comparison.* https://github.com/sanjaikanth/LCSLACSPhraseMatchComparison

van der Linden, S. (2022, March). Misinformation: Susceptibility, spread, and interventions to immunize the public. *Nature Medicine, 28*(3).

Visser, J., Lawrence, J., & Reed, C. (2020, November). Reason-checking fake news. *Communications of the ACM, 63*(11), 38–40.

Vuong, Q.-H., Le, T.-T., La, V.-P., Nguyen, H., Ho, M.-T., Khuc, Q., & Nguyen, M.-H. (2022, January 18). Covid-19 vaccines production and societal immunization under the serendipity-mindsponge-3D knowledge management theory and conceptual framework. *Humanities & Social Sciences Communications, 9*(1), 22. doi:10.105741599-022-01034-6

Wikipedia. (n.d.). *Longest common subsequence problem.* https://en.wikipedia.org/wiki/Longest_common_subsequence_problem

WordNet. (n.d.). *A lexical database for English.* https://wordnet.princeton.edu/

Xamarin. (n.d.). *Cross-platform with Xamarin.* https://dotnet.microsoft.com/en-us/apps/xamarin/cross-platform

Zhou, X. & Zafarani, R. (2020, October). A survey of fake news: fundamental theories, detection methods, and opportunities. *ACM Computing Surveys, 53*(5), 1-40.

Chapter 9
Social Media:
A Gateway for Online Child Grooming

Desmond Onyemechi Okocha
https://orcid.org/0000-0001-5070-280X
Bingham University, Nigeria

Judith Oyiza Isah
Bingham University, Nigeria

Samuel Akpe
Bingham University, Nigeria

ABSTRACT

Advances in technology have provided people with unparalleled opportunities to communicate efficiently and in real time. Adults with an inappropriate sexual interest in children have also benefited from developments in information and communications technology, using it to establish contact with them, to develop relationships, and to groom potential victims for sexual abuse and exploitation. Based on this, this study examined how social media has become a gateway for online child grooming. The study was anchored on the luring communication theory. The study adopted in-depth interview as its research design. The study used purposive sampling technique to draw a sample size of 15 experts. Findings from the study revealed that since the introduction of social media platforms, the amount of child sexual abuse content has been increasing yearly as these platforms have become a channel that offenders use in soliciting and sharing of explicit images and videos of minors.

DOI: 10.4018/978-1-6684-5991-1.ch009

INTRODUCTION

Social Media platforms have become an essential part of present-day life as they play major roles in the educational and social growth of children. However, they also expose children to new and advancing forms of sexual exploitation by sexual predators (Brown, 2017). One of the increasing risks is online child grooming. Online child grooming simply put, is when someone who disguises as a minor, befriends a child online, builds up their trust and develops a relationship with the child, with the intention of exploiting and harming the child (Childnet, n.d.). Every child has the possibility of being groomed, regardless of age, gender, race or location. Some children may have higher chances of getting groomed online due to special educational needs, disabilities, or other vulnerabilities and may find gaining support from an adult they trust hard ("Childnet", n.d.).

The fast growth of technologies, boost in mobile infiltration and successive growth of the use of the internet (Roser, Ritchie & Ortiz-Ospina, 2015) led to many studies of the effect of the latter. One of the frequently used points of view in favor of providing children with access to the internet is its positive impact on their academic performance (Carter, Greenberg & Walker, 2016). Having access to a technology device at home and internet connection seems to be as essential as self-learning skills (Yesilyurt et al., 2014) and it is effectively used as a subsidiary learning source in schools (Siraj et al., 2015). Presently, the internet is a preferable way of getting swift and varied data than going to mainstream sources such as libraries (Kumah, 2015). Alongside the positive features linked with the growth of the internet, there are various risks children can become exposed to online and the effect these risks can have on children is significant. Online child abuse experiences can lead to psychological, emotional, safety and health-related issues for children (Alqahtan et al., 2017).

A topic drawing an increasing level of media and research attention in recent years is the safety of children online especially children on social media platforms. In accordance to the study of 11 countries done by Silver, 79% of responders are very worried about children's exposure to vile and dangerous content online (Silver et al., 2019). Understanding the scale of the concern requires deliberation of multiple aspects. Nearly every age group of children is represented online in some capacity. For example, among the 12- to 15-year-old group, 83% have their own smart phones and among 5- to 7-year-olds, 42% have their own tablets usually with connection to the internet (Ofcom, 2019). Between 80% and 93% of children have access to social media platforms on their phones; nearly 60% are reported to have more than 100 friends and 65% of children who have social media profiles connect with "new friends" online (GSMA, 2016). In the environment of social media, half of the children set up their profiles to public and 20% of them have no idea on how to make their profiles private (Alqahtan et al., 2017). The blend of these factors means children are extremely represented online and later on highly open to online sexual predatory behaviors, leading to online grooming, sexual abuse and exploitation. This research studies how social media has become a gateway for online child grooming.

The status of a moral agent presumes moral duties, what one must do or avoid doing. The moral duty not to commit child sex abuse is universal and that the duty to reduce the individual risk of child sex abuse is specific to the offenders. Society has a moral duty to help reduce the rate at which online child grooming and child abuse is increasing by reporting child sexual abuse contents they see on social media platforms but societies rarely provide such opportunities and hence fail in their moral duty, as most people turn a blind eye to so many immoral contents seen online (Cherry, 2021).

RESEARCH OBJECTIVES

This study was anchored on the following four objectives, which would clearly establish the importance of this chapter. They are to be analysed or examined using the findings of the study.

1. To examine the factors that influence online child grooming
2. Analyse the consequences of online child grooming
3. Examine government laws and regulations against online child grooming
4. Examine how online child grooming can be prevented.

Questions would be posed to the study participants based on these objectives. Findings from the chosen population would be used to analyse these objectives.

THEORETICAL FRAMEWORK

Two relevant theoretical frameworks were chosen to handle this topic. They are the Luring Communication Theory and the Kohlberg's Theory of Moral Development. Both were found to be appropriate in examining the issue in line with the objectives of the chapter.

Luring Communication Theory

Olson et al. (2007) developed a luring communication theory model (LCT) that divides predation into five stages: obtaining access, deceptive trust creation, grooming, isolation, and approach.

Gaining access is the first step in the tempting process, according to Olson et al. (2007), in which the predator must be motivated and capable of gaining access to potential victims and their families. According to Olson et al., deceptive trust creation is defined as the ability of a perpetrator to cultivate relationships with potential victims and possibly their families in order to promote the perpetrator's personal sexual desire. Beyond grooming, the sexual predator must physically and emotionally isolate the victim, whether online or in person. Physical isolation is described as scheduling time alone with the victim, but mental isolation is defined as increasing emotional reliance on the predator for things like friendship and direction. While complete physical isolation is impossible to obtain over the Internet, the predator creates seclusion by ensuring the victim chats are unsupervised. In Olson et al. the initial physical touch or verbal lead-ins that occur before the actual sexual act are characterized as approach in the LCT model. Approach is the final phase in the online model of luring communication, when the predator wants to meet the victim offline with the goal of starting a sexual connection (Olson et al., 2007).

Kohlberg's Theory of Moral Development

Kohlberg's moral development theory is a study of how children acquire morality and moral reasoning. According to Kohlberg's theory, moral development unfolds in six stages. Moral logic, according to the theory, is primarily concerned with obtaining and sustaining justice. Kohlberg's theory can be divided into three tiers. There are two stages of moral development at each level. Kohlberg argued that not everyone proceeds to the highest stages of moral growth, just as Piaget believed that not everyone reaches the highest levels of moral development.

The earliest phase of moral development is level one (1), which is pre-conventional morality. It lasts until a child reaches the age of nine. Children's decisions at this age are mostly influenced by adult expectations and the penalties of breaking rules. Within this level, there are two stages: the first is obedience and punishment, and the second is individualism and exchange. Level two (2) is Conventional Morality, which is distinguished by acceptance of social conventions about what is good and moral. Adolescents and adults internalize the moral principles they have learnt from their role models and society during this time. Accepting authority and adhering to the group's rules are also important during this time. At this level of morality, there are two stages: the first is the development of good interpersonal relationships, and the second is the maintenance of social order. Post-conventional Morality is the third level of moral development, where people develop a knowledge of abstract moral principles. The social contract and individual rights, as well as universal principles, are the two stages at this level. Only a small number of people, according to Kohlberg, ever reach the post-conventional stages.

LITERATURE REVIEW

In reviewing previous studies by experts on this subject, this chapter will examine the pre and post internet grooming stages, effects of sexual grooming on children, how online grooming can be prevented, statistics on online child grooming, Instagram: A major platform for online grooming, and law and against child grooming. Three countries where laws on online grooming are applicable would be examined.

Pre and Post Internet Grooming Stages

Pre and post internet grooming stages and strategies are almost the same with just a little difference. (Ringenberg et al., 2021). Before the internet grooming stages included;

Targeting the child and getting to know everything about the child, the child's weakness and find ways to exploit them. Gaining the child's trust by getting to know their needs, and discovering ways to provide for those needs (whether emotional or material needs), gaining the trust of the parents/guardians in order to lower suspicion and gain access to the child by providing superficially warm yet planned attention and support. Isolating the child to strengthen their relationship with the child by making settings in which they are alone together. Sexualizing the relationship by talking about sexual acts with the child, asking the child for illicit pictures or sending illicit pictures of themselves to the child. Then maintaining control of that child's continuous participation in the relationship either through secrecy, blame or threat to the child, the child's family or friends (Raising Children, 2022).

Grooming stages during the internet era, now consists of targeting the child, sending a follow or friend request, chatting the child up and trying to gain the child's trust by creating a friendship or relationship and providing for their needs, risk assessment - online predator will begin to assess the level of threat parents or guardians pose to them, isolating the child, sexualizing the relationship, and finally maintaining control of the relationship and the child's continuous participation in the relationship (Ringenberg et al., 2021).

The Effects of Sexual Grooming, Abuse and Exploitation on Children

The effect or consequences of online child abuse on a child can be short term or long term. In the short term, a child victim of sexual abuse can display regressive behaviors (e.g. sucking of their thumb and bed-wetting in younger children), insomnia, eating problems, behavior and/or performance issues at school and reluctance to participate in school or social activities (UNICEF, 2016). Long-term consequences for a child victim may include, mental and physical issues like self-harm or attempt to commit suicide, the idea of being visually exposed permanently online, ignoring a child's right to be forgotten can be a traumatic factor for most victims. An abused minor may learn to use sexual conduct to get affection, attention, presents, and privileges as a result of this type of trauma. Other possible outcomes include the feeling of betrayal by adults and inability to trust them because the person they relied on caused them tremendous harm or failed to protect them. Abused children may feel powerless; victims feel ashamed and accountable for their mistreatment. As a result of their images or films appearing on the internet, victims may experience distress, anger and shame due to the fact that it may be seen by not just perpetrators but also their own friends and relatives, and there is a continuous circle of sexual violence, as victims can be re-victimized (UNICEF, 2016).

It is essential to have safety nets in place for children who are experiencing the horrifying aftermath of grooming, sexual abuse and exploitation whether online and offline. Many parents, schools, organizations, religious groups etc. are aware of this and provide some assistance, such as professional counselling services adjusted to the needs of victims of grooming, sexual abuse and exploitation (UNICEF, 2016).

How Online Child Grooming Can Be Prevented

Here are some suggestions on how the undesirable online child grooming can be prevented:

- Parents should discuss with their children about the difference between online and offline friends, it is important to point out that, however nice a new friend online can seem or however long they have spoken to them for, those online friends are still strangers.
- Parents should talk to their children about the red flags in chats which are very necessary to report, block and tell an adult or authority about. Such chats would include if the online friend suggested to meet up offline and requested the child to come alone or tell no one, asking for personal information about

them of their family or to send explicit photos or videos, chats moving to private messages to avoid being seen by others, or asking them to keep secrets.

- Parents should figure out where the block buttons are located on their children's devices and applications. Social media platforms, phone and tablet apps, online games and websites all offer reporting and blocking buttons.

- Parents should always make sure their children know that they are there to help when needed (either emotional or materialistic needs). Children who worry about how a parent or guardian will react to certain issues are prevented from asking for help. Ensure that your child knows that, no matter what has occurred, you are there to do your best to help them through it all.

Statistics on Online Child Grooming

Social media platforms appeal to online predators because of direct and often unsupervised approach to children. In 2019, the National Center for Missing and Exploited Children (NCMEC) received a total of 19,174 reports of online child grooming (also known as online child enticement) and in 2020 they received a total of 37,872 reports, that is a 97.5% increase and the major contribution is attributed to the COVID-19 lockdown. According to the report, 98% of reported offenders were apparently unknown to the child offline and 78 percent of victims were female, 13 percent were male, while 9% of reports had no gender information. ("Online Enticement", n.d.). To be able to have better understanding of the scale of online child grooming and online child sexual abuse, it is worth looking into the official statistics on yearly produced child sexual abuse content (CSAC). There is a legal responsibility for companies to report CSAC to the US National Center for Missing and Exploited Children (NCMEC) ("18 U.S. Code § 2258A - Reporting requirements of providers", n.d.) and this offers the opportunity to track data trends in this area. In the past few years, law enforcement agencies have seen a fast upward trend in CSAC. In 2018, the National Center for Missing and Exploited Children (NCMEC) received 18.4 million reports of suspected online child sex offenses from all around the world. ("NCMEC Data", n.d.). In 2018 NCA received 3 times more UK-specific online case referrals compared to 2016: 113,948 versus 43,072 reports correspondingly (Brennan et al., 2022).

In 2019, the Internet Watch Foundation (IWF) assessed 260,426 reports on child sexual abuse content, 132,730 were confirmed as containing sexual abuse content and out of this 38,424 were confirmed as self-generated content ("IWF Annual Report 2019", n.d.). And in 2020, the IWF assessed a total number of 153,383 child sexual abuse contents reports and that was a 16% increase from 2019 and IWF analysts confirmed 153,350 reports of child sexual abuse content in total for 2020, 68,000 cases were confirmed to be self-generated content which accounts for almost half

(44%) the content IWF took action on in 2019. This is a 77% increase on 2019's total of 38,400 reports which included self-generated content. New analysis by the IWF shows that in 80% of these cases, the victims were 11 to 13-year-old girls. In 2019, 92% of the child abuse content were confirmed to be female, 3% were male and 3% were of both genders. In 2020, 93% of the child abuse content were confirmed to be female, 3% were male and 3% were of both genders (IWF", n.d.).

In Nigeria, though there are just a few reported cases and no annual statistics of online child grooming and online sexual abuse contents, there are still some stories online on blogs or online newspapers (Sun News online, 2022). Most times it is just few of these stories that make the news and most never get reported because of the stigma these victims face.

Instagram: A Major Platform for Online Grooming

As of December 2021, the number of monthly active Instagram users increased to 2 billion (Statista, 2022). As part of Instagram's terms and conditions, children under 13 are not permitted to have Instagram accounts (Instagram Help Centre", n.d.). According to the official statistics only thirteen- to seventeen-year-old children are on Instagram and they consist of 6.2% of all Instagram users worldwide (Statista", n.d.). In applying, children below 13 years can easily beat age related rules and also get entry to the platform as Instagram is not requesting for their users age when registering, even though this procedure cannot still fully guarantee that children don't get access to the platform when they are not meant to. There are several ways to avoid these processes; they can lie about their age, use their parents' social media accounts, or ask adults to open up an account for them.

In 2021, whistleblower Frances Haugen revealed that Meta had behaved in bad faith by concealing information of Instagram's damages to minors, particularly females. Rather than making significant modifications to mitigate the effects, Meta focused its resources on the creation of Instagram for Kids in order to expand its user base and attract children at a younger age to its brand (Ghaffary, 2021).

Instagram is frequently mentioned as a top platform for child sex trafficking and grooming. According to the Human Trafficking Institute's 2020 Federal Human Trafficking Report, 65% of child sex trafficking victims recruited on social media platforms were gotten on Facebook, with Instagram being the second most popular platform used (14 percent) (2020 Federal Human Trafficking Report, 2020).

Instagram was the most often used site for grooming in 2020, according to the latest data from the UK's National Society for the Prevention of Cruelty to Children (NSPCC), with police identifying the platform in 32% of incidents (NSPCC, 2022). In May 2021, 'Thorn', a child welfare non-profit, revealed some highly insightful quantitative analysis based on data collected in 2020 (Thorn, 2021). According to the study, Instagram was the second most popular social media platform among minors, with 76 percent of the 9 - 17-year-olds questioned said to be using it (50 percent, at least once a day); it was only second to Youtube, with 97 percent (Thorn, 2021). Given Instagram's high rankings for both minors' use and threats posed to minors, it is very necessary for Instagram to address this; they must take all reasonable steps to safeguard the safety of the children who use their platform.

Thorn is not the only one who has looked into Instagram's negative effects on minors. Instagram's owner, Facebook, undertook similar research and found Instagram to be damaging to kids (particularly young females) in a variety of ways. However, in the face of its own study, Facebook failed to behave honestly and ethically, and instead chose to keep the findings hidden from the public (Nealon, 2021). The revelations of a whistleblower and following hearings in the US Senate confirmed what many had believed for a long time: that Facebook constantly prioritized business over child safety and well-being (Nealon, 2021).

A big challenge for child protection on Facebook-owned platforms is end to end encryption; which means that only users involved in the communication have access to the data (WhatsApp, 2022.). Neither Facebook nor the law enforcement will be able to access private communication data. This modification was caused by the amplified pressure on Facebook to protect data privacy. This is why, taking into account the present state and difficulty of managing child welfare on social media platforms, it is vital to note that all parties (technology and social media companies, law enforcement, educational institutions, charity organizations and parents) have a responsibility for guaranteeing proper experiences for children's online activities.

Government Law and Regulations against Child Grooming

Grooming has already been designated as a criminal offense in some countries. According to a review of these regulations, some may be redundant due to existing legislation and practices in their respective countries.

Nigeria

In Nigeria, law and regulations for online child grooming have not yet been drafted. However, Article 27 of the African Charter on the Rights and Welfare of the Child, 1990, makes child pornography, grooming, and sexual abuse illegal in Nigeria (African Charter on the Rights and Welfare of the Child, n.d.). Child's Right Act (2003) is the law that guarantees the rights of all children (children as defined by Child's Right Act is any person under the age of 18) in Nigeria and so far 24 out of 36 states of Nigeria have adopted the CRA as a state law, making 12 states out of 36 yet to implement this act. Under the Child Right Act (2003) section 31 and 32, makes it an offence to have unlawful sexual intercourse and to sexually abuse or exploit a child. Under section 31 the penalty is imprisonment for life if found guilty and under section 32 the penalty is 14-years imprisonment if found guilty (2, n.d.)

United States

In the United States, 18 U.S. Code § 2251 Sexual exploitation of children, subsection A, makes child grooming a federal offense that carries a maximum sentence of 15 years in jail, subsection E (18 U.S. Code § 2251 - Sexual exploitation of children, n.d.). 18 U.S.C section 2422 makes it a federal offence to use mail or any facility or means to intentionally persuade or entice a minor to be involved in prostitution or any sexual activity, which is punishable by 10years or life imprisonment (18 U.S. Code § 2422 - Coercion and enticement, n.d.). 18 U.S.C section 2425 makes it a federal offence to intentionally share personal information such as the name, address, telephone number, etc. of a person under 16 years, with the intention to entice, the minor to be involved in any form of sexual activity, the offender can be imprisoned for 5 years (18 U.S. Code § 2425 - Use of interstate facilities to transmit information about a minor, n.d.)".

United Kingdom

In England and Wales, it is illegal to set up a meeting with a child under the age of 16 for oneself or someone else with the intention of sexually abusing the child under section 14 and 15 of the Sexual Offences Act 2003. The meeting of a minor has been declared illegal. The criminal faces a maximum penalty of ten years in prison, as well as an immediate ban from working with children or vulnerable persons. A similar clause was included in Scotland's Protection of Children and Prevention of Sexual Offences (Scotland) Act 2005 (Wikipedia, 2022).

Despite all of these laws and bans, incidents continue to spread like wildfire, particularly during the COVID-19 shutdown, and these have sadly not been thoroughly and methodically investigated. Because of its online, remote, and anonymous nature, it is one of the least reported forms of abuse. It's a covert crime, with the vast majority of victims and perpetrators remaining anonymous, including abused children who share a home with their parents. Because of the anonymous nature of the internet, discovering and deterring online sexual abuse is challenging; yet, detecting that a kid is mistreated online remains the primary job of the parents (Mbaegbu, 2020).

RESEARCH METHOD

To anchor this study, the qualitative research method is used. In-depth Interview was used to collect primary data. Using purposive sampling technique fifteen participants were chosen for this study by the literacy level and exposure of participants with regard to the subject of study and they were identified as participants 1 – 15. Research has shown that when undertaking studies aimed at accessing hidden population, a manageable population becomes necessary because of the difficulties in reaching willing participants or respondents (Daniela, 2020). In another study, it is a settled fact that in qualitative research, the sample size is contextually determined; and that in-depth qualitative research does not require larger population as is the case in qualitative research "oriented towards positivism" (Boddy, 2016). Again, Mills et al. (2009), cited by Sarfo et al. (2021) state that the choice on the size of a sample for any research depends both on the "research questions and the epistemological assumption." In other words, as already confirmed by Boddy (2016), the choice is contextual, not fixed. Knowing the cultural sensitivity of the issue focused on in this study, it was only necessary to choose the population among those who have been witnesses to the issue and not necessarily only the victims who would feel inconvenienced to come under probe.

The discussion was conducted over the phone, face to face and also through interview guides for two weeks. Additionally, it should be highlighted that the interview guide included 13 semi-open-ended questions that justified the objectives of this study. This structure allowed for statistical analyses.

The demographic details of participants were represented in tabular form. Information obtained cut across gender, participants' age, location, and profession.

DATA ANALYSIS

In Table 1 above, the study indicates the demographic arrangement of respondents. First is the number of male and female respondents, followed by the age range which is between 25 and above 40 years. The Table also shows the locations of the respondents across the areas focused on, and their professions.

Having established the demographics of the study as indicated in Table 1, the study zeroed into raising questions and getting answers. The question started with the preferred platform used by each of the respondents. The responses revealed interesting findings in terms the age differences and the referred platforms.

Table 1. Demographic details

Sex	Frequency
Male	6
Female	9
Total	**15**
Age Range	**Frequency**
25-30	6
31-35	3
36-40	1
40 & above	5
Total	**15**
Location	**Frequency**
Abuja	5
Plateau	5
Nasarawa	2
Benue	1
Port Harcourt	1
Abeokuta	1
Total	**15**
Occupation	**Frequency**
Medical Doctors	4
NGOs	6
Lecturers	1
Public/Civil Servants	2
Unemployed	2
Total	**15**

Source: Field Study, 2022

Q1: Social Media Platform Usage Preference

Following a brief discussion which checked to see the participants' preference of social media platforms and reasons for their preference, the participants were asked to choose which social media platform they preferred as their first question in the first category. This question saw that four (4) participants chose Twitter as their preferred app, while three (3) picked WhatsApp, three (5) indicated that Instagram was their favorite, and three (3) listed Facebook as their preference.

Again, within the four (4) participants that chose Twitter, the participants were 30, 32 and 34 years old, while one (1) was 46 years old. This suggests that Twitter may appeal to users in their mid-thirties. A participant, P12 said,

I prefer Twitter because it is entertaining and I can keep up with world news and also news on different investments on twitter.

Among the three (3) participants who preferred Facebook, two (2) were individuals of older age group, 58 and 60, and just one participant was middle aged, 39. It stands to reason that older people prefer Facebook as it has been around for a long while.

Q2: How Often Participants' Use Social Media Platforms

An enquiry on how often participants' use social media was made, to which fourteen out of fifteen participants answered "Very often" and one (1) answered "Not often" because he's always busy with work he forgets to check social media at times. P1 said,

If not for WhatsApp, I'd be sending text message every time probably would be spending lots of money on credit, but now I subscribe my data for a month on my phone and also Mifi and I can chat with my family and friends.

Q3: Awareness of Online Child Grooming

All the participant demonstrated knowledge of online child grooming, some were fully aware of it, while others only grasped the surface of the subject. P8 said that she had an idea of the concept of online child grooming but did not have a deep knowledge on it. P14 said,

Online child grooming is when an adult becomes friends a child with the intention of sexually abusing the child.

Q4: Factor Responsible for Online Child Grooming

Participants agreed that there are combinations of factors responsible for this however, to give a concise answer to this, P3 identified the degradation of culture and over-exposure to sex-inducing content online as factors that influence online child grooming. For P11, it was the increase of children in the social media platforms. Furthermore, P2 stated that,

Children having access to the internet at an early age. Children want to explore, they are curious, so if devices are made that would make them want to explore, they would use it. Baits are also a factor that influence online child grooming, children have emotional and material needs that sometime they can't get from their parents or guardians, so when groomers offer them gifts or special attention they are easily mislead and begin to do things to keep the attention or the flow of gifts. Factors that influence online child grooming from the adult, can be adults who don't find emotional or sexual satisfaction or balance/stability and also have no control in their "adult" relationships or marriages, tend to look for those stability in minors and also to control them.

Q5: Consequences of Online Child Grooming on the Child

Participants said mental disorders, low self-esteem, the child's inability to trust anyone after the experience, lack of concentration and participation in school, and substance abuse, are consequences of online child grooming (abuse) on the child/ victim. Additionally, P2 stated,

There's a lot of consequences, a few are, the groomer could influence a child up to the extent of telling the child to run away from home and come to her/him which could lead to illegal migration or child sex trafficking or the child's organs could be harvested. Mental disorders and substance abuse etc.

Participant P4, also stated that,

Self-harm, physical injuries such as cuts, bruises, or broken bones, emotional and psychological problems, such as impaired social-emotional skills or anxiety, self-blame, depressions and low self-esteem, nightmares and trouble sleeping, anxiety and panic attacks, issues at school, for example, finding it hard keeping up with schoolwork or behavioral issues.

Q6: Prevention of Online Child Grooming

To P6, government should create laws against such with penalty for offenders, schools should educate children on preventive measures, social media platforms should put more restrictions, parents should guide and monitor social media use by children, and CSOs should advocate for preventive measures and treatment.

Furthermore, P2 responded that,

Government should create awareness and orientations through infomercials on the media, community town halls meetings and also there should be social and behavioral change education or risk communication for primary to tertiary school levels. Government should also introduce laws and regulations that set out the punishment of online child grooming for offenders and justice for the victims. Schools should carry out exposure education and it should be incorporated into their curriculums, teach them all about online child grooming and abuse and also do awareness sessions during assemblies, through drama and debate clubs etc. Social Media Platforms should be able to trace and remove immoral contents and also find stricter ways of verifying ages of users signing up for their platforms. Parents should practice censorship; they should develop a habit of routine check of their child's devices and internet/social media usage. Parents should educate their children about social media, because the parents won't be there always to check the child's phone, children will go to school and parents will go to work, so educating their children about the dangers of social media, also sex and moral education. Social media education should come first, sex and moral education next and finally censorship. And finally, CSOs can prevent it through campaigns, awareness creation via infomercials, jingles etc.

Q7: Participants' Child or Minor is on Social Media

Majority of the participants disclosed that their children or the child under their care does have a social media account. Among 15 participants, the children of two (2) participant's, P3 and P5, whose children are two and five-year old respectively, gave "No" as their answer and explained their children are not on social media. P10 also explained that:

I allowed them to be on social media but once in a while I check what their looking at and who they're chatting with. Because if you don't let them join social media, they will find a way to do it behind your back.

Q8: Screen-time Awareness Level by the Participants

Most participants expressed a good level of awareness of what their children are doing when they use their devices and are connected to the internet. Sometimes they might not be aware of what their child/minor is doing due to an inability to be physically present next to the child. During the conversation, P15 stated,

I am very aware of my junior ones' screen-time. He doesn't have a smart phone, so he uses my phone for anything he does online, so once he's done, I go through

my browser history and chats and his social media accounts to see what he's doing and the kind of people he chats with. I know it can be seen as invasion of privacy, but it has to be done.

Q9: What does the Child/Minor do with Devices?

Majority of the participants stated that entertainment, educational researches, playing games, and chatting are the things they know their children use their devices for. For P11 affirmed that chatting, watching cartoons and movies, playing games and browsing of assignments, are what her younger one uses his phone for.

Q10: Child/Minor's Supervised vs. Unsupervised Time

P 12 said,

Due to the fact that I'm always busy and traveling I put a parental guidance software on my child's phone and linked his phone to my watch, so I get to limit his what he accesses with his device and also get to see who he chats with.

Participants who have older children disclosed that they cannot really supervise what their children do or who they are chat with when they use devices and are connected to the internet. P7 disclosed that,

When I'm walking towards my daughter, she locks her phone screen or turns her phone upside down so I won't see who she's chatting with, so how am I meant to supervise her screen-time? She won't even let me. So, I have a mother-daughter talk with her once in a while about the dangers of social media and ask about who she chats with and hope she doesn't entertain immoral conversations with online strangers. And when I see a video when scrolling through Facebook about an incident that involved social media and the dangers, I send her the video.

Q11: Heard of or Faced any Online Sexual Predatory Behaviors

Majority of the participant disclosed that they have heard of or faced online predatory behaviors. P11 said that,

On social media platforms especially Facebook, all you'll do is accept a friend request and next thing you'll see is some random guy sending you a picture of his dick on messenger and asking for your nudes, or some random guy sending you sex-chats. I instantly block and remove the person from my following of Facebook.

And the funny thing is, most of the guys/men, in fact a 100% of them are from a certain geographical zone. So, I've stopped accepting friend request from men, even women (from those areas) because it might be a disguise.

Q12: Types of Sexual Predatory Behaviors Children Could be exposed to Online

All participants gave different predatory behaviors children could be exposed to online. Child pornography to bait from adults they met online, were some of the types of sexual predatory behaviors participants listed. P12 said,

Virtual pedophilia pages, pornographic images and videos, online sexual games.

P8 adds that even if children refused to go to places where immoral contents are shown, now, it just pops up on their screens as they scroll through social media or when they browse on the internet and out of curiosity, the children may click it to see what it is about.

Q13: Examples of Grooming Phrases

On one hand, it looks really innocent and appropriate in certain instances, but on the other hand, can be very alarming, especially when a stranger online says it to a thirteen-year-old child, said P14. For P1, stated

"You know I love you so much, right?"

P6 adds that when a predator is grooming a child, they always shower the child with compliments in order for the child to lower their resolve and feel good. Some grooming phrases that P6 identified are,

"You are pretty". "You are special". "You are the best"

DISCUSSION

Results obtained from the in-depth interviews show that there are many factors that influence online child grooming. This can be traced from early exposure of a child to social media to the various features theses platforms have to the need for a child to be validated and have attention particularly if the child is neglected at home and has low self-esteem.

Responses also indicate that certain negative behavioral consequences on the child are traced to online child grooming. These include mental disorders, eating disorders, depression, bad performances and lack of participation at school, lack of trust, and in worst cases children can be suicidal. These are the after effects of online child grooming on children. This is in sync with a study UNICEF (2016), which found that, in the short term, child victims of sexual abuse can exhibit regressive behaviors, sleep and eating disorders, behavior or performance issues at school and an unwillingness to participate in school or social activities and long-term complications, including emotional and physical issues such as immune deficiency, chromosome erosion and missing brain tissue or might even commit suicide.

In examining government laws and regulations against online child grooming, it was discovered that there are laws set in place by 3 nations, Nigeria, the United States and the United Kingdom. Despite all of these laws and bans, incidents continue to spread like wildfire, particularly during the COVID-19 shutdown, and these have sadly not been thoroughly and methodically investigated. Because of its online, remote, and anonymous nature, it is one of the least reported forms of abuse.

This chapter, based on results obtained from the sampled population, revealed certain challenges regarding prevention of online child grooming. Because of the anonymous nature of the internet, discovering and preventing online sexual abuse is challenging; yet, detecting that a kid is mistreated online remains the primary job of the parents During the interview process, participants took the topic of children's online safety seriously and understood the need for thorough parental supervision. This, according to Ktoridou, Eteokleous, and Zahariadou (2012) can influence the quality of children's experiences online and prevent abuse. The strategy common for every participant regardless of a child's age is being physically present or being able to listen to the activities a child is engaged in being online.

FINDINGS

Our findings have in most cases reinforced previous beliefs or findings by previous scholars. They have also thrown up certain new scientific information and challenges that would form the bases for further research.

This chapter found out that Facebook-owned platforms (Instagram, WhatsApp and Facebook-Messenger) also known as the Metaverse now, are the social media platforms majorly used by offenders for grooming, abusing and exploiting children. These platforms also have the highest rate for child sexual abuse content being shared around the world.

Findings from this study show that most parents or guardians and the public in general are not familiar with the complexity of the grooming process and see certain behaviors as individual rather than connected harmful activities. In turn, this means that parents or others may react appropriately to some grooming stages and miss others.

The use of social media platforms for online grooming has been growing rapidly over the past years. As more children sign-up for these platforms so does the rate of online child grooming increase because adults looking to abuse children will go where kids can be found. As a result, grooming can apparently happen anywhere.

Social media has both great risk and advantage for children. However, key factors that may tip the outcome of use in either direction is bent on what the children are using it for, what they are viewing and sensitization of the children/minor about the dangers of social media.

The most noteworthy predatory behavior children are going to be exposed to on any social media platform is immoral content (child sexual abuse content). This disadvantage was largely emphasized by majority of the participant who partook in the study and also the literature review.

The effect of problems created by online child grooming (abuse) can be disastrous and long term, ranging from mental disorders to children being suicidal after having such experiences, in addition victims can be re-victimized again as adults.

With the laws and regulations that have been placed by the government, groomers are still lurking in hidden and dark places on these social media platforms, finding more ways of hiding their identity and avoiding being caught.

RECOMMENDATIONS

Based on examination of the responses from our population as a result of the in-depth interview and discussions, and having used the same responses in analysing and justifying the objectives of the study, here are some recommendations based on the already discussed findings.

In view of the information provided by this chapter, the chapter recommends that it is time for government to not penalize the offenders but also sanction social media platforms that fail to behave honestly and ethically, and instead chose to keep the findings hidden from the public and prioritize business over child safety and well-being.

Parents and guardians should have a close relationship with their children and pay close attention to their children in order to notice change in behavior. They are to ensure the children have constant access to them and are not afraid to tell them anything and should also monitor their children's online activities (especially younger ones).

Social media platforms should play their part and report child sexual abuse contents and offenders' accounts to the government authorities so they can trace and penalize the offenders. They should also restrict minors from accessing immoral contents on their platforms.

It is essential to have safety nets in place for children who are going through the horrifying aftermath of sexual abuse and exploitation whether online and offline. Many parents, schools, organizations, religious groups etc. are aware of this and provide some assistance, such as professional counselling services adjusted to the needs of victims of sexual abuse and exploitation.

Individuals should catalyze their deepest moral and help reduce the rate at which online child grooming and child abuse is increasing by reporting child sexual abuse contents they see on social media platforms to government authorities or organizations that has been set up such as Internet Watch Foundation (IWF) and US National Center for Missing and Exploited Children (NCMEC).

CONCLUSION

With the above scientific findings, it is believed that government, lawmakers, the judiciary, non-governmental organizations, operators of social media platforms, families and individuals will rise to the challenge of protecting our children from this moral corruption. They are expected to apply stricter measures to ensure that children are not misled into immoral acts by those who should be protecting their interests. Social media can be a source of disciplined behaviour among our youths instead of being turned into an avenue for corrupt manners.

The internet and Social Media platforms have become an essential part of present-day life, and play a major role in the educational and social growth of children. However, they also reveal children to new and advancing forms of sexual exploitation by sexual predators.

The study found that social media is the most dangerous place for a child, causing more harm than good, and that early exposure to social media is a major factor that influences online child grooming, because the child is naive and unaware of the dangers that social media poses, making it easy for groomers to entice and exploit them. The study also found that, while social media platforms such as Facebook promises to disclose online child abuse information to authorities, the Facebook whistleblower's revelation reveals that they disguise how destructive their site is for children because they (children/minors) are the major users. The consequences of online child grooming or abuse are damaging and can last a long time; victims may develop mental or eating disorders, low self-esteem, difficulty trusting others, and, in the worst-case scenario, suicide ideation. Victims and even adults might be re-victimized.

Instead of using parental control, parents or guardians frequently utilize physical presence as a risk mitigation approach and rely on creating trust with their children. The findings are important for a variety of organizations, including parents, technological businesses, educational institutions, and governments, because of their diversity. This research provides a solid platform for future qualitative and quantitative research in the field of online child safety. It is anticipated that further studies would incorporate responses from direct child victims of online grooming, how their lifestyles or behaviors have been influenced, and in their own opinion and what should be done by parents and government or other community of interest groups to control the situation

REFERENCES

Alqahtan, N., Atkinson, S., Furnell, S., & Stengel, I. (2017). *Internet risks for children: Parents' perceptions and attitudes: An investigative study of the Saudi Context.* Retrieved from https://pearl.plymouth.ac.uk/bitstream/handle/10026.1/13613/ITAPaper.pdf?sequence=1

Boddy, C. R. (2016). Sample size for qualitative research. *Qualitative Market Research, 19*(4), 426-432. https://doi-org/1 doi:0.1108/QMR-06-2016-0053

Brennan, M., Perkins, D., Merdian, H., Tyrrell, E., Babchishin, K., McCartan, K., & Kelly, R. (2022). *Best Practice in the Management of Online Sex Offending.* Retrieved 26 March 2022, from https://pearl.plymouth.ac.uk/handle/10026.1/14331

Carter, S., Greenberg, K., & Walker, M. (2016). The impact of computer usage on academic performance: Evidence from a randomized trial at the United States Military Academy. *Economics of Education Review, 56.* Advance online publication. doi:10.1016/j.econedurev.2016.12.005

Cherry, K. (2021). *Levels of Developing Morality in Kohlberg's Theories.* Retrieved 23 March 2022, from https://www.verywellmind.com/kohlbergs-theory-of-moral-development-2795071#:~:text=Kohlberg's%20theory%20of%20moral%20development%20is%20a%20theory%20that%20focuses,on%20seeking%20and%20maintaining%20justice

Child grooming. (2022). In *Wikipedia*. Retrieved 24 February 2022, from https://en.wikipedia.org/wiki/Child_grooming

Child Sexual Exploitation and grooming by Victoria State Government. (n.d.). www.education.vic.gov.au

Children's use of mobile phones: An international comparison 2015. (2016). Retrieved 24 February 2022, from https://www.gsma.com/publicpolicy/wp-content/uploads/2016/10/GSMA_Report_Childrens-use-of-mobile-phones-An-international-comparison-2015.pdf

Code, U. S. § 2258A - Reporting requirements of providers. Retrieved 26 March 2022, from https://www.law.cornell.edu/uscode/text/18/2258A

Daniela, R. M. (2020). *Determining the sample size in qualitative research*. 1 doi:0.26520/mcdsare.2020.4.181-187

Face the facts. (2020). *Internet Watch Foundation Annual Report*. Retrieved 26 March 2022, from https://www.iwf.org.uk/about-us/who-we-are/annual-report/

Ghaffary, S. (2021). *Why this Facebook scandal is different*. Vox. Available at: https://www.google.com/amp/s/www.vox.com/platform/amp/recode/2021/10/3/22707940/frances-haugen-facebook-whistleblower-60-minutes-teen-girls-instagram

Grooming: Recognising the signs. (2022). Retrieved 24 February 2022, from https://raisingchildren.net.au/school-age/safety/online-safety/grooming-signs#:~:text=Signs%20of%20grooming%20in%20children%20aged%20 0%2D11%20years,-Many%20of%20the&text=has%20unexplained%20gifts%20 like%20new,lot%20of%20time%20with%20them

Instagram monthly active users. (n.d.). *Statista*. Retrieved 26 March 2022, from https://www.statista.com/statistics/253577/number-of-monthly-active-instagram-users/

IWF Annual Report. (2019). Retrieved 26 March 2022, from https://www.yumpu.com/en/document/read/63240486/iwf-annual-report-2019

Kumah, C. (2015). *A Comparative Study of use of the Library and the Internet as Sources of Information by Graduate Students in the University Of Ghana*. Retrieved from https://digitalcommons.unl.edu/libphilprac/1298?utm_source=digitalcommons.unl.edu%2Flibphilprac%2F1298&utm_medium=PDF&utm_campaign=PDFCoverPages

Lawsofnigeria.placng.org. (n.d.). Available at: http://lawsofnigeria.placng.org/laws/C38.pdf

Legal Information Institute. (n.d.a). *18 U.S. Code § 2251 - Sexual exploitation of children*. Available at: https://www.law.cornell.edu/uscode/text/18/2251

Legal Information Institute. (n.d.b). *18 U.S. Code § 2425 - Use of interstate facilities to transmit information about a minor.* Available at: https://www.law.cornell.edu/uscode/text/18/2425

Mbaegbu, I. (2020). Children Can Become Victims of Online Sexual Abuse Without Parents Knowing. *The Whistler Nigeria.* Available at: https://thewhistler.ng/children-can-become-victims-of-online-sexual-abuse-without-parents-knowing/

Nealon, L. (2021). How social media preys on children. *Newsweek.* Available at: https://www.newsweek.com/how-social-media-preys-children-opinion-1637132

NSPCC. (2022). *Record high number of recorded grooming crimes lead to calls for stronger online safety legislation.* Available at: https://www.nspcc.org.uk/about-us/news-opinion/2021/online-grooming-record-high/

Olson, L., Daggs, J., Ellevold, B., & Rogers, T. (2007). Entrapping the Innocent: Toward a Theory of Child Sexual Predators? Luring Communication. *Communication Theory, 17*(3), 231–251. doi:10.1111/j.1468-2885.2007.00294.x

Online Enticement. (n.d.). Retrieved 26 March 2022, from https://www.missingkids.org/theissues/onlineenticement

Online grooming. (n.d.). *Childnet.* Retrieved 26 February 2022, from https://www.childnet.com/help-and-advice/online-grooming/

Protecting Children from Online Sexual Exploitation. (2016). *A guide to action for religious leaders and communities.* Retrieved 3 March 2022, from https://www.unicef.org/media/73506/file/FBO-Guide-for-Religious-Leaders-Communities-2016.pdf.pdf

Responding to Online Threats: Minors' Perspectives on Disclosing, Reporting, and Blocking. (2021). Available at: https://info.thorn.org/hubfs/Research/Responding%20to%20Online%20Threats_2021-Full-Report.pdf?utm_campaign=H2D%20report&utm_source=website

Ringenberg, T., Seigfried-Spellar, K., Rayz, J., & Rogers, M. 2022. A scoping review of child grooming strategies: pre- and post-internet. *Child Abuse & Neglect, 123.* Available at: https://www.sciencedirect.com/science/article/abs/pii/S0145213421004610#!

Roser, M., Ritchie, H., & Ortiz-Ospina, E. (2015). *Internet.* Retrieved 24 February 2022, from https://ourworldindata.org/internet

Sarfo, J. O., Debrah, T., Obeng, P., & Jubey, S. (2021). Qualitative research designs, sample size and saturation: Is enough always enough. Journal of Advocacy. *Research in Education*, 8(3), 60–65. doi:10.13187/jare.2021.3.60

Silver, L., Smith, A., Johnson, C., Taylor, K., Jiang, J., Anderson, M., & Rainie, L. (2019). *Mobile Connectivity in Emerging Economies*. Retrieved 24 February 2022, from https://www.pewinternet.org/wp-content/uploads/sites/9/2019/03/PI_2019.03.07_Mobile-Connectivity_FINAL.pdf

Siraj, H., Salam, A., Hasan, N., Jin, T., Roslan, R., & Othman, M. (2015). Internet Usage and Academic Performance: A Study in a Malaysian Public University. *International Medical Journal*, 22(2), 83–86. https://www.researchgate.net/publication/275833912_Internet_Usage_and_Academic_Performance_A_Study_in_a_Malaysian_Public_University

Underage Children. (n.d.). *Instagram Help Centre*. Retrieved 26 March 2022, from https://help.instagram.com/290666591035380

UNICEF Division of Communication. (2017). *Children in a Digital World*. Retrieved from https://www.unicef.org/media/48601/file

WhatsApp Help Center. (n.d.). *About end-to-end encryption*. Retrieved 26 March 2022, from https://faq.whatsapp.com/general/security-and-privacy/end-to-end-encryption

Yesilyurt, M., Basturk, R., Yesilyurt, F., & Kara, I. (2014). The effect of technological devices on student's academic success: Evidence from Denizli. *Journal of Internet Applications And Management*, 5(1), 39–47. doi:10.5505/iuyd.2014.83007

KEY TERMS AND DEFINITIONS

Child Prostitution: Prostitution involving a child, and it is a form of commercial sexual exploitation of children. The term normally refers to prostitution of a minor, or person under the legal age of consent.

Child Sexual Abuse: Also called child molestation, is a form of child abuse in which an adult or older adolescent uses a child for sexual stimulation.

Cybersex Trafficking: Is a cybercrime involving sex trafficking and the live streaming of coerced sexual acts and/or rape on webcam. Cybersex trafficking is distinct from other sex crimes. Victims are transported by traffickers to 'cybersex dens'.

Fantasy Defense: Where a defendant accused of attempting a crime (enticing minors into sexual activity, for example) claims that they never intended to complete the crime. Instead, they claim they were engaged in a fantasy and, in the case of luring a minor, believed they were dealing with an adult.

Kohlberg's Moral Development Theory: Is a study of how children acquire morality and moral reasoning.

Minor: Someone under a certain age, usually the age of majority, which legally demarcates childhood or an underage individual from adulthood. The age of majority depends upon jurisdiction.

Online Child Grooming: Simply put, is when someone (under disguise or not) as a minor befriends a child online and builds up their trust and develops a relationship with the child, with the intention of exploiting and harming the child.

Pedophilia: A psychiatric disorder in which an adult or older adolescent experiences a primary or exclusive sexual attraction to prepubescent children.

Compilation of References

Abbas, S. G., Vaccari, I., Hussain, F., Zahid, S., Fayyaz, U. U., Shah, G. A., Bakhshi, T., & Cambiaso, E. (2021). Identifying and mitigating phishing attack threats in IoT use cases using a threat modelling approach. *Sensors (Basel)*, *21*(14), 4816. doi:10.339021144816 PMID:34300556

Abreu, Z., & Pereira, L. (2022). Privacy protection in smart meters using homomorphic encryption: An overview. *WIREs*, *12*(4), 1–16. doi:10.1002/widm.1469

Abu, M. S., Selamat, S. R., Ariffin, A., & Yusof, R. (2018). Cyber threat intelligence – issue and challenges. *Indonesian Journal of Electrical Engineering and Computer Science*, *10*(1), 371–379. doi:10.11591/ijeecs.v10.i1.pp371-379

Afzaliseresht, N., Miao, Y., Michalska, S., Liu, Q., & Wang, H. (2020). From logs to stories: Human-centred data mining for cyber threat intelligence. *IEEE Access : Practical Innovations, Open Solutions*, *8*, 19089–19099. doi:10.1109/ACCESS.2020.2966760

Agarwal, A., Walia, H., & Gupta, H. (2021, September). Cyber Security Model for Threat Hunting. In *2021 9th International Conference on Reliability, Infocom Technologies and Optimization (Trends and Future Directions)(ICRITO)* (pp. 1-8). IEEE. 10.1109/ICRITO51393.2021.9596199

Aggarwal, C. C. (2005). *On k -Anonymity and the Curse of Dimensionality*. Academic Press.

Agrawal, D., & Aggarwal, C. C. (2001). On the design and quantification of privacy preserving data mining algorithms. *Proceedings of the Twentieth ACM SIGMOD-SIGACT-SIGART Symposium on Principles of Database Systems - PODS '01*, 247–255. 10.1145/375551.375602

Agrawal, R., Kiernan, J., & Srikant, R. (2002). *Hippocratic Database*. In *28th International Conference on Very Large Data Bases*, Hong Kong, China.

Ahmed, B., Ali, G., Hussain, A., Baseer, A., & Ahmed, J. (2021, April). Analysis of text feature extractors using deep learning on fake news. *Engineering, Technology, & Applied Scientific Research*, *11*(2), 7001–7005.

Ahmed, Y., Naqvi, S., & Josephs, M. (2019). Cybersecurity Metrics for Enhanced Protection of Healthcare IT Systems. *13th International Symposium on Medical Information and Communication Technology (ISMICT)*, 1-9. 10.1109/ISMICT.2019.8744003

Aldwairi, M., & Alwahedi, A. (2018, November 5). Detecting fake news in social media networks. *Procedia Computer Science, 141*, 215–222. doi:10.1016/j.procs.2018.10.171

Al-Fuqaha, A., Guizani, M., Mohammadi, M., Aledhari, M., & Ayyash, M. (2015). Internet of things: A survey on enabling technologies, protocols, and applications. *IEEE Communications Surveys and Tutorials, 17*(4), 2347–2376. doi:10.1109/COMST.2015.2444095

Alhajri, M., Salehi, A., & Rudolph, C. (2022). Privacy of Fitness Applications and Consent Management in Blockchain. In *Australasian Computer Science Week 2022 (ACSW 2022)*. ACM. 10.1145/3511616.3513100

Ali, Q. E., Ahmad, N., Malik, A. H., Ali, G., & ur Rehman, W. (2018). Issues, challenges, and research opportunities in intelligent transport system for security and privacy. In *Applied Sciences (Switzerland), 8*(10). doi:10.3390/app8101964

Alqahtan, N., Atkinson, S., Furnell, S., & Stengel, I. (2017). *Internet risks for children: Parents' perceptions and attitudes: An investigative study of the Saudi Context.* Retrieved from https://pearl.plymouth.ac.uk/bitstream/handle/10026.1/13613/ITAPaper.pdf?sequence=1

Anjum, A., Ahmad, N., Malik, S. U. R., Zubair, S., & Shahzad, B. (2018). An efficient approach for publishing microdata for multiple sensitive attributes. *The Journal of Supercomputing, 74*(10), 5127–5155. doi:10.100711227-018-2390-x

Armel, K., Gupta, A., Shrimali, G., & Albert, A. (2013). Is disaggregation the holy grail of energy efficiency? The case of electricity. *Energy Policy, 52*(1), 213–234. doi:10.1016/j.enpol.2012.08.062

Arnaboldi, L., Czekster, R. M., Morisset, C., & Metere, R. (2020). Modelling load-changing attacks in cyber-physical systems. *Electronic Notes in Theoretical Computer Science, 353*, 39–60. doi:10.1016/j.entcs.2020.09.018

Asghar, M. R., Lee, T., Baig, M. M., Ullah, E., Russello, G., & Dobbie, G. (2017). A Review of Privacy and Consent Management in Healthcare: A Focus on Emerging Data Sources. *IEEE 13th International Conference on e-Science (e-Science)*, 518-522. 10.1109/eScience.2017.84

Asghar, M. R., Dán, G., Miorandi, D., & Chlamtac, I. (2017). Smart meter data privacy: A survey. *IEEE Communications Surveys and Tutorials, 19*(4), 2820–2835. doi:10.1109/COMST.2017.2720195

Asghar, M., & Russello, G. (2012). Flexible and Dynamic Consent Capturing. In J. Camenisch & D. Kesdogan (Eds.), Lecture Notes in Computer Science: Vol. 7039. *Open Problems in Network Security. iNetSec 2011.* Springer. doi:10.1007/978-3-642-27585-2_10

Asghar, M., & Russello, G. (2015). Automating Consent Management Lifecycle for Electronic Healthcare Systems. In A. Gkoulalas-Divanis & G. Loukides (Eds.), *Medical Data Privacy Handbook.* Springer. doi:10.1007/978-3-319-23633-9_14

Ashfield, J., Shroyer, D., & Brown, D. (2012, October 23). *Location based authentication of mobile device transactions.* Google Patents. (US Patent 8,295,898)

Bace, R., & Mell, P. (2001). NIST special publication on intrusion detection systems. In Nist Special Publication.

Backes, M., & Melser, S. (2012). Differentially private smart metering with battery recharging. *IACR Cryptology*, 183. https://eprint.iacr.org/2012/183

Bahrami, M., & Singhal, M. (2015). A light-weight permutation based method for data privacy in mobile cloud computing. *Proceedings - 2015 3rd IEEE International Conference on Mobile Cloud Computing, Services, and Engineering, MobileCloud 2015*, 189–196. 10.1109/MobileCloud.2015.36

Balasubramaniam, A., Paul, A., Hong, W. H., Seo, H., & Kim, J. (2017). Comparative Analysis of Intelligent Transportation Systems for Sustainable Environment in Smart Cities. *Sustainability*, *9*(7), 1120. doi:10.3390u9071120

Ball, P., & Maxmen, A. (2020). The epic battle against coronavirus misinformation and conspiracy theories. *Nature*, *581*(7809), 371–374. doi:10.1038/d41586-020-01452-z PMID:32461658

Bang, Y., Lee, D.J., Bae, Y.S., & Ahn, J.H. (2012). Improving information security management: An analysis of id–password usage and a new login vulnerability measure. *International Journal of Information Management, 32* (5), 409–418.

Banu, M. N., & Banu, S. M. (2013). A comprehensive study of phishing attacks. *International Journal of Computer Science and Information Technologies*, *4*(6), 783–786.

Barnum, S. (2012). Standardizing cyber threat intelligence information with the Structured Threat Information eXpression (STIX). *Mitre Corporation*, *11*, 1–22.

Bayardo, R. J., & Agrawal, R. (n.d.). Data Privacy through Optimal k-Anonymization. *21st International Conference on Data Engineering (ICDE'05)*, 217–228. 10.1109/ICDE.2005.42

Beal, C. D., & Flynn, J. (2015). Toward the digital water age: Survey and case studies of Australian water utility smart-metering programs. *Utilities Policy*, *32*, 2–37. doi:10.1016/j.jup.2014.12.006

Benaloh, J., Chase, M., Horvitz, E., & Lauter, K. (2009). Patient controlled encryption. *Proceedings of the 2009 ACM Workshop on Cloud Computing Security - CCSW '09*, 103. 10.1145/1655008.1655024

Berady, A., Jaume, M., Tong, V. V. T., & Guette, G. (2021). From TTP to IoC: Advanced persistent graphs for threat hunting. *IEEE eTransactions on Network and Service Management*, *18*(2), 1321–1333. doi:10.1109/TNSM.2021.3056999

Bhardwaj, A., & Goundar, S. (2019). A framework for effective threat hunting. *Network Security*, *2019*(6), 15–19. doi:10.1016/S1353-4858(19)30074-1

Bhardwaj, A., & Goundar, S. (2021). Comparing single tier and three tier infrastructure designs against DDoS attacks. In *Research Anthology on Combating Denial-of-Service Attacks* (pp. 541–558). IGI Global. doi:10.4018/978-1-7998-5348-0.ch028

Bhuyan, S.S., Kabir, U.Y., Escareno, J.M., Ector, K., Palakodeti, S., Wyant, D., Kumar, S., Levy, M., Kedia, S., Dasgupta, D., & Dobalian, A. (2020). Transforming Healthcare Cybersecurity from Reactive to Proactive: Current Status and Future Recommendations. *Journal of Medical Systems, 44*(5), 98. doi:10.1007/s10916-019-1507-y

Blocki, J., Harsha, B., & Zhou, S. (2018). *On the economics of offline password cracking. In 2018 ieee symposium on security and privacy (sp).* IEEE.

Boddy, C. R. (2016). Sample size for qualitative research. *Qualitative Market Research, 19*(4), 426-432. https://doi-org/1 doi:0.1108/QMR-06-2016-0053

Bonnici, C. J., & Coles-Kemp, L. (2010). Principled Electronic Consent Management A Preliminary Research Framework. *2010 International Conference on Emerging Security Technologies*, 119-123. 10.1109/EST.2010.21

Boudguiga, A., Klaudel, W., Boulanger, A., & Chiron, P. (2016). A simple intrusion detection method for controller area network. *2016 IEEE International Conference on Communications, ICC 2016.* IEEE. 10.1109/ICC.2016.7511098

Bozdal, M., Samie, M., Aslam, S., & Jennions, I. (2020). Evaluation of can bus security challenges. In Sensors (Switzerland), 30(8). doi:10.339020082364

Braintree. (2007). *Top 5 vulnerabilities leading to credit card data breaches.* Braintree Payments. https://www.braintreepayments.com/blog/top-5-vulnerabilities-leading-to-credit-card-data-breaches/

Brand, R. (2002). *Microdata Protection through Noise Addition.* 1 doi:0.1007/3-540-47804-3_8

Brennan, M., Perkins, D., Merdian, H., Tyrrell, E., Babchishin, K., McCartan, K., & Kelly, R. (2022). *Best Practice in the Management of Online Sex Offending.* Retrieved 26 March 2022, from https://pearl.plymouth.ac.uk/handle/10026.1/14331

Brennen, J. S., Simon, F. M., & Nielsen, R. K. (2021). Beyond (mis) representation: Visuals in COVID-19 misinformation. *The International Journal of Press/Politics, 26*(1), 277–299. doi:10.1177/1940161220964780

Brickell, J., & Shmatikov, V. (2008). The cost of privacy: Destruction of data-mining utility in anonymized data publishing. *Proceedings of the ACM SIGKDD International Conference on Knowledge Discovery and Data Mining*, 70–78. 10.1145/1401890.1401904

Britton, T. C., Stewart, R. A., & O'Halloran, K. R. (2013). Smart metering: Enabler for rapid and effective post meter leakage identification and water loss management. *Journal of Cleaner Production, 54*, 166–176. doi:10.1016/j.jclepro.2013.05.018

Brunschwiler, C. (2013). *Wireless M-Bus security.* Black Hat.

Buinevich, M., & Vladyko, A. (2019). Forecasting Issues of Wireless Communication Networks' Cyber Resilience for An Intelligent Transportation System: An Overview of Cyber Attacks. *Information (Basel), 10*(1), 27. doi:10.3390/info10010027

Burch, L. L., & Carter, S. R. (2010, June 15). *Methods and systems for multi-factor authentication.* Google Patents. (US Patent 7,739,744)

Burger, E. W., Goodman, M. D., Kampanakis, P., & Zhu, K. A. (2014, November). Taxonomy model for cyber threat intelligence information exchange technologies. In *Proceedings of the 2014 ACM Workshop on Information Sharing & Collaborative Security* (pp. 51-60). ACM. 10.1145/2663876.2663883

Byun, J.-W., Sohn, Y., Bertino, E., & Li, N. (2006). *Secure Anonymization for Incremental Datasets.* 1 doi:0.1007/11844662_4

Byun, J. W., Bertino, E., & Li, N. (2005). Purpose Based Access Control of Complex Data for Privacy Protection. In *Proceedings of the tenth ACM symposium on Access control models and technologies (SACMAT '05).* Association for Computing Machinery. 10.1145/1063979.1063998

California Public Utilities Commission. (2014). *Decision adopting rules to provide access to energy usage and usage-related data while protecting privacy of personal data.* CPUC. https://docs.cpuc.ca.gov/PublishedDocs/Published/G000/M090/K845/90845985.PDF

Can, O. (2018). Personalised anonymity for microdata release. *IET Information Security, 12*(4), 341–347. doi:10.1049/iet-ifs.2016.0613

Carsten, P., Andel, T. R., Yampolskiy, M., & McDonald, J. T. (2015). In-Vehicle Networks. *Proceedings of the 10th Annual Cyber and Information Security Research Conference,* (pp. 1–8). ACM. doi:10.1145/2746266.2746267

Carter, S., Greenberg, K., & Walker, M. (2016). The impact of computer usage on academic performance: Evidence from a randomized trial at the United States Military Academy. *Economics of Education Review, 56.* Advance online publication. doi:10.1016/j.econedurev.2016.12.005

Cate, F. H., & Mayer-Schonberger, V. (2013). Notice and consent in a world of Big Data, Tomorrow's Privacy. *International Data Privacy Law, 3*(2), 2013. doi:10.1093/idpl/ipt005

Chand, H. V., & Karthikeyan, J. (2018). Survey on the role of IoT in intelligent transportation system. *Indonesian Journal of Electrical Engineering and Computer Science, 11*(3), 936–941. doi:10.11591/ijeecs.v11.i3.pp936-941

Chase, M., & Chow, S. S. M. (2009). Improving privacy and security in multi-authority attribute-based encryption. *Proceedings of the 16th ACM Conference on Computer and Communications Security - CCS '09,* 121. 10.1145/1653662.1653678

Chauduri, S., Kaushik, R., & Ramamurthy, R. (2011). *Database Access Control & Privacy: Is there a Commom Ground.* 5th Biennial Conference on Innovative Data Systems Research (CIDR '11), Asilomar, CA.

Checkoway, S., McCoy, D., Kantor, B., Anderson, D., Shacham, H., Savage, S., Koscher, K., Czeskis, A., Roesner, F., & Kohno, T. (2011). Comprehensive experimental analyses of automotive attack surfaces. *Proceedings of the 20th USENIX Security Symposium.* USENIX.

Chen, W. D., Hancke, G. P., Mayes, K. E., Lien, Y., & Chiu, J. H. (2010). Using 3g network components to enable nfc mobile transactions and authentication. In 2010 ieee international conference on progress in informatics and computing (Vol. 1). IEEE.

Chen, Y. (2007). A bayesian network model of knowledge-based authentication. *AMCIS 2007 Proceedings, 423.* AMC.

Chen, D., Irwin, D., Shenoy, P., & Albrecht, J. (2014). *Combined heat and privacy: Preventing occupancy detection from smart meters.* In *2014 IEEE International Conference on Pervasive Computing and Communications,* (pp. 208–215). IEEE.

Chen, F., Dai, J., Wang, B., Sahu, S., Naphade, M., & Lu, C.-T. (2011). *Activity analysis based on low sample rate smart meters.* In *Proceedings of the 17th ACM International Conference on Knowledge Discovery and Data Mining,* (pp. 240–248). ACM. 10.1145/2020408.2020450

Cheng, Z., Pang, M.-S., & Pavlou, P. A. (2020). Mitigating Traffic Congestion: The Role of Intelligent Transportation Systems. *Information Systems Research, 31*(3), 653–674. doi:10.1287/isre.2019.0894

Chen, Y., & Liginlal, D. (2007). Bayesian networks for knowledge-based authentication. *IEEE Transactions on Knowledge and Data Engineering, 19*(5), 695–710. doi:10.1109/TKDE.2007.1024

Cherry, K. (2021). *Levels of Developing Morality in Kohlberg's Theories.* Retrieved 23 March 2022, from https://www.verywellmind.com/kohlbergs-theory-of-moral-development-2795071#:~:text=Kohlberg's%20theory%20of%20moral%20development%20is%20a%20theory%20that%20focuses,on%20seeking%20and%20maintaining%20justice

Chiew, K. L., Yong, K. S. C., & Tan, C. L. (2018). A survey of phishing attacks: Their types, vectors and technical approaches. *Expert Systems with Applications, 106,* 1–20. doi:10.1016/j.eswa.2018.03.050

Child grooming. (2022). In *Wikipedia.* Retrieved 24 February 2022, from https://en.wikipedia.org/wiki/Child_grooming

Child Sexual Exploitation and grooming by Victoria State Government. (n.d.). www.education.vic.gov.au

Children's use of mobile phones: An international comparison 2015. (2016). Retrieved 24 February 2022, from https://www.gsma.com/publicpolicy/wp-content/uploads/2016/10/GSMA_Report_Childrens-use-of-mobile-phones-An-international-comparison-2015.pdf

Chi-Wing, R., Li, J., Fu, A. W.-C., & Wang, K. (2006). (α, k)-anonymity. *Proceedings of the 12th ACM SIGKDD International Conference on Knowledge Discovery and Data Mining - KDD '06,* 754. 10.1145/1150402.1150499

Choi, K., Lee, J. L., & Chun, Y. T. (2017). Voice phishing fraud and its modus operandi. *Security Journal, 30*(2), 454–466. doi:10.1057j.2014.49

Chokhani, S. (2004). Knowledge based authentication (kba) metrics. In Kba symposium-knowledge based authentication: Is it quantifiable. CSRC.

Ciriani, V., Vimercati, S. D. C., Foresti, S., & Samarati, P. (n.d.). *k-Anonymity*. Academic Press.

City Circle Line. (2022, June).

Clarke, R. (2002). eConsent: A critical element of trust in ebusiness. *Proceedings of the 15th Bled Electronic Commerce Conference*, 338-360.

Code, U. S. § 2258A - Reporting requirements of providers. Retrieved 26 March 2022, from https://www.law.cornell.edu/uscode/text/18/2258A

Coiera, E., & Clarke, R. (2004, March-April). e-Consent: The Design and Implementation of Consumer Consent Mechanisms in an Electronic Environment. *Journal of the American Medical Informatics Association*, *11*(2), 129–140. doi:10.1197/jamia.M1480 PMID:14662803

Collins, B., Hoang, D. T., Nguyen, N. T., & Hwang, D. (2021). Trends in combating fake news on social media – a survey. *Journal of Information and Telecommunication*, *5*(2), 247–266. doi:10.1080/24751839.2020.1847379

Connolly, J., Davidson, M., & Schmidt, C. (2014). The Trusted Automated eXchange of Indicator Information (TAXII), 1-20. The MITRE Corporation.

Conti, M., Dargahi, T., & Dehghantanha, A. (2018). Cyber threat intelligence: challenges and opportunities. In *Cyber Threat Intelligence* (pp. 1–6). Springer. doi:10.1007/978-3-319-73951-9_1

Contributor, T. T. (2014, December). What is mobile authentication? *Tech Target*. https://www.techtarget.com/searchsecurity/definition/mobile-authentication

Cormen, T. H., Leiserson, C. E., Rivest, R. L., & Stein, C. (2009). *Introduction to algorithms* (3rd ed.). MIT Press and McGraw-Hill.

Council, F. F. I. E. (2005). *Authentication in an internet banking environment. FFIEC agencies.* FFIE Council.

Court of Justice of the European Union. (2010). *Joint Case C-92/09 and C-93/09 (2010). Volker und Markus Schecke GbR (C-92/09) and Hartmut Eifert (C-93/09) v. Land Hessen.* [*Volker und Markus Schecke GbR (C-92/09) and Hartmut Eifert (C-93/09) v. Land Hessen.*] Europea. https://curia.europa.eu/juris/liste.jsf?num=C-92/09

Court of Justice of the European Union. (2013). *Case C-473/12. Institut professionnel des agents immobiliers (IPI) v Geoffrey Englebert and Others.* [*Professional Institute of Realtors (IPI) v Geoffrey Englebert and Others.*]. Europa. https://curia.europa.eu/juris/liste.jsf?num=C-473/12

Court of Justice of the European Union. (2014). Case C-212/13. *František Ryneš v Úřad pro ochranu osobních údajů.* [*František Ryneš in the Office for Personal Data Protection.*] Europa. https://curia.europa.eu/juris/liste.jsf?num=C-212/13

Court of Justice of the European Union. (2016). Case C-582/14. *Patrick Breyer v. Bundesrepublik Deutschland.* Europea. https://curia.europa.eu/juris/liste.jsf?num=C- 582/14

Court of Justice of the European Union. (2017). Case C-13/16. *Valsts policijas Rīgas reģiona pārvaldes Kārtības policijas pārvalde v. Rīgas pašvaldības SIA "Rīgas satiksme".* [*Order Police Department of the Riga Region Administration of the State Police v. Riga Municipality Ltd. "Rīgas* satiksme".]. Europea. https://curia.europa.eu/juris/liste.jsf?num=C-13/16

Court of Justice of the European Union. (2018a). Case C-210/16. *Unabhängiges Landeszentrum für Datenschutz Schleswig-Holstein v Wirtschaftsakademie Schleswig-Holstein GmbH.* [*Unabhängiger Landeszentrum für Datenschutz Schleswig-Holstein v Wirtschaftsakademie Schleswig-Holstein GmbH.*]. Europa. https://curia.europa.eu/juris/liste.jsf?num=C-210/16

Court of Justice of the European Union. (2018b). Case C-25/17. *Jehovah witness.* Europa. *https:// curia.europa.eu/juris/liste.jsf?num=C-25/17*

Court of Justice of the European Union. (2019a). Case C-708/18. *TK v. Asociaţia de Proprietari bloc M5A-ScaraA.* [*TK v. Association of Owners block M5A-ScaraA.*]. Europa. https://curia. europa.eu/juris/liste.jsf?num=C-708/18

Court of Justice of the European Union. (2019b). Case C-40/17. *Fashion ID GmbH & Co.KG v Verbraucherzentrale NRW eV.* https://curia.europa.eu/juris/liste.jsf?num=C- 40/17

Court of Justice of the European Union. (2020). Case C-311/18. *Data Protection Commissioner v. Facebook Ireland Limited a Maximillian Schrems.* Europa. https://curia.europa.eu/juris/liste. jsf?num=C- 311/18

Court of Justice of the European Union. (2022). Case C-175/20. *„SS" SIA v. Valsts ieņēmumu dienests.* [*"SS" Ltd. v. State Revenue Service.*] https://curia.europa.eu/juris/liste.jsf?num=C- 175/20

CRYPTO-IT. (2020, -03-09). Frequency analysis (Vol. 2020) (No. 29th June). *Crypto.* http:// www.crypto-it.net/eng/attacks/frequency-analysis.html#:~:text=Frequency%20analysis%20 is%20one%20of,are%20used%20with%20different%20frequencies.&text=Based%20on%20 that%2C%20one%20can,texts%20written%20in%20other%20languages

Cuijpers, C., & Koops, B.-J. (2008). The 'smart meters' bill: A privacy test based on article 8 of the ECHR. *Study commissioned by the Dutch Consumers' Association.* English version available from the authors, see Cuijpers, C., & Koops, B.-J. (2012), footnote 39.

Cuijpers, C., & Koops, B.-J. (2012). Smart metering and privacy in Europe: Lessons from the Dutch case. In *European data protection: Coming of age* (pp. 269–293). Springer.

Czekster, R. M., Metere, R., & Morisset, C. (2022a). cyberaCTIve: a STIX-based Tool for Cyber Threat Intelligence in Complex Models. *arXiv preprint arXiv:2204.03676.*

Czekster, R. M., Metere, R., & Morisset, C. (2022b). Incorporating Cyber Threat Intelligence into Complex Cyber-Physical Systems: A STIX Model for Active Buildings. *Applied Sciences (Basel, Switzerland), 12*(10), 5005. doi:10.3390/app12105005

Dale, W. (2021, 7 Sep). The top 12 password-cracking techniques used by hackers (Vol. 2022) (No. 02/02/). *IT Pro.* https://www.itpro.co.uk/security/34616/the-top-password-cracking-techniques-used-by-hackers

Dalenius, T., & Reiss, S. P. (1982). Data-swapping: A technique for disclosure control. *Journal of Statistical Planning and Inference, 6*(1), 73–85. doi:10.1016/0378-3758(82)90058-1

Daly, M. K. (2009). Advanced persistent threat. *Usenix, Nov, 4* (4), 2013–2016.

Daniela, R. M. (2020). *Determining the sample size in qualitative research.* 1 doi:0.26520/mcdsare.2020.4.181-187

Das, D., & Bhattacharyya, D. K. (2012). Decomposition+: Improving ℓ-Diversity for Multiple Sensitive Attributes. In *International Conference on Computer Science and Information Technology* (pp. 403–412). 10.1007/978-3-642-27308-7_44

Daszczyszak, R., Ellis, D., Luke, S., & Whitley, S. (2019). *TTP-Based Hunting.* MITRE CORP MCLEAN VA.

Davies, J. (2018). *The 10 biggest U.S. healthcare data breaches of 2018.* Retrieved from https://healthitsecurity.com/news/the-10-biggest-u.s.-healthcaredata-breaches-of-2018

de Aguiar, E. J., Faiçal, B. S., Krishnamachari, B., & Ueyama, J. (2020). A Survey of Blockchain-Based Strategies for Healthcare. *ACM Computing Surveys, 53*(2), 1–27. doi:10.1145/3376915

de Boer, M. H., Bakker, B. J., Boertjes, E., Wilmer, M., Raaijmakers, S., & van der Kleij, R. (2019). Text mining in cybersecurity: Exploring threats and opportunities. *Multimodal Technologies and Interaction, 3*(3), 62. doi:10.3390/mti3030062

de Capitani di Vimercati, S., Foresti, S., Livraga, G., Paraboschi, S., & Samarati, P. (2018a). *Confidentiality Protection in Large Databases.* 1 doi:0.1007/978-3-319-61893-7_27

de Capitani di Vimercati, S., Foresti, S., Paraboschi, S., Pelosi, G., & Samarati, P. (2018b). *Access Privacy in the Cloud.* 1 doi:0.1007/978-3-030-04834-1_10

de Capitani di Vimercati, S., Foresti, S., Livraga, G., & Samarati, P. (2019). Data security and privacy in the cloud. In S. S. Agaian, S. P. DelMarco, & V. K. Asari (Eds.), *Mobile Multimedia/Image Processing, Security, and Applications 2019* (p. 15). SPIE. doi:10.1117/12.2523603

de Guzman, J. A., Thilakarathna, K., & Seneviratne, A. (2020). Security and Privacy Approaches in Mixed Reality. *ACM Computing Surveys, 52*(6), 1–37. doi:10.1145/3359626

de Melo e Silva, A., Costa Gondim, J. J., de Oliveira Albuquerque, R., & García Villalba, L. J. (2020). A methodology to evaluate standards and platforms within cyber threat intelligence. *Future Internet, 12*(6), 108. doi:10.3390/fi12060108

Debar, H., Curry, D., & Feinstein, B. (2007). The intrusion detection message exchange format (IDMEF). *IETF Request for Comments, 4765.*

Dejan, T. (2018, December 3,). How to prevent brute force attacks with 8 easy tactics. *Phoenix Nap.* https://phoenixnap.com/kb/prevent-brute-force-attacks

di Natale, M., Zeng, H., Giusto, P., & Ghosal, A. (2012). Understanding and using the controller area network communication protocol: Theory and practice. In *Understanding and Using the Controller Area Network Communication Protocol.* Theory and Practice., doi:10.1007/978-1-4614-0314-2

Digital, Data & Technology. (2022*). UK. Detecting the Unknown: A Guide to Threat Hunting.* HO Digital.. https://hodigital.blog.gov.uk/wp-content/uploads/sites/161/2020/03/Detecting-the-Unknown-A-Guide-to-Threat-Hunting-v2.0.pdf

Dimitrakopoulos, G., & Demestichas, P. (2010). Intelligent Transportation Systems. *IEEE Vehicular Technology Magazine, 5*(1), 77–84. doi:10.1109/MVT.2009.935537

Ding, W., Nayak, J., Swapnarekha, H., Abraham, A., Naik, B., & Pelusi, D. (2021). Fusion of intelligent learning for COVID-19: A state-of-the-art review and analysis on real medical data. *Neurocomputing, 457*, 40–66. doi:10.1016/j.neucom.2021.06.024 PMID:34149184

Domingo-Ferrer, J., & Mateo-Sanz, J. M. (2002). Practical data-oriented microaggregation for statistical disclosure control. *IEEE Transactions on Knowledge and Data Engineering, 14*(1), 189–201. doi:10.1109/69.979982

Domingo-Ferrer, J., & Soria-Comas, J. (2017). Steered Microaggregation: A Unified Primitive for Anonymization of Data Sets and Data Streams. *2017 IEEE International Conference on Data Mining Workshops (ICDMW)*, 995–1002. 10.1109/ICDMW.2017.141

Drokov, I., Punskaya, E., & Tahar, E. (2015, January 27). *System and method for dynamic multifactor authentication.* Google Patents. (US Patent 8,943,548)

Dunkelberger, P. (2018). Fido2 puts biometrics at heart of web security. *Biometric Technology Today, 2018*(8), 8–10. doi:10.1016/S0969-4765(18)30126-7

Dürmuth, M., Angelstorf, F., Castelluccia, C., Perito, D., & Chaabane, A. (2015). OMEN: Faster password guessing using an ordered markov enumerator. In Engineering Secure Software and Systems: 7th International Symposium, ESSoS 2015, Milan, Italy, March 4-6, 2015. [Springer International Publishing.]. *Proceedings, 7*, 119–132.

Dushyant, K., & Muskan, G. Annu, Gupta, A. and Pramanik, S. (2022). Utilizing Machine Learning and Deep Learning in Cybesecurity: An Innovative Approach. In M. M. Ghonge, S. Pramanik, R. Mangrulkar and D.-N. Le (eds.) Cyber Security and Digital Forensics. doi:10.1002/9781119795667.ch12

Dutta, A., & Kant, S. (2020, December). An overview of cyber threat intelligence platform and role of artificial intelligence and machine learning. In *International Conference on Information Systems Security* (pp. 81-86). Springer, Cham. 10.1007/978-3-030-65610-2_5

Eden, T., & Avigad, B. (2012). *Location based authentication system.* (US Patent US8321913B2)

Edwards, M., Larson, R., Green, B., Rashid, A., & Baron, A. (2017). Panning for gold: Automatically analysing online social engineering attack surfaces. *Computers & Security, 69,* 18–34. doi:10.1016/j.cose.2016.12.013

Elabd, E., Abdulkader, H., & Mubark, A. (2015). L–Diversity-Based Semantic Anonymaztion for Data Publishing. *International Journal of Information Technology and Computer Science,* 7(10), 1–7. doi:10.5815/ijitcs.2015.10.01

Ellison, G., Hodges, J., & Landau, S. (2002). Security and privacy concerns of internet single sign-on. *Liberty v1*(6).

Enterprise, V. (2017). 2017 data breach investigations report. Verizon Enterprise.

Enterprise, V. (2016). *Data breach investigations report. Report.* Verizon Enterprise.

Erol-Kantarci, M., & Mouftah, H. T. (2013). Smart grid forensic science: Applications, challenges, and open issues. *IEEE Communications Magazine, 51*(1), 68–74. doi:10.1109/MCOM.2013.6400441

Esmaeilzadeh, P., & Mirzaei, T. (2019, June 20). The Potential of Blockchain Technology for Health Information Exchange: Experimental Study From Patients' Perspectives. *Journal of Medical Internet Research, 21*(6), e14184. doi:10.2196/14184 PMID:31223119

Esposito, C., & Ciampi, M. (2015). On security in publish/subscribe services: A survey. *IEEE Communications Surveys and Tutorials, 17*(2), 966–997. doi:10.1109/COMST.2014.2364616

EU Commission website . (n.d.). https://ec.europa.eu/commission/priorities/justice-and%02fundamental-rights/data-protection/2018-reform-eu-data-protection-rules_en.%0A

European Commission. (2011). Article 29 Data Protection Working Party. *Opinion 12/2011 on smart metering.* Europea. https://ec.europa.eu/justice/article-29/documentation/opinion recommendation/files/2011/wp183_en.pdf

European Commission. (2011). Programming Mandate M/487 EN. *Programming mandate addressed to CEN, CENELEC and ETSI to establish security standards.* European Commission. https://ec.europa.eu/growth/tools-databases/mandates/index.cfm?fuseaction=search. detail&id=472

European Commission. (2012). Recommendation 2012/148/EU. *Commission Recommendation of 9 March 2012 on preparations for the roll-outroll-out of smart metering systems. Official Journal of the European Union, L,* 73(9), 9–22.

European Commission. (2013). Article 29 Data Protection Working Party. *Opinion 05/2013 on purpose limitation.* Europea. https://ec.europa.eu/justice/article-29/documentation/opinion-recommendation/files/2013/wp203_en.pdf

European Commission. (2014). Article 29 Data Protection Working Party. *Opinion 05/2014 on anonymization techniques.* Europea. https://ec.europa.eu/justice/article-29/documentation/opinion-recommendation/files/2014/wp216_en.pdf

European Commission. (2014). Recommendation 2014/724/EU. *Commission Recommendation of 10 October 2014 on the data protection impact assessment template for smart grid and smart metering systems. Official Journal of the European Union, L, 300*(63), 63–68.

European Data Protection Board. (2021). *Recommendations 01/2020 on measures that supplement transfer tools to ensure compliance with the EU level of protection of personal data Version 2.0.* Europa. https://edpb.europa.eu/system/files/2021-06/edpb_recommendations_202001vo.2.0_supplementarymeasurestransferstools_en.pdf

European Parliament and Council. (2016). *General Data Protection Regulation (GDPR). Regulation 2016/679/EU. Official Journal of the European Union* L 119, 4.5.2016, 1–88.

European Parliament and Council. (2018). Directive 2018/2002/EU. *Amending Directive 2012/27/EU on energy efficiency. European Parliament and Council. Official Journal of the European Union* L 328, 21.12.2018, p. 210–230.

European Parliament and Council. (2019). Directive 2019/944/EU. *On common rules for the internal market for electricity and amending Directive 2012/27/EU*. European Parliament and Council. Official Journal of the European Union L *158, 14.6.2019, 125–199.*

European Parliament. (2021) *European Parliament Resolution 2021/C 494/11. European Parliament Resolution of 25 March 2021 on the Commission evaluation report on the implementation of the General Data Protection Regulation two years after its application (2020/2717(RSP)). European Parliament. Official Journal of the European Union* C 494/129-138.

Face the facts. (2020). *Internet Watch Foundation Annual Report*. Retrieved 26 March 2022, from https://www.iwf.org.uk/about-us/who-we-are/annual-report/

Faden, R. R., & Beauchamp, T. L. (1986). *A History and Theory of Informed Consent*. Oxford University Press.

Fang, Y., Ashrafi, M. Z., & Ng, S. K. (2011). *Privacy beyond Single Sensitive Attribute*. 1 doi:0.1007/978-3-642-23088-2_13

Fang, Y., Kao, I.-L., Milman, I. M., & Wilson, G. C. (2001, June 5). *Single sign-on (sso) mechanism personal key manager*. Google Patents. (US Patent 6,243,816)

Fan, W., Lwakatare, K., & Rong, R. (2017). Social engineering: Ie based model of human weakness for attack and defense investigations. *International Journal of Computer Network & Information Security, 9*(1), 1–11. doi:10.5815/ijcnis.2017.01.01

Fernández-Alemán, J. L., Señor, I. C., Lozoya, P. Á., & Toval, A. (2013, June). Security and privacy in electronic health records: A systematic literature review. *Journal of Biomedical Informatics, 46*(3), 541–562. doi:10.1016/j.jbi.2012.12.003 PMID:23305810

Ferraiolo, D. F., & Kuhn, D. R. (1992). Role-Based Access Controls. *15th National Computer Security Conference*, 554–563.

Ferraiolo, D. F., Sandhu, R., Gavrila, S., Kuhn, D. R., & Chandramouli, R. (2001). Proposed NIST Standard for Role-Based Access Control. *ACM Transactions on Information and System Security*, *4*(3), 222–274. doi:10.1145/501978.501980

Fleming, N. (2020, June 17). Coronavirus misinformation, and how scientists can help to fight it. *Nature*, *583*(7814), 155–156. doi:10.1038/d41586-020-01834-3 PMID:32601491

Flu, K. (2015). *Knowledge-based authentication (kba). for Cybersecurity*. HSGAC. https://www.hsgac.senate.gov/imo/media/doc/Testimony-Fu-2015-06-02-REVISED%2021.pdf

Fonseca, M., Karkaletsis, K., Cruz, I. A., Berler, A., & Oliveira, I. C. (2015). OpenNCP: A novel framework to foster cross-border e-Health services. *Studies in Health Technology and Informatics*, *210*, 617–621. PMID:25991222

Friedman, B., Felten, E., & Millett, L.I. (2000). *Informed Consent Online: A Conceptual Model and Design Principles*. CSE Technical Report.

Fung, B. C. M., Wang, K., Chen, R., & Yu, P. S. (2010). Privacy-preserving data publishing: A survey of recent developments. *ACM Computing Surveys*, *42*(4), 1–53. Advance online publication. doi:10.1145/1749603.1749605

Fung, B. C. M., Wang, K., & Yu, P. S. (n.d.). Top-Down Specialization for Information and Privacy Preservation. *21st International Conference on Data Engineering (ICDE'05)*, 205–216. 10.1109/ICDE.2005.143

Fung, B. C., Wang, K., Fu, A. W. C., & Philip, S. Y. (2010). *Introduction to privacy-preserving data publishing: Concepts and techniques*. Chapman and Hall/CRC. doi:10.1201/9781420091502

Gadad, V., & Sowmyarani, C. N. (2019). A novel utility metric to measure information loss for generalization and suppression techniques in Privacy Preserving Data publishing. *CSITSS 2019 - 2019 4th International Conference on Computational Systems and Information Technology for Sustainable Solution Proceedings*, *4*, 1–5. doi:10.1109/CSITSS47250.2019.9031014

Gadad, V., Sowmyarani, C. N., Kumar, R., & Dayananda, P. (2020). Role of privacy attacks and utility metrics in crowdsourcing for urban data analysis. *CEUR Workshop Proceedings*, *2557*, 17–31.

Gafni, R., & Nissim, D. (2014). To social login or not login? exploring factors affecting the decision. *Issues in Informing Science and Information Technology*, *11*(1), 57–72. doi:10.28945/1980

Galpottage, P. A. B., & Norris, A. C. (2005). Patient consent principles and guidelines for e-consent: A New Zealand perspective. *Health Informatics Journal*, *11*(1), 5–18. doi:10.1177/1460458205050681

Gal, T. S., Chen, Z., & Gangopadhyay, A. (2008). A Privacy Protection Model for Patient Data with Multiple Sensitive Attributes. *International Journal of Information Security and Privacy*, *2*(3), 28–44. doi:10.4018/jisp.2008070103

Gao, P., Shao, F., Liu, X., Xiao, X., Qin, Z., Xu, F., Mittal, P., Kulkarni, S. R., & Song, D. (2021, April). Enabling efficient cyber threat hunting with cyber threat intelligence. In 2021 *IEEE 37th International Conference on Data Engineering (ICDE)* (pp. 193-204). IEEE. 10.1109/ ICDE51399.2021.00024

Gardiyawasam Pussewalage, H. S., & Oleshchuk, V. A. (2016). Privacy preserving mechanisms for enforcing security and privacy requirements in E-health solutions. *International Journal of Information Management*, *36*(6), 1161–1173. doi:10.1016/j.ijinfomgt.2016.07.006

GDPR. (2016). *The European Parliament and of the council. 2016. Directive 95/46/EC (General data protection regulation)*. Retrieved from https://eur-lex.europa.eu/legal-content/EN/TXT/ PDF/?uri=CELEX:32016R0679

Ghaffary, S. (2021). *Why this Facebook scandal is different*. Vox. Available at: https://www. google.com/amp/s/www.vox.com/platform/amp/recode/2021/10/3/22707940/frances-haugen-facebook-whistleblower-60-minutes-teen-girls-instagram

Ghani, N.A., Selamat, H., & Sidek, Z.M. (2012). Analysis of Existing Privacy-Aware Access Control for Ecommerce Application. *Global Journal of Computer Science and Technology*, *12*(4).

Ghazvini, A., & Shukur, Z. (2013). Security challenges and success factors of electronic healthcare system. *4th International Conference of Electrical Engineering and Informatics (ICEEI)*. 10.1016/j.protcy.2013.12.183

Ghinita, G., Tao, Y., & Kalnis, P. (2008). On the Anonymization of Sparse High-Dimensional Data. *2008 IEEE 24th International Conference on Data Engineering*, 715–724. 10.1109/ ICDE.2008.4497480

Ghinita, G., Kalnis, P., & Tao, Y. (2011). Anonymous publication of sensitive transactional data. *IEEE Transactions on Knowledge and Data Engineering*, *23*(2), 161–174. doi:10.1109/ TKDE.2010.101

Ghinita, G., Karras, P., Kalnis, P., & Mamoulis, N. (2007). Fast data anonymization with low information loss. *33rd International Conference on Very Large Data Bases, VLDB 2007 - Conference Proceedings*, 758–769.

Gisondi, M., Barber, R., Faust, J., Raja, A., Strehlow, M., Westafer, L., & Gottlieb, M. (2022, February). A deadly infodemic: Social media and the power of COVID-19 misinformation. *Journal of Medical Internet Research*, *24*(2), e35552. doi:10.2196/35552 PMID:35007204

Gmiden, M., Gmiden, M. H., & Trabelsi, H. (2017). An intrusion detection method for securing in-vehicle CAN bus. *2016 17th International Conference on Sciences and Techniques of Automatic Control and Computer Engineering, STA 2016 - Proceedings*. IEEE. doi:10.1109/ STA.2016.7952095

Goyal, V., Pandey, O., Sahai, A., & Waters, B. (2006). Attribute-based encryption for fine-grained access control of encrypted data. *Proceedings of the 13th ACM Conference on Computer and Communications Security - CCS '06*, 89–98. 10.1145/1180405.1180418

Granger, S. (2001). Social engineering fundamentals, part i: Hacker tactics. *Security Focus*, (December), 18.

Greer, L., Fraser, J. L., Hicks, D., Mercer, M., & Thompson, K. (2018). *Intelligent transportation systems benefits, costs, and lessons learned: 2018 update report*. DT.

Griffioen, H., Booij, T., & Doerr, C. (2020, October). Quality evaluation of cyber threat intelligence feeds. In *International Conference on Applied Cryptography and Network Security* (pp. 277-296). Springer, Cham. 10.1007/978-3-030-57878-7_14

Gritzalis, D., Iseppi, G., Mylonas, A., & Stavrou, V. (2018). Exiting the risk assessment maze: A meta-survey. [CSUR]. *ACM Computing Surveys*, *51*(1), 1–30. doi:10.1145/3145905

Grooming: Recognising the signs. (2022). Retrieved 24 February 2022, from https://raisingchildren.net.au/school-age/safety/online-safety/grooming-signs#:~:text=Signs%20of%20grooming%20in%20children%20aged%200%2D11%20years,-Many%20of%20the&text=has%20unexplained%20gifts%20like%20new,lot%20of%20time%20with%20them

Gruschka, N., Mavroeidis, V., Vishi, K., & Jensen, M. (2018). Privacy Issues and Data Protection in Big Data: A Case Study Analysis under GDPR. *2018 IEEE International Conference on Big Data (Big Data)*, 5027–5033. 10.1109/BigData.2018.8622621

Gunson, N., Marshall, D., Morton, H., & Jack, M. (2011). User perceptions of security and usability of single-factor and two-factor authentication in automated telephone banking. *Computers & Security*, *30*(4), 208–220. doi:10.1016/j.cose.2010.12.001

Gunter, T. D., & Terry, N. P. (2005). The Emergence of National Electronic Health Record Architectures in the United States and Australia: Models, Costs, and Questions. *Journal of Medical Internet Research*, *7*(1), e3. doi:10.2196/jmir.7.1.e3 PMID:15829475

Guo, B., Ding, Y., Yao, L., Liang, Y., & Yu, Z. (2020, September 4). The future of false information detection on social media: new perspectives and trends. *ACM Computing Surveys*, *53*(4), 1-36.

Gupta, A., Verma, A., & Pramanik, S. (2022). Advanced security system in video surveillance for COVID-19. In *An Interdisciplinary Approach to Modern Network Security* (pp. 131–151). CRC Press. doi:10.1201/9781003147176-8

Gupta, L., Gasparyan, A. Y., Misra, D. P., Agarwal, V., Zimba, O., & Yessirkepov, M. (2020, July 13). Information and misinformation on COVID-19: A cross-sectional survey study. *Journal of Korean Medical Science*, *35*(27), e257. doi:10.3346/jkms.2020.35.e256 PMID:32657090

Gylling, A., Ekstedt, M., Afzal, Z., & Eliasson, P. (2021, July). Mapping Cyber Threat Intelligence to Probabilistic Attack Graphs. In *2021 IEEE International Conference on Cyber Security and Resilience (CSR)* (pp. 304-311). IEEE. 10.1109/CSR51186.2021.9527970

Hahn, D., Munir, A., & Behzadan, V. (2021). Security and privacy issues in intelligent transportation systems: Classification and challenges. *IEEE Intelligent Transportation Systems Magazine*, *13*(1), 181–196. doi:10.1109/MITS.2019.2898973

Compilation of References

Hammad, A., & Faith, P. (2017). *Location based authentication.* (US Patent US10163100B2)

Han, J., Luo, F., Lu, J., & Peng, H. (2013). SLOMS: A privacy preserving data publishing method for multiple sensitive attributes microdata. *Journal of Software, 8*(12), 3096–3104. doi:10.4304/jsw.8.12.3096-3104

Harber, L. M. (2022, January 19th). Fake gps: top 5 vpns for spoofing your location. *Tom's Guide.* https://www.tomsguide.com/uk/best-picks/fake-gps-vpn

Harman, L. B., Flite, C. A., & Bond, K. (2012). Electronic Health Records: Privacy, Confidentiality and Security. *The Virtual Mentor, 14.* PMID:23351350

Harvey, J., & Kumar, S. (2020). A Survey of Intelligent Transportation Systems Security: Challenges and Solutions. *Proceedings - 2020 IEEE 6th Intl Conference on Big Data Security on Cloud, BigDataSecurity 2020, 2020 IEEE Intl Conference on High Performance and Smart Computing, HPSC 2020 and 2020 IEEE Intl Conference on Intelligent Data and Security, IDS 2020.* IEEE. 10.1109/BigDataSecurity-HPSC-IDS49724.2020.00055

Hasan, A. S. M. T., Jiang, Q., Chen, H., Wang, S., Liu, F., Jia, Y., Han, W., Science, C., Liao, W., He, J., Zhu, S., Chen, C., Guan, X., Maheshwarkar, N., Pathak, K., Choudhari, N. S., Xu, Y., Ma, T., Tang, M., ... Siva Kumar, A. P. (2018b). Anonymization and Analysis of Horizontally and Vertically Divided User Profile Databases with Multiple Sensitive Attributes. *Journal of Big Data, 8*(10), 768–772. doi:10.1109/ICMLC.2017.8108955

Hasan, A., Jiang, Q., Chen, H., & Wang, S. (2018a). A New Approach to Privacy-Preserving Multiple Independent Data Publishing. *Applied Sciences (Basel, Switzerland), 8*(5), 783. doi:10.3390/app8050783

Hathaliya, J.J., Tanwar, S., Tyagi, S., & Kumar, N. (2019) Securing electronics healthcare records in Healthcare 4.0: a biometric-based approach, *Comput. Electr. Eng., 76,* 398–410. 1.2019.04.017 doi:0.1016/j.compeleceng

Haydari, A., & Yilmaz, Y. (2018). Real-Time Detection and Mitigation of DDoS Attacks in Intelligent Transportation Systems. *2018 21st International Conference on Intelligent Transportation Systems (ITSC),* 157–163. 10.1109/ITSC.2018.8569698

He, X., Xiao, Y., Li, Y., Wang, Q., Wang, W., & Shi, B. (2012). *Permutation Anonymization: Improving Anatomy for Privacy Preservation in Data Publication.* 1 doi:0.1007/978-3-642-28320-8_10

Heinze, O., Birkle, M., Köster, L., & Bergh, B. (2011). Architecture of a consent management suite and integration into IHE-based regional health information networks. *BMC Medical Informatics and Decision Making, 11*(1), 58. doi:10.1186/1472-6947-11-58 PMID:21970788

History of the CAN technology. (n.d.). CAN. Https://Www.Can-Cia.Org/Can-Knowledge/Can/Can-History/

Hitaj, B., Gasti, P., Ateniese, G., & Perez-Cruz, F. (2019). Passgan: A deep learning approach for password guessing. In *International conference on applied cryptography and network security* (p. 217-237). Springer. 10.1007/978-3-030-21568-2_11

Ho, G., Sharma, A., Javed, M., Paxson, V., & Wagner, D. (2017). Detecting credential spearphishing in enterprise settings. In *26th USENIX security symposium (USENIX security 17)* (p. 469-485). Springer.

Horawalavithana, S., Bhattacharjee, A., Liu, R., Choudhury, N. O., Hall, L., & Iamnitchi, A. (2019, October). Mentions of security vulnerabilities on reddit, twitter and github. In *IEEE/WIC/ACM International Conference on Web Intelligence* (pp. 200-207). IEEE. 10.1145/3350546.3352519

Hu, V. C., Ferraiolo, D., Kuhn, R., Schnitzer, A., Sandlin, K., Miller, R., & Scarfone, K. (2014) *Guide to Attribute Based Access Control (ABAC) Definition and Considerations.* NIST Special Publication 800-162.

Hu, C., Li, C., Zhang, G., Lei, Z., Shah, M., Zhang, Y., Xing, C., Jiang, J., & Bao, R. (2022). CrowdMed-II: A blockchain-based framework for efficient consent management in health data sharing. *World Wide Web (Bussum), 25*(3), 1489–1515. doi:10.100711280-021-00923-1 PMID:35002477

Humayed, A., Lin, J., Li, F., & Luo, B. (2017). Cyber-physical systems security – A survey. *IEEE Internet of Things Journal, 4*(6), 1802–1831. doi:10.1109/JIOT.2017.2703172

Huq, N., Vosseler, R., & Swimmer, M. (2017). Cyberattacks against intelligent transportation systems. *TrendLabs Research Paper.*

Husari, G., Al-Shaer, E., Ahmed, M., Chu, B., & Niu, X. (2017, December). TTPDrill: Automatic and accurate extraction of threat actions from unstructured text of CTI sources. In *Proceedings of the 33rd Annual Computer Security Applications Conference* (pp. 103-115). ACM. 10.1145/3134600.3134646

Hu, W.-C., Ritter, G. X., & Schmalz, M. S. (1998, April). Approximating the longest approximate common subsequence problem. *Proceedings of the 36th Annual ACM Southeast Conference,* 166-172. 10.1145/275295.283951

Iakovidis, I. (1998). Towards Personal Health Record: Current situation, obstacles and trends in implementation of Electronic Healthcare Records in Europe. *International Journal of Medical Informatics, 52*(128), 105–117. doi:10.1016/S1386-5056(98)00129-4 PMID:9848407

Inkoom, S., Sobanjo, J., & Chicken, E. (2020). Competing Risks Models for the Assessment of Intelligent Transportation Systems Devices: A Case Study for Connected and Autonomous Vehicle Applications. *Infrastructures, 5*(3), 30. doi:10.3390/infrastructures5030030

Instagram monthly active users. (n.d.). *Statista.* Retrieved 26 March 2022, from https://www.statista.com/statistics/253577/number-of-monthly-active-instagram-users/

Isha Priyavamtha, U. J., Vishnu Vardhan Reddy, G., Devisri, P., & Manek, A. S. (2021). Fake news detection using artificial neural network algorithm. In Data Science and Computational Intelligence. ICInPro. Communications in Computer and Information Science. Springer. doi:10.1007/978-3-030-91244-4_26

Islam, M. R., Liu, S., Wang, X., & Xu, G. (2020). Deep learning for misinformation detection on online social networks: A survey and new perspectives. *Social Network Analysis and Mining*, *10*(1), 82. doi:10.100713278-020-00696-x PMID:33014173

ISO/IEC. (2007, -10). Identification cards part 2: Cards with contacts. ISO.

ISO/TC 22/SC 31. (2006). *ISO 11898-3:2006: Road vehicles — Controller area network (CAN) — Part 3: Low-speed, fault-tolerant, medium-dependent interface.* ISO 11898-3:2006.

ISO/TC 22/SC 31. (2015). *ISO 11898-1:2015: Road vehicles -- Controller area network (CAN) -- Part 1: Data link layer and physical signaling.* In ISO 11898-1:2015.

ISO/TC 22/SC 31. (2016). *ISO 11898-2:2016: Road vehicles — Controller area network (CAN) — Part 2: High-speed medium access unit.* ISO 11898-2:2016.

IWF Annual Report. (2019). Retrieved 26 March 2022, from https://www.yumpu.com/en/document/read/63240486/iwf-annual-report-2019

Iyengar, V. S. (2002). Transforming data to satisfy privacy constraints. *Proceedings of the ACM SIGKDD International Conference on Knowledge Discovery and Data Mining*, 279–288. 10.1145/775047.775089

Jablon, D. P. (1997). Extended password key exchange protocols immune to dictionary attack. In *Proceedings of ieee 6th workshop on enabling technologies: Infrastructure for collaborative enterprises* (p. 248-255). IEEE. 10.1109/ENABL.1997.630822

Jajodia, S. (1996). Managing security and privacy of information. *ACM Computing Surveys*, *28*(4es), 79. doi:10.1145/242224.242327

Janušová, L., & Čičmancová, S. (2016). Improving Safety of Transportation by Using Intelligent Transport Systems. *Procedia Engineering*, *134*, 14–22. doi:10.1016/j.proeng.2016.01.031

Jin, S., Chung, J. G., & Xu, Y. (2021). Signature-based intrusion detection system (IDS) for in-vehicle CAN bus network. *Proceedings - IEEE International Symposium on Circuits and Systems, 2021-May*. IEEE. doi:10.1109/ISCAS51556.2021.9401087

Jo, H. J., & Choi, W. (2021). A Survey of Attacks on Controller Area Networks and Corresponding Countermeasures. *IEEE Transactions on Intelligent Transportation Systems*. doi:10.1109/TITS.2021.3078740

Jøsang, A. (2018). *Lecture 9: User authentication.* UIO. https://www.uio.no/studier/emner/matnat/ifi/IN2120/h18/lectures/in2120-2018-l09-user-authentication.pdf

Joseph, T., Bruchim, G. Z., Gofman, I., & Ashkenazy, I. G. (2021, August 31). *Credential spray attack detection.* Google Patents. (US Patent 11,108,818)

Journal, I., Giri, S. S., & Mukhopadhyay, N. (n.d.). *Overlapping Slicing with New Privacy Model A Novel Framework for Privacy Conserving Data Publishing and Handling High Dimensional Data.* Academic Press.

Kaatz, J. (2017). Resolving the conflict between new and old: A comparison of New York, California and other state DER proceedings. *The Electricity Journal, 30*(9), 6–13. doi:10.1016/j.tej.2017.10.005

Kabir, M. E., & Wang, H. (2009) Conditional Purpose Based Access Control Model for Privacy Protection. *20th Australasian Database Conference (ADC 2009)*, Wellington, New Zealand.

Kalogridis, G., Efthymiou, C., Denic, S., Lewis, T., & Cepeda, R. (2010). Privacy for smart meters: towards undetectable appliance load signatures. In *2010 First IEEE International Conference on Smart Grid Communications*, 232–237. 10.1109/SMARTGRID.2010.5622047

Kang, M. J., & Kang, J. W. (2016). Intrusion detection system using deep neural network for in-vehicle network security. *PLoS One, 11*(6), e0155781. doi:10.1371/journal.pone.0155781 PMID:27271802

Karat, J., Karat, C.M., Bertino, E., Li, N., Ni, Q., Brodie, C., Lobo, J., Calo, S.B., Cranor, L.F., Kumaraguru, P., & Reeder, R.W. (2009). Policy framework for security and privacy management. *IBM J. Res. Dev., 53*(2). 1 doi:0.1147/JRD.2009.5429046

Kargupta, H., Datta, S., Wang, Q., & Sivakumar, K. (2005). Random-data perturbation techniques and privacy-preserving data mining. *Knowledge and Information Systems, 7*(4), 387–414. doi:10.100710115-004-0173-6

Kelly, J., & Knottenbelt, W. (2015). The UK-DALE dataset, domestic appliance-level electricity demand and whole-house demand from five UK homes. *Scientific Data, 2*(1), 1–14. doi:10.1038data.2015.7 PMID:25984347

Khan, H. Z. U., & Zahid, H. (2010). Comparative study of authentication techniques. *International Journal of Video & Image Processing and Network Security IJVIPNS, 10*(04), 9.

Khan, R., Tao, X., Anjum, A., Sajjad, H., & Malik, S. (2020). ur R., Khan, A., & Amiri, F. (2020). Privacy Preserving for Multiple Sensitive Attributes against Fingerprint Correlation Attack Satisfying c -Diversity. *Wireless Communications and Mobile Computing*, 1–18. doi:10.1155/2020/8416823

Khan, T., Michalas, A., & Akhunzada, A. (2021, September 15). Fake news outbreak 2021: Can we stop the viral spread? *Journal of Network and Computer Applications, 190*, 103112. doi:10.1016/j.jnca.2021.103112

Kifer, D., & Gehrke, J. (2006). Injecting utility into anonymized datasets. *Proceedings of the ACM SIGMOD International Conference on Management of Data*, 217–228. 10.1145/1142473.1142499

Knapp, E. D., & Samani, R. (2013). *Applied cyber security and the smart grid*. Elsevier Inc.

Knyrim, R., & Trieb, G. (2011). Smart metering under EU data protection law. *International Data Privacy Law*, *1*(2), 121–128. doi:10.1093/idpl/ipr004

Koloveas, P., Chantzios, T., Tryfonopoulos, C., & Skiadopoulos, S. (2019, July). A crawler architecture for harvesting the clear, social, and dark web for IoT-related cyber-threat intelligence. In *2019 IEEE World Congress on Services (SERVICES)* (Vol. 2642, pp. 3-8). IEEE. 10.1109/SERVICES.2019.00016

Komninos, N., Philippou, E., & Pitsillides, A. (2014). Survey in smart grid and smart home security: Issues, challenges and countermeasures. *IEEE Communications Surveys and Tutorials*, *16*(4), 1933–1954. doi:10.1109/COMST.2014.2320093

Konigs, H.-P. (1991). Cryptographic identification methods for smart cards in the process of standardization. *IEEE Communications Magazine*, *29*(6), 42–48. doi:10.1109/35.79401

Koscher, K., Czeskis, A., Roesner, F., Patel, S., Kohno, T., Checkoway, S., McCoy, D., Kantor, B., Anderson, D., Snachám, H., & Savage, S. (2010). Experimental security analysis of a modern automobile. *Proceedings - IEEE Symposium on Security and Privacy*. IEEE. 10.1109/SP.2010.34

Koutny, T., & Sykora, J. (2010). Lessons learned on enhancing performance of networking applications by ip tunneling through active networks. *International Journal on Advances in Internet Technology*, *3*(3 & 4), 2010.

Koyun, A., & Janabi, E. A. (2017). Social engineering attacks. [JMEST]. *Journal of Multidisciplinary Engineering Science and Technology*, *4*(6), 7533–7538.

Krivolapova, O. (2017). Algorithm for Risk Assessment in the Introduction of Intelligent Transport Systems Facilities. *Transportation Research Procedia*, *20*, 373–377. doi:10.1016/j.trpro.2017.01.056

Krombholz, K., Hobel, H., Huber, M., & Weippl, E. (2015). Advanced social engineering attacks. *Journal of Information Security and applications*, *22*, 113-122.

Kula, S., Choraś, M., Kozik, R., Ksieniewicz, P., & Woźniak, M. (2020). Sentiment analysis for fake news detection by means of neural networks. In Lecture Notes in Computer Science (vol. 12140). Springer. doi:10.1007/978-3-030-50423-6_49

Kulandaivel, S., Jain, S., Guajardo, J., & Sekar, V. (2021). CANNON: Reliable and stealthy remote shutdown attacks via unaltered automotive microcontrollers. *Proceedings – IEEE Symposium on Security and Privacy, 2021-May*. IEEE. doi:10.1109/SP40001.2021.00122

Kumah, C. (2015). *A Comparative Study of use of the Library and the Internet as Sources of Information by Graduate Students in the University Of Ghana*. Retrieved from https://digitalcommons.unl.edu/libphilprac/1298?utm_source=digitalcommons.unl.edu%2Flibphilprac%2F1298&utm_medium=PDF&utm_campaign=PDFCoverPages

Kumari, E. H. J., & Kannammal, A. (2009). Privacy and security on anonymous routing protocols in manet. In *2009 second international conference on computer and electrical engineering* (*Vol. 2*, pp. 431–435). IEEE. 10.1109/ICCEE.2009.147

Kumar, P., Lin, Y., Bai, G., Paverd, A., Dong, J. S., & Martin, A. (2019). Smart grid metering networks: A survey on security, privacy and open research issues. *IEEE Communications Surveys and Tutorials, 21*(3), 2886–2927. doi:10.1109/COMST.2019.2899354

Kundalwal, M. K., Chatterjee, K., & Singh, A. (2019). An improved privacy preservation technique in health-cloud. *ICT Express, 5*(3), 167–172. doi:10.1016/j.icte.2018.10.002

Kunyu, P., Jiande, Z., & Jing, Y. (2009). *An identity authentication system based on mobile phone token. In 2009 ieee international conference on network infrastructure and digital content*. IEEE.

Kuo, C.-C., & Lo, M. (1999, December 14). *Secure open smart card architecture.* Google Patents. (US Patent 6,003,134)

Lakshmipathi Raju, N. V. S., Seetaramanath, M. N., & Srinivasa Rao, P. (2018). An enhanced dynamic KC-slice model for privacy preserving data publishing with multiple sensitive attributes by inducing sensitivity. *Journal of King Saud University - Computer and Information Sciences.* 1 doi:0.1016/j.jksuci.2018.09.013

Lamssaggad, A., Benamar, N., Hafid, A. S., & Msahli, M. (2021). A Survey on the Current Security Landscape of Intelligent Transportation Systems. In IEEE Access (Vol. 9). IEEE doi:10.1109/ACCESS.2021.3050038

Lance, S. (2019, June 27,). Time for password expiration to die. *SANS.* https://www.sans.org/security-awareness-training/blog/time-password-expiration-die

Larrucea, X., Moffie, M., Asaf, S., & Santamaria, I. (2020). Towards a GDPR compliant way to secure European cross border Healthcare Industry 4.0. *Computer Standards & Interfaces, 69.* doi:10.1016/j.csi.2019.103408

Lawsofnigeria.placng.org. (n.d.). Available at: http://lawsofnigeria.placng.org/laws/C38.pdf

Lee, H., Jeong, S. H., & Kim, H. K. (2018). OTIDS: A novel intrusion detection system for in-vehicle network by using remote frame. *Proceedings - 2017 15th Annual Conference on Privacy, Security and Trust, PST 2017.* IEEE. doi:10.1109/PST.2017.00017

Lee, Y. J., & Lee, K. H. (2017). Re-identification of medical records by optimum quasi-identifiers. *2017 19th International Conference on Advanced Communication Technology,* 428–435. 10.23919/ICACT.2017.7890125

Lee, D., & Hess, D. J. (2021). Data privacy and residential smart meters: Comparative analysis and harmonization potential. *Utilities Policy, 70,* 101188. doi:10.1016/j.jup.2021.101188

Lefevre, K., Dewi, D. J., Ramakrishnan, R., & Boulos, G. W. (2009). *Mondrian Mul+dimensional K-Anonymity.* Academic Press.

LeFevre, K., DeWitt, D., & Ramakrishnan, R., I. (2005). Efficient Full-Domain Kanonymity. *ACM SIGMOD International Conference on Management of Data.*

Legal Information Institute. (n.d.a). *18 U.S. Code § 2251 - Sexual exploitation of children.* Available at: https://www.law.cornell.edu/uscode/text/18/2251

Legal Information Institute. (n.d.b). *18 U.S. Code § 2425 - Use of interstate facilities to transmit information about a minor.* Available at: https://www.law.cornell.edu/uscode/text/18/2425

Lehtonen, M., Michahelles, F., & Fleisch, E. (2007). Probabilistic approach for location-based authentication. In *1st international workshop on security for spontaneous interaction iwssi* (Vol. 2007). IEEE.

Leszczyna, R. (2018). A review of standards with cybersecurity requirements for smart grid. *Computers & Security, 77*, 262–276. doi:10.1016/j.cose.2018.03.011

Le, V. H., den Hartog, J., & Zannone, N. (2018). Security and privacy for innovative automotive applications: A survey. *Computer Communications, 132*, 17–41. doi:10.1016/j.comcom.2018.09.010

Li, J., Wong, R. C.-W., Fu, A. W.-C., & Pei, J. (2006). *Achieving k-Anonymity by Clustering in Attribute Hierarchical Structures.* 1 doi:0.1007/11823728_39

Li, V. G., Dunn, M., Pearce, P., McCoy, D., Voelker, G. M., & Savage, S. (2019). Reading the tea leaves: A comparative analysis of threat intelligence. In 28th USENIX Security Symposium (USENIX Security 19) (pp. 851-867).

Liao, H. J., Richard Lin, C. H., Lin, Y. C., & Tung, K. Y. (2013). Intrusion detection system: A comprehensive review. In Journal of Network and Computer Applications, 36(1). doi:10.1016/j.jnca.2012.09.004

Liao, X., Yuan, K., Wang, X., Li, Z., Xing, L., & Beyah, R. (2016, October). Acing the IoC game: Toward automatic discovery and analysis of open-source cyber threat intelligence. In *Proceedings of the 2016 ACM SIGSAC Conference on Computer and Communications Security* (pp. 755-766). ACM. 10.1145/2976749.2978315

Liberati, F., Garone, E., & Di Giorgio, A. (2021). Review of Cyber-Physical Attacks in Smart Grids: A System-Theoretic Perspective. *Electronics (Basel), 10*(10), 1153. doi:10.3390/electronics10101153

Li, C.-T., & Hwang, M.-S. (2010). An efficient biometrics-based remote user authentication scheme using smart cards. *Journal of Network and Computer Applications, 33*(1), 1–5. doi:10.1016/j.jnca.2009.08.001

Li, D., He, X., Cao, L., & Chen, H. (2016). Permutation anonymization. *Journal of Intelligent Information Systems, 47*(3), 427–445. doi:10.100710844-015-0373-4

Liew, A. (2013). DIKIW: Data, information, knowledge, intelligence, wisdom and their interrelationships. *Business Management Dynamics, 2*(10), 49.

Lima, C. A. F., & Navas, J. R. F. (2012). Smart metering and systems to support a conscious use of water and electricity. *Energy*, *45*(1), 528–540. doi:10.1016/j.energy.2012.02.033

Lim, C. H., & Kwon, T. (2006). Strong and robust rfid authentication enabling perfect ownership transfer. In *International conference on information and communications security* (p. 1-20). Springer. 10.1007/11935308_1

Li, N., Li, T., & Venkatasubramanian, S. (2010). Closeness: A New Privacy Measure for Data Publishing. *IEEE Transactions on Knowledge and Data Engineering, 22*(7), 943–956. doi:10.1109/TKDE.2009.139

Li, N., Qardaji, W., & Su, D. (2012). On sampling, anonymization, and differential privacy or, k -anonymization meets differential privacy. *Proceedings of the 7th ACM Symposium on Information, Computer and Communications Security - ASIACCS '12*, 32. 10.1145/2414456.2414474

Ling, C., & Feng, D. (2012). An algorithm for detection of malicious messages on CAN buses. *Proceedings of the 2012 National Conference on Information Technology and Computer Science, CITCS 2012*. Springer. 10.2991/citcs.2012.161

Lishchenko, T. (2021, January 14). *Intelligent Transport System: Trends, best practices, success stories*.

Lisovich, M. A., Mulligan, D. K., & Wicker, S. B. (2010). Inferring personal information from demand-response systems. *IEEE Security and Privacy*, *8*(1), 11–20. doi:10.1109/MSP.2010.40

Li, T., & Li, N. (2008). Towards optimal k-anonymization. *Data & Knowledge Engineering, 65*(1), 22–39. doi:10.1016/j.datak.2007.06.015

Li, T., & Li, N. (2009). On the tradeoff between privacy and utility in data publishing. *Proceedings of the ACM SIGKDD International Conference on Knowledge Discovery and Data Mining*, 517–525. 10.1145/1557019.1557079

Li, T., Li, N., Zhang, J., & Molloy, I. (2012). Slicing: A new approach for privacy preserving data publishing. *IEEE Transactions on Knowledge and Data Engineering*, *24*(3), 561–574. doi:10.1109/TKDE.2010.236

Liu, F., Jia, Y., & Han, W. (2012). A new k-anonymity algorithm towards multiple sensitive attributes. *Proceedings - 2012 IEEE 12th International Conference on Computer and Information Technology, CIT 2012*, 768–772. 10.1109/CIT.2012.157

Liu, J., & Luo, J. (n.d.). *Rating: Privacy preservation for multiple attributes with different sensitivity requirements*. Retrieved July 20, 2021, from https://ieeexplore.ieee.org/abstract/document/6137444/

Liu, A., Giurco, D., & Mukheibir, P. (2015). Motivating metrics for household water-use feedback. *Resources, Conservation and Recycling*, *103*, 29–46. doi:10.1016/j.resconrec.2015.05.008

Liu, B., Ding, M., Shaham, S., Rahayu, W., Farokhi, F., & Lin, Z. (2021). When Machine Learning Meets Privacy. *ACM Computing Surveys*, *54*(2), 1–36. doi:10.1145/3436755

Li, X., Niu, J., Khan, M. K., & Liao, J. (2013). An enhanced smart card based remote user password authentication scheme. *Journal of Network and Computer Applications*, *36*(5), 1365–1371. doi:10.1016/j.jnca.2013.02.034

Li, X., Niu, J.-W., Ma, J., Wang, W.-D., & Liu, C.-L. (2011). Cryptanalysis and improvement of a biometrics-based remote user authentication scheme using smart cards. *Journal of Network and Computer Applications*, *34*(1), 73–79. doi:10.1016/j.jnca.2010.09.003

Li, X., Xiong, Y., Ma, J., & Wang, W. (2012). An efficient and security dynamic identity based authentication protocol for multi-server architecture using smart cards. *Journal of Network and Computer Applications*, *35*(2), 763–769. doi:10.1016/j.jnca.2011.11.009

Lokman, S.-F., Othman, A. T., & Abu-Bakar, M.-H. (2019). Intrusion detection system for automotive Controller Area Network (CAN) bus system: A review. *EURASIP Journal on Wireless Communications and Networking*, *2019*(1), 184. doi:10.118613638-019-1484-3

Loukides, G., & Shao, J. (2007). Capturing data usefulness and privacy protection in K-anonymisation. *Proceedings of the ACM Symposium on Applied Computing*, 370–374. 10.1145/1244002.1244091

Luo, F., Han, J., & Lu, J. (n.d.). *ANGELMS: A privacy preserving data publishing framework for microdata with multiple sensitive attributes*. Retrieved July 20, 2021, from https://ieeexplore.ieee.org/abstract/document/6747576/

Lyastani, S. G., Schilling, M., Neumayr, M., Backes, M., & Bugiel, S. (2020). Is fido2 the kingslayer of user authentication? a comparative usability study of fido2 passwordless authentication. In 2020 ieee symposium on security and privacy (sp) (pp. 268–285). IEEE.

Lynch, K. M., Marchuk, N., & Elwin, M. L. (2016). Chapter 21. Sensors. Embedded Computing and Mechatronics with the PIC32.

Machanavajjhala, A., Kifer, D., Gehrke, J., & Venkitasubramaniam, M. (2007). ℓ-diversity: Privacy beyond k-anonymity. *ACM Transactions on Knowledge Discovery from Data*, *1*(1), 3. Advance online publication. doi:10.1145/1217299.1217302

Mandl, K. D., Szolovits, P., & Kohane, I. S. (2001, February 3). Public standards and patients' control: How to keep electronic medical records accessible but private. *BMJ (Clinical Research Ed.)*, *322*(7281), 283–287. doi:10.1136/bmj.322.7281.283 PMID:11157533

Mangiaracina, R., Perego, A., Salvadori, G., & Tumino, A. (2017). A comprehensive view of intelligent transport systems for urban smart mobility. *International Journal of Logistics Research and Applications*, *20*(1), 39–52. doi:10.1080/13675567.2016.1241220

Marchetti, M., & Stabili, D. (2017). Anomaly detection of CAN bus messages through analysis of ID sequences. *IEEE Intelligent Vehicles Symposium, Proceedings*. IEEE. 10.1109/IVS.2017.7995934

March, H., Morote, Á.-F., Rico, A.-M., & Saurí, D. (2017). Household smart water metering in Spain: Insights from the experience of remote meter reading in Alicante. *Sustainability*, *9*(4), 582. doi:10.3390u9040582

Marforio, C., Masti, R. J., Soriente, C., Kostiainen, K., & Capkun, S. (2016). Hardened setup of personalized security indicators to counter phishing attacks in mobile banking. In *Proceedings of the 6th workshop on security and privacy in smartphones and mobile devices* (p. 83-92). ACM. 10.1145/2994459.2994462

Martin, D. J., Kifer, D., Machanavajjhala, A., Gehrke, J., & Halpern, J. Y. (2007). Worst-case background knowledge for privacy-preserving data publishing. *Proceedings - International Conference on Data Engineering*, 126–135. 10.1109/ICDE.2007.367858

Martinelli, F., Mercaldo, F., Nardone, V., & Santone, A. (2017). Car hacking identification through fuzzy logic algorithms. *IEEE International Conference on Fuzzy Systems*. IEEE. 10.1109/FUZZ-IEEE.2017.8015464

Martino, L. D., Ni, Q., Lin, D., & Bertino, E. (2008). Multi-domain and Privacy-aware Role Based Access Control in eHealth. *Second International Conference on Pervasive Computing Technologies for Healthcare*, 131-134. doi: 10.1109/PCTHEALTH.2008.4571050

Matthan, R. (2017). *Beyond Consent: A new paradigm for data protection*. Discussion Document 2017-2003.

Matvej Yli-Olli. (2019). *Machine Learning for Secure Vehicular Communication: an Empirical Study*. Aalto University.

Mavroeidis, V., & Bromander, S. (2017, September). Cyber threat intelligence model: an evaluation of taxonomies, sharing standards, and ontologies within cyber threat intelligence. In *2017 European Intelligence and Security Informatics Conference (EISIC)* (pp. 91-98). IEEE. 10.1109/EISIC.2017.20

Mbaegbu, I. (2020). Children Can Become Victims of Online Sexual Abuse Without Parents Knowing. *The Whistler Nigeria*. Available at: https://thewhistler.ng/children-can-become-victims-of-online-sexual-abuse-without-parents-knowing/

McKenna, E., Richardson, I., & Thomson, M. (2012). Smart meter data: Balancing consumer privacy concerns with legitimate applications. *Energy Policy*, *41*, 807–814. doi:10.1016/j.enpol.2011.11.049

McLaughlin, S., McDaniel, P., & Aiello, W. (2011). Protecting consumer privacy from electric load monitoring. In *Proceedings of the 18th ACM Conference on Computer and Communications Security*, (pp. 87–98). ACM. 10.1145/2046707.2046720

Medlin, B. D., Cazier, J. A., & Foulk, D. P. (2008). Analyzing the vulnerability of US hospitals to social engineering attacks: How many of your employees would share their password? [IJISP]. *International Journal of Information Security and Privacy*, *2*(3), 71–83. doi:10.4018/jisp.2008070106

Mehmood, R., Katib, S. S. I., & Chlamtac, I. (2020). *Smart infrastructure and applications*. Springer International Publishing. doi:10.1007/978-3-030-13705-2

Mendes, R., & Vilela, J. P. (2017). Privacy-Preserving Data Mining: Methods, Metrics, and Applications. *IEEE Access: Practical Innovations, Open Solutions, 5*, 10562–10582. doi:10.1109/ACCESS.2017.2706947

Menges, F., Sperl, C., & Pernul, G. (2019, August). Unifying cyber threat intelligence. In *International Conference on Trust and Privacy in Digital Business* (pp. 161-175). Springer, Cham.

Mengozzi, P. (2018). Opinion of Advocate General Mengozzi. *CJEU Case C-25/17, ECLI:EU:C:2018:57.* https://curia.europa.eu/juris/liste.jsf?num=C-25/17

Mian, A. & Khan, S. (2020, March). Coronavirus: The spread of misinformation. *BMC Medinine, 18*(89).

Miller, C., & Valasek, C. (2015). Remote Exploitation of an Unaltered Passenger Vehicle. *Defcon, 23*, 2015.

Ming, L., Zhao, G., Huang, M., Kuang, X., Li, H., & Zhang, M. (2018). Security analysis of intelligent transportation systems based on simulation data. *Proceedings - 2018 1st International Conference on Data Intelligence and Security, ICDIS 2018.* IEEE. 10.1109/ICDIS.2018.00037

Miron-Shatz, T., & Elwyn, G. (2011). To serve and protect? Electronic health records pose challenges for privacy, autonomy and person-centered medicine. *International Journal of Person Centered Medicine, 1*(2), 405–409.

Mishra, S., & Soni, D. (2019). Sms phishing and mitigation approaches. In *2019 twelfth international conference on contemporary computing (ic3)* (p. 1-5). IEEE. 10.1109/IC3.2019.8844920

Mittal, S., Das, P. K., Mulwad, V., Joshi, A., & Finin, T. (2016, August). Cybertwitter: Using twitter to generate alerts for cybersecurity threats and vulnerabilities. In *2016 IEEE/ACM International Conference on Advances in Social Networks Analysis and Mining (ASONAM)* (pp. 860-867). IEEE. 10.1109/ASONAM.2016.7752338

MLB9252. (2011). How to calculate pass- word entropy. *RIT Cyber Self Defense.* https://ritcyberselfdefense.wordpress.com/2011/09/24/how-to-calculate-password-entropy/

Mohassel, R. R., Fung, A., Mohammadi, F., & Raahemifar, K. (2014). A survey on advanced metering infrastructure. *Electrical Power and Energy Systems, 63*, 473–484. doi:10.1016/j.ijepes.2014.06.025

Monbiot, G. (2004). *The Age of Consent- A Manifesto For A New World Order.* Harper Perennial.

Monedero, I., Biscarri, F., Guerrero, J. I., Roldán, M., & León, C. (2015). An approach to detection of tampering in water meters. *Procedia Computer Science, 60*, 413–421. doi:10.1016/j.procs.2015.08.157

Moriarty, K. (2012). *Real-time Inter-network defense (RID) (RFC6545).* Tools. https://tools.ietf.org/html/rfc6545

Muralidhar, K., & Sarathy, R. (1999). Security of random data perturbation methods. *ACM Transactions on Database Systems*, 24(4), 487–493. doi:10.1145/331983.331986

Murthy, A. S., Ganesan, K., Mangam, P. M., Jandhyala, S. S., & Walter, M. (2020, January 28). *Multifactor authentication as a network service.* Google Patents. (US Patent 10,547,600)

Nadhamuni, S., John, O., Kulkarni, M., Nanda, E., Venkatraman, S., Varma, D., Balsari, S., Gudi, N., Samantaray, S., Reddy, H., & Sheel, V. (2021). Driving digital transformation of comprehensive primary health services at scale in India: An enterprise architecture framework. *BMJ Global Health*, 6(Suppl 5), e005242. doi:10.1136/bmjgh-2021-005242 PMID:34312149

Naehrig, M., Lauter, K., & Vaikuntanathan, V. (2011). Can homomorphic encryption be practical? *Proceedings of the 3rd ACM Workshop on Cloud Computing Security Workshop - CCSW '11*, 113. 10.1145/2046660.2046682

Narayanan, A., & Shmatikov, V. (2005). Fast dictionary attacks on passwords using time-space tradeoff. *In Proceedings of the 12th acm conference on computer and communications security* (p. 364-372). ACM. 10.1145/1102120.1102168

Narayanan, S. N., Mittal, S., & Joshi, A. (2016). OBD-SecureAlert: An Anomaly Detection System for Vehicles. *2016 IEEE International Conference on Smart Computing, SMARTCOMP 2016*. IEEE. 10.1109/SMARTCOMP.2016.7501710

Nathaniel, A., Baal, L., & Broda, G. (2019). Design and Implementation of a Blockchain-Based Consent Management System. *Computing Research Repository.* 1. doi:0.48550/ARXIV.1912.09882

NCSC. (2019) *Most hacked passwords revealed as uk cyber survey exposes gaps in online security.* NCSC. https://www.ncsc.gov.uk/news/most-hacked-passwords-revealed-as-uk-cyber-survey-exposes-gaps-in-online-security

Nealon, L. (2021). How social media preys on children. *Newsweek.* Available at: https://www.newsweek.com/how-social-media-preys-children-opinion-1637132

New York State Public Service Commission. (2018). *Order Adopting Whole Building Energy Data Aggregation Standard.* NYPSC.https://documents.dps.ny.gov/public/Common/ViewDoc.aspx?DocRefId=%7B4C4CE28E-54CC-4514-967D-B513678E3F37%7D

Ni, Q., Trombetta, A., Bertino, E., & Lobo, J. (2007). Privacy-aware role based access control. *Proceedings of the 12th ACM symposium on Access control models and technologies*, 41-50. 10.1145/1266840.1266848

NSPCC. (2022). *Record high number of recorded grooming crimes lead to calls for stronger online safety legislation.* Available at: https://www.nspcc.org.uk/about-us/news-opinion/2021/online-grooming-record-high/

O'Keefe, C. M., Greenfield, P., & Goodchild, A. (2005). A Decentralised Approach to Electronic Consent and Health Information Access Control. *Journal of Research and Practice in Information Technology*, 37(2).

Olson, L., Daggs, J., Ellevold, B., & Rogers, T. (2007). Entrapping the Innocent: Toward a Theory of Child Sexual Predators? Luring Communication. *Communication Theory*, *17*(3), 231–251. doi:10.1111/j.1468-2885.2007.00294.x

Olufowobi, H., Young, C., Zambreno, J., & Bloom, G. (2020). SAIDuCANT: Specification-Based Automotive Intrusion Detection Using Controller Area Network (CAN) Timing. *IEEE Transactions on Vehicular Technology*, *69*(2), 1484–1494. doi:10.1109/TVT.2019.2961344

Ometov, A., Bezzateev, S., Davydov, V., Shchesniak, A., Masek, P., Lohan, E. S., & Koucheryavy, Y. (2019). Positioning information privacy in intelligent transportation systems: An overview and future perspective. *Sensors (Switzerland)*, *19*(7), 1603. doi:10.339019071603 PMID:30987097

Onashoga, S., & Bamiro, B. (2017). *KC-Slice: A dynamic privacy-preserving data publishing technique for multisensitive attributes*. Taylor & Francis. 1 doi:0.1080/19393555.2017.1319522

Online Enticement. (n.d.). Retrieved 26 March 2022, from https://www.missingkids.org/theissues/onlineenticement

Online grooming. (n.d.). *Childnet*. Retrieved 26 February 2022, from https://www.childnet.com/help-and-advice/online-grooming/

Onuiri, E., Sunday, I., & Komolafe, O. (2015). Electronic Health Record Systems and Cyber Security Challenges. *International Conference on African Development Issues*, 98–105.

openEHR. (2022). *openEHR - EHR Information Model*. Retrieved from https://specifications.openehr.org/releases/RM/latest/ehr.html

Orlando, D., & Vandelvelde, W. (2021). Smart meters' roll out, solutions in favour of a trust enhancing law in the EU. *Journal of Law. Technology & Trust*, *2*(1). Advance online publication. doi:10.19164/jltt.v2i1.1071

Ota, K., Kumrai, T., Dong, M., Kishigami, J., & Guo, M. (2017). Smart infrastructure design for smart cities. *IT Professional*, *19*(5), 42–49. doi:10.1109/MITP.2017.3680957

Padmanabhan, P. (2017). *The NHS ransomware event and security challenges for the U.S. healthcare system*. Retrieved from https://www.cio.com/article/3196706/cyber-attacks-espionage/thenhs-ransomware-event-and-security-challenges-for-the-u-s-healthcaresystem.html

ParthDutt. (n.d.). Understanding rainbow table attack (Vol. 2020) (No. 29th June). Retrieved from https://www.geeksforgeeks.org/understanding-rainbow-table-attack/

Pascual, D., Amirshahi, A., Aminifar, A., Atienza, D., Ryvlin, P., & Wattenhofer, R. (2021). EpilepsyGAN: Synthetic Epileptic Brain Activities With Privacy Preservation. *IEEE Transactions on Biomedical Engineering*, *68*(8), 2435–2446. doi:10.1109/TBME.2020.3042574 PMID:33275573

Peleg, M., Beimel, D., Dori, D., & Denekamp, Y. (2008). Situation-Based Access Control: Privacy management via modeling of patient data access scenarios. *Journal of Biomedical Informatics*, *41*(6), 1028–1040. doi:10.1016/j.jbi.2008.03.014 PMID:18511349

Pillitteri, V., & Brewer, T. (2014). *Guidelines for Smart Grid Cybersecurity, NIST Interagency/ Internal Report (NISTIR).* National Institute of Standards and Technology. doi:10.6028/NIST. IR.7628r1

Poh, N., Bengio, S., & Korczak, J. (2002). A multi-sample multi-source model for biometric authentication. In *Proceedings of the 12th ieee workshop on neural networks for signal processing* (p. 375-384). IEEE. 10.1109/NNSP.2002.1030049

Polčák, L., & Matoušek, P. (2022). *Metering homes: do energy efficiency and privacy need to be in conflict?* In *Proceedings of the 19th International Conference on Security and Cryptography,* Lisboa, Portugal. 10.5220/0011139000003283

Pop, M. D., Pandey, J., & Ramasamy, V. (2020). Future Networks 2030: Challenges in Intelligent Transportation Systems. *ICRITO 2020 - IEEE 8th International Conference on Reliability, Infocom Technologies and Optimization (Trends and Future Directions).* IEEE. 10.1109/ ICRITO48877.2020.9197951

Pradhan, D., Sahu, P. K., Goje, N. S., Ghonge, M. M., Tun, H. M., Rajeswari, R., & Pramanik, S. (2022). Security, Privacy, Risk, and Safety Toward 5G Green Network (5G-GN). *Cyber Security and Network Security,* 193-216.

Prasdika, & Sugiantoro, B. (2013). A Review Paper On Big Data And Data Mining. *International Journal on Informatics for Development, 7*(1), 33–35.

Protecting Children from Online Sexual Exploitation. (2016). *A guide to action for religious leaders and communities.* Retrieved 3 March 2022, from https://www.unicef.org/media/73506/ file/FBO-Guide-for-Religious-Leaders-Communities-2016.pdf.pdf

Rahimi, M., Bateni, M., & Mohammadinejad, H. (2015). Extended K-Anonymity Model for Privacy Preserving on Micro Data. *International Journal of Computer Network and Information Security, 7*(12), 42–51. doi:10.5815/ijcnis.2015.12.05

Raju, N. V. S. L., Seetaramanath, M. N., & Rao, P. S. (2019a). A Novel Dynamic KCi - Slice Publishing Prototype for Retaining Privacy and Utility of Multiple Sensitive Attributes. *International Journal of Information Technology and Computer Science, 11*(4), 18–32. doi:10.5815/ ijitcs.2019.04.03

Raju, N. V. S. L., Seetaramanath, M. N., & Rao, P. S. (2019b). An optimal dynamic KC<SUB align="right">i-slice model for privacy preserving data publishing of multiple sensitive attributes adopting various sensitivity thresholds. *International Journal of Data Science, 4*(4), 320. doi:10.1504/IJDS.2019.105264

Ram Mohan Rao, P., Murali Krishna, S., & Siva Kumar, A. P. (2018). Privacy preservation techniques in big data analytics: A survey. *Journal of Big Data, 5*(1), 33. doi:10.118640537- 018-0141-8

Ramsdale, A., Shiaeles, S., & Kolokotronis, N. (2020). A comparative analysis of cyber-threat intelligence sources, formats and languages. *Electronics (Basel)*, *9*(5), 824. doi:10.3390/electronics9050824

Rayani, P. K., Bhushan, B., & Thakare, V. R. (2018). Multi-Layer Token Based Authentication Through Honey Password in Fog Computing. [IJFC]. *International Journal of Fog Computing*, *1*(1), 50–62. doi:10.4018/IJFC.2018010104

Raza, M., Iqbal, M., Sharif, M., & Haider, W. (2012). A survey of password attacks and comparative analysis on methods for secure authentication. *World Applied Sciences Journal*, *19*(4), 439–444.

Reddy, H., Raj, N., Gala, M., & Basava, A. (2020, February 18). Text-mining-based fake news detection using ensemble methods. *International Journal of Automation and Computing*, *17*(2), 210–221. doi:10.100711633-019-1216-5

Reiss, S. P. (1984). Practical data-swapping: The first steps. *ACM Transactions on Database Systems*, *9*(1), 20–37. doi:10.1145/348.349

Responding to Online Threats: Minors' Perspectives on Disclosing, Reporting, and Blocking. (2021). Available at: https://info.thorn.org/hubfs/Research/Responding%20to%20Online%20Threats_2021-Full-Report.pdf?utm_campaign=H2D%20report&utm_source=website

Rial, A., Danezis, G., & Kohlweiss, M. (2018). Privacy-preserving smart metering revisited. *International Journal of Information Security*, *17*(1), 1–31. doi:10.100710207-016-0355-8

Ringenberg, T., Seigfried-Spellar, K., Rayz, J., & Rogers, M. 2022. A scoping review of child grooming strategies: pre- and post-internet. *Child Abuse & Neglect*, *123*. Available at: https://www.sciencedirect.com/science/article/abs/pii/S0145213421004610#!

Roberts, A. (2021). *Cyber threat intelligence: The no-nonsense guide for CISOs and security managers*. Apress. doi:10.1007/978-1-4842-7220-6

Roozenbeek, J., Schneider, C. R., Dryhurst, S., Kerr, J., Freeman, A. L. J., Recchia, G., van der Bles, A. M., & van der Linden, S. (2020, October 14). Susceptibility to misinformation about COVID-19 around the world. *Royal Society Open Science*, *7*(10), 201199. doi:10.1098/rsos.201199 PMID:33204475

Roser, M., Ritchie, H., & Ortiz-Ospina, E. (2015). *Internet*. Retrieved 24 February 2022, from https://ourworldindata.org/internet

Rouse, M. (2018). challenge-response authentication. *Search Security*. https://searchsecurity.techtarget.com/definition/challenge-response-system

Ruan, C., & Varadharajan, V. (2003). An Authorization Model for E-consent Requirement in a Health Care Application. In J. Zhou, M. Yung, & Y. Han (Eds.), Lecture Notes in Computer Science: Vol. 2846. *Applied Cryptography and Network Security. ACNS 2003*. Springer. doi:10.1007/978-3-540-45203-4_15

Ruj, S., Stojmenovic, M., & Nayak, A. (2012). Privacy Preserving Access Control with Authentication for Securing Data in Clouds. *2012 12th IEEE/ACM International Symposium on Cluster, Cloud and Grid Computing (Ccgrid 2012)*, 556–563. 10.1109/CCGrid.2012.92

Russello, G., Dong, C., & Dulay, N. (2008). Consent-Based Workflows for Healthcare Management. *IEEE Workshop on Policies for Distributed Systems and Networks*, 153-161. 10.1109/POLICY.2008.22

Salahdine, F., & Kaabouch, N. (2019). Social engineering attacks: A survey. *Future Internet*, *11*(4), 89. doi:10.3390/fi11040089

Salamatian, S., Huleihel, W., Beirami, A., Cohen, A., & Medard, M. (2020). Centralized vs decentralized targeted brute-force attacks: Guessing with side-information. *IEEE Transactions on Information Forensics and Security*, *15*, 3749–3759. doi:10.1109/TIFS.2020.2998949

Samarati, P., & Sweeney, L. (1998). Generalizing data to provide anonymity when disclosing information (abstract). *Proceedings of the Seventeenth ACM SIGACT-SIGMOD-SIGART Symposium on Principles of Database Systems - PODS '98*, 188. 10.1145/275487.275508

Samtani, S., Abate, M., Benjamin, V., & Li, W. (2020). Cybersecurity as an industry: A cyber threat intelligence perspective. The Palgrave Handbook of International Cybercrime and Cyberdeviance, 135-154.

Sandhu, R. S., Coyne, E. J., Feinstein, H. L., & Youman, C. E. (1996). Role-Based Access Control Models. *IEEE Computer*, *29*(2), 38–47. doi:10.1109/2.485845

Sarfo, J. O., Debrah, T., Obeng, P., & Jubey, S. (2021). Qualitative research designs, sample size and saturation: Is enough always enough. Journal of Advocacy. *Research in Education*, *8*(3), 60–65. doi:10.13187/jare.2021.3.60

Savage, N. (2021, March 12). Fact-finding mission. *Communications of the ACM*, *64*(3), 18–19. doi:10.1145/3446879

Schneier, B. (2005). The failure of two-factor authentication. *Schneier.* https://www.schneier.com/blog/archives/2005/03/the_failure_of.html

Schuster, T., Schuster, R., Shah, D. J., & Barzilay, R. (2020). The limitations of stylometry for detecting machine-generated fake news. *Computational Linguistics*, *46*(2), 499–510. doi:10.1162/coli_a_00380

Seol, K., Kim, Y.-G., Lee, E., Seo, Y.-D., & Baik, D.-K. (2018). Privacy-Preserving Attribute-Based Access Control Model for XML-Based Electronic Health Record System. *IEEE Access: Practical Innovations, Open Solutions*, *6*, 9114–9128. doi:10.1109/ACCESS.2018.2800288

Sethi, R. J., Rangaraju, R., & Shurts, B. (2019, May 30). Fact checking misinformation using recommendations from emotional pedagogical agents. Intelligent Tutoring Systems.

Shablygin, E., Zakharov, V., Bolotov, O., & Scace, E. (2013). *Token management.* (US Patent US8555079B2)

Compilation of References

Shah, J. R., Murtaza, M. B., & Opara, E. (2014). Electronic Health Records: Challenges and Opportunities. *Journal of International Technology and Information Management*, *23*(3), 10. doi:10.58729/1941-6679.1082

Sharma, K., Qian, F., Jiang, H., Ruchansky, N., Zhang, M., & Liu, Y. (2019, May). Combating fake news: a survey on identification and mitigation techniques. *ACM Transactions on Intelligent Systems and Technology*, *10*(3), 1-42.

Sharma, O., & Bhargav, P. A. (n.d.). *Controller area network*.

Sharma, S. (2005). *Location based authentication*. Sharma.

Shay, R., Komanduri, S., Durity, A. L., Huh, P. S., Mazurek, M. L., Segreti, S. M, & Cranor, L. F. (2014). Can long passwords be secure and usable? In *Proceedings of the sigchi conference on human factors in computing systems* (p. 2927-2936). ACM. 10.1145/2556288.2557377

Shi, Y., Zhang, Z., Chao, H.-C., & Shen, B. (2018). Data Privacy Protection Based on Micro Aggregation with Dynamic Sensitive Attribute Updating. *Sensors (Basel)*, *18*(7), 2307. doi:10.339018072307 PMID:30013012

Shrivastava, S., & Srikanth, T. K. (2021). A Dynamic Access Control Policy for Healthcare Service Delivery in Healthcare Ecosystem using Electronic Health Records. *International Conference on COMmunication Systems & NETworkS (COMSNETS)*, 662-667. 10.1109/COMSNETS51098.2021.9352812

Shrivastava, S., Srikanth, T. K., & Dileep, V. S. (2020). e-Governance for healthcare service delivery in India: challenges and opportunities in security and privacy. In *Proceedings of the 13th International Conference on Theory and Practice of Electronic Governance (ICEGOV 2020)*. ACM. 10.1145/3428502.3428527

Shu, X., Araujo, F., Schales, D. L., Stoecklin, M. P., Jang, J., Huang, H., & Rao, J. R. (2018, October). Threat intelligence computing. In *Proceedings of the 2018 ACM SIGSAC Conference on Computer and Communications Security* (pp. 1883-1898). ACM. 10.1145/3243734.3243829

Silver, L., Smith, A., Johnson, C., Taylor, K., Jiang, J., Anderson, M., & Rainie, L. (2019). *Mobile Connectivity in Emerging Economies*. Retrieved 24 February 2022, from https://www.pewinternet.org/wp-content/uploads/sites/9/2019/03/PI_2019.03.07_Mobile-Connectivity_FINAL.pdf

Simmons, M., & Lee, J. S. (2020). Catfishing: A look into online dating and impersonation. In *International conference on human-computer interaction* (p. 349-358). Springer. 10.1007/978-3-030-49570-1_24

Sinha, H. S., & Sharma, Y. (2021). Text-convolutional neural networks for fake news detection in Tweets. In Evolution in Computational Intelligence. Advances in Intelligent Systems and Computing. Springer.

Siraj, H., Salam, A., Hasan, N., Jin, T., Roslan, R., & Othman, M. (2015). Internet Usage and Academic Performance: A Study in a Malaysian Public University. *International Medical Journal*, 22(2), 83–86. https://www.researchgate.net/publication/275833912_Internet_Usage_and_Academic_Performance_A_Study_in_a_Malaysian_Public_University

Sitaula, N., Mohan, C. K., Grygiel, J., Zhou, X., & Zafarani, R. (2020). Credibility-based fake news detection. In K. Shu, S. Wang, D. Lee, & H. Liu (Eds.), *Disinformation, misinformation, and fake news in social media, Lecture Notes in Social Networks* (pp. 163–182). Springer. doi:10.1007/978-3-030-42699-6_9

Slatman, H. (2022, April 26). hslatman/awesome-threat-intelligence. General format. https://github.com/hslatman/awesome-threat-intelligence

Smith, N. (2018). Hotp vs totp: What's the difference? *Microcosm*. https://www.microcosm.com/blog/hotp-totp-what-is-the-difference

Sowmyarani C. N., & Dayananda P. (n.d.). *Analytical Study on Privacy Attack Models in Privacy Preserving Data Publishing*. 1 doi:0.4018/978-1-5225-1829-7.ch006

Sowmyarani, C. N., Gadad, V., & Dayananda, P. (2021). (P+, A, T)-Anonymity Technique Against Privacy Attacks. *International Journal of Information Security and Privacy*, 15(2), 68–86. doi:10.4018/IJISP.2021040104

Sowmyarani, C. N., & Srinivasan, G. N. (2015). A robust privacy preserving model for data publishing. *2015 International Conference on Computer Communication and Informatics (ICCCI)*, 1–6. 10.1109/ICCCI.2015.7218095

Spanakis, E. G., Bonomi, S., Sfakianakis, S., Santucci, G., Lenti, S., Sorella, M., . . . Magalini, S. (2020, July). Cyber-attacks and threats for healthcare–a multi-layer thread analysis. In *2020 42nd Annual International Conference of the IEEE Engineering in Medicine & Biology Society (EMBC)* (pp. 5705-5708). IEEE. 10.1109/EMBC44109.2020.9176698

Stasiukonis, S. (2006). Social engineering, the usb way. *Dark Reading, 7*.

Steinberger, J., Sperotto, A., Golling, M., & Baier, H. (2015, May). How to exchange security events? overview and evaluation of formats and protocols. In *2015 IFIP/IEEE International Symposium on Integrated Network Management (IM)* (pp. 261-269). IEEE. 10.1109/INM.2015.7140300

Stephen, M. (2019, Jan 2,). Phishing attacks in the banking industry. *Info Institute*. https://resources.infosecinstitute.com/category/enterprise/phishing/the-phishing-landscape/phishing-attacks-by-demographic/phishing-in-the-banking-industry/

Stojanović, B., Hofer-Schmitz, K., & Kleb, U. (2020). APT datasets and attack modeling for automated detection methods: A review. *Computers & Security*, 92, 101734. doi:10.1016/j.cose.2020.101734

Strom, B. E., Applebaum, A., Miller, D. P., Nickels, K. C., Pennington, A. G., & Thomas, C. B. (2018). *MITRE ATT&CK: Design and philosophy*. Technical report.

Studnia, I., Alata, E., Nicomette, V., Kaâniche, M., & Laarouchi, Y. (2018). A language-based intrusion detection approach for automotive embedded networks. *International Journal of Embedded Systems, 10*(1), 89430. doi:10.1504/IJES.2018.089430

Sun, X., Wang, H., Truta, T. M., Li, J., & Li, P. (2008). (p+, α)-sensitive k-anonymity: A new enhanced privacy protection model. *Proceedings - 2008 IEEE 8th International Conference on Computer and Information Technology, CIT 2008*, 59–64. 10.1109/CIT.2008.4594650

Sun, X., Sun, L., & Wang, H. (2011). Extended k-anonymity models against sensitive attribute disclosure. *Computer Communications, 34*(4), 526–535. doi:10.1016/j.comcom.2010.03.020

Sun, X., Wang, H., Li, J., & Truta, T. M. (2008). Enhanced P -Sensitive K-Anonymity Models for Privacy Preserving Data Publishing. *Health (San Francisco), 1*, 53–66.

Supreme Administrative Court of the Czech Republic. (2021). *Internet Mall, a.s. v. Úřad pro ochranu osobních údajů [Internet Mall, a.s. Office for Personal Data Protection].* SACCR. https://www.nssoud.cz/files/SOUDNI_VYKON/2021/0238_1As__2100033S_20211111111159.pdf

Susan, V. S., & Christopher, T. (2016). Anatomisation with slicing: A new privacy preservation approach for multiple sensitive attributes. *SpringerPlus, 5*(1), 964. Advance online publication. doi:10.118640064-016-2490-0 PMID:27429874

Sweeney, L. (2002a). A model for protecting privacy. *IEEE Security and Privacy, 10*(5), 1–14.

Sweeney, L. (2002b). Privacy protection using generalization and suppression 1. *IEEE Security and Privacy, 10*(5), 1–18.

Takabi, H. (2014). Privacy aware access control for data sharing in cloud computing environments. *Proceedings of the 2nd International Workshop on Security in Cloud Computing - SCC '14*, 27–34. 10.1145/2600075.2600076

Takahashi, T., Landfield, K., & Kadobayashi, Y. (2014). *RFC 7203: An Incident Object Description Exchange Format (IODEF) Extension for Structured Cybersecurity Information. Internet Engineering Task Force.* IETF.

Tang, J., Cui, Y., Li, Q., Ren, K., Liu, J., & Buyya, R. (2016). Ensuring Security and Privacy Preservation for Cloud Data Services. *ACM Computing Surveys, 49*(1), 1–39. doi:10.1145/2906153

Tao, Y., Chen, H., Xiao, X., Zhou, S., & Zhang, D. (2009). ANGEL: Enhancing the Utility of Generalization for Privacy Preserving Publication. *IEEE Transactions on Knowledge and Data Engineering, 21*(7), 1073–1087. doi:10.1109/TKDE.2009.65

Tariq, S., Lee, S., Kim, H. K., & Woo, S. S. (2020). CAN-ADF: The controller area network attack detection framework. *Computers & Security, 94*, 101857. Advance online publication. doi:10.1016/j.cose.2020.101857

Tariq, S., Lee, S., & Woo, S. S. (2020). CANTransfer: Transfer learning based intrusion detection on a controller area network using convolutional LSTM network. *Proceedings of the ACM Symposium on Applied Computing.* ACM. 10.1145/3341105.3373868

Taylor, A., Leblanc, S., & Japkowicz, N. (2016). Anomaly detection in automobile control network data with long short-term memory networks. *Proceedings - 3rd IEEE International Conference on Data Science and Advanced Analytics, DSAA 2016*. IEEE. 10.1109/DSAA.2016.20

Taylor, A., Japkowicz, N., & Leblanc, S. (2016). Frequency-based anomaly detection for the automotive CAN bus. *2015 World Congress on Industrial Control Systems Security, WCICSS 2015*. IEEE. doi:10.1109/WCICSS.2015.7420322

Taylor, L., Zhou, X. H., & Rise, P. (2018). A tutorial in assessing disclosure risk in microdata. *Statistics in Medicine, 37*(25), 3693–3706. doi:10.1002im.7667 PMID:29931695

Tech Target. (2019) What is Intelligent transportation system (ITS): Applications and Examples. *Tech Target*.

Thomas, B. (2017). All that's needed to hack gmail and rob bitcoin: A name and a phone number. *Forbes*. https://www.forbes.com/sites/thomasbrewster/2017/09/18/ss7-google-coinbase-bitcoin-hack/#338f7a5f41a4

Tith, D., Lee, J., Suzuki, H., Wijesundara, W. M. A. B., Taira, N., Obi, T., & Ohyama, N. (2020). Patient Consent Management by a Purpose-Based Consent Model for Electronic Health Record Based on Blockchain Technology. *Health Information Research, 26*(4), 265-273. 1 doi:0.4258/hir.2020.26.4.265

Tiwari, A., Sanyal, S., Abraham, A., Knapskog, S. J., & Sanyal, S. (2011). A multi-factor security protocol for wireless payment-secure web authentication using mobile devices. arXiv preprint arXiv:1111.3010

Toch, E., Bettini, C., Shmueli, E., Radaelli, L., Lanzi, A., Riboni, D., & Lepri, B. (2018). The Privacy Implications of Cyber Security Systems. *ACM Computing Surveys, 51*(2), 1–27. doi:10.1145/3172869

Tomlinson, A., Bryans, J., & Shaikh, S. A. (2018b). Using a one-class compound classifier to detect in-vehicle network attacks. *GECCO 2018 Companion - Proceedings of the 2018 Genetic and Evolutionary Computation Conference Companion*. doi:10.1145/3205651.3208223

Tomlinson, A., Bryans, J., & Shaikh, S. A. (2018a). Towards Viable Intrusion Detection Methods For The Automotive Controller Area Network. *Proceedings of the 2nd ACM Computer Science in Cars Symposium, 9*. ACM.

Tools, R. S. (n.d.). *Password cracking tools*. Google. https://sites.google.com/site/reusablesec/Home/password-cracking-tools

Tounsi, W., & Rais, H. (2018). A survey on technical threat intelligence in the age of sophisticated cyber attacks. *Computers & Security, 72*, 212–233. doi:10.1016/j.cose.2017.09.001

Trojahn, M., & Marcus, P. (2012). *Towards coupling user and device locations using biometrical authentication on smartphones. In 2012 international conference for internet technology and secured transactions*. IEEE.

Truta, T. M., Campan, A., Abrinica, M., & Miller, J. (2008). A comparison between local and global recoding algorithms for achieving microdata-sensitive-anonymity. *Acta Universitatis Apulensis. Mathematics-Informatics*, *15*, 213–233.

Truta, T. M., & Vinay, B. (2006). Privacy Protection: p-Sensitive k-Anonymity Property. *22nd International Conference on Data Engineering Workshops (ICDEW'06)*, 94–94. 10.1109/ICDEW.2006.116

Tsai, F. S. (2010). Security Issues in e-Healthcare. *Journal of Medical and Biological Engineering*, *30*(4), 209–214. doi:10.5405/jmbe.30.4.04

Turnbull, R. S., & Gedge, R. (2012). *Location based authentication.* (US Patent US8321913B2)

Turner, D. M. (2016, 01 August). Digital authentication - the basics. *Cryptomathic.* https://www.cryptomathic.com/news-events/blog/digital-authentication-the-basics

Underage Children. (n.d.). *Instagram Help Centre.* Retrieved 26 March 2022, from https://help.instagram.com/290666591035380

UNICEF Division of Communication. (2017). *Children in a Digital World.* Retrieved from https://www.unicef.org/media/48601/file

United States Court of Appeals for the Seventh Circuit. (2018). *Naperville Smart Meter Association v. Naperville - Seventh Circuit Decision.* United States Court of Appeals for the Seventh Circuit.

V, K., & K.P, T. (2012). Protecting Privacy When Disclosing Information: K Anonymity and its Enforcement through Suppression. *International Journal of Computing Algorithm*, *1*(1), 19–22. 1 doi:0.20894/ijcoa.101.001.001.004

Vadakkethil Somanathan Pilla, E. S. (2022). *LCS, LACS, and phrase match comparison.* https://github.com/sanjaikanth/LCSLACSPhraseMatchComparison

Vallant, H., Stojanović, B., Božić, J., & Hofer-Schmitz, K. (2021). Threat Modelling and Beyond-Novel Approaches to Cyber Secure the Smart Energy System. *Applied Sciences (Basel, Switzerland)*, *11*(11), 5149. doi:10.3390/app11115149

van der Heijden, R. W., Dietzel, S., Leinmüller, T., & Kargl, F. (2018). Survey on misbehavior detection in cooperative intelligent transportation systems. *IEEE Communications Surveys and Tutorials*, *21*(1), 779–811. doi:10.1109/COMST.2018.2873088

van der Linden, S. (2022, March). Misinformation: Susceptibility, spread, and interventions to immunize the public. *Nature Medicine*, *28*(3).

Vargas, J. C. (2019). Blockchain Cyber-attacks and threats for healthcare – a multi-layer thread analysis -based consent manager for GDPR compliance. In Open Identity Summit 2019, Lecture Notes in Informatics (LNI). Gesellschaft für Informatik.

Vel´asquez, I., Caro, A., & Rodr´ıguez, A. (2018). Authentication schemes and methods: A systematic literature review. *Information and Software Technology, 94*, 30-37.

Visser, J., Lawrence, J., & Reed, C. (2020, November). Reason-checking fake news. *Communications of the ACM*, *63*(11), 38–40.

Vuong, Q.-H., Le, T.-T., La, V.-P., Nguyen, H., Ho, M.-T., Khuc, Q., & Nguyen, M.-H. (2022, January 18). Covid-19 vaccines production and societal immunization under the serendipity-mindsponge-3D knowledge management theory and conceptual framework. *Humanities & Social Sciences Communications*, *9*(1), 22. doi:10.105741599-022-01034-6

Wagner, C., Dulaunoy, A., Wagener, G., & Iklody, A. (2016, October). MISP: The design and implementation of a collaborative threat intelligence sharing platform. In *Proceedings of the 2016 ACM on Workshop on Information Sharing and Collaborative Security* (pp. 49-56). ACM. 10.1145/2994539.2994542

Wagner, I., & Eckhoff, D. (2018). Technical Privacy Metrics. *ACM Computing Surveys*, *51*(3), 1–38. doi:10.1145/3168389

Wagner, T. D., Mahbub, K., Palomar, E., & Abdallah, A. E. (2019). Cyber threat intelligence sharing: Survey and research directions. *Computers & Security*, *87*, 101589. doi:10.1016/j.cose.2019.101589

Wang, G., Zhu, Z., Du, W., & Teng, Z. (2008). Inference analysis in privacy-preserving data re-publishing. *Proceedings - IEEE International Conference on Data Mining, ICDM*, 1079–1084. 10.1109/ICDM.2008.118

Wang, Q., Lu, Z., & Qu, G. (2019). An Entropy Analysis Based Intrusion Detection System for Controller Area Network in Vehicles. *International System on Chip Conference, 2018-September*. doi:10.1109/SOCC.2018.8618564

Wang, M., Jiang, Z., Zhang, Y., & Yang, H. (2018). T-Closeness slicing: A new privacy-preserving approach for transactional data publishing. *INFORMS Journal on Computing*, *30*(3), 438–453. doi:10.1287/ijoc.2017.0791

Wang, R., Zhu, Y., Chen, T.-S., & Chang, C.-C. (2018). Privacy-Preserving Algorithms for Multiple Sensitive Attributes Satisfying t-Closeness. *Journal of Computer Science and Technology*, *33*(6), 1231–1242. doi:10.100711390-018-1884-6

Weir, C. M. (2010). *Using probabilistic techniques to aid in password cracking attacks*.

Weir, M., Aggarwal, S., Medeiros, B. D., & Glodek, B. (2009). Password cracking using probabilistic context-free grammars. In *2009 30th ieee symposium on security and privacy* (p. 391-405). IEEE. 10.1109/SP.2009.8

WhatsApp Help Center. (n.d.). *About end-to-end encryption*. Retrieved 26 March 2022, from https://faq.whatsapp.com/general/security-and-privacy/end-to-end-encryption

Wikipedia. (n.d.). *Longest common subsequence problem*. https://en.wikipedia.org/wiki/Longest_common_subsequence_problem

Win, K. T. (2005). A review of security of electronic health records. *Health Information Management, 34*(1), 13-18.

WordNet. (n.d.). *A lexical database for English.* https://wordnet.princeton.edu/

Wu, Y., Ruan, X., Liao, S., & Wang, X. (2010). P-cover k-anonymity model for protecting multiple sensitive attributes. *ICCSE 2010 - 5th International Conference on Computer Science and Education, Final Program and Book of Abstracts*, 179–183. 10.1109/ICCSE.2010.5593663

Wu, W., Li, R., Xie, G., An, J., Bai, Y., Zhou, J., & Li, K. (2020). A Survey of Intrusion Detection for In-Vehicle Networks. *IEEE Transactions on Intelligent Transportation Systems, 21*(3), 919–933. doi:10.1109/TITS.2019.2908074

XACML. (2022). *OASIS eXtensible Access Control Markup Language (XACML).* Retrieved from https://www.oasis-open.org/committees/tc_home.php?wg_abbrev=xacml

Xamarin. (n.d.). *Cross-platform with Xamarin.* https://dotnet.microsoft.com/en-us/apps/xamarin/cross-platform

Xiao, X., & Tao, Y. (2006a). Anatomy: Simple and effective privacy preservation. *VLDB 2006 - Proceedings of the 32nd International Conference on Very Large Data Bases*, 139–150.

Xiao, X., Yi, K., & Tao, Y. (2010). The hardness and approximation algorithms for L-diversity. *Advances in Database Technology - EDBT 2010 - 13th International Conference on Extending Database Technology, Proceedings*, 135–146. 10.1145/1739041.1739060

Xiao, X., & Tao, Y. (2006b). Personalized privacy preservation. *Proceedings of the 2006 ACM SIGMOD International Conference on Management of Data - SIGMOD '06*, 229. 10.1145/1142473.1142500

Xiao, X., Tao, Y., & Chen, M. (2009). Optimal random perturbation at multiple privacy levels. *Proceedings of the VLDB Endowment International Conference on Very Large Data Bases, 2*(1), 814–825. doi:10.14778/1687627.1687719

Xu, J., Wang, W., Pei, J., Wang, X., Shi, B., & Fu, A. W.-C. (2006). Utility-based anonymization using local recoding. *Proceedings of the 12th ACM SIGKDD International Conference on Knowledge Discovery and Data Mining - KDD '06*, 785. 10.1145/1150402.1150504

Xu, Y., Ma, T., Tang, M., & Tian, W. (2014). A Survey of Privacy Preserving Data Publishing using Generalization and Suppression. *Applied Mathematics & Information Sciences, 8*(3), 1103–1116. doi:10.12785/amis/080321

Yang, W., Li, N., Qi, Y., Qardaji, W., McLaughlin, S., & McDaniel, P. (2012). *Minimizing private data disclosures in the smart grid.* In ACM Conference on Computer and Communications Security, Raleigh, North Carolina. 10.1145/2382196.2382242

Yang, X.-C., Wang, Y.-Z., Wang, B., & Yu, G. (2009). Privacy Preserving Approaches for Multiple Sensitive Attributes in Data Publishing. *Chinese Journal of Computers, 31*(4), 574–587. doi:10.3724/SP.J.1016.2008.00574

Yang, Y., Wu, L., Yin, G., Li, L., & Zhao, H. (2017). A survey on security and privacy issues in Internet-of-Things. *IEEE Internet of Things Journal*, *4*(5), 1250–1258. doi:10.1109/JIOT.2017.2694844

Ye, Y., Liu, Y., Wang, C., & Lv, D. (2009). Decomposition: privacy preservation for multiple sensitive attributes. *Springer, 5463*, 486–490. 1 doi:0.1007/978-3-642-00887-0_42

Ye, Y., Wang, L., & Han, J. (n.d.). *An anonymization method combining anatomy and permutation for protecting privacy in microdata with multiple sensitive attributes*. Retrieved July 20, 2021, from https://ieeexplore.ieee.org/abstract/document/8108955/

Yesilyurt, M., Basturk, R., Yesilyurt, F., & Kara, I. (2014). The effect of technological devices on student's academic success: Evidence from Denizli. *Journal of Internet Applications And Management*, *5*(1), 39–47. doi:10.5505/iuyd.2014.83007

Yi, T., & Shi, M. (2015). *Privacy Protection Method for Multiple Sensitive Attributes Based on Strong Rule*. 1 doi:0.1155/2015/464731

Yin, X., Zhu, Y., & Hu, J. (2021). A Comprehensive Survey of Privacy-preserving Federated Learning. *ACM Computing Surveys*, *54*(6), 1–36. doi:10.1145/3460427

Young, C., Zambreno, J., Olufowobi, H., & Bloom, G. (2019). Survey of Automotive Controller Area Network Intrusion Detection Systems. *IEEE Design & Test*, *36*(6), 48–55. doi:10.1109/MDAT.2019.2899062

Yuan, X., Ma, X., Zhang, L., Fang, Y., & Wu, D. (2021). Beyond Class-Level Privacy Leakage: Breaking Record-Level Privacy in Federated Learning. *IEEE Internet of Things Journal*. 1 doi:0.1109/JIOT.2021.3089713

Yu, J. J. Q. (2021). Sybil Attack Identification for Crowdsourced Navigation: A Self-Supervised Deep Learning Approach. *IEEE Transactions on Intelligent Transportation Systems*, *22*(7), 4622–4634. doi:10.1109/TITS.2020.3036085

Yüksel, B., Küpçü, A., & Özkasap, Ö. (2017). Research issues for privacy and security of electronic health services. *Future Generation Computer Systems*, *68*, 1–13. doi:10.1016/j.future.2016.08.011

Zeifman, M., & Roth, K. (2011). Nonintrusive appliance load monitoring: Review and outlook. *IEEE Transactions on Consumer Electronics*, *57*(1), 76–84. doi:10.1109/TCE.2011.5735484

Zhang, F., Kondoro, A., & Muftic, S. (2012). Location-based authentication and authorization using smart phones. In *2012 ieee 11th international conference on trust, security and privacy in computing and communications* (p. 1285-1292). IEEE. 10.1109/TrustCom.2012.198

Zhang, Q., Koudas, N., Srivastava, D., & Yu, T. (2007). Aggregate Query Answering on Anonymized Tables. *2007 IEEE 23rd International Conference on Data Engineering*, 116–125. 10.1109/ICDE.2007.367857

Compilation of References

Zhang, A., Bacchus, A., & Lin, X. (2016). Consent-based access control for secure and privacy-preserving health information exchange. *Security and Communication Networks*, *9*(16), 3496–3508. doi:10.1002ec.1556

Zhang, L., Tan, C., & Yu, F. (2017). An improved rainbow table attack for long passwords. *Procedia Computer Science*, *107*, 47–52. doi:10.1016/j.procs.2017.03.054

Zhang, P., Jin, H., Dong, H., Song, W., & Bouguettaya, A. (2020). Privacy-Preserving QoS Forecasting in Mobile Edge Environments. *IEEE Transactions on Services Computing*, 1–1. doi:10.1109/TSC.2020.2977018

Zhao, J., Yan, Q., Li, J., Shao, M., He, Z., & Li, B. (2020). TIMiner: Automatically extracting and analyzing categorized cyber threat intelligence from social data. *Computers & Security*, *95*, 101867. doi:10.1016/j.cose.2020.101867

Zhao, Y., Wang, J., Luo, Y., & Le, J. (2009). (α,β,κ)-anonymity: An effective privacy preserving model for databases. *Proceedings of the International Symposium on Test and Measurement*, *1*, 412–415. 10.1109/ICTM.2009.5412903

Zheng, B., Sayin, M. O., Lin, C.-W., Shiraishi, S., & Zhu, Q. (2017). Timing and security analysis of VANET-based intelligent transportation systems: (Invited paper). *2017 IEEE/ACM International Conference on Computer-Aided Design (ICCAD)*, (pp. 984–991). IEEE. 10.1109/ICCAD.2017.8203888

Zhou, X. & Zafarani, R. (2020, October). A survey of fake news: fundamental theories, detection methods, and opportunities. *ACM Computing Surveys*, *53*(5), 1-40.

Zhou, S., & Brown, M. A. (2016). Smart meter deployment in Europe: A comparative case study on the impact of national policy schemes. *Journal of Cleaner Production*, *144*, 22–32. doi:10.1016/j.jclepro.2016.12.031

About the Contributors

Carlos Rabadão is Coordinator Professor at Department of Computer Science Engineering at School of Technology and Management of Polytechnic of Leiria (ESTG). He is the Head of Computer Science and Communication Research Centre (CIIC) of Polytechnic of Leiria and Chair of the Technical-Scientific Council of ESTG. He received his PhD degree in Computer Science Engineering from University of Coimbra, Portugal, in 2007, his MSc degree in Electronics and Telecommunications Engineering, from University of Aveiro, Portugal, in 1996 and his BSc degree in Electrical Engineering, specialization in Telecommunications and Electronics, from University of Coimbra, Portugal, in 1989. He has more than 24 years of teaching and research experience in Computer Engineering, namely in the areas of Cybersecurity and Computer Networks. He has published around 50 papers in international conferences and journals in the areas of Cybersecurity, Computer Science and Data Communications. He has participated in more than 20 national and international R&D projects, having coordinated 5 of these. His major research interests include Information and Networks Security, Information Security and Privacy Management, Security Incident Response Systems for Industry 4.0, Next Generation Networks and Services and Wireless Networks.

Leonel Santos is Assistant Professor at Department of Computer Science Engineering at School of Technology and Management of Polytechnic of Leiria (ESTG). He is Full member of Computer Science and Communication Research Centre (CIIC) of Polytechnic of Leiria, Forensic computer expert of the Cybersecurity and Computer Forensics Laboratory - LabCIF, at Polytechnic of Leiria, and member of the Scientific-Pedagogical Committee of BSc degree in Computer Engineering of ESTG. He received his PhD degree in Computer Science from University of Trás-os-Montes e Alto Douro, Portugal, in 2020 and his BSc degree in Computer Engineering, specialization in Communication Networks and Systems, from Polytechnic of Leiria, Portugal, in 2006. He has more than 14 years of teaching and research experience in Computer Engineering, namely in the areas of Cybersecurity and Computer Networks. He has published papers in journals and international conferences in the areas of Cybersecurity, Information and Networks Security, and Computer Science. He has participated in national R&D projects. His major research interests include Cybersecurity, Information Security, Networks Security, Internet of Things, Intrusion Detection Systems, and Computer Forensics.

Rogério Luís de Carvalho Costa received a PhD in Computer Engineering from the University of Coimbra (UC), Portugal, in 2011, and an MSc in Informatics from the Pontifícia Universidade Católica do Rio de Janeiro (PUC-Rio), Brazil, in 2002. He has over 15 years of teaching experience. He participated in research projects in Brazil and Portugal and published papers at international conferences and leading journals. Rogério also held technical and managerial positions in software development companies. He is currently a researcher at the Polytechnic of Leiria, Portugal. His research interests include big data, machine learning, cybersecurity and privacy, and data integration and quality.

* * *

Samuel Matthew Akpe is a PhD candidate in the Department of Mass Communication, Bingham University, Nigeria. He holds a Bachelor of Arts degree in Communication Arts and a Master of Arts in Mass Communication from the University of Uyo, Akwa Ibom State. Aside being a media consultant and a biographer, his areas of research interest include Journalism, Media Studies and Political Communication.

Sowmyarani C. N. is working as an Associate Professor for Department of Computer Science and Engineering, RVCE Bangalore. Research Areas include computer security & privacy.

Ricardo Czekster is currently a Lecturer in Computer Science at Aston University, in Birmingham/UK. His career focus is directed to dependability plus cyber-security tackling quantitative analysis. He has worked with modelling and simulation throughout his career. More recently, he is concerned about higher level representations of cyber-physical security incidents in smart infrastructure such as Attack Trees and Fault Tree Analysis, in combination with Markovian processes, among other topics. Ricardo is interested in modelling adversaries in cyber-physical systems and dependability intersections with cybersecurity, combining techniques and methodologies as diverse as Attack Modelling Techniques (AMT), automated risk assessment, threat modelling, and intrusion detection. Nowadays he has been investigating Cyber Threat Intelligence (CTI) and the integration of multiple datasets with cyber-security modelling languages and standardised formats, for instance, using the STIX framework.

Luis da Bernarda holds BS. in Computer Science and currently is finishing a MS. in Computer Science - Mobile Computing, his academic path allowed him to investigate about solutions based on internet of things as emergent technology applied to Industry 4.0 and many others.

Wen-Chen Hu received a PhD in Computer Science from the University of Florida in 1998. He is currently an associate professor in the Department of Computer Science of the University of North Dakota. He is the Editor-in-Chief of the International Journal of Handheld Computing Research (IJHCR), the general chairs of a number of international conferences, and associate editors of several journals. In addition, he has acted more than 100 positions as editors and editorial advisory/review board members of international journals/books, and track/session chairs and program committee members of international conferences. Dr. Hu has been teaching more than 10 years at the US universities and over 10 different computer/IT-related courses, and advising/consulting more than 100 graduate students. He has published over 100 articles in refereed journals, conference proceedings, books, and encyclopedias, and edited more than 10 books and conference proceedings. His current research interests include handheld/mobile/smartphone/tablet computing, location-based services, web-enabled information system such as search engines, electronic and mobile commerce systems, and web technologies.

Judith Isah is a postgraduate student, Department of Mass Communication, Bingham University, Nigeria.

Desmond Onyemechi Okocha, PhD, is a Social Scientist with specialisation in Journalism, Corporate Communication. He has over 16 years experience in consulting, research and lecturing. He obtained his B.A. degree in Management from the United Kingdom, holds a M.A and PhD in Journalism and Mass Communication, both from India. Additionally, has PGDs in Education Management and Leadership and another in Logistics and Supply Chain Management. He was the pioneer National Knowledge Management and Communication Coordinator for the International Fund for Agricultural Development project in the Niger Delta. He is presently, an Associate Professor and Head, Department of Mass Communication, Bingham University, Nigeria and Research Fellow, University of Religions and Denominations, Iran. He is the Founder of Institute for Leadership and Development Communication, Nigeria. He has published over 80 articles in refereed journals, conference proceedings, books and 2 edited books. His current research interests include digital journalism, immersive communication, mass media and society, digital activism, social media, development communication, and corporate communication. As an international voice, Dr. Okocha is a frequent speaker in conferences across continents. In 2018, he was invited to speak at Harvard University, USA, Vienna University, Austria, and at the MIRDEC-8th, International Academic Conference on Social Sciences, Portugal.

Libor Polcák is an assistant professor and researcher on the Faculty of Information Technology, Brno University of Technology with focus on security and data protection in networking and on the web. His area of interests include law interception, device identification, network identities, privacy, and data protection. He finished his Ph.D. studies on the Faculty of Information Technology, Brno University of Technology in 2017. In 2018, he received Czech Minister of the Interior award for outstanding results in the area of security research. From 2022, he is a member in Pool of Experts of European Data Protection Board. He works on the JShelter web extension.

Guilherme Santo holds BS in Computer Science and currently is finishing a MS. in Computer Science - Mobile Computing.

Swapnil Shrivastava is presently Senior Architect and Research Scholar in eHealth Research Centre (EHRC) at IIIT Bangalore. During her prior two-decade stint at C-DAC she has spearheaded and effectively contributed towards Applied Research Projects, Mission Mode Projects and Turnkey Projects. She has contributed towards technical papers, book chapter, keynote address and tutorial sessions in events organized by IETE, IEEE, ACM, IGI and Springer. She has delivered invited talks in various professional courses and workshops organized by professional bodies and institutes.

T. K. Srikanth obtained his Ph.D. in Computer Science from Cornell University in 1986, and has a B.Tech (Mech. Eng) from the Indian Institute of Technology, Madras. His research interests are in the areas of Computer Graphics, Geometric Modeling and 3D Printing, mobile and internet based applications, and data privacy. He is a co-convenor of the E-Health Research Center at IIITB (ehrc.iiitb.ac.in), and is actively involved in multiplee collaborative research projects in healthcare.

Aminu B. Usman is the Associate Head of Computer and Data Science, York St John University in UK. He received a Computer Science degree from Bayero Universidad, Kano, a Master's degree in Network Security from Middlesex University, London, and a Ph.D. in Network Security from Auckland University of Technology. His current research is on Security and Authentication methods, IoT, next-generation networks and security issues in wireless networks

Sanjaikanth E. Vadakkethil Somanathan Pillai is a Senior Systems Analyst for Visa Inc. with 16 years of industry experience. Sanjaikanth completed his bachelor's degree from The University of Calicut, India, and his Master's in Electrical and Computer Engineering (Software Engineering) from The University of Texas at Austin. He is currently studying toward a Ph.D. in Computer Science at The University of North Dakota. His expertise includes application programming, automation, performance optimization, and data research.

Alec Wells is a postgraduate PhD student at York St John University in the UK. He received a Master's by Research degree also at York St John University in the UK. His research interests include cyber security, authentication, biometrics and IoT.

Index

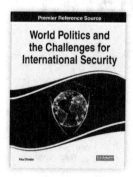

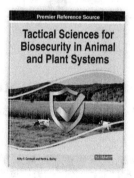

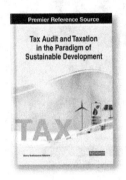
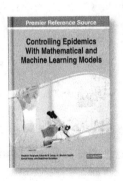

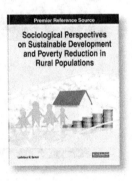

Printed in the United States
by Baker & Taylor Publisher Services